Writing and the English Renaissance

Crosscurrents

General Editors:
Professor J B Bullen, University of Reading
Dr Neil Sammells, Bath College of Higher Education
Dr Paul Hyland, Bath College of Higher Education

Published titles:

William Zunder and Suzanne Trill, *Writing and the English Renaissance*

Writing and the English Renaissance

Edited by

William Zunder and Suzanne Trill

LONGMAN
London and New York

Longman Group Limited
Longman House, Burnt Mill,
Harlow, Essex CM20 2JE, England
and associated Companies throughout the world.

Published in the United States of America
by Longman Publishing, New York.

First published 1996

ISBN 0 582 22974X CSD
ISBN 0 582 229758 PPR

British Library Cataloguing-in-Publication Data

A catalogue record of this book is
available from the British Library

Library of Congress Cataloging-in-Publication Data
Also available

Set by 7XX in 10/12 sabon

Produced by Longman Singapore Publishers (Pte) Ltd.
Printed in Singapore

Contents

Preface

This is a volume for the new era in higher education: the era of modularity, of increased access, and of interdisciplinarity. We have accordingly made the volume open and accessible; we have extended the canon to include new – especially women – writers; and we have gone beyond traditional notions of the literary to include other kinds of writing, in particular history. We have been greatly assisted in this endeavour by the general editors, who have applied a light but steering hand; by Francis Dodd at Longman, who gave crucial editorial help at an early stage; and by our contributors, who have cheerfully and willingly acceded to all our requests. We owe a special debt to Marion Wynne-Davies, who originally brought us together in what has proved to be a happy and fruitful partnership.

We would like to thank the Academic Council of Queen's University, Belfast for their practical assistance with this project.

Chronology

1572   Society of Antiquaries founded
John Donne, Ben Jonson born
1579   Spenser publishes *The Shepherd's Calendar*
1580   Sir Francis Drake completes circumnavigation of the world
John Webster born
1586   Colonization of Munster
Death of Philip Sidney
1588   Defeat of the Spanish Armada
1593   George Herbert born
Death of Marlowe
1599   Death of Spenser
1600   East India Company founded
1603   Accession of James VI of Scotland as James I
1604   Hampton Court Conference: James rejects Puritan requests
for reform of the Church of England
1606   Shakespeare's *King Lear* acted before James at Whitehall
1607   Colonization of Virginia
1608   John Milton born
1609   Gerrard Winstanley born
1610   Galileo publishes *Sidereal Messenger*
1611   Authorized Version of the Bible is published
1616   Death of Shakespeare
1620   Pilgrim Fathers leave for America
1621   Andrew Marvell born
Death of Mary Sidney
1625   Accession of Charles I
1628   John Bunyan born
1629   Charles dissolves Parliament and rules without it
1631   Death of Donne
1633   Death of Herbert
1634   Death of Webster
1637   Death of Jonson
1640   Long Parliament meets
1642   Civil war starts between Charles and Parliament
Theatres are closed by ordinance
Anna Trapnel begins to prophesy
Isaac Newton born
Death of Galileo
1645   Use of the *Book of Common Prayer* forbidden
1646   Episcopacy abolished

1649   Execution of Charles by Parliament
          Monarchy and the House of Lords abolished
          England declared to be a Commonwealth
          Sacking of Drogheda and Wexford
          Diggers begin to work at St George's Hill, Surrey

1650   Marvell writes 'An Horatian Ode upon Cromwell's Return from Ireland'

1651   Navigation Act restricts colonial trade to English shipping

1653   Oliver Cromwell becomes Lord Protector

1655   Jamaica captured from Spain

1658   Richard Cromwell becomes Lord Protector
          Trapnel ceases to prophesy

1660   Restoration of Charles II
          House of Lords restored
          Episcopacy restored
          Royal Society for the promotion of science founded
          Theatres reopened

1661   Clarendon Code imposes penalties on nonconformists

1662   *Book of Common Prayer* reissued
          Final Act of Uniformity

1667   Milton publishes *Paradise Lost*

1674   Death of Milton

1676   Death of Winstanley

1678   Death of Marvell

1685   Accession of James II

1687   Newton publishes *Mathematical Principles of Natural Philosophy*

1688   Glorious Revolution removes James from throne
          Death of Bunyan

1689   Accession of William III and Mary II
          Bill of Rights establishes parliamentary supremacy

1694   Bank of England founded

Introduction

The Renaissance

The Renaissance reached England late. From its origins in the northern city-states of fourteenth- and fifteenth-century Italy, especially Florence, it finally began to inform English culture at the beginning of the sixteenth century: in the work of such writers as Thomas More, whose satirical and idealizing prose work, *Utopia* – written in Latin for a humanist and European élite – appeared in 1516; Sir Thomas Wyatt, whose rewriting of the fourteenth-century Italian poet, Francesco Petrarch, was undertaken in the 1520s and '30s; and Henry Howard, Earl of Surrey, whose version of the Roman poet Virgil's epic, the *Aeneid*, first appeared in 1554, and established the blank verse line as the norm for English poetry virtually until the modernist moment at the beginning of the twentieth century. By the last decades of the sixteenth century, the humanist project to reinvent contemporary culture in terms of the classical past was firmly established, indeed dominant, within English society; and this dominance is marked by the publication in 1579 of Edmund Spenser's pastoral sequence, *The Shepherd's Calendar*. The poems not only revealed Spenser as an authoritative, specifically humanist voice: a characteristically Renaissance writer; but, in their widespread contemporary reception as constituting a new departure in English writing, they revealed the extent to which humanist ideals and practices were by then accepted as normal.

This dominance continued for at least the next half-century. All the writers traditionally accepted as major and discussed in the present collection – Spenser himself, Christopher Marlowe, John Donne, George Herbert, Andrew Marvell – took for granted and variously applied the principles of the humanist project. In the work of John Milton, with which the collection effectively concludes, the project is carried to the last decades of the seventeenth century. *Paradise Lost*, published in 1667, in a sense completes Surrey's aim of regrounding classical epic, particularly Virgil, in English writing.

It would be a mistake, however, to see the Renaissance simply in terms of literary production. It was a time of many profound shifts in European culture. Fundamentally, it was the moment that saw the shift from feudalism to capitalism. Although this shift had its precursors and antecedents in continental Europe – fifteenth-century Florence under the great banking family of the Medici, for example – it was actually a development that took place in England between the beginning of the fourteenth century and the early years of the eighteenth, with the sixteenth and seventeenth centuries – especially the decades around 1600 – crucial in the developing crisis of the transition.

It was the moment that saw the fracturing of Europe in the Reformation: from its beginning in Martin Luther's 95 theses nailed to the Palace Church door in Wittenberg in 1517 through John Calvin's seminal *Institutes of the Christian Religion* of 1536 to the emergence of the radical sects of the English Revolution of the mid-seventeenth century. All the writers discussed in this volume, not only the consciously religious writers like Mary Sidney or Herbert, lived their lives to different extents within the variously inflected discursive formation of protestantism.

Less disruptive at the time, but equally momentous in the long run, was the rise of science. Nicolaus Copernicus published his heliocentric theory in 1543; and it was progressively confirmed by the work of Tycho Brahe, Johann Kepler, and in particular the Italian physicist, Galileo Galilei, whose *Sidereal Messenger*, published in Latin in 1610 and describing his observations with his telescope, had such an impact on Donne.[1] But it was an Englishman, Isaac Newton, working at the end of the seventeenth century, and the founding of the Royal Society in London in 1660, that completed the scientific revolution and laid the foundation for the world-view of the Enlightenment. As Alexander Pope put it in 1730, 'God said, *Let Newton be!* and All was *Light*'.[2]

More particularly, there was developing political disruption in England. The English Reformation had been carried through in the 1530s by the crown acting in concert with Parliament, especially the House of Commons where the gentry were dominant. But by the end of the sixteenth century this alliance was beginning to break down, and be replaced by a growing opposition between an increasingly puritan House of Commons and a crown under James I, and more strongly under his son Charles I, which had strengthening ambitions towards absolutism. In 1642 this opposition became armed conflict; and in 1649 Parliament beheaded the King: an event unthinkable a generation earlier. The revolutionary decades of 1640–60 saw a political intensification of the economic and social changes of the previous century. The Navigation Act passed by the Long Parliament in 1651, for instance, aimed to establish an English monopoly in colonial trade; and by the time Milton's epic reached its final form, the country was only a decade away from the Glorious Revolution of 1688, which saw England take its modern shape: capitalist, imperialist, protestant, under a constitutional monarchy.

By the end of the seventeenth century England was a major imperial power, with extensive possessions in North America and the West Indies. Marvell's poem, 'Bermudas', probably written shortly after the 1651 Act, is a celebration of the imperial project. But overseas expansion was, again, in origin a continental development. Remarkably soon after Christopher Columbus set foot on Cuba in 1492, Hernando Cortés took Mexico for Spain in 1521. By 1534 Francisco Pizarro had taken Peru. But, despite earlier attempts, English overseas expansion is a seventeenth-century phenomenon: Virginia colonized in 1607; New England in 1620; and Maryland in 1632.

The great exception to this, of course, was Ireland. In 1542 Henry VIII had proclaimed himself King of Ireland. And by the 1590s England was involved in a protracted colonial war on Irish soil; a war Spenser was deeply implicated in from 1580 onwards, first as secretary to Lord Grey de Wilton, Elizabeth's Lord Deputy of Ireland, and later as owner of the estate of Kilcolman in County Cork. It was a struggle that was to continue until Oliver Cromwell crushed the Irish resistance with a parliamentary army in 1649, an event commemorated by Marvell in his 'Horatian Ode upon Cromwell's Return from Ireland'.

Ideology

Ideologically, the reaction of English governments in the sixteenth century to these changes was to reformulate and enforce the hierarchical assumptions about reality and society inherited from the preceding feudal period. It was an attempt by the superstructure, necessarily doomed, to impose on the base an order that had long since been lost. The principal vehicle for achieving this was the *Homilies*, a series of sermons written, among others, by Thomas Cranmer, Henry VIII's Archbishop of Canterbury, first printed in 1547, and reprinted and augmented throughout the century. The ideology suffered from the contradiction of emanating from a national church that both stressed its subordination to the crown – the monarch was the head of the church – and claimed to express a universal truth. But the *Homilies* had to be read every Sunday and holy day in churches that people had to attend; and their characteristic emphasis is on social stasis and hierarchy, and on obedience to the crown.[3]

The *Homilies* as an instrument of control did not survive the sixteenth century. But the *Book of Common Prayer*, again largely the creation of Cranmer, had its use enforced by successive Acts of Uniformity between 1549 and 1662; and imposed on a variously willing populace not only a particular version of protestant discourse but also, especially in terms of sexual relations, a highly traditional morality.[4]

The traditional view

Until recently, the dominant view of the Renaissance within English studies was that, at least until the middle of the seventeenth century, English culture was essentially unified. E. M. W. Tillyard, whose *Elizabethan World Picture* was first published in 1943, expounded the ideology of the Tudors, and claimed to be explicating the basic assumptions taken for granted by 'ordinary educated' people between 'the ages of Henry VIII and Charles I', between 1509 and 1649.[5] This view of the period was widely influential, and itself taken for granted for a generation.[6] But with the impact of new theoretical approaches around 1980, all this began to change.

New perspectives

Tillyard stressed the hierarchical nature of society in the Elizabethan era, portraying it as a 'Golden Age' in which social relations were stable and every individual knew his (*sic*) place. According to Tillyard, 'the dominant ruling idea of Renaissance England . . . was the belief in a cosmic order which governed both human institutions and natural phenomenona';[7] the monarch represented the centre of power and the rest of society was rigidly stratified in relation to that centre in descending order, from the nobility and gentry, through the ranks of the 'middling sort', to the labourers and vagabonds at the bottom of the human 'Chain of Being'. History was the narrative of those at the top of the hierarchy and events were viewed from their perspective; consequently, those at the bottom, those deemed to be outside of the centres of power, were not perceived to have played a significant role in historical events. Correspondingly, the 'great literature' of the period, produced by such well-known, canonical authors as Spenser, Shakespeare and Milton, was perceived to embody and reflect the interests of the élite and to reinforce contemporary social mores. However, recent developments in literary criticism have challenged this approach and have produced a rather different picture of Renaissance society and literature; as one critic put it recently, whereas Tillyard 'found order, many now find disorder, or anxiety about order. Where he projected an agreed consensus among Elizabethans as to what the world picture consisted of, we now discover contention and subversion.'[8] How, then, did this change in perspective occur and what are its implications for studying Renaissance literature?

If it is possible to locate such a shift in perspective to one critical text, then an obvious contender would be Stephen Greenblatt's *Renaissance Self-Fashioning*.[9] First published in 1980, this book has proved to be highly influential both within and beyond Renaissance literary studies; as well as introducing the term 'self-fashioning' into literary critics' vocabulary, it is one of the founding texts of the school of criticism now known as new historicism, although Greenblatt himself initially used the term 'cultural poetics'.[10] While it has subsequently become renowned for its heterogeneity, there are certain key assumptions that identify new historicists' approach to literary studies.[11] Rather than positing a transhistorical, universal human essence, new historicism reveals its debt to Michel Foucault in its assumption that human subjectivity is socially constructed within contemporary cultural codes or discourses; put most simply, a discourse is a particular area of language use (for example, law, theology, literature, science) and the individual is 'fashioned' or shaped by such discourses, which both produce and limit the subject position(s) that an individual can occupy at any given time. The critic's task, therefore, is to examine the way in which such discourses 'intersect, contradict, destabilize, cancel or modify each other' in order to 'arrive at an understanding of the broader ideological codes that order all discourse in that particular culture'.[12] To that end, new historicists examine the way in which such codes are present in both literary and non-literary texts, thereby breaking down the evaluative distinctions between 'good' and 'bad' writing, and simultaneously collapsing the distinction between 'literature' and 'history'.

Unlike Tillyard's formulation in which literature is a passive receptacle that unproblematically reflects an external historical reality, new historicists suggest that literature plays a constitutive or active role in 'constructing a culture's sense of reality'; thus, 'instead of [positing] a hierarchical relationship in which literature figures as the parasitic reflector of historical fact, one imagines a complex textualized universe in which literature participates in historical processes and in the political management of reality'.[13] Rather than seeking a monolithic, unitary, historical 'master narrative', new historicism's emphasis upon conflict and contradiction, both within and between different discourses, focuses upon discontinuities and explores the possibility of other histories. This is, in part, due to the fact that new historicists do not see power as being confined to those in authority, or to the monarch as in traditional historical narratives; again revealing a Foucauldian influence, they tend to see power as more widely dispersed throughout the different levels of society and, to varying degrees, within different cultural and literary forms. The fact that literature plays a part in constituting subjectivity and is seen as exercising influence in the 'political management of reality' raises the question of quite how, and to what extent, it both affects and is influenced by the period or culture in which it is produced. Thomas Healy, for example, argues that in Greenblatt's work

> [l]iterature is seen as often (perhaps unconsciously) acting in a subversive relation with [the power exercised by the state's dominant institutions], contending with it, questioning its norms. The real force of literature's subversive power, though, is ultimately contained because its texts are sanctioned by the state to play a subversive role, a role which state institutions can control.[14]

According to this model, then, literature can provoke questions about power and authority, but in the last resort it does not promote any real challenge to the authorities; for even its subversion has been legitimated by them and, therefore, on some level its political effectiveness has been contained.

Despite its tendency to emphasize the containment of potentially subversive elements, new historicism's focus upon the possibility of divergent or contradictory viewpoints draws attention to the fact that history is not an objective or disinterested discipline. Rather new historicists argue that history is only ever a *partial* representation of the past, and can itself be seen as a narrative that, like literary texts, needs to be read and interpreted; for a historical narrative is itself a construction and one which is heavily influenced by the historian's (or the 'author's') own position: 'the historiographer is never simply describing or retrieving the past but is engaged in constructing a past'.[15] The emphasis upon interpretation and partiality is both one of the major strengths and one of the major weaknesses of new historicist thought. It is its strength insofar as it acknowledges, in Louis Montrose's famous phrase, the 'historicity of texts and the textuality of history' (that is, the cultural specificity and ideological nature of literary texts, and the fact that history is only knowable through the mediation of texts) and enables its practitioners to explore the 'intertextual relations between canonical literary texts and other kinds of cultural data'; for one effect of this approach has been to challenge the notion of the literary canon 'and thereby to change not only *how* we read but *what* we read'.[16] In order to understand the significance of the formulation of a particular discourse within a literary text, new historicism emphasizes the need to examine how this discourse was articulated within other contemporary texts; for example, court records, diaries, autobiographies. These texts have traditionally been seen as 'historical' sources, but by emphasizing the fact that ideas circulate within a culture, new historicism argues that literature and history cannot be separated; rather, we need to study the way in which they influence each other. But this intertextual approach has also opened new historicism up to charges of arbitrariness; for the problem with any intertextual reading is how to justify the connections one is making. Why, for example, are these particular texts chosen and not others? And how representative are they of the issue under discussion?

While the question of 'arbitrariness' is a problematic aspect of new historicist approaches, there are other ways in which it has been challenged that are potentially more significant; firstly, there is the question of its political efficacy, and secondly, the extent to which it obscures issues of gender and sexuality. While it is an over-simplification to see *all* new historicists as emphasizing containment and *all* cultural materialists as stressing subversion, this distinction does indicate rather different political concerns.[17] From the latter perspective in *Radical Tragedy*, Jonathan Dollimore 'finds in [the theatre of Renaissance England] a substantial challenge'; while acknowledging that it offers 'not a vision of political freedom so much as a subversive knowledge of political domination' and that the rehearsal of threats can serve to contain them, he also points out that

> to contain a threat by rehearsing it one must first give it a voice, a part, a presence – in the theatre, as in the culture. Through this process the very condition of something's containment may constitute the terms of its challenge: opportunities for resistance become apparent, especially on the stage and even as the threat is being disempowered.[18]

Such an analysis acknowledges the material constraints that limit the enactment of opposition, but it also recognizes that it is often precisely the articulation of the subordinate nature of one's position that performs a critique. However, the extent of the subversiveness of such an articulation is not unqualified; as Dollimore explains elsewhere; 'not only does the idea have to be conveyed, it has also actually to be used to refuse authority *or* be seen by authority as capable and likely of being so used'.[19] In other words, the material consequences of the articulation of the 'subversive' or oppositional ideas has to be established in order to assess the degree to which it had an effect. And that can also mean examining the methods by which it was repressed: for 'such repression emerges not because the subversive was always contained, subversion being a ruse of power to consolidate itself, but because the challenge really *was* unsettling'.[20]

While Dollimore forcefully defends cultural materialism from being subsumed within new historicism, particularly by undermining Carol Thomas Neely's critique in which she conflates the two under the 'neologism' of 'cult-historicists', he rather too easily dismisses some other legitimate points that she raises.[21] For Neely points to the fact that although new historicists and cultural materialists are concerned with different histories and different points of view, much of their work replicates 'traditional' criticism insofar as it concentrates primarily upon male canonical authors (most often Shakespeare) and 'high' literary genres (such as tragedy). Furthermore, Judith Lowder Newton registers a concern that current discussion of both these theoretical approaches is 'often carried on as if their assumptions and practices had been produced by men' when they were, at least in part, influenced by the questions posed by feminist theory.[22] In this way, feminist critics have challenged not only traditional approaches to

Renaissance studies, but have also questioned the terms upon which more recent theories have been developed. For feminist critics have also interrogated the 'objectivity' of historical narratives, have examined the extent to which the subject is socially and culturally constructed, and have read texts that have not been traditionally viewed as literary (primarily because women's writing has been consistently excluded from the literary 'canon'). However, just as new historicist and cultural materialist critics have their differences, so too do feminist critics: while the latter group share a commitment to the struggle against patriarchy and sexism, the methods they employ to achieve this vary enormously.

Broadly speaking, feminist literary criticism can be divided into two general approaches, defined by Elaine Showalter as 'feminist critique' (focusing on woman as reader) and 'gynocriticism' (focusing on woman as writer), although as more writing by women becomes available it is increasingly possible to combine these two approaches.[23] But within these two broad categories, the specific approach taken by an individual critic reveals different nuances. At the heart of Neely's criticism of 'the new Renaissance discourses', for example, is a distrust of the poststructuralist influence upon them which she sees as having the potential to erase the subject; this, for her, precludes the possibility of practising feminist criticism, as she argues that '[i]f feminist criticism abandons the notion of the subject, replacing it with the much more slippery concept of subject positions, and by doing so calls into question the notion of gendered subjects, gendered authors, gendered texts, the ground of its critique is eliminated'.[24] But for critics influenced by the psychoanalytic theories of Hélène Cixous and Julia Kristeva, and those influenced by poststructuralist theory, the 'slippery concept of subject positions' is the very factor which facilitates a feminist critique.[25] Indeed, Neely's insistence upon the need for a subject could be seen as one of the problems which faces feminist criticism, that is the tendency to 're-essentialise Woman' in much the same way (although for different reasons) that Neely herself criticizes new historicists for 'reproducing' traditional history.

This difficulty is present not only in the performance of feminist critique, but also in the process of rediscovering women writers. While much valuable work has been done in this area, including the ground-breaking books *Redeeming Eve* and *The Virtue of Necessity*, and is continuing in the production of both new critical texts focusing on women's writing and anthologies which make their texts more widely available, one critic in particular has called attention to the need to examine the premises upon which the new 'canon' of women's writing is being established: Margaret J. Ezell warns against replicating the formation of a traditional male canon and imposing nineteenth- and twentieth-century assumptions upon Renaissance women writers by pointing out that '[b]ecause of the way we have defined authorship, audience, and literature, we have effectively silenced a large number of early women's voices in our very attempt to preserve and celebrate women's writings'.[26] Ezell makes the important point that our selection of women's writing can distort our understanding of women's literary and social history, for example, either by devaluing manuscript circulation or by silencing women's voices that are not deemed to be oppositional enough; in other words, Ezell is warning against complicity in silencing women's voices because they are not easily assimilated into contemporary 'feminist' concerns. While much work remains to be done, feminist critics have achieved a great deal, both by making a real, material difference to the current availability of texts by editing and anthologizing previously unpublished or 'forgotten' texts by women and producing critical texts which challenge historical categories; for example, *Rewriting the Renaissance* takes its cue from Joan Kelly-Gadol's question 'Did women have a Renaissance?', and *Women, Writing, History* poses the questions that 'we need to go on asking, What "women"? Whose "writing"? Which "history"?'.[27]

While new historicism, cultural materialism, and feminist criticism present a wide range of interpretive strategies, corporately they have transformed the nature of literary studies, especially perhaps Renaissance literary studies. Each of them recognizes the way in which human subjects and literary texts are socially constructed and the importance of examining different perspectives on history, which encourages us to read texts that have not been examined within the traditional literary canon; and each of them, at least in theory, encourages a self-conscious reflection upon critical practice and the categories or narratives by which we seek to understand the past.

The present collection

The present collection aims to provide a representative overview of the writing produced in the English Renaissance; and is very conscious of operating within these new parameters. It has a nucleus of canonical writers. But it sees them within the new perspectives. Marion Wynne-Davies, for example, discusses Spenser, especially the *Faerie Queene*, Book I, in terms of the Elizabethan system of patronage, focusing on the contradictory nature of a material, social practice which, nevertheless, claims to utter a metaphysical, transcendent truth. William Zunder sees the work of Marlowe, both the plays and the poetry, as crossed by a dialectic between traditional discourses of hierarchy and monarchy and a radical discourse of individualism. There is a marxist subtext here: the traditional discourses are seen as stemming from the superseded feudalism of the Middle Ages and the new individualism as stemming from the emergent capitalism of the 1580s and '90s. Bruce Woodcock, drawing on the work of the French theorist, Michel Foucault, sees the work of Donne and the seventeenth-century metaphysical poets as exhibiting an anxiety about male gender identity not dissimilar from that of our own time. In a discussion centring on the work of Herbert, Helen Wilcox places the seventeenth-century religious lyric, by women as well as men, in the ideological context of the age, and sees it as constituting a discourse at once personal and public, private and political. John Hoyles offers an interpretation of the whole of Marvell's work, poetry and prose, in the context of the mid-seventeenth-century revolution, in particular of the Engagement controversy of 1649–52, and sees it as registering a dialectic between sexual and political commitment and non-commitment. And Tony Davies, drawing on both poststructuralist and feminist perspectives, sees Milton's work as inscribing patriarchy, yet, in its shifting ascriptions of gender, also opening up a space in which patriarchy can be interrogated, even refused.

The collection also extends the canon: into the women's writing of the period and into kinds of writing not traditionally considered to be literary – or sufficiently literary. Kathleen McLuskie, for instance, argues that commercial pressure on the new capitalist theatre of the late sixteenth century and the demands of theatrical pleasure led to the destabilization of high tragedy, and of the male revenger in particular, and led in turn to the emergence of a new tragic form centring on women and on the authenticity of actual, recorded experience. Domestic tragedy is thus moved from the wings of traditional discussions of Renaissance drama to centre-stage. Melanie Hansen, drawing in part on the work of Roland Barthes in *Mythologies* (1957), discusses the variety of texts mapping the new geography of Renaissance England produced by the Society of Antiquaries from

1572, and sees them as disrupting the traditional discourse of monarchy (hence James I's hostility), and subserving the class interest of the new gentry. Mark Thornton Burnett, in a discussion of the popular culture of the time that draws ultimately on the insights of the Italian theorist, Antonio Gramsci, sees popular representations of women, women servants, and apprentices as characteristically ambivalent, both supporting and interrogating traditional structures of gender and class. Garthine Walker, in a parallel discussion of representations of criminal women in the pamphlet writing of the time, argues, differently, that representations of women and gender there were not oppositional but integral to general representations of order and hierarchy, sin and repentance. Suzanne Trill, utilizing poststructuralist concepts, especially those of Jacques Derrida, argues that translation was central to the humanist project, just as the Psalms of the Old Testament were central to the construction of protestant subjectivity, and so places Mary Sidney's translation of the Psalms at the centre of the English Renaissance. In the last two contributions to the collection, Christopher Kendrick relates the discursive and symbolic dimensions of the Digger project in the middle years of the seventeenth century, in particular the writing of Gerrard Winstanley, to the developing class relations of early agrarian capitalism; and Kate Chedgzoy discusses the writing of the Fifth Monarchist, Anna Trapnel, again in the revolutionary moment in the middle of the seventeenth century, focusing on the representative ambiguity of a woman writer who constructs her own identity by denying herself any autonomy from God.

William Zunder
Suzanne Trill

Notes

1. See 'The First Anniversary', lines 205–18, in *John Donne: The Complete English Poems*, ed. A. J. Smith (Harmondsworth, 1971), p. 276.
2. 'Epitaph. Intended for Sir Isaac Newton, In Westminster-Abbey', line 2, in *The Poems of Alexander Pope*, ed. John Butt (London, 1963), p. 808.
3. See the extract from the 'Exhortation Concerning Good Order and Obedience to Rulers and Magistrates', quoted in the *Documents* section below, pp. 257–8.
4. See the excerpt from the 'Solemnisation of Matrimony' in the *Documents* section, pp. 258–9.

5. E. M. W. Tillyard, *The Elizabethan World Picture* (London, 1943; reprinted Harmondsworth, 1972), pp. 7–9.
6. Not by everyone, though. See, for example, Hiram Haydn, *The Counter-Renaissance* (New York, 1950).
7. Thomas Healy, *New Latitudes: Theory and English Renaissance Literature* (London, 1992), p. 7.
8. Ibid., p. 9.
9. Stephen Greenblatt, *Renaissance Self-Fashioning: From More to Shakespeare* (Chicago, 1980). Obviously, Greenblatt's book did not effect this change on its own: the change in perspective in Renaissance studies has also been affected by broader developments in literary criticism. However, Greenblatt's book does represent an important shift in critical approaches to Renaissance studies in particular.
10. Ibid., p. 5.
11. H. Aram Veeser summarizes them as follows: 1. every expressive act is embedded in a network of material practices; 2. every act of unmasking, critique, and opposition uses the tools it condemns and falls prey to the practice it exposes; 3. literary and non-literary 'texts' circulate inseparably; 4. no discourse, imaginative or archival, gives access to unchanging truths nor expresses inalterable human nature: see *The New Historicism*, ed. H. Aram Veeser (New York and London, 1989) p. xi.
12. Don E. Wayne, 'New historicism', in *Encyclopedia of Literature and Criticism*, ed. Martin Coyle, Peter Garside, Malcolm Kelsall, and John Peck (New York and London, 1990), pp. 795, 793.
13. Jean E. Howard, 'The new historicism in Renaissance studies', *English Literary Renaissance*, 15 (1985), 13–43 (25).
14. Healy, *New Latitudes*, p. 75.
15. Wayne, 'New Historicism', in Coyle *et al.*, eds, *Encyclopedia*, p. 795.
16. Louis A. Montrose, 'Professing the Renaissance; the poetics and politics of culture', in Veeser, ed., *The New Historicism*, p. 20, and Wayne, 'New Historicism', in Coyle *et al.*, eds, *Encyclopedia*, p. 801.
17. This distinction is succinctly illustrated by Jonathan Dollimore in 'Shakespeare, cultural materialism, feminism and marxist humanism', *New Literary History (NLH)* 21 (1990), 471–93 (472).
18. Idem, *Radical Tragedy: Religion, Ideology and Power in the Drama of Shakespeare and his Contemporaries*, 2nd edn (Hemel Hempstead, 1989), p. xxi.
19. Idem, 'Shakespeare, cultural materialism and the new historicism', in *Political Shakespeare: New Essays in Cultural Materialism* (Manchester and New York, 1985), p. 13.
20. Idem, in *NLH* 21 (1990), 482.
21. Ibid., 472. Dollimore is, in part, responding to Carol Thomas Neely's article, 'Constructing the subject; feminist practice and the new

Renaissance discourses', in *English Literary Renaissance (ELR)* 18 (1988), 5–18.

22. Judith Lowder Newton, 'History as usual? Feminism and the "new historicism" ', in Veeser, ed., *The New Historicism*, p. 153.

23. Elaine Showalter, 'Toward a feminist poetics', in *The New Feminist Criticism*, ed. Elaine Showalter (London, 1989 [1985]), p. 128.

24. Neely, in *ELR* 18 (1988), 13.

25. For an exploration of the importance of French feminism, see Toril Moi, *Sexual/Textual Politics: Feminist Literary Theory* (London and New York, 1985). For a discussion of the advantages and disadvantages of poststructuralism for feminist criticism, see Chris Weedon, *Feminist Practice and Poststructuralist Theory* (Oxford, 1993 [1987]) and Janet Ransom, 'Feminism, difference and discourse: the limits of discursive analysis for feminism', in *Up Against Foucault: Explorations of Some Tensions between Foucault and Feminism*, ed. Caroline Ramazanoglu (London and New York, 1993), pp. 123–46.

26. Elaine V. Beilin, *Redeeming Eve: Women Writers of the English Renaissance* (Princeton, 1987); Elaine Hobby, *The Virtue of Necessity: English Women's Writing 1646–1688* (London, 1988); Margaret J. M. Ezell, *Writing Women's Literary History* (Baltimore, 1993), p. 38.

27. *Rewriting the Renaissance: The Discourses of Sexual Difference in Early Modern Europe*, ed. Margaret W. Ferguson, Maureen Quilligan, and Nancy J. Vickers (Chicago and London, 1986), p. xxx; *Women, Writing, History 1640–1740*, ed. Isobel Grundy and Susan Wiseman (London, 1992), p. 14.

Part I

1 'If we shadows have offended': Edmund Spenser and the Elizabethan world of patronage

Marion Wynne-Davies

I

The quotation in the title of this essay is taken from the epilogue to Shakespeare's play, *A Midsummer Night's Dream* (1595), where Puck turns to the audience and requests their response to the dramatic entertainment just witnessed. The full speech runs as follows:

> If we shadows have offended,
> Think but this, and all is mended,
> That you have but slumber'd here
> While these visions did appear.
> And this weak and idle theme,
> No more yielding but a dream,
> Gentles, do not reprehend:
> If you pardon, we will mend.
> And, as I am an honest Puck,
> If we have unearned luck
> Now to 'scape the serpent's tongue,
> We will make amends ere long;
> Else the Puck a liar call.
> So, goodnight unto you all.
> Give me your hands, if we be friends,
> And Robin shall restore amends.
>
> (V. i. 409–24)[1]

This epilogue allows one of the characters in the play to refer to his own and the text's fictional nature, while at the same time eliciting a critical judgement from the real men and women sitting in the auditorium. Puck offers a choice between being 'offended', thereby rejecting the play as a meaningless dream, or of being 'friends' with the 'visions', so that they become a truth as potent as that of the sixteenth-century reality outside the Globe Theatre. Of course, Puck constructs the audience as choosing the latter option, since the conventions of play-going demand the applause – 'Give me your hands . . .' – which he asserts will signify the assurance of enjoyment. The epilogue thus functions as a point of exchange between the playwright and the play-goers, where the former acknowledges his need for the latter's patronage, while at the same time demanding that they acknowledge the power of his art. This mutuality of interest, which is endemic to the Elizabethan discourse of patronage, pervades the poetry of Edmund Spenser just as it is evidenced in the plays of William Shakespeare. There is, however, one significant difference: the poet's constructed 'audience' consisted, not of the socially diverse theatre-going public, but of a single and autocratic monarch – Elizabeth I.

The importance of patronage to Spenser becomes apparent when tracing his career. Born in London (c. 1552), he belonged to the growing class of 'gentlemen' who, because they did not belong to the nobility, had to rely upon education and political employment to gain them acceptance in court circles. Spenser was educated as a 'poor scholar' at the Merchant Taylor's School (1561), before taking a degree at Cambridge (1573) and entering the service of the powerful Earl of Leicester as a confidential emissary (1579). As the foremost of the Queen's favourites and the centre of his own influential faction, Leicester's support clearly benefited Spenser, who subsequently became acquainted with other Elizabethan court writers, such as Sir Philip Sidney, as well as being awarded the lucrative post of private secretary to Lord Grey de Wilton, the newly appointed Lord Deputy of Ireland. Spenser travelled with Grey to Ireland in 1580, thereby commencing his rise through the administration of the province, which culminated in his selection as sheriff-designate of Cork in 1598. During this period Spenser also established his reputation in the literary and court circles of London with the publication of several well-received works. These include: the pastoral sequence, *The Shepheardes Calender* (1579); the unfinished romance epic, *The Faerie Queene* (Books I–III published in 1590 and Books IV–VI in 1596); the satirical *Complaints* (1591) and allegory of the court, *Colin Clout's Come Home Again* (1595); three groups of love poems, *Amoretti* and *Epithalamion* (both 1595) and *Prothalamion* (1596); two elegies, *Daphnaida* (1591) and – for Sir Philip Sidney – *Astrophel* (1595); the neoplatonic *Fowre Hymnes* (1596); and finally, his prose treatise, *A Viewe of the Present State of Ireland* (registered in 1598, but not published until 1633).[2] Thus, by the late 1590s Spenser could claim to have achieved a certain measure of success in both political and literary spheres: he had become a landed gentleman in Ireland and a well-respected author at home. However, only a few months after being made sheriff and registering *A Viewe*, his castle and lands were totally destroyed by Irish forces during the Tyrone rebellion against English rule, and he returned to London, dying on 13 January 1599. Spenser's funeral was paid for by Leicester's stepson, the Earl of Essex (Leicester having died in 1588), and was attended by poets and courtiers alike. He was buried at Westminster Abbey with orders from the Queen that a memorial be erected, although this was not carried out until 1620.

What is immediately apparent from this history is that Spenser created a dialectical identity for himself: he was both a clever and opportunistic courtier who was deeply enmeshed in Elizabethan politics, as well as a brilliant poet and man of letters. For a twentieth-century reader, the divide appears virtually unbreachable – after all, how many of today's politicians could qualify for the Nobel Prize in literature? In the English Renaissance, however, such a combination of literary skill and governmental interests would have been less surprising; for example, two of Spenser's associates, Sidney and Sir Walter Raleigh, pursued a similarly bifurcated career. Partly, their self-expectations were derived from the humanist ideal of courtly behaviour, which had been typified in Baldassare Castiglione's *The Courtier* (1528; translated into English by Sir Thomas Hoby in 1561), as encouraging physical prowess, moral integrity, artistic skill and diplomatic dexterity.[3] But, as courtiers dependent upon the bounty of a powerful Renaissance prince, they also needed to entertain and impress their near-omnipotent patrons. Therefore, since both literary and political talent was used to define the courtier's identity in relation to the monarch they served, no division of interest was immediately apparent, and if Elizabeth I admired shrewd advisors, she also prized the display of keen, imaginative wit. For Spenser this meant that his poetic flourishes were as important to his advancement at court as governmental accomplishments in Ireland, and that success was measured according to the Queen's reception of his activities. Like Shakespeare, he required his audience-of-one to be 'friends', and not 'offended'.

Patronage, however, cannot sustain itself through a one-way system of perpetual praise. Rather, it is a practice of exchange, the artist's celebratory investment being repaid with the patron's recognition of the worth of their creation – usually with a monetary recompense. As John Barrell writes in his analysis of Shakespeare's 29th sonnet:

> Among the characteristics of the discourse of patronage . . . are that it represents personal relations as economic relations . . . and that it represents personal reputation as something to be measured in terms not of moral worth or worthlessness, but in terms of honour and shame and their equivalents, which it estimates in terms of material success.[4]

Thus, when Spenser addresses his monarch at the beginning of *The Faerie Queene*, he states explicitly that, while it is she who has inspired him to write, he expects her to read what he has written:

> O Goddesse heauenly bright,
> Mirrour of grace and Maiestie diuine,
> Great Lady of the greatest Isle, whose light
> Like *Phoebus* lampe throughout the world doth shine,
> Shed thy faire beames into my feeble eyne,
> And raise my thoughts too humble and too vile,
> To thinke of that true glorious type of thine,
> The argument of mine afflicted stile:
> The which to heare, vouchsafe, O dearest dred a-while.
>
> (I Proem 4)[5]

The text is required to fulfil a double function, conveying pleasure to the reader through overt compliment and literary skill, as well as demanding that the power of the author to command that response is acknowledged and rewarded. Thus a curious split runs through works of art which participate in the discourse of patronage: they simultaneously offer and subvert the expected laudation. In the quotation above Spenser refers to Elizabeth I as a 'Goddesse heauenly bright', but the next words undercut her magnificence, since she is described merely as a 'Mirrour of grace', rather than its source. While the Queen is praised for her magnificence, she is simultaneously reminded that the light is not generated by her, but simply a reflection of 'Maiestie diuine', that is, God's glory. The poet instructs the patron that, while her immediate greatness has animated the poet, she is simply a debased material reflection of a higher power, which has in reality supplied the motivation for the artistic endeavour. *The Faerie*

Queene might superficially praise Elizabeth I, but when Spenser lays claim to the higher spiritual authority of God, he succeeds in displacing the Queen from her position of eminence, while at the same time positing his poem as a more accurate reflection of God's splendour. This shift of interest, from poet to patron and back again, existed within and contributed towards the Renaissance discourse of patronage. The patron's desire to be praised, in order to enhance their own social standing, was equalled by the author's expectation of material reward; and the assertion of the text's ability to transcend material concerns, thereby guaranteeing the patron's fame, existed only at the expense of, and/or acceptance of, the author's pre-eminence. These differing claims could not co-exist in harmony, and, not surprisingly, the literature of the Elizabethan court, like Spenser's *The Faerie Queene*, is fraught with the conflicting investments of patrons and poets.[6] In the remainder of this essay I intend to discuss *The Faerie Queene* in the context of patronage, and to examine the roles of Arthur and Gloriana in Book I (cantos vii–ix) more closely, uncovering the conflict inherent in the yoking together of political and religious allegiances through the rhetorical device of allegory.

II

The Faerie Queene, even though Spenser never finished writing the twelve books he originally planned, is one of the longest and most intricate poems in the English language. It was originally published in two parts, Books I–III celebrating the virtues of holiness, temperance and chastity with their respective champions, the Red Cross Knight, Guyon and Britomart, and Books IV–VI exemplifying the virtues of concord, justice and courtesy through their particular representative knights, Cambel and Telamond, Artegal and Calidore. There are two characters who link the separate books: the first is Prince Arthur who embodies the sum of all virtues – magnificence – and who travels through faery land rescuing the other figures and questing for his love, the Faery Queen. The second associative character is Gloriana, the Faery Queen herself, who, although she never actually appears in the poem, is the inspirational centre of the whole. It is from Cleopolis, the unseen court of Gloriana, that the knights depart on their missions, and, through Arthur's persistent search, the poem gravitates in a return motion towards that court and its monarch. Explained in this manner, the poem appears to combine moral didacticism with courtly romance, and the archaic language Spenser uses certainly affirms the text's medieval overtones. However, *The Faerie Queene* does not rest upon these basic narrative and instructive levels.

Spenser explains how the poem should be understood in an introductory letter addressed to Raleigh, where he writes:

> Sir knowing how doubtfully all Allegories may be construed, and this booke of mine, which I haue entituled the Faery Queene, being a continued Allegory, or darke conceit, I haue thought good . . . to discouer vnto you the general intention and meaning . . .   (p. 737)

He then proceeds to identify certain characters and devices within the text, such as Arthur representing 'magnificence', the Red Cross Knight, 'Holynes', and,

> In that Faery Queene I meane glory in my generall intention, but in my particular I conceiue the most excellent and glorious person of our soueraine the Queene, and her kingdome in Faery Land.   (p. 737)

There are, therefore, two ways of interpreting the poem: firstly as a 'generall' moral allegory, and secondly, as a 'particular' or political allegory. In this manner Prince Arthur may be both a symbol of perfection, as well as suggesting the Tudor inheritance of a mythic British greatness, and Gloriana may signify both glorious virtue and Elizabeth I.[7] In both cases, what Spenser relies upon is the ability of his readers to interpret the 'continued Allegory'. An Elizabethan readership would have been familiar with the conventions of allegory; for example, Henry Peacham in *The Garden of Eloquence* (1577) defines 'alligoria' as 'when a sentence hath another meaning, then the proper signyfication doth expresse',[8] and George Puttenham in *The Arte of English Poesie* (1589) comments that

> *Allegoria* is when we do speak in sence translative and wrested from the owne signification, nevertheless applied to another not altogether contrary.[9]

The device of allegory, therefore, demands that the text be read on two levels: firstly as a simple narrative or description, and secondly, as having another, more covert, signification, which is imbued with greater resonance and power by the very fact that it has been partially concealed. Such a practice of reading requires skill and knowledge to decode the allegory, in addition to the simple processes of pleasure more commonly employed in literary enterprise.

The description of Arthur's armour in Book I, canto vii, stanzas 29–36, provides us with a good example of how Spenser employs allegory in *The Faerie Queene*. The champion of Book I, the Red Cross Knight, has been defeated by the witch Duessa and the giant Orgoglio, and has left the virtuous lady Una without a defender. In her search for aid, Una sees a knight riding towards her, and the subsequent passage appears almost cinematographic in style, in that the figure appears to get closer and closer, increasing the focus from the first hazy impression of magnificence to a sharp depiction of the minute details of the Prince's armour. The individual symbols of sword, shield and helmet are thus placed within the context of a shifting temporality: like Una, the reader 'sees' and interprets each emblematic unit, but is also aware of a gradual movement forward in time and place, so that, by the last stanza of the portrait, Arthur's function has become clear on both planes of allegoric connotation. On the simplest level, therefore, Arthur is a brave knight who has been brought into the story to rescue Una and her defeated champion; however, by decoding his 'arms' the other concealed meanings may be uncovered.

At first, Una perceives only the reflected light from Arthur's 'glitterand armour' (29.4), but she then begins to distinguish sharper points of light through the general sheen:

> Athwart his brest a bauldrick braue he ware,
> That shynd, like twinkling stars, with stons most pretious rare.
>
> And in the midst thereof one pretious stone
>   Of wondrous worth, and eke of wondrous mights,
>   Shapt like a Ladies head, exceeding shone,
>   Like *Hesperus* emongst the lesser lights,
>   And strove for to amaze the weaker sights.
>
> (I. vii. 29. 8–9 and 30. 1–5)

Although the shift from armour to baldric (a sword-belt worn across the shoulder) accords perfectly with the visual impression of the approaching figure, the thematic choice of giving a decorated belt pre-eminence seems somewhat inappropriate for a puissant knight. Why not, for example, describe Arthur's sword or shield? The unexpectedness of the symbol halts our progress through the narrative and makes us look more closely at this starry accoutrement. The clue to its inner identity is the central stone, which is 'Shapt like a Ladies head' and is compared to the star '*Hesperus*'. Another name for Hesperus is 'Venus' which suggests, through an allusion to the goddess of love, the romantic nature of the Prince's quest; an interpretation which is affirmed by the fact that the stone depicts a lady, and by its central position over the Prince's heart. In this sense, the primary situation of the baldric as symbol gives prominence to Arthur's identity as courtly lover, as well as privileging his connection with Gloriana and, hence, the poem's political allegory. Thus, as the Prince enters the poem, his moral and chivalric perfection is transposed from the fictional world, through the double meaning of the allegory, onto Spenser's real-life sixteenth-century patron, Elizabeth I. Praise for Arthur becomes praise for the Queen. Moreover, the use of light as a metaphor increases the associative faculties of the baldric, allowing a play of reflections to occur through the poem: Elizabeth I's 'light' (1 Proem 4.3) is mirrored by the text, which in turn allows Arthur's fictional self to 'shine . . . farre away', shedding reflected and renewed glory back onto the Renaissance monarch. But Arthur's baldric is not the only aspect of his description which 'amaze[s] weaker sights'.

The last piece of armour to be described is Arthur's shield, which is 'all closely couer'd' (33.1), perhaps explaining why Una appears not to see it until the Prince has almost reached her. The shield is made out of diamond which not only resists all weapons because of its strength, but has the power to defeat all enchantments when it is displayed:

> For so exceeding shone his glistring ray,
> That *Phoebus* golden face it did attaint,
> As when a cloud his beames doth ouer-lay;
> And siluer Cynthia wexed pale and faint,
> As when her face is staynd with magicke arts constraint.
>
> No magicke arts hereof had any might,
> Nor bloudie wordes of bold Enchaunters call,
> But all that was not such, as seemd in sight,
> Before that shield did fade, and suddeine fall:
> And when him list the raskall routes appall,
> Men into stone therewith he could transmew,
> And stones to dust, and dust to nought at all.
>
> (I. vii. 34. 5–9 and 35. 1–7)

Arthur's diamond shield is a Christian symbol; its sources are the biblical shield of faith in Ephesians 6.16, and in Tasso's spiritual epic *Gerusalem Liberata* (1581) where the diamond shield defends those faithful to God.[10] Moreover, its power to defeat magic enchantments affirms its holy signification, while its timeless quality – 'stones to dust, and dust to nought at all' – reminds us of God's eternal power. Arthur's shield accords perfectly with his identity within the religious allegory of Book I where, for example, he is described as 'heauenly grace' (viii. 1.3) and rescues the Red Cross Knight from the sin of pride (Orgoglio) and false truth (Duessa). But while it elevates the fictional character of the Prince within the spiritual interpretation of the text, it simultaneously distances him from the political allegory and Gloriana/Elizabeth I. Unlike his armour and baldric, which shine like the sun and stars, Arthur's shield is so bright that it makes Phoebus and Cynthia (the sun and moon) look dull in comparison. Elizabeth I's glory has already been compared to that of Phoebus (1 Proem 4.3–4), and she was often depicted as the goddess Cynthia, the virgin huntress, in contemporary literature.[11] Therefore, by being brighter than either, Arthur's shield establishes itself as the more potent source of power, the religious allegory superseding the political identifications at this point.

Initially, there appears to be no overt diminishing of Elizabeth's monarchic role, since she would, after all, have expected her worldly authority to be on a lower scale than God's heavenly omnipotence, even though she might reasonably have assumed no direct threat to her rule would ever emerge from that divine being. However, the problem with Arthur's shield is that instead of being clearly presented, like the other arms, it is covered up. To begin with, the only way in which the reader can access what lies beneath the concealment is by relying upon what the author tells us is there. Spenser presents himself to us and, more significantly, to his most important reader Elizabeth I, as more capable of interpreting the true Christian faith signified by the shield than either ourselves or the Queen. Indeed, Spenser makes it explicit that he has chosen to veil the shield because its naked power would be unbearable to the mortal eye: 'The same to wight he neuer wont disclose' (34.1). This veiling process is repeated at several points in the poem: for example, Una's face (I.4) is concealed because Christian truth is too strong to be perceived by humankind in their postlapsarian state. The poet must therefore act as a conveyor for, but also a protector of, spiritual truth; he or she becomes, in Sidney's phrase, a 'vates', or prophetic counsellor. Sidney defines the poet's vatic role in *An Apologie for Poetrie* (1595):

> For these third [poets] be they which most properly do imitate to teach and delight, and to imitate borrow nothing of what is, hath been, or shall be; but range, only reined with learned discretion, into the divine consideration of what may be and should be.[12]

This practice allows, even demands, Spenser to engineer a shift away from the concerns of patronage – 'what is' – towards the metaphysical and timeless interests of moral and spiritual perfection – 'what may be and should be'. The fictional character, Prince Arthur, while conveying praise of Elizabeth I within the political allegory, is thus simultaneously developed into the more highly valued ideal of Christian faith in the religious allegory, and by contriving this shift of interest, the poet is likewise transported from the material to the holy realm.

There is one final element in the description of the covered shield which develops further the way in which the poet stresses his superior worth within the discourse of patronage. As has already been pointed out, *The Faerie Queene* relies upon allegory to convey differing levels of meaning, and the way in which this is managed is partly elucidated by Spenser in the letter to Raleigh, where he acknowledges that some readers will be displeased with such 'shadow[s]', in which meaning is 'clowdily enwrapped in Allegorial devices' (p. 737). Spenser's choice of vocabulary indicates that he uses allegory to enwrap his meanings, just as the true faith of Arthur's shield is 'closely couer'd. In *The Faerie Queene* the veiling image acts as a metaphor for the device of allegory, here commuting the shield into further symbolic signification, that of the text itself. The central stone of the baldric with its suggestion of Elizabeth I might well shine brightly enough to 'amaze the weaker sights' (30.5), but the light of the shield, with its Christian overtones and identification with Spenser's text, is so brilliant that it defies time itself. The Queen as patron remains caught within the mortal world, but Spenser lays claim to a timeless permanence for the poem's metaphysical truth and, more particularly, for the text itself – if *The Faerie Queene* may be identified with the shield, then it too may defy time 'turning all to dust'. In a classic form of the negotiation between patron and poet, the text becomes both an assurance of the former's continued fame, while at the same time reminding the patron of his or her own mutability.

By stressing the text's immutable and universal qualities, the writer may imply a system of unchanging meaning which the contemporary reader finds as easily accessible as his or her sixteenth-century counterpart, and, until recently, twentieth-century criticism has read *The Faerie Queene* in the light of this interpretative process. This view is expressed by Isabel MacCaffrey in *Spenser's Allegory* (1976), one of the most detailed studies of the poem, where she writes that 'allegorical fictions develop within a "mental space" which is analogically related to the spaces realizing God's "great idea", the macrocosmic spaces of the universe'.[13] For MacCaffrey the two levels of allegorical interpretation are identified with immediate circumstance and an eternal infinity, so that Arthur may be associated with Tudor propaganda, but his essential and true meaning is that of heavenly grace. However, by the end of the 1970s, and certainly through the '80s, the understanding of 'allegory' was to change radically. Maureen Quilligan's *The Language of Allegory* (1979) suggested that, rather than offer a fixed meaning, allegory necessitated a perpetual shifting of signification: 'the process of interpretation can go on indefinitely, as it is in fact supposed to with allegory'.[14] Instead of reading *The Faerie Queene* as projecting a veiled, but nevertheless unified, meaning, criticism began to suggest that the poem encourages the reader to quest for a single truth, but that, at the same time, fulfilment is perpetually deferred, intimating that perhaps no ultimate signification exists after all. Like Arthur searching for the character (the faery queen), the reader pursues the meaning of the text (*The Faerie Queene*), and, like the fictional Prince, we too are doomed to fail.

Allegory can never satisfy the desire for a single truth since it inevitably includes the element of temporality; as Spenser pointed out in his letter to Raleigh it must be 'continued'. When static interpretation is used, the figurative device is called symbolism, but as soon as a movement through time and space is added to the signification, we have allegory. Thus, the separate pieces of Arthur's armour may be recognized as symbols, but the total description of the Prince requires a visualization of the character moving slowly towards Una, thereby signifying allegory. In addition, there is a more emphatic underlining of the poem's invocation of mutability. At the very end of our first sight of Arthur and the presentation of his armour, we are unexpectedly informed of his death:

> But when he dyde, the Faerie Queene it brought
> To Faerie lond, where yet it may be seene, if sought.
>
> (36.9–9)

The perception of the character immediately changes to encompass fictional and real time, as well as the dynamic existing between the two. The lines place *The Faerie Queene* in the context of Arthurian narrative, where Spenser's contribution occupies a position at the start of Arthur's career: in Spenser's poem he is still an untried prince and not the king of legend. The plot has already been fixed and most readers would have been aware that Arthur will die in a last climactic battle, his body being conveyed to the fairy isle of Avalon by three unidentified queens, one of whom might be – if we follow Spenser's tale – Gloriana.[15] By referring to the broader fictional context, Spenser places the Prince within a temporal context, which posits a previous and subsequent existence, as well as inescapable loss and negation. Yet, in a further twist, Spenser refers to the armour which may still be seen in faery land if the reader chooses to look for it. Here, through the direct address from poet to reader, the timescale jumps into a contemporary framework, demanding that we enter faery land, that is the poem, and quest for the moral and Christian idealism presented to us through the previous eight stanzas of allegory. This is, of course, in some ways exactly what has happened through the practice of decoding and interpretation, but while Spenser propels us into the search, he simultaneously informs us of its futile nature. All we can ever discover are the glorious and glittering arms, since the inner identity, that which exists within the armour, has long since died. All we may read are the attractive and dazzling words – the inner meaning of the poem can never be understood, since it does not exist. As Jonathan Goldberg comments in his analysis of Spenser's poetry, *Endlesse Worke: Spenser and the Structures of Discourse* (1981):

> In *The Faerie Queene*, how difficult it is to fix meanings in the endless flood of signifiers, always, it seems, equally far from arriving at a signified.[16]

What we are left with is a nostalgia for an ideal past, a golden Arthurian era, where truth, both in its moral and textual guises, was realizable. But we are concurrently presented with a bitter recognition of mutability, where nothing is certain and the dark shadows of mortality threaten.

III

The existence of *The Faerie Queene* is as precariously balanced between two alternative discourses, as Spenser's life and work was poised between the two-fold demands of Renaissance patronage. The text shifts from political propaganda, overtly praising Elizabeth I, to spiritual idealism, where the vatic poet instructs his patron in the eternal laws of God. The author has similarly to negotiate a passage between the demands of his monarch to be served before all others, and the need to project a fictional entity which will outlast the vicissitudes of contemporary fashion. Both poem and poet are caught in the knot of time: they must answer the requirements of their immediate position within history, and yet attempt to propel themselves into a timeless and universal system. While remaining in the present, they must conform to the rules of patronage, praising the patron because he or she controls the discourse within that time and place. Hence, Spenser must celebrate Elizabeth I if he wishes to attain preferment in the material society of the late sixteenth-century British court. On the other hand, the very requirements of patronage – to offer continued fame – pitches author and text into a universalized system of meaning, where history becomes unimportant and the fictional discourse supplants the political one. In *The Faerie Queene* Elizabeth might be eulogized, but she is also reminded of her own mortality in the face of the text's higher and more eternal ideological tenets. If we think of these alternate demands as two lines of power – the synchronic one emphasizing historical and political discourse, and the diachronic one signifying the universal and timeless discourse – we can envisage *The Faerie Queene* at the intersection, and Spenser opening his poem to the two conflicting ideological forces. Clark Hulse describes this 'residual entanglement of the political and mythical' and the 'pressure to pull the two apart' in 'Spenser: myth, politics, poetry', where he concludes:

> Poetic myth might indeed be a language of counsel that reminds the prince of his strength and warns him of its limits, but neither goal can be achieved by simple flattery or panegyric, or pompous moralizing. Poetic language must be analytical as much as it is celebratory, laying bare the basis of power and the ways – good or bad, successful or flawed – that it is wielded by the prince or by the poet.[17]

Allegory illustrates this dialectical allegiance perfectly, since it can convey, simultaneously, both discourses through its own cloven form. But what allegory also suggests is that the diachronic may be negated by the synchronic, just as the synchronic is subverted by the diachronic. In other words, the material concerns of patronage are undercut by the metaphysical aspirations of the poem and the vatic subjectivity of the poet, but similarly, any universalized identity claimed by author and text is immediately frustrated by allegory's recognition of the power of temporality and the inevitability of mortality.

The relationship between Prince Arthur and the Faery Queen acts as a trope within the poem for this aporia. Indeed, on one level, the quest by a mythical and fictional character for a sixteenth-century English monarch was always doomed to fail. The chasm between the two figures is too great, divided as they are by myth and history, text and reality, and fiction and materialism. They represent the powerful forces which cut through the text, continually structuring its practice, but simultaneously leaving only a void at their intersection. Or do they?

When Arthur has triumphed over the forces of evil in Book I and rescued Una and the Red Cross Knight, he explains his quest to them and describes the dream vision which has driven him to enter faery land:

> For-wearied with my sports, I did alight
>   From loftie steed, and downe to sleepe me layd;
>   The verdant gras my couch did goodly dight,
>   And pillow was my helmet faire displayd:
>   Whiles euery sence the humour sweet embayd,
>   And slombring soft my hart did steale away,
>   Me seemed, by my side a royall Mayd
>   Her daintie limbes full softely down did lay:
> So faire a creature yet saw neuer sunny day.
>
> Most goodly glee and louely blandishment
>   She to me made, and bad me loue her deare,
>   For dearly sure her loue was to me bent,
>   And when iust time expired should appeare.
>   But whether dreames delude, or true it were,
>   Was neuer hart so rauisht with delight,
>   Ne liuing man like words did euer heare,
>   As she to me deliuered all that night;
> And at her parting said, She Queene of Faeries hight.
>
> (I. ix. 13–14)

When Arthur awakes he is uncertain as to whether he has merely dreamed of the Faery Queen – 'dreames delude' – or whether Gloriana has actually been with him – 'true it were' – but he sets out to find his lost love regardless. For the Prince the question of metaphysical vision and material reality becomes inconsequential, since the pleasure of the experience is such – 'so rauisht with delight' – that he must attempt to regain it. Arthur is like the audience of *A Midsummer Night's Dream*, in that, while he is perfectly aware of the implausibility of the 'visions' and 'dream', he too gives his 'hands' and offers applause. When Arthur confides in Una about his dream vision, he echoes Puck's final address to the audience, affirming that the power of the poem and the potency of the performance lie, not in the cloven allegiances of the diachronic and synchronic axes, but in the provocation of desire and the delight of the imagination when these two lines meet and, momentarily, ignite.

Notes

1. William Shakespeare, *A Midsummer Night's Dream*, ed. Harold F. Brooks (London, 1979), pp. 127–8.
2. Spenser's biography and all his works may be found in *The Works of Edmund Spenser – A Variorum Edition*, ed. Edwin Greenlaw *et al.* (Baltimore, 1932–49), 10 vols. A more readily available edition of the poetry is *Poetical Works*, ed. J. C. Smith and E. de Selincourt (Oxford, 1912).
3. Baldassare Castiglione, *The Courtier* (New York, 1967).
4. John Barrell, *Poetry, Language and Politics* (Manchester, 1988), p. 22.
5. All quotations from *The Faerie Queene* are taken from Edmund Spenser, *The Faerie Qveene*, ed. A. C. Hamilton (London, 1977); subsequent references will be given parenthetically in the text.
6. See Guy Fitch Lytle and Stephen Orgel, eds, *Patronage in the Renaissance* (Princeton, 1981).
7. For a discussion of Arthur's incorporation into the Tudor myth, see E. Greenlaw, *Studies in Spenser's Historical Allegory* (Baltimore, 1932), and Sidney Anglo, 'The *British History* in Early Tudor Propaganda', *Bulletin of the John Ryland's Library* 44 (1961), 17–48.
8. Henry Peacham, *The Garden of Eloquence* (London, 1577), pp. Di^r–Di^v.
9. George Puttenham, *The Arte of English Poesie* (London, 1589), p. 197.
10. Spenser, *The Faerie Qveene*, ed. Hamilton, p. 103.
11. For example, John Lyly's play *Endimion* (1591), where Cynthia is generally identified with Elizabeth I and Endimion with the Earl of Leicester; in *The Complete Works of John Lyly*, ed. R. Warwick Bond (Oxford, 1902), III, pp. 5–103.

12. Philip Sidney, *An Apologie for Poetrie* (1595), ed. Geoffrey Shepherd (Manchester, 1973), p. 114.
13. Isabel MacCaffrey, *Spenser's Allegory* (Princeton, 1976), p. 6.
14. M. Quilligan, *The Language of Allegory* (Ithaca, 1979), p. 22.
15. This version may be found in Sir Thomas Malory's *Works*, ed. Eugene Vinaver (Oxford, 1954). However, it is important to remember that Spenser would have used Caxton's version of Malory's Arthurian narrative, *Le Morte Darthur* (London, 1485). All variations are recorded by Vinaver.
16. J. Goldberg, *Endlesse Worke: Spenser and the Structures of Discourse* (Baltimore, 1981), pp. 24–5.
17. C. Hulse, 'Spenser: myth, politics, poetry' *Studies in Philology* 85 (1988), 378–89 (381).

2 Discourse and dialectic: the work of Christopher Marlowe

William Zunder

Marlowe belonged to the generation of Elizabethan writers which succeeded that of Spenser. It included Shakespeare and Donne, and came to consciousness in the late 1580s and early 1590s. Typically of this generation, Marlowe was born into the urban middle class, at the heart of the capitalist economy that was emerging in the last decades of the sixteenth century. Born in 1564, he was the son of a Canterbury shoemaker; and his work reveals a fascinating dialectic between a radical discourse of individualism and the dominant discourses of hierarchy and monarchy that marked the culture of his day.

The *Homily* 'Of Obedience', for example, regularly read out in church since 1547 and deeply familiar to Marlowe's generation, begins by stressing the order established by God in nature. The heavens and the earth, in all their plenitude, 'keep their comely course and order'. Human subjectivity is correspondingly ordered: 'Man himself . . . hath all his parts both within and without, as soul, heart, mind, memory, understanding, reason, speech, with all and singular corporal members of his body, in a profitable, necessary, and pleasant order'; and the whole discourse is founded, quite unequivocally, on social and gender hierarchy:

> Every degree of people, in their vocation, calling, and office, hath appointed to them their duty and order. Some are in high degree, some in low; some kings and princes, some inferiors and subjects; priests and laymen, masters and servants, fathers and children, husbands and wives, rich and poor; and every one have need of other.

Without it, 'all things shall be common; and there must needs follow all mischief and utter destruction both of souls, bodies, goods, and commonwealths'.[1]

The first part of *Tamburlaine*, which Marlowe probably wrote in 1587, articulates a position that deliberately challenges this discourse. In one crucial speech, the play articulates an explicit ideology of individualism. It is an individualism that both refuses limit and grounds itself in the contemporary centre of power. The speech is delivered by Tamburlaine directly to the audience; and is carefully structured to confront the opening of the *Homily* virtually point by point:

> Nature, that fram'd us of four elements
> Warring within our breasts for regiment,
> Doth teach us all to have aspiring minds.
> Our souls, whose faculties can comprehend
> The wondrous architecture of the world,
> And measure every wand'ring planet's course,
> Still climbing after knowledge infinite,
> And always moving as the restless spheres,
> Wills us to wear ourselves and never rest
> Until we reach the ripest fruit of all,
> That perfect bliss and sole felicity,
> The sweet fruition of an earthly crown.
>
> (Part I, II. vii. 18–29)[2]

The *Homily* continues, moreover, to centre order on the monarchy, in a politicizing turn of thought characteristic of the dominant view: 'God hath sent us his high gift, our most dear Sovereign Lady Queen Elizabeth, with godly, wise, and honourable counsel, with other superiors and inferiors, in a beautiful order and goodly'; and Marlowe does not challenge this. In fact, he intensifies the absolutist tendency of the discourse by transferring to it the power of traditional religious language. Perfect 'bliss' is to be found not in a heavenly, but an 'earthly' crown (lines 28–9). The conclusion of the speech is at once surprising and insistent. Nevertheless, the refusal of limit subverts the *Homily*'s insistence on social stasis and on obedience to established authority: 'Let us all obey, even from the bottom of our hearts, all their godly proceedings, laws, statutes, proclamations, and injunctions, with all other their godly orders' (*Homilies*, p. 106).[3]

The ruling ideology was unambiguous in its condemnation of social rising, and in its insistence that wrongdoing will always be punished. 'All subjects', says the *Homily*, are bounden to obey their magistrates, and for no cause to resist (or withstand), rebel, or make any sedition against them, yea, although they be wicked men. And let no man think that he can escape unpunished that committeth treason, conspiracy, or rebellion against his Sovereign Lord the King, though he commit the same never so secretly, either in thought, word, or deed, never so privily in his privy chamber by himself, or openly communicating and consulting with other. For treason will not be hid; treason will out at the length.   (*Homilies*, p. 113)

And it cites examples from scripture of the punishment visited by God on the presumptuous, among them Absalom (p. 113). The *Homily* 'Against Disobedience', issued in 1570 in the aftermath of the northern rebellion of the previous year, is if anything more emphatic: 'Such subjects as are disobedient or rebellious against their princes disobey God, and procure their own damnation' (*Homilies*, p. 553).

Marlowe weaves this discourse into *Tamburlaine*, especially Part I. Cosroe, for instance, asks, 'What means this devilish shepherd to aspire / With such a giantly presumption?' (Part I, II. vi. 1–2). And this prompts one to expect that Tamburlaine will be punished; that, like Absalom for attempting to displace his king and father David, he will suffer a 'strange and notable death' ('Of Obedience', *Homilies*, p. 113). His irresistible rise to power, however, and the triumphant conclusion to Part I manifestly deny this; but the discourse of Part II, which Marlowe also seems to have written in 1587, is more complex.[4]

In Act II, Scene iv, Zenocrate dies; and the text articulates the sense of an external, threatening force: 'the malice of the angry skies' (line 11). In fact, Zenocrate is simply ill; and after the opening hyperbole of the scene ('Black is the beauty of the brightest day . . . ', lines 1–37), Marlowe makes Tamburlaine ask, 'Physicians, will no physic do her good?' (line 38). The question is matter-of-fact, as is the reply: 'My lord . . . /And if she pass this fit, the worst is past' (lines 39–40). Tamburlaine's words to Zenocrate, moreover, though marked by playfulness and concern, are ordinary: 'Tell me, how fares my fair Zenocrate?' (line 41). Zenocrate's reply is a crucial moment in the drama. It is the moment that gives centre and presence to this aspect of the play's multiple discourse. Elsewhere, in both plays, Zenocrate tends to be at once idealized and subordinated, but here she speaks with the full authority of the text:

I fare, my lord, as other empresses,
That, when this frail and transistory flesh

> Hath suck'd the measure of that vital air
> That feeds the body with his dated health,
> Wanes with enforc'd and necessary change.
>
> (Part II, II. iv. 42–6)

The moment registers a sense of limit which had been refused so recently in the earlier play. But it is an intrinsic, natural limit: a matter of fact. The body has a 'dated health' (line 45). And the limit is universal. Even the most exalted – even Elizabeth herself – wane with 'enforc'd and necessary change' (line 46).

And the appropriate response to this is the stoic one: 'bear and forbear'. Zenocrate dies patiently: 'Let me die, my love; yet, let me die; / With love and patience let your true love die' (lines 66–7); and the text marks her death as exemplary. 'Sweet sons, farewell!', she says:

> In death resemble me,
> And in your lives your father's excellency.
>
> (Part II, II. iv. 75–6)

Tamburlaine's response is actually one of impatience. He calls on Techelles to wound the earth, descend with him to hell, and take revenge on the fates; and on Usumcasane and Theridamas to shatter the universe with their cannon (lines 96–108). The passage is marked by a return to hyperbole; and Marlowe signals the inappropriateness of the response. 'Behold me here, divine Zenocrate', he makes Tamburlaine declare of himself, 'Raving, impatient, desperate and mad' (lines 111–12). And there is a final advocacy of stoicism through Theridamas: 'Ah, good my lord, be patient! She is dead, / And all this raging cannot make her live . . . / Nothing prevails, for she is dead, my lord' (lines 119–24).

Tamburlaine learns the lesson of stoicism. The drama is seen to enact its own morality. In Act III, Scene ii, after the burning of Larissa, he accepts Zenocrate's death: 'Sorrow no more, my sweet Casane, now. / Boys' – to his sons – 'leave to mourn' (lines 44–5). They, nevertheless, continue to mourn. And he responds briskly: 'But now, my boys, leave off, and list to me' (line 53); and launches energetically into his speech about the 'rudiments of war' (lines 54–92). In reply, Calyphas emerges as weak and pitiful; and Tamburlaine reacts by cutting his arm. The emblematic nature of the action is foregrounded by the text. 'Let the burning of Larissa walls', Tamburlaine proclaims,

> My speech of war, and this my wound you see,
> Teach you, my boys, to bear courageous minds.
>
> (Part II, III. ii. 141–3)

And he takes up the struggle with the Turks. The stoic acceptance of death is followed by the active prosecution of war. The play acts out Zenocrate's injunction to resemble her in death, and Tamburlaine's prowess in life.

When, however, Tamburlaine first feels ill, his response is one of defiance: 'Whatsoe'er it be, / Sickness or death can never conquer me' (V. i. 219–end); and it continues into the play's last scene. Its unfittingness, however, is signified not only in the hyperbole of his command to Theridamas: 'haste to the court of Jove; / Will him to send Apollo hither straight / To cure me, or I'll fetch him down myself' (V. iii. 61–3); but also in Theridamas' and Techelles' comments: 'Ah good my lord, leave these impatient words, / Which add much danger to your malady' (V. iii. 54–5). As with Zenocrate's death, Marlowe emphasizes the naturalness of Tamburlaine's illness; and Tamburlaine comes to accept his mortality – reluctantly at first: 'Sit still, my gracious lord; this grief will cease, / And cannot last, it is so violent' . . . 'Not last, Techelles? No, for I shall die' (V. iii. 64–6). Then more firmly:

> my martial strength is spent;
> In vain I strive and rail against those powers
> That mean t'invest me in a higher throne.
>
> (Part II, V. iii. 119–21)

The lesson of stoicism is relearned.

Marlowe presents the succession in the same naturalistic terms as Tamburlaine's illness. It is a natural inheritance that achieves a kind of immortality. 'Here, lovely boys', he makes Tamburlaine say after surveying the unconquered lands, 'what death forbids my life, / That let your lives command in spite of death' (V. iii. 159–60); and a little later: 'My flesh, divided in your precious shapes, / Shall still retain my spirit, though I die, / And live in all your seeds immortally' (V. iii. 172–4). And he does the same with Tamburlaine's death. Amyras is overcome with grief at its prospect; but Tamburlaine composes the moment with a magisterial pronouncement:

> Let not thy love exceed thine honour, son,

> Nor bar thy mind that magnanimity
> That nobly must admit necessity.
>
> (Part II, V. iii. 199–201)

It is, in fact, a key assertion in the play, with its twin concepts of acceptance and natural limit: 'admit necessity' (line 201); and it is endorsed through Theridamas:

> My lord, you must obey his majesty,
> Since fate commands and proud necessity.
>
> (Part II, V. iii. 204–5)

Tamburlaine's death, in short, is presented, subversively, not as retribution for the violation of hierarchy, but as part of natural process; the result, like his wife's death, of 'enforc'd and necessary change'. And the proper response to this is acceptance, not grief.

In *Edward II*, which Marlowe most likely wrote some four years later in 1591, the recruitment of Baldock and the elevation of Gaveston and Spencer by Edward are endorsed. As Theridamas says, 'he is gross and like the massy earth / That moves not upwards' (*Tamburlaine*, Part I, II. vii. 31–2). And this, despite their cynicism and hypocrisy; and despite the violation of hierarchical principle involved. But the attitude to Mortimer is very different.

At the beginning of the play, Mortimer is little more than one of the unruly barons. But after the execution of Lancaster and Warwick, the barons as a class disappear from the text; and Mortimer starts his solitary rise to power. Immediately, his words are those of *Tamburlaine*. His defiance of Edward has the accents and the key terms – 'virtue', 'aspires' – of the earlier work. 'What, Mortimer!', he says as he is taken off to the Tower,

> Can ragged stony walls
> Immure thy virtue that aspires to heaven?
> No Edward, England's scourge, it may not be;
> Mortimer's hope surmounts his fortune far.
>
> (III. iii. 71–4)

And his words to Gurney after his ascendancy has been achieved rewrite the famous lines of Tamburlaine to Theridamas: 'I hold the Fates bound fast in iron chains, / And with my hand turn Fortune's wheel about' (Part I, I. ii. 174–5). Gurney is exhorted to make the life of Edward a misery, 'as', says Mortimer,

thou intend'st to rise by Mortimer,
Who now makes Fortune's wheel turn as he please.

(V. ii. 52–3)

The high point of Mortimer's rise is reached just before the King's murder; and it is expressed in one of the outstanding speeches of the play – a soliloquy that extends the naturalism emergent in Marlowe further in the direction of interiority:

> The Prince I rule, the Queen do I command,
> And with a lowly congé to the ground
> The proudest lords salute me as I pass.
> I seal, I cancel, I do what I will;
> Fear'd am I more than lov'd: let me be fear'd,
> And when I frown, make all the court look pale.
> I view the Prince with Aristarchus' eyes,
> Whose looks were as a breeching to a boy.
> They thrust upon me the Protectorship,
> And sue to me for that that I desire:
> While at the council-table, grave enough
> And not unlike a bashful puritan,
> First I complain of imbecility,
> Saying it is *onus quam gravissimum*,
> Till being interrupted by my friends,
> *Suscepi* that *provinciam*, as they term it;
> And, to conclude, I am Protector now.
> Now all is sure: the Queen and Mortimer
> Shall rule the realm, the King; and none rule us.
> Mine enemies will I plague, my friends advance,
> And what I list command, who dare control?
> *Maior sum quam cui possit fortuna nocere.*

(V. iv. 48–69)

The speech, all the same, does not create the sense of assured achievement and ensuing peace that is created at the high point of Tamburlaine's rise (Part I, V. i. 504–end). Instead, there is an ironical sense of tragic villainy. Mortimer is represented as having replaced the barons as the principal source of disorder in the play. Unfettered individualism has replaced feudal intransigence. Once more, the subject rules the ruler: 'the Queen and Mortimer / Shall rule the realm, the King; and none rule us' (lines 65–6); and though the agency is new, the world is again turned upside down.

The irony of the speech stems fundamentally from the character's misconception of his position; a position that the text privileges the audience to recognize: '*Maior sum quam cui possit fortuna nocere*' (line 69), 'I am greater than anyone that fortune could harm'. Like Tamburlaine before the death of Zenocrate, he claims to transcend all external limit; in particular, to be above every restraint upon his political will: 'What I list command, who dare control?' (line 68). In a sense, though, his downfall is already present in the text. In the first place, it was part of the familiar Elizabethan narrative of feudal history; and in the second, the intertextuality with Ovid brings it ineluctably into the drama. Niobe's words, which Marlowe makes Mortimer quote here, come when she claims to be superior to the goddess Latona and, as a result, provokes her own destruction: transformation into a pillar of weeping stone (*Metamorphoses*, VI. 195).[5] Niobe was a classic instance of pride that was justly punished; and the intertextuality inevitably brings the whole dominant ideology to bear on the speech. The subject position which Marlowe constructs for the audience is one of traditional disapprobation.

The actual downfall takes place in the brief, final scene of the play: in Mortimer's last speech. It is not, strictly speaking, a soliloquy. The stage is full; and the occasion is a highly public one: the dispensation of royal justice. Part of it, too, is spoken to Isabella. But the effect at the beginning is one of alienated interiority:

> Base Fortune, now I see, that in thy wheel
> There is a point, to which when men aspire,
> They tumble headlong down; that point I touch'd,
> And seeing there was no place to mount up higher,
> Why should I grieve at my declining fall?
> Farewell, fair Queen, weep not for Mortimer,
> That scorns the world, and as a traveller
> Goes to discover countries yet unknown.
>
> (V. vi. 59–66)

It is a marvellous moment. The tragic defiance has a special poignancy; and one that was to echo throughout Elizabethan and Jacobean tragedy. But Marlowe is very deliberate in his use of the wheel of fortune, and of the crucial term 'aspire' (line 60). In *Tamburlaine*, they had been used with revolutionary significance. Here they are used to situate the growing individualism of the 1580s and '90s, registered textually in a developing interiority and stemming ultimately from the new economy, within a dominant frame of reference. Mortimer is represented as proud; as having presumed to rise too far; and as justly – even divinely – punished. Young Edward calls on God to exact retribution from him:

> So may his limbs be torn, as is this paper:
> Hear me, immortal Jove, and grant it too.
>
> (V. i. 142–3)

And in the very last moment, his head is produced on stage and placed on Edward's hearse by the new king (V. vi. 93–end). The tension implicit in *Tamburlaine* between individualism and monarchy, and provisionally contained within the text, becomes an explicit contradiction in *Edward II*. Faced by monarchy, the commitment to open-ended individualism is closed down.

The dominant ideology is reproduced in the drama in another way: in its advocacy of strong monarchy and a unified state. As Marlowe makes Edward say, 'Two kings in England cannot reign at once' (V. i. 58). Strong rule, however, is something that Edward is unable to achieve, at least consistently; and his weakness is brought out at various moments. But it is emphasized by Marlowe in Act II, Scene ii, when Mortimer and Lancaster speak their mind frankly to him (lines 153–98). Given the hierarchical assumptions of the time, in particular that of the pre-eminence of the ruler, it is an occasion of profound humiliation for him. The accusations are, nevertheless, endorsed: self-indulgence, favouritism, mismanagement of revenues, over-taxation, military weakness, loss of prestige at home and abroad. It is a catalogue of archetypal errors. Marlowe intensifies the historical narrative here, and adds to it; and its specificity is that of the 1590s. Although there was war with Ireland in Edward's reign, for example, it was not central to it, whereas it was central to Elizabeth's; and 'the wild O'Neill, with swarms of Irish kerns' (line 162) was a source of anxiety to her, but not to Edward.

It would be a mistake, nevertheless, to see Edward as simply a weak monarch; and to see the play as simply presenting an example to be eschewed: exorcizing a fear. Towards the end of Act III, Marlowe shows Edward to be capable of decisive action. He defeats the barons and executes their leaders; and the event functions as a renewal of monarchy within the play. 'Edward this day', Marlowe gets him to declare, 'hath crown'd him king anew' (III. iii. 76); though the old irresponsibility lingers. Three scenes later, when we next see him, he is with the two Spencers. And though his first words are acceptably patriotic: 'Thus after many threats of wrathful war, / Triumpheth England's Edward' (IV. iii. 1–2), he adds: 'with his friends' (IV. iii. 2); and then voices a totally unacceptable sentiment: 'And triumph Edward with his friends uncontroll'd' (IV. iii. 3). The prospect is of a return to the debilitating favouritism that prevailed while Gaveston was alive.

More importantly, there is a marked shift in attitude towards Edward after his defeat by Mortimer and Isabella in Act IV, Scene v. The event marks a real change in the drama. Affectively, it generates sympathy for Edward by creating a sense of pity towards him. Marlowe situates the audience for this through the Abbot early on. 'My heart with pity earns' – grieves – 'to see this sight', he says of him (IV. vi. 70); but the pity is less for Edward as a man than it is for Edward as a king. Discursively, Marlowe induces a sense of pathos at the decline of a ruler in order to elevate the notion of kingship; and again the audience is situated for this through the Abbot: 'A king to bear these words and proud commands!' (IV. vi. 71). Marlowe, in short, reinforces the absolutist turn of the dominant ideology; and he does this by accentuating monarchy rather than the monarch: the institution rather than the individual. It is something apparent in practically every speech Edward utters in the final phase of the play. Indeed, after his capture, Marlowe explicitly differentiates the subject from the monarch, and emphasizes the otherness of rule. 'The griefs of private men', he makes Edward assert,

> are soon allay'd,
> But not of kings: the forest deer being struck
> Runs to an herb that closeth up the wounds,
> But when the imperial lion's flesh is gor'd
> He rends and tears it with his wrathful paw,
> And highly scorning that the lowly earth
> Should drink his blood, mounts up into the air:
> And so it fares with me.
>
> (V. i. 8–15)

It is with this emphasis that Marlowe includes the episode of Edward's forcible shaving in puddle water. It is a moment of further humiliation for him that looks forward to the final humiliation of his murder two scenes later. But, in fact, Marlowe lessens the pathos of the narrative and the humanizing of monarchy that it entailed. Edward refused cold water. 'Will ye or nill ye', he said, 'I will have warm water: and that he might keep his promise, he began to weep and to shed tears plentifully'.[6] It is the climax of the narrative; but Marlowe omits it. Instead, he stresses the violation of monarchical sanctity. Turning away from Matrevis and Gurney, and perhaps facing the audience, Edward exclaims:

> Immortal powers, that knows the painful cares
> That waits upon my poor distressed soul,
> O level all your looks upon these daring men,
> That wrongs their liege and sovereign, England's king.
>
> (V. iii. 37–40)

The play concludes with a movement parallel to that at the end of *Tamburlaine*, Part II: with the succession assured, the state unified, and monarchical power forcefully affirmed. Edward III, who is viewed sympathetically throughout, is crowned on stage in Act V, Scene iv; but he does not confront Mortimer until after his father's death. When he does, there is a sense of strong monarchy at last. 'Traitor', he says directly to him, 'in me my loving father speaks, / And plainly saith, 'twas thou that murd'redst him' (V. vi. 41–2). He is supported by his nobles. 'Fear not, my lord, know that you are a king', the first lord prompts him (V. vi. 24). They are anonymous; the feudal baron has been replaced by the court functionary. And the dispensation of justice is open and impartial. There is no favouritism towards Isabella. 'Mother . . . ', Edward addresses her, 'If you be guilty, though I be your son, / Think not to find me slack or pitiful' (V. vi. 78, 81–2); although he is shown to possess common human feelings which – rightly – he suppresses. 'Away with her', he tells the lords, 'her words enforce these tears, / And I shall pity her if she speak again' (V. vi. 85–6). The difference between this and his father's indulgence is clearly presented as a pregnant one.

By the close of the play, however, there is no criticism of Edward. His suffering, his religious death, and the filial devotion of his son, all function to absolve him from blame. Rather, opprobrium is directed towards Mortimer: the representation of unbridled self-assertion that threatens monarchy. In a gesture that rewrites the conclusion of the first part of *Tamburlaine*, the young king puts on funeral robes: inaugurating a new order. And placing Mortimer's head on his father's hearse as a sign of Mortimer's submission and defeat, he completes the final tableau:

> Sweet father here, unto thy murder'd ghost,
> I offer up this wicked traitor's head;
> And let these tears distilling from mine eyes
> Be witness of my grief and innocency.
>
> (V. vi. 99–end)

In the historical mythology of the time, the reign of Edward III was one of archetypal greatness; just as that of his father was one of archetypal weakness. Marlowe here both draws on and reproduces this duality; and shares with the audience the proleptic knowledge that the events which will follow the conclusion of the drama will form a moment of high achievement in English history. Rejecting feudal particularism, and uncomfortable with capitalist self-interest, Marlowe chooses to occupy the only other terrain open to his generation: that of royal absolutism.[7]

Edward is the weak king he is because of his love for Gaveston; later, because of his love for Spencer. And it is here that Marlowe enforces a radical transgression of the ruling ideology. For the relationship between Edward and Gaveston is sexual.

The dominant discourse saw homosexuality as wrong; one among many deviations from the exclusive heterosexual union of marriage. Quoting St Paul (1 Corinthians 6. 9–10), the *Homily* 'Against Whoredom and Uncleanness' warned that 'neither whoremongers . . . nor adulterers, nor softlings, nor sodomites . . . shall inherit the kingdom of God' (*Homilies*, p. 131); while Leviticus is quite explicit: 'The man . . . that lieth with the male, as one lieth with a woman, they have both committed abomination: they shall die the death' (20.13).[8] And in 1563 Parliament revived earlier legislation to make the 'detestable and abominable vice of buggery' punishable by death. And yet the relationship is presented as humanly valid; as valid as any relationship in the play. The commitment to absolutism, itself a departure from traditional notions of limited monarchy, is complemented by a radical homosexuality.

This homosexuality is reinforced in *Hero and Leander*, which Marlowe seems to have written just before he was killed in 1593. Although Hero and Leander are represented as young, adolescent lovers, their love is nevertheless put forward as representative, even archetypal. The effect of the authorial interventions that mark the writing is, quite deliberately, to generalize and universalize the experience being handled. The text aims to disclose the essence of human love. In particular, it embraces not only heterosexual, but also homosexual, male-to-male relationships; and it makes no fundamental distinction between them.

As Leander swims the Hellespont to reach Hero immediately before the description of their lovemaking, he himself is made love to by Neptune (II. 155–226). The episode is a tale of unrequited love, in which Leander plays Hero's part and Neptune, Leander's. When Leander leaps into the water, Neptune imagines it is Ganymede, the beautiful cupbearer of Jupiter, who has left heaven. Leander is so desirable – is the implication. At the end of the sixteenth century, 'Ganymede' was a codeword for a young homosexual; and 'the lusty god embraced him, called him love, / And swore he never should return to Jove' (lines 167–8). Even the waves desire him. In a witty image, they 'mounted up, intending to have kissed him, / And fell in drops like tears because they missed him' (lines 173–4), as Neptune beats them down with his mace.

The pathos and absurdity felt elsewhere for Hero are here felt in relation to Leander, who,

> being up, began to swim,
> And, looking back, saw Neptune follow him;
> Whereat aghast, the poor soul 'gan to cry,
> 'O let me visit Hero ere I die.'

> (II. 175–8)

And Marlowe resumes the witty imagery in a passage that describes the movement of water round a swimmer's body, just as the previous image had depicted the breaking of the waves, but which is also a frank description of homosexual lovemaking; though, teasingly, he omits the most erotic caresses. Neptune 'clapped' Leander's 'plump cheeks', and

> with his tresses played,
> And smiling wantonly, his love bewrayed.
> He watched his arms, and as they opened wide
> At every stroke, betwixt them would he slide
> And steal a kiss, and then run out and dance,
> And as he turned, cast many a lustful glance,
> And threw him gaudy toys to please his eye,
> And dive into the water, and there pry
> Upon his breast, his thighs, and every limb,

And up again, and close beside him swim,
And talk of love.

(II. 181–91)

There is the same distance between youthful innocence and adult experience that there is elsewhere in the poem, this time in terms of homosexual passion; and on this occasion, presented ironically. To Neptune's words of love 'Leander made reply.' ' "You are deceived" ', he said, ' "I am no woman, I" '. 'Thereat smiled Neptune' (lines 191–3).

Leander, however, is indifferent to Neptune's advances; and Neptune's mood darkens. As with the love between Hero and Leander, the text reveals the tragic insistence of sexuality (lines 207–9). There is an absurdity in Neptune's sudden change of heart, as love then makes him relent (lines 209–10); and the wound inflicted on his hand conveys the inescapable pain of personal relationships (lines 211–12). 'Neptune', writes Marlowe, 'was angry' that Leander

> gave no ear,
> And in his heart revenging malice bare:
> He flung at him his mace, but as it went,
> He called it in, for love made him repent.
> The mace returning back, his own hand hit,
> As meaning to be venged for darting it.

(II. 207–12)

The pathos of the narrative now centres on Neptune, who misreads Leander's ordinary human pity for his wound as love; and Marlowe intervenes in the story in order to generalize from this, and so foreground what is presented as the essentially tragic uncertainty at the heart of sexual experience. 'Love', he pronounces, 'is too full of faith, too credulous, / With folly and false hope deluding us' (lines 221–2). And in one of the sudden modulations of tone characteristic of the whole work, the pessimism latent in this observation shifts to the near-cynicism of the wit that the episode concludes with. Neptune rushes off to the ocean floor to find presents that will captivate Leander's affections. ' 'Tis wisdom to give much', Marlowe notes finally, 'a gift prevails / When deep persuading oratory fails' (lines 225–6).[9]

The text constructs a male homosexual subjectivity. Marlowe begins the poem with a portrait of Hero (I. 5–50); but he immediately follows this with a description of Leander. The portrait of Hero is external. It is largely of her clothes. And Marlowe presents her as a typical Renaissance princess or great lady. But the description of Leander is very different in character (I. 51–90). It is predominantly physical and highly erotic. 'His body', Marlowe declares,

> was as straight as Circe's wand;
> Jove might have sipped out nectar from his hand.
> Even as delicious meat is to the taste,
> So was his neck in touching, and surpassed
> The white of Pelops' shoulder. I could tell ye
> How smooth his breast was, and how white his belly,
> And whose immortal fingers did imprint
> That heavenly path with many a curious dint
> That runs along his back.
>
> (I. 61–9)

Especially powerful in creating a sense of sexual pleasure is the synaesthesia of lines 63–4, with their comparison of touching flesh to tasting food.

Apart, though, from the reference to 'succeeding times' in line 54, and the implicit comparison of him in lines 59–60 to Endymion, who was loved by Cynthia the moon, Leander is seen exclusively in terms of his attractiveness to men. Jason and the Argonauts, says Marlowe, with the nice hyperbole that is characteristic of the description, would have hazarded more for his 'dangling tresses' than they did for the golden fleece (lines 55–8). Jupiter, the chief of the gods, would have drunk from a cup held in his hand: the Ganymede motif once more (line 62). And if 'wild Hippolytus', devoted to chastity and hunting, had seen him, Marlowe claims, 'enamoured of his beauty had he been' (lines 77–8). For Leander's 'presence' affected the least cultivated. It 'made the rudest peasant melt, / That in the vast uplandish country dwelt' (lines 79–80). Even the 'barbarous Thracian soldier', an archetype in classical times of masculine brutality and inhumanity – 'moved with nought', as Marlowe puts it – 'was moved with him, and for his favour sought' (lines 81–2).

As in *Edward II*, there is no criticism of homosexual relationships. The love that Neptune has for Leander may be tragic, on occasion even absurd; but it is not wrong. And as with the earlier work, this is a position that goes right against the morality of the time. Yet the description of Leander ends with a moment that is even more radical than this.

The dominant ideology of the age assumed that sexual relationships were normally between men and women, and that heterosexual love found its natural expression in marriage. Any other kind of sexuality was a perversion: an 'abomination', as Leviticus termed homosexual relations (20.13); and this gender-specific sexuality was subsumed under the larger, in fact all-embracing, discourse of hierarchy. As the monarch was superior to his subjects, so the husband was superior to his wife.[10] Marlowe effectively ignores marriage. He certainly does not disapprove of either Leander or Hero for wanting or having sex outside it. Nevertheless, to an extent, the dominant ideology prevails in the poem. Although the relationship between Leander and Hero, like that between Neptune and Leander, is seen as typically predatory, it is also perceived as essentially hierarchical. The male Leander is represented as superior to, more active than, the passive, female Hero; just as the older Neptune dominates the less experienced Leander. Towards the conclusion of the description of Leander, however, the text separates sexuality from gender. 'Some swore', Marlowe writes, that Leander was 'a maid in man's attire', for

> in his looks were all that men desire,
> A pleasant smiling cheek, a speaking eye,
> A brow for love to banquet royally.

> (I. 83–6)

The sentiment here is male-directed. It is a matter of what 'men' desire (line 84); not of what women, or men and women, desire. But in place of the gender-specific sexuality of the dominant discourse, the lines affirm a sexuality that is free to find satisfaction in either gender. It makes no difference whether Leander is male or female. In his beauty men are able to find everything they are looking for.

The description closes with an endorsement of sexual love: 'love's holy fire', as Marlowe expresses it later (I. 193). Those who knew that Leander was a man, says Marlowe – homosexual orientation again – would urge him to make love. ' "Leander" ', they would declare, ' "thou art made for amorous play: / Why art thou not in love?" ' (lines 88–9). Then Marlowe adds: ' "and loved of all?" ' (line 89). Not 'why are you not married?'. But 'why are you not available to everyone, regardless of gender?'.

And Marlowe finishes with an exhortation, which is both reported within the narrative as being spoken to Leander and addressed directly to the reader, who is assumed to be male. ' "Though thou be fair" ', Marlowe writes, ' "yet be not thine own thrall" ' (line 90). Do not be like Narcissus, the beautiful young man of mythology who figures a little earlier in the description (lines 73–6), who 'leapt into the water for a kiss / Of his own shadow' (lines 74–5), and drowned; and who became a powerful symbol of self-love and auto-eroticism. Here he is also used to signify a human waste. 'Despising many', Marlowe asserts, he 'died ere he could enjoy the love of any' (lines 75–6). Sexuality is to be shared, is the implication of the text. 'For', as Marlowe maintains later in the poem, 'from the earth to heaven is Cupid raised, / Where fancy is in equal balance peised' (II. 31–2). It is to be shared without reference to the form a relationship takes: whether married or unmarried; and it is to be shared irrespective of gender. Taken together, lines 83–90 of the description constitute a moment that is deeply disintegrative of the morality of the time.

The radical individualism of Part I of *Tamburlaine* which saw no boundary of any kind to human aspiration, moderated by a sense of natural limit in Part II to a subversive stoicism and rigorously curtailed in the interest of monarchy in *Edward II*, survived at Marlowe's death in a radical sexuality that acknowledged no restriction on the satisfaction of human sexual desire.

Notes

1. *The Two Books of Homilies* (Oxford, 1859), pp. 105–6. Quotation is from this edition. See also the *Documents* section below, pp. 257–8.
2. Quotation of Marlowe is from *The Plays of Christopher Marlowe*, ed. Roma Gill (Oxford, 1971), and *Christopher Marlowe: The Complete Poems and Translations*, ed. Stephen Orgel (Harmondsworth, 1971).
3. The speech has been read ironically: by, for example, Catherine Belsey, *Critical Practice* (London, 1980), pp. 94–5.
4. The conclusion of Part I is sometimes viewed as ironical. See, for instance, Simon Shepherd, *Marlowe and the Politics of Elizabethan Theatre* (Brighton, 1986), pp. 23–4, 37–8.
5. See *Ovid in Six Volumes*, Vol. 3, ed. and tr. Frank Justus Miller, 2nd edn (Cambridge, Massachusetts, 1921).
6. Quoted from John Stow's *Chronicles of England* (1580), in *Edward the Second: Christopher Marlowe*, ed. Charles R. Forker (Manchester, 1994), p. 360.
7. For the view, however, that Edward III's minority questions the stability

of the play's ending, see Michael Hattaway, *Elizabethan Popular Theatre* (London, 1982), pp. 143–4.

8. Quotation is from *The Geneva Bible* [1560], introduced by Lloyd E. Berry (Madison, Milwaukee, 1969).

9. There seems no reason to doubt the authenticity of the narrative voice. For the contention, nevertheless, that the narrator is dramatized and unreliable, see W. L. Godshalk, '*Hero and Leander*: the sense of an ending', in '*A Poet and a filthy Play-maker*', ed. Kenneth Friedenreich *et al.* (New York, 1988), pp. 293–314.

10. On the ideology of marriage in the sixteenth century (and later), see the *Documents* section, pp. 258–9.

3 'Anxious to amuse': metaphysical poetry and the discourse of Renaissance masculinity[1]

Bruce Woodcock

The explosion in lyric love poetry written by men in England from the sixteenth century onwards has a distinct historical context. One element in this was a combination of literary influences from abroad. The traditions of courtly love in the medieval period had, of course, been as strong in Britain as they had been on the Continent – witness great courtly love poems such as *Gawain and the Green Knight* or secular love lyrics such as the marvellous 'Now wold I fayn some mirthes make' from the mid-fifteenth century. But with the sixteenth century and the appearance in Britain of translations of Petrarch's sonnets, the *Canzoniere* of 1366, a whole new wave of love poetry was created, with an apparently individualized address by the male subject to a particular beloved. Petrarch was translated and imitated by English poets like Wyatt and Surrey, and had a pervasive influence on Sir Philip Sidney.

I say apparently individualized because of course the poetry was *not* the spontaneous outpouring of feelings which some modern readers still (wrongly) assume poetry should be. It was, in fact, written very much within the parameters of Petrarchan convention, in which an idealized female (Laura in Petrarch's poems) was both the cause of the male lover's sorrows, leading to his anguished endurance of extremes of emotion, and at the same time became the moral dynamic to lead to his spiritual improvement. The trick for the poets following Petrarch was to reinvigorate those conventions with a distinctive life of their own, a voice characteristic of the poet himself. So in Wyatt, Surrey and Sidney we have three consummate masters of the Petrarchan mode who manage to reinvent it for themselves, and to some degree parody it, without seriously undermining its attitudes.

But increasingly Petrarchism became a cliché: what John Donne calls the 'whining poetry'[2] of the melancholic male lover swinging between the poles of fierce desire and freezing depression became increasingly predictable. This is not to suggest that Donne was *anti*-Petrarchan. Indeed, as Donald Guss argued as long ago as 1966, to miss Donne's saturation in Petrarchan imagery, subject and themes is to misread him. But Petrarchism was not a static thing: on the contrary, it was a repository of stock material which awaited the transforming virtuosity of some new master, just as electric blues guitar riffs which are decades old are totally transformed when played by experts as diverse as Jimi Hendrix, Mark Knopfler or J. J. Cale. Donne was the first English exponent of what Guss describes as extravagant or witty Petrarchism, already initiated in Italian writers like Serafino, Tasso or Guarino. What Donne added was his own individual flair and invention, a more strenuous inversion of stock attitudes, a more fantastic drama and expressive extravagance to the conceits.[3]

What also helped give male love poets like Donne a new possible direction was the impact of another set of literary influences from abroad – the rediscovery and reassimilation of classical love poetry from Roman times. The love poetry of Catullus (c. 84–c. 54 BC) and Ovid (43 BC–AD 18) was retranslated and republished in new editions throughout the sixteenth century: one translation of Ovid's *Amores* was made by Christopher Marlowe, Shakespeare's famous predecessor. Here, English male love poets could find verse which offered a quite different model for love poetry, one which engaged with the physical, erotic and bawdy sides of physical passion in a way which the Petrarchan tradition had not done and in a language which was down-to-earth if not downright obscene. As Donne was to realize in the poem 'Love's Growth', 'Love's not so pure, and abstract, as they use / To say, which have no mistress but their Muse' (*CEP*, p. 69).

The case of Ovid was particularly apt since he too had lived at a time when the conventions of love poetry had seemed exhausted. He managed to revitalize them partly through parody: Ovid took the established models of the classical love elegy, inherited from Tibullus (c. 48–19 BC) and Propertius (c. 50–c. 16 BC), and injected into them an irony and self-knowingness which brought them back to life.[4] In Marlowe's translation of the *Amores*, for example, we find the declaration 'I love but one, and her I love change never, / If men have faith, I'll live with thee for ever',[5] a sincere profession of constancy which simultaneously ironizes the elegiac love scenario through the sceptical hypothesis about faith.

Though they are two quite different poets, the analogy between Ovid and Donne is instructive, since Donne did something similar with the Petrarchan tradition. But the point of interest for our investigation is not so much one of literary influences as the way in which this tension between the dominant discourse of Petrarchan love poetry and these other emergent possibilities allowed Donne to create poetic texts which embody contradictions in male attitudes to love expressive of the tensions in attitudes to masculinity. What this reveals is an uncertainty about male gender identity not dissimilar to our own time's.

Perhaps this is a dangerously ahistorical suggestion. After all, many recent theorists have argued that gender identity is predominantly a construction whose nature changes according to historical and material social forces. Necessarily, then, the experiences of masculinity during Donne's time and ours are likely to be very different, as indeed the experiences of masculinity between different social groups within the *same* time are likely to be very different. Equally, as modern theory on masculinity increasingly indicates, the notion of male gender identity, as with any sexual identity, is itself provisional, contingent and troubled by fractures.

In addition, we need to ask what was the status of masculinity in England during the late sixteenth and early seventeenth centuries? It is no doubt an impossible question to answer: it is difficult enough these days to put together an account of male gender identity or of the male subject, despite, or perhaps because of, the immense amount of work that is being done in these areas. To imagine that we might describe the construction of male subjectivity during the late Elizabethan and early Jacobean period would therefore be unrealistic. Yet it undoubtedly mattered: John Donne's epigram 'Manliness' reads:

> Thou call'st me effeminate, for I love women's joys,
> I call not thee manly, though thou follow boys.
>
> (*CEP*, p. 152)

And Elegy 4, 'The Perfume', talks of 'the greatest stain to man's estate . . . to be called effeminate' (*CEP*, p. 100).

Of course, it is dangerous to generalize from such evidence. Bruce Smith in his book *Homosexual Desire in Shakespeare's England* has indicated how categories of homosexuality and heterosexuality are specifically twentieth-century constructions of sexuality and form a distinction which would not have had the same meaning during the Renaissance period. This is because our notions of such sexual identities are themselves post-nineteenth-century phenomena, and because homosexual acts would not have led a man 'to think of himself as fundamentally different from his peers. Just the opposite was true. Prevailing ideas asked him to castigate himself for falling into the general depravity to which *all* mankind is subject'. Nevertheless, Smith continues, 'that does not mean . . . that there were no men in early modern England whose sexual desires were turned primarily towards other men'.[6]

While bearing Smith's cautions in mind, what the above extracts suggest is an uncertainty about male gender identity which informs the love poetry written by men throughout the Elizabethan and Jacobean periods, of which John Donne forms an intriguing example. Rather than read off Donne's poems against some mythical model or impossible template of what constitutes masculinity either in his time or ours, the interrogation proposed here is a reading of his love poems as contentious sites within which we can discern the slippages and contradictions to be found in any attempt to establish a 'masculine' position. As Helen Carr has pointed out,[7] Donne's use of the word 'masculine' to mean gender identity in describing 'my words' masculine persuasive force' in 'Elegy 16' (*CEP*, p. 118) predates the *OED*'s allocation of the first use to 1629. In so far as Donne's writing took part in the ongoing construction and reconstruction of male gendered subjectivity during this period, the 'masculine persuasive force' in the language of his love poems often displays an anxiety which lets us see some of the different masks of masculinity.

A number of previous readers have noted anxiety as an undercurrent in Donne's love poetry. John Carey, for example, suggests that the *Songs and Sonnets* exhibit a 'perpetual worry about fidelity and falseness . . . a profound anxiety about the permanence of relationships'.[8] The apparently assured male lovers who speak in the poems are in fact far from assured; but to discover this depends, Carey suggests, on 'our detecting lapses and contradictions'[9] in the arguments of the poems. Yet the anxiety is not simply about the security of relationships; it is more specifically an insecurity over power – the power of being able to capture women, of being able to capture a woman's body, and of being then able to enact the fantasy of capture through possession. As David Aers and Gunther Kress have noted, 'male egotism, in all its conventional sexual jauntiness, is a product of anxiety as well as being an attempt to exploit the woman's own anxiety'.[10]

Bruce Smith is right to insist that we pay attention to 'the imaginative dimension to sexual experience', since 'sexual acts are acts of the imagination as well as acts of the body'.[11] In the case of poems, however, acts of the body and acts of the imagination have been mediated and replaced by acts of language. So, because what we are dealing with is *texts* rather than *acts*, the traces of this anxiety manifest themselves in the language effects of the poems. I would not want to minimize the extent to which, as a poet, Donne is self-consciously jokey in his lyrics, playfully invoking love conventions in order to display his own inventiveness *and* just have *fun*. But behind the diverse tones – the swaggering arrogance of 'The Sunne Rising', the reverence of 'The Canonization' or 'Aire and Angels', the lasciviousness of 'Community', the cynicism of 'The Apparition' – we can also trace an underlying concern whose focus is the male subject himself and the nature of his male identity. The women in the poems, in so far as there *are* any women *in* the poems, are frequently merely the counters in an enactment of male imaginative fantasy whose true subject is the uncertainties of a male speaker and whose aim is an impossible attempt at reassurance. In their eagerness to mark themselves out as masculine and thereby distance themselves from 'the greatest stain to man's estate . . . to be called effeminate' (*CEP*, p. 100), Donne's love poems reveal the contradictions of this enterprise *through* the 'words' masculine persuasive force', the struggle to enact the desired fantasies, or the agonized recognition of the fragility of male sexual identity.

One sign of that fragility is the lament for the brevity of male sexuality displayed in a poem like 'Farewell to Love' (*CEP*, pp. 56–7). This takes familiar notions surrounding the well-known saying *post coitum triste*, 'after intercourse, sadness' – the depression after sexual climax, the threat of orgasm shortening life and so on, all of which were common views enshrined in forms such as the popular sex manual *Aristotle's Masterpiece or the Secrets of Generation* or in the eleventh-century Arab physician Avicenna's claim 'that one ejaculation is more debilitating than forty blood-lettings'.[12] But the poem gives them a peculiarly male twist in the way the language plays with itself, hinting at sexual innuendos and at the same time revealing a sense of frustration at the incapacities of male sexual experience.

In verse three, for example, Nature's decree that sex diminishes life-expectancy is made to apply to the penis:

> Ah cannot we,
> As well as cocks and lions jocund be,
>   After such pleasures? Unless wise
> Nature decreed (since each such act, they say,
> Diminisheth the length of life a day)
>   This; as she would man should despise
>   The sport,
> Because that other curse of being short,
>   And only for a minute made to be
> Eager, desires to raise posterity.
>
>   (*CEP*, p. 57)

It is only to be expected that the 'cocks and lions' who remain 'jocund' after their pleasures should contain a bawdy pun on the inability of the human cock to remain jocund after orgasm; but we should also notice that the language in this verse invites a kind of self-disgust in its emphasis. There is an awareness not just of the conventional threat of orgasm to diminish life-expectancy, but also of the shortness of the pleasure itself – perhaps also the shortness of the male organ? Certainly the shortness of its ability to sustain its energies is ironized in the explicit contrast made between its hopes – it 'desires to raise posterity' – and its absurd limits – 'only for a minute made to be / Eager'.[13] The placing of that word 'Eager' at the beginning of the line with its eager capital letter raising its head is itself a wry reminder of the male organ's inability to raise itself after detumescence. Nature's decree, then, seems to insist man should not simply 'depise / The sport' but also despise the tools of the sport; and this is confirmed by the sarcastic ending. Having vowed to avoid love in future and turn his mind to higher things, the poem's speaker acknowledges that in the (likely) event of failure he has one desperate remedy: ' 'Tis but applying worm-seed to the tail'. 'Worm-seed' we can take, as the Penguin editor A. J. Smith does, as a harsh anaphrodisiac applied to the penis to dissuade it from further activity, but it is also by innuendo death itself, the only desperate remedy which is likely to stop the elastic cock winking his eye as the ladies go by.

It might be objected that many of Donne's poses in these poems are purely conventional deriving from previous models. So we might find similar such anxieties in male poetry from Catullus onwards. There is, for example, Ovid's humorous agony over penile limpness: 'notwithstanding, like one dead it lay, / Drooping more than a rose picked yesterday' in the seventh elegy of his *Amores*, Book Three.[14] Or there is Rochester's 'The Imperfect Enjoyment' with its agonies about premature ejaculation, or Philip Larkin's dissatisfactions with the process of ejaculation in 'Dry Point'. It risks universalism, but it is intriguing that male poets should return with such persistence to their dissatisfaction with sexuality and male performance. The self-disarming humour common to many of these examples is itself a deflationary strategy which simultaneously tries to make light of the problem of impotence, dismissing it through the jokiness of tone, and by doing so reveals the disruptive effects of the experience, the deep insecurity it generates in male sexual identity. It speaks of a more general fracture in the armoury of male power, one which displays the contradictions in the very notion of power itself.

One of the best examples is Donne apparently at his most full-bloodedly sensual in the famous 'Elegy 19: To His Mistress Going to Bed' (*CEP*, p. 124). This opens with commanding assurance and a marvellous innuendo for the modern ear in the very first word:

> Come, Madam, come, all rest my powers defy,
> Until I labour, I in labour lie.
> The foe oft-times having the foe in sight,
> Is tired with standing though they never fight.

Behind that opening image is anxiety at drooping ardour, and the arrogance masks insecurity over the temporariness of male desire: if she doesn't 'come' soon, he may 'come' before she arrives. The famous passage from line 25 on speaks simultaneously of desire for power over woman's body and uncertainty about that power: it is *she* who licenses him, who gives him the power to rove over her body, who captures him in the economy of love and the bonds of sexual trade. So whilst fantasizing about mining her precious deposits and lording it over her body as a ruler over a kingdom, the voice of the poem is also troubled by the contradictions of being in thrall to the power of his own attraction to the female body, a troubling which also surfaces as a fear of the invasions of other men into this imaginary kingdom, 'safeliest when with one man manned' (*CEP*, p. 125).

For, of course, that is precisely what it is – *imaginary*. It has long been recognized that some of Donne's love poems were often occasioned not so much by actual female subjects to whom they were addressed as by the demands of a male audience of court wits for whom the poems were partly an exercise in competitive extravagance and partly in titillating entertainment.[15] This is true of other male metaphysical poets too. A poem like Thomas Carew's 'A Rapture' contains a similar linguistic indulgence in the imaginary possibilities of a female body and the sexual capabilities of the male body:

> Thou like a sea of milk shall lie display'd,
> Whilst I the smooth calm ocean invade
> With such a tempest, as when Jove of old
> Fell down on Danaë in a storm of gold;
> Yet my tall pine shall in the Cyprian strait
> Ride safe at anchor and unlade her freight:
> My rudder with thy bold hand, like a tried
> And skilful pilot, thou shalt steer.[16]

Like Elegy 19, this is a contradictory mixture: the poem imagines male sexual power (the tempest), heroically grand (Jove) and of ponderous proportions (the penis as a ship's mast); yet it also desires security (safe at anchor), and a sense of being taken over and serviced by a female.

In both these poems we see male fantasy catering to the imaginations of its male readers and examples of that male imagination at work: a verbal capture of the woman to be probed by words. Frank Kermode has argued that, in Donne's work, 'it is impossible not to admire the translation of sexual into mental activity'.[17] But rather than merely admired, that is precisely what should be *observed*, critically. What is going on in such poems is moves in a game constructed and activated by the male sexual imagination. The women in the texts are not actually 'women' at all; they are counters to be played with in a game of sexual fantasy whose functions are a complex interaction of the imposition and reinforcement of a sense of power, coupled with a process of self-reassurance and consolation. In that game, the subjection of the figure of the woman to the needs of the male imagination is paramount. What makes Donne's poetry so fascinating is that this subjection is effected in a variety of ways which, because of their complexity and diversity, themselves yield up and reveal the undercurrents of the male imagination at work.

Why is it that John Donne in particular should have been able to create texts which register the contradictions and disturbances in male attitudes to love and sexuality – because it is undoubtedly true that Donne's poems present the most complex and interesting case among the male love poets of his time? By comparison the Cavalier poets such as Suckling seem notably one-dimensional. One reason may be to do with the ambivalence of Donne's social position. In relation to the dominant social order of the day, the court hegemony and its associated discourses, he was both an outsider and an insider at the same time. As John Carey's engaging biography shows, his life is remarkable for its ambiguities and displacements. Born a catholic and brought up, as he himself tells us, among 'men of a suppressed and afflicted Religion',[18] Donne came from a social background which was marginalized and persecuted: his brother went to Newgate prison for harbouring a priest. Donne himself converted to Anglicanism early in his life and this allowed him to enter the Inns of Court, a stepping-stone for a young man with ambition for a court career. And despite his sarcastic satire of the court to be found in Satire 4, this is exactly what Donne pursued through the 1590s, no doubt with the distinctive energy which finds its way into his verse.

From being an outsider, then, he translated himself into an aspiring insider. Did that betrayal of his background trouble him? John Carey suggests that it did and that the love poetry was written partly out of an impetus to fill 'the crater left by apostasy'.[19] This might help explain the peculiar intensity Donne gives to his transfer of otherwise quite conventional metaphors and conceits from religion to love in poems like 'The Canonization'. Nevertheless, Donne's apparently secure insider status was shattered in 1601, and *because* of love: he married Ann More without following the usual protocol of asking the permission of her father. His explanatory letter to Sir George More (2 February 1602) attempted to explain why he and Ann had thus 'adventured' their fortunes, indicating that to have acquainted Sir George with their plans would have been 'to impossibilate the whole matter'. Not surprisingly, this did nothing to placate the angry father. As a result, Donne and his new wife were summarily thrown out of court and spent the next ten years of his life in what he called in a letter of 1609 'the barbarousness and insipid dulnesse of the Country'.[20]

For a man of Donne's energy and disposition the stagnancy of country life after the dazzle of the court must have been immensely frustrating. Is it surprising that during this period he should write his extraordinary meditation on suicide, the *Biathanatos (1609)*? From being a brilliantly promising insider, suddenly he was again an obscure outsider, what David Aers and Gunther Kress call 'a classic example of an excluded intellectual';[21] and they quote a powerful letter from 1608 in which Donne expresses his despair at being made 'nothing' in terms which make it quite plain that he feels this *as* a man: he speaks of his 'impotency' and writes that 'men of wit and delightful conversation [are] but as moles for ornament, except they be so incorporated into the body of the world that they contribute something to the sustentation of the whole'.[22]

This dislocation in his career hopes, triggered as it was by a conflict between his personal life and his public life as a man, helps us contextualize the contradictions over masculinity in his love poetry. This is particularly true if we take up the argument of David Morse's book *England's Time of Crisis*,[23] which suggests that the majority of Donne's most famous poems were written between 1607 and 1614, after his exile from court. In a sense the anxieties in Donne's love poems around masculinity and male power are the marks of his own personal position in relation to the dominant discourse of the day. Everything in the public world of men urged him to overcome the disadvantages of his background in order to compete with the best for the glittering prize of success in court; but in the private world of his relationship with Ann More the imperatives were different and urged him to sacrifice his career for the satisfaction of his heart.

Donne can be seen as a victim of the conflict between the dominant hierarchy of the court order with its more or less fixed notions of what constituted success for a man of the world and the emergent ethic of individualism on which the expansion of trade and the values of puritanism were basing themselves. Ironically, as David Aers and Gunther Kress note, the very love poetry which he excelled at 'was a literature avidly consumed by those who had place and status in the world which excluded him, an elite who sacrificed nothing for love but ensured that it was carefully controlled in the interests of property, patriarchy and the family'.[24] Having sacrificed *all* for love, perhaps this is partly why Donne is so energetic in challenging and undermining the assumptions and conventions of the court love poetry. The opening of a poem like 'The Canonization', a poem generally accepted as having been written after Donne lost his court position, dramatically records the tension between public and private precisely in terms of the irreconcilable views of what might be important to its male speaker:

For God's sake hold your tongue, and let me love,
   Or chide my palsy, or my gout,
My five grey hairs, or ruined fortune flout.

(CEP, p. 47)

This may well exploit a conventional Petrarchan *topos*, but Donne transforms it with a newly inflected rhetorical gesture. The explosive dramatic tone is of frustrated anger, as the speaker rejects the criticisms of his implied companion who we imagine has chastised him for sacrificing his career and wellbeing for love. We can read the next few lines with an increasingly sarcastic bite in the emphasis as the speaker's impatience mounts with his realization, perhaps, of exactly what he *has* given up for love:

With wealth *your* state, *your* mind with arts improve,
   Take *you* a course, get *you* a place. (my emphases)

We can see here something of what David Morse means when he suggests that, after his exclusion from a court career, Donne's 'very sanity was at risk as he struggled like a drowning man to rise to the surface of his depression. The writing of some of the *Songs and Sonnets* may have been part of an infinitely protracted and only partial cure'.[25] He goes on to argue that the love poems should not be read simply as love poems at all; that they were also attempts to counteract the conditions of depression and spiritual isolation; they were therapeutic as much as expressive.

Such a view complements the thesis we are investigating. What is partly at work in these poems is the attempted translation of sex into discourse, an attempt at constructing an imaginary domain of power, a possible compensation for non-existent or compromised power in the 'real' world. This links with arguments presented by Foucault in *The History of Sexuality: An Introduction*. As is well known, Foucault sees sex as a historical construct, produced and changing in/through history; and he also sees sex as increasingly articulated and deployed by being put into discourse, mapping an intensification of knowledge/talk/words about sex as a form of power/control.[26]

In Donne's texts, this often takes the form of seeing woman as a material body to be celebrated, and a subjection of the female body to the probing investigations and invasions of the male word with its 'masculine persuasive force'. The poems thus achieve a verbal capture of the female body as the object of male fantasy in language which is in the service of the male imagination. John Carey has suggested that power is a 'shaping principle in Donne's verse'.[27] We can see it in his sometimes imperious and dictatorial attitudes to women, the unrelenting violence of his arguments and language, the manipulations he enforces. Yet as Foucault's arguments imply, the will to power masks awareness of insecurity; power is often conditional on insecurity, a product of it. In these poems, Donne attempts to possess imaginary women as material bodies (images of exploration, trades, treasure, etc.), but it is a possession enacted through the fantasy power of language, subjecting the idea or image of the woman to verbal investigation and invasion. This is essentially a translation of sexual desire into mental activity, into discourse, and as such it is at a safe distance from actual sexual activity; it doesn't require the participation of another (female) body, merely the poet's command of his material (words) and the indulgence of his (male) readership. There is a hidden subject here – that of male narcissism, or even homoeroticism.

One unusual example in the Donne corpus is the elegy/epistle 'Sappho to Philænis'. The authorship of this text has been questioned, but for our argument this is less pertinent since what is under consideration is not *the* man Donne but *a* man 'Donne', or more specifically a male institution under the name of 'Donne'. As the work of Jacques Derrida has indicated, the 'name' of an author is an institution whose composition has been as much an effect of literary history as of the activities of the historical individual who, in our case, bore the name 'John Donne' between the years 1572 and 1631.[28] The name of the institution and the body of work which makes it up may be open to disputation, but the contradictions of its gender mark are indisputable. They are written into the language of the poems.

'Sappho to Philænis' takes another convention familiar from Ovid, this time the fictionalized letters between famous lovers found in the *Heroides*. This erotic epistle is cast in the voice of Sappho, the lesbian classical poet (born c. mid-seventh century BC). Choosing her voice as the vehicle for an erotic fantasy initiates a number of strategies. One is to create a voyeuristic vantage-point for the male reader allowing privileged access to a common male fantasy, the sexual activities of lesbian lovers. Yet what is notable about the central section of the poem is not that it indulges in erotic fantasy on behalf of male sexuality so much as that it does so at the expense of male sexuality and 'silly' men:

Thy body is a natural paradise,
  In whose self, unmanured, all pleasure lies,
Nor needs perfection; why shouldst thou then
  Admit the tillage of a harsh rough man?

(CEP, p. 128)

This makes the obvious analogy between the body and the garden of Eden, but it inverts the conventional order by seeing the garden as first belonging not to Adam but to Eve, and as being at its most paradisal *before* cultivation. The pun in 'un*man*ured' emphasizes that male 'tillage' is an invasion, an unnatural intrusion of culture into nature, a penetration of the body/garden which is unnecessary for female pleasure. The definition of male sexuality in terms of 'harsh rough' penetrative intercourse is challenged as an imposition, a 'sin' of theft which leaves its traces on the body; whereas the 'dalliance' between the two females is natural and unobtrusive: 'no more signs there are, / Than fishes leave in streams, or birds in air' (*CEP*, p. 128).

This anxiety about avoiding defacing the body is intriguing, not least as the rest of the poem invites the male reader to entertain himself with a fantasy not of lesbian sexual enjoyment but of female masturbation. Sappho is arguing what would seem obvious and redundant if this were a woman writing/reading the poem – that she and her lover can not only achieve all sexual pleasure between themselves without the need of men, but that their two bodies are so alike that this too is an argument for their mutual congress. Furthermore:

Likeness begets such strange self flattery,
  That touching myself, all seems done to thee.
Myself I embrace, and mine own hands I kiss,
  And amorously thank myself for this.

(CEP, p. 128)

Male fantasies of female masturbation may be as common as male fantasies of lesbian sex, but they both have the same impetus – a titillation which is also an implicit invitation to the male reader to imagine masturbating himself. What is unusual here is that this comes after the explicit denigration of the effects of male penetrative sexual activity. In that sense, it can be read as a surreptitious invitation to the male reader to *enjoy* himself by enjoying *himself*. In other words, as the women don't need men, so the man doesn't need a woman.

Under the veil of female homoeroticism, this Donne text is in fact an invitation to male narcissism or homoeroticism. This point receives some support from the arguments put by Eve Kosofsky Sedgwick, following Gayle Rubin, that in patriarchal heterosexuality women become 'exchangeable, perhaps symbolic, property for the primary purpose of cementing the bonds of men with men': the man 'uses a woman as a "conduit of a relationship" in which the true partner is a man'.[29] Equally, the historical context provides supportive material. According to Lawrence Stone, there is evidence to suggest that attitudes towards homoeroticism among the middle and upper classes in Donne's time were more pragmatic and less persecutory than in other parts of Europe.[30] Certainly it appears that among the colleges of Oxford and Cambridge it was not uncommon for young male students to encounter some homosexual practices by virtue of the fact that they often shared their sleeping quarters with a number of other students and a tutor. Stone mentions the confessional autobiography of David Baker as alleging that homosexuality among students was common in Broadgate Hall in the 1590s.[31]

Equally, despite Shakespeare's Sonnet 129, attitudes to masturbation seem generally to have had less of the obsessive anxiety and policing that became evident from the eighteenth century onwards, signalled by the first popular pamphlet of 1710.[32] For late sixteenth- and early seventeenth-century medical theory, moderate masturbation seems to have coincided with the notion of evacuating surplus fluids in order to balance bodily humours.[33] As Thomas Cogan put it in 1589: 'the commodities which come by moderate evacuation thereof [semen] are great. For it procureth appetite to meat and helpeth concoction; it maketh the body more light and nimble, it openeth the pores and conduits, and purgeth phlegm; it quickeneth the mind, stirreth up the wit, reneweth the senses, driveth away sadness, madness, anger, melancholy, fury'.[34]

No wonder, then, that in his poem 'The Blossom', Donne could suggest that when his renegade heart, infatuated as it was with an unyieldingly stiff woman, should rejoin himself and his body 'at London . . . Twenty days hence', it will find him 'fresher, and more fat, by being with men, / Than if I had stayed still with her and thee' (*CEP*, p. 45). Perhaps this also helps explain the degree of anxiety we find in Donne's poems over the constancy of women and the dependability of their love. Such anxiety about the possibility of women's 'treason' can invade an otherwise apparently assured and celebratory poem such as 'The Anniversary', where in lines 25–8 the celebration turns into a plea for a continuity to love which the speaker seems less than certain of:

> Who is so safe as we? where none can do
> Treason to us, except one of us two.

(CEP, p. 42)

It is such anxieties which might tend to encourage that cynicism or misogyny to be found in the 'libertine' poems such as 'Community' or 'Confined Love', whereby women are best viewed as disposable commodities.

Francis Barker, in *The Tremulous Private Body*, has shown similar strategies of subjection to a male voice at work in Marvell's 'To His Coy Mistress'. Presenting his view as 'an anti-reading' of Marvell's poem which allows for an 'underside' to the text, Barker recognizes alongside the persuasive and cajoling male voice, a silent woman in the text whose resistance can be seen as her refusal to enter into dialogue with the male voice. This, for Barker, defines 'a mute limit of the penetrative capacity of the male voice', from which position 'the male voice can be understood as crying vain-gloriously and even somewhat pathetically into a silence it doesn't notice. No actual "woman" is listening, or, if listening, only negligently and with scorn . . . . The gendered voice . . . revolves alone, and completely within the speaking of its own "dialectic" '.[35]

Here we have the contradiction of such male 'love' poetry, and it is one which, in my experience, some women student readers find difficult to accept. My sense that this is the case has grown increasingly clear over the last few years, not so much because I have encountered women students who have any more of an emphatically feminist analysis of these poems but because I myself have come to recognize more clearly how irritating or even irrelevant in their address these texts can be to women readers. These are male texts which speak of men, for men, through men and about men. The genre title of 'love poem' really seems a misnomer for texts whose subject is themselves, a recognition which goes back at least as far as Catullus's 16. Catullus berates his friends Furius and Aurelius for accusing him of not being chaste because his poems aren't:

You miss the point; my poetry
Is simply not the same as me.
But all my verses really owe
Their wit and charm and all their salt
To spicy, merry, sexy flow
Of words that even stir up halt
And hairy grandads.[36]

The recognition that the poems aren't Catullus is equally apt for us. Donne's love poems weren't Donne in any confessional sense, even if confessional writing itself can somehow be unproblematically seen as equatable with its author. The question as to how Donne saw his love poetry is attached to this problem. Did it function, as in John Carey's suggestion, as 'a private theatre in which un-resolvable questions could be entertained as they could not in the decisive business of life',[37] or as some kind of exploration or constitution of self? Or were poems, as Donne himself dismissively wrote, merely 'evaporations' of his wit?[38]

Such speculations are intriguing but unanswerable. What remains the case, however, is indicated by the rest of Catullus's remarks – the masculine parameters which somehow define the activity and function of these love poems. They are anxious to amuse and entertain other men with fantasies which, however, inadvertently display other anxieties about the security of the male speaking voice. We would do more justice to the material if, as male critics, we stopped masquerading such poems as somehow complimentary of women or as 'faithful to natural experience', and instead embraced them as what they are – love poems addressed to the male ego; surreptitious or overt reinforcements to the spurious security of male sexual identity. We might then see more clearly what they have to say to us about the masks of our own masculinities.

Notes

1. Thanks should go to William Zunder, John Hoyles, Lucy Vulliamy and Robin Wells for their extremely useful and sometimes provocative suggestions about this piece.
2. John Donne, 'The Triple Fool', in *The Complete English Poems*, ed. A. J. Smith (Harmondsworth, 1977), p. 81; referred to hereafter as *CEP*.
3. Donald L. Guss, *John Donne, Petrarchist: Italianate Conceits and Love Theory in 'The Songs and Sonnets'* (Detroit, Michigan 1966). Guss

comments on the theory that, as what he terms 'a manly realist, Donne repudiates Elizabethan Petrarchism', saying that 'This theory prevents a true reading of Donne's poems. And it is involved with so many misconceptions, critical and historical, that it can hardly be answered except through a new understanding of Petrarchan imitation' (p. 34).

4. In his introduction to a recent translation of Ovid, E. J. Kennedy describes Ovid as a poet who 'takes the genre by the scruff of the neck and shows it who is to be master'. See Ovid, *The Love Poems*, tr. A. D. Melville (Oxford, 1990), p. xvi.

5. Christopher Marlowe, *The Complete Poems and Translations*, ed. Stephen Orgel (Harmondsworth, 1971), p. 116. The Melville translation for the same passage gives more of a sense of Ovid's playfulness with the conventions: 'I'm not love's acrobat to leap from bed / To bed. Believe me, you'll be mine always' (Ovid, *The Love Poems*, ed. Melville, p. 6).

6. Bruce R. Smith, *Homosexual Desire in Shakespeare's England: A Cultural Poetics* (Chicago and London, 1991), pp. 11–12. A good recent example of the impact of masculinity theory on literary criticism is Joseph A. Boone and Michael Cadden, eds, *Engendering Men: The Question of Male Feminist Criticism* (London, 1990). It contains some essays relevant to this period as well as a reasonable bibliography. The present author's book *Male Mythologies: John Fowles and Masculinity* (Brighton, 1984), was an early example applied to a contemporary author. It is at present out of print.

7. Helen Carr, 'Donne's masculine persuasive force', in Clive Bloom, ed., *Jacobean Poetry and Prose: Rhetoric, Representation and the Popular Imagination* (London, 1988), p. 97.

8. John Carey, *John Donne: Life, Mind and Art* (London 1981), p. 37.

9. Ibid., p. 47.

10. David Aers, Bob Hodge and Gunther Kress, *Literature, Language and Society in England 1580–1680* (Dublin, 1981), p. 55.

11. Smith, *Homosexual Desire*, p. 15.

12. Lawrence Stone, *The Family, Sex and Marriage in England 1500–1800*, abridged edn (Harmondsworth, 1979), p. 311.

13. There is a textual crux here which is discussed and interpreted differently by A.J. Smith in his *Literary Love: The Role of Passion in English Poems and Plays of the Seventeenth Century* (London, 1983), p. 112, as well as in his notes to his edition of Donne's poems. I can't see that this renders my interpretation implausible.

14. Ovid, *The Love Poems*, ed. Melville, p. 69.

15. See the research in Arthur F. Marotti, *John Donne, Coterie Poet* (Madison, Wisconsin, 1986), pp. 3–24.

16. Thomas Carew, *Poems*, ed. Arthur Vincent (London, no date), pp. 72–3. The whole poem is quoted in the *Documents* section below, pp. 259–63.

17. Frank Kermode, *Shakespeare, Spenser, Donne* (London, 1971), p. 133.
18. John Donne, *Selected Prose*, ed. Helen Gardner and Timothy Healy (Oxford, 1967), p. 26.
19   Carey, *John Donne*, p. 45.
20. Donne, *Selected Prose*, ed. Gardner and Healy, p. 134.
21. Aers, Hodge and Kress, *Literature, Language and Society*, p. 36.
22. Ibid, p. 50.
23. David Morse, *England's Time of Crisis. From Shakespeare to Milton – A Cultural History* (Basingstoke, 1989).
24. Aers, Hodge and Kress, *Literature, Language and Society*, pp. 64–5.
25. Morse, *England's Time of Crisis*, pp. 277–8.
26. See Michel Foucault, *The History of Sexuality: An Introduction*, tr. Robert Hurley (Harmondsworth, 1981), pp. 105, 155.
27. Carey, *John Donne*, p. 117.
28. See Derrida's deconstruction of Nietzsche in the essay 'Otobiographies: the teaching of Nietsche and the politics of the proper name', in *The Ear of the Other*, ed. Christie McDonald (Lincoln, Nebraska, and London, 1988), pp. 3–38; or Michel Foucault, 'What is an author?', in *The Foucault Reader*, ed. Paul Rabinow (Harmondsworth, 1984), pp. 101–20.
29. Eve Kosofsky Sedgwick, *Between Men: English Literature and Male Homosocial Desire* (Columbia, Ohio, 1985), pp. 25–6.
30. Stone, *The Family, Sex and Marriage*, p. 309.
31. Ibid., pp. 322–3.
32. Ibid., pp. 320–1.
33. Ibid., p. 319; Smith, *Homosexual Desire*, p. 87, quotes Follopius to this effect.
34. Stone, *The Family, Sex and Marriage*, p. 313.
35. Francis Barker, *The Tremulous Private Body: Essays on Subjection* (London, 1984), pp. 92–3.
36. Catullus, *The Complete Poems for Modern Readers*, tr. Reney Myers and Robert J. Ormsby (London, 1972), pp. 30–1.
37. Carey, *John Donne*, p. 46.
38. Donne, *Selected Prose*, ed. Gardner and Healy, p. 132.
39. Smith, *Literary Love*, p. 105.

4 'When the bad bleed': Renaissance tragedy and dramatic form

Kathleen E. McLuskie

I

'Tragedy', wrote Sir Philip Sidney, 'maketh kings fear to be tyrants and tyrants to manifest their tyrannical humours'.[1] This apparent manifesto for the social application of tragic art is often quoted by modern critics who wish to claim an oppositional role for early modern tragic drama, locating it within the struggles for power which attended the formation of the early modern state.[2] Yet there is, in Sidney's *Defense*, a fundamental gap between the high ideals which he claimed for Poetry and a dissatisfaction with the work of mere practitioners of the art. He found

> Our tragedies and comedies not without cause cried out against, observing rules neither of honest civility nor skilful poetry.[3]

For Sidney, only those works which conformed to classical ideals of art could hope to fulfil the poet's highest purpose, which was to create a golden world of poetic truth in contrast to the leaden world of everyday reality. The only tragedy which he admired, Sackville and Norton's *Gorboduc* (1562), was a formal piece in which dramatic action was separated out into allegorical dumbshows while the eloquent speeches debated their political implications. It was, moreover, produced by student lawyers at the Inns of Court and its didactic purpose ensured by the context of its performance.

This special relationship between high moral purpose, rhetorical form and a non-commercial, private performance is highlighted in the Preface to the Reader of the printed text. The Preface reminds the reader that this Tragedie was for furniture of part of the grand Christmasse in the Inner Temple first written about nine yeares agoe . . . and after shewed before her Maiestie.[4]

These aristocratic origins were no doubt part of the appeal for the purchaser of the book, but the Preface goes on to remind him of the precariousness of such privacy with the story of how the text had been pirated and corrupted by money. The text is compared to a virgin violently dishonoured by exposure to the public world, but the printer's convoluted efforts to distinguish between the prostitution of a corrupted text and the honest commerce of his own publication reveal the contradictions which surrounded the discourses of commercialized culture. They reworked the conflict between high and low art and in feminizing the text revealed an anxiety over the control of unruly elements in the society as well as the culture. Together with Sidney's concern over the political and formal requirements for true tragedy they indicate the axes of commerce, form and politics around which the development of tragedy was negotiated in early modern culture.

As drama became more commercial, available in the professional theatres for anyone who had the price of entry and distanced from a privileged access to the seats of power, dramatists complained of the detrimental effects on their art.[5] All their comments reflect the tension between high social and aesthetic ideals and the working conditions imposed by a commercial theatre. Nevertheless, the forms of Renaissance tragedy did adapt to those working conditions and developed out of the creative interaction of different traditions of dramatic writing. The role of commerce was less to mitigate high artistic ideals than to offer new and competing kinds of theatrical pleasure.

An appeal to theatrical pleasures was not as incompatible with political ideals as the exponents of an exclusive high culture would have claimed. Indeed, the tension between high and low culture in the development of tragic form itself complicated the plays' political impact. In *Cambises* (1558–69), for example, the classical analogues of the prologue and the explicit political appeal of its epilogue announce the play's relevance for kings and suggest that the play took itself seriously as a contribution to the social role of English tragedy. With its Vice, its morality figures and its mixture of emblematic and mimetic form the play defied classical theories of tragedy, but it offered a compendium of available dramatic pleasures and indicated the complex relationship between its political and its theatrical effects.

The play is constructed in two contrasting movements, the first dealing with the cruelty and downfall of the unjust councillor Sisamnes, and the second with Cambises' own unfitness for the role of king. The story of the corrupt justice is recounted to King Cambises by the allegorical figure of Commons Cry, aided by Proof and Trial. Like the prologue or the emblematic presentation of 'SHAME, *with a trump black*' (line 340, Stage Direction), this episode enacts the explicit political theme of the unhappy end of unjust rulers which is also the explicit moral of Cambises' own gory end.

The conflict between demands of teaching and entertaining has its formal counterpart in the different styles of the play's dramatization. The stage directions throughout are vividly explicit, but they also indicate the difficulty of realizing both political and theatrical aims with the stage devices available. In the episode of Sisamnes' death, for example, the moral point is quite explicit, but the theatrical effect of the scene in which he is punished is more complex. The executioner is instructed to '*Smite him in the neck with a sword to signify his death*' and '*Flay him with a false skin*'. T. W. Craik, in his edition, notes that

> this flaying of the covetous judge was a proverbial example which moralists had already urged rulers to imitate.[6]

However, this political message may have been muted, if not suppressed, by the spectacular effect of the theatrical trick.

Tension between the didactic and the spectacular is complicated elsewhere in this scene by a similar conflict between the political moral and the pleasures of an emotional response. Sisamnes' son, Otian, who has been appointed to succeed him as justice, is called to witness his father's execution as a warning 'Lest thou do purchase the like death ere ever it be long'. The moral precept, however, has no power to silence Otian's grief:

> The grievous griefs and strained sighs my heart doth break in twain,
> And I deplore, most woeful child, that I should see you slain.
> O false and fickle frowning dame, that turneth as the wind,
> Is this the joy in father's age, thou me assign'st to find?
> O doleful day, unhappy hour, that loving child should see
> His father dear before his face thus put to death should be!
> Yet, father, give me blessing thine, and let me once embrace
> Thy comely corpse in folded arms, and kiss thy ancient face.
>
> (lines 447–54)

The representation of Otian's grief evokes powerful images of Fortune's falseness and the reversal of natural hopes; the culminating stage image of the father's and son's tearful embrace carries an emotional power which all but unbalances the political argument. Sisamnes is being justly executed as a corrupt judge, but the clear moral line is somewhat obscured by the pathos and horror of his end.[7]

Cambises' own death is sudden and theatrically stunning: he appears *'without a gown, a sword thrust up into his side, bleeding'*, and, after a speech of terror, dies in evident anguish: *Here let him quake and stir*. Its moral point, however, has to be stressed in the Lords' accompanying comment, which is a curious mixture of providential commonplace and narrative practicalities:

A just reward for his misdeeds, the God above hath wrought:
For certainly the life he led, was to be counted nought.
Yet a princely burial he shall have, according to his estate:
And more of him here at this time, we have not to dilate.

(lines 1187–91)

The conflict between the political and the theatrical dimensions is further complicated by the figure of Ambidexter who orchestrates the audience's responses. His impertinent way with the audience presents him as a figure who mediates not only between audience and stage but between abstract concepts and their dramatization. He 'cannot choose but weep for the queen', and encourages the audience's moral judgement on Cambises' murder of his brother. He tells the audience to laugh and cry, to be apprehensive and relieved, and reminds them not only of the nature of the action but also of its moral significance. In classical tragedy these are the functions of the chorus, but Ambidexter is far from reliable as a chorus to a tragedy. Like the audience he is both involved in the action and distanced from it. He tempts Sisamnes to become corrupt – a necessary action for the plot to move on – but also deplores the ensuing evil; he stirs up the low-life figures to fight and then sends in the whore to beat them. His emotional reaction to the events of the play, moreover, is also a role. After the death of the king's brother at the hands of Cruelty and Murder, Ambidexter is instructed by a stage direction to 'weep'. He tells the audience:

If I should have had a thousand pound, I could not forbear weeping.
Now Jesus have his blessed soul in keeping!

> Ah good lord! to think on him, how it doth me grieve!
> I cannot forbear weeping, ye may me believe.
>
> (lines 736–9)

But his emotion only lasts for a moment and at the end of the speech
he can exclaim:

> Nay, I have done, in faith, now, and God give you good morrow!
> Ha! ha! Weep? Nay, laugh, with both hands to play!
> The king through his cruelty hath made him away.
>
> (lines 740–4)

Ambidexter's startling shift from tears to laughter is partly a
manifestation of the double-handedness (or even-handedness) which
his name implies. However, it is also an example of the complex
relationship between performer and audience, narrative and
interpretation, character and persona which is central to the impact of
Elizabethan and Jacobean tragedy. His line effects a shift from
emotional reaction to explanation and the next episode of the
narrative. He moves back and forth across the boundary between the
audience and the world of the play, sharing both their emotional
involvement in and their moral judgement of the action; but his
cheerful acceptance of the new situation suggests that the emotional
and the moral are held in check by the pleasures of narrative.
Ambidexter thus acts as a conduit and control for the audience's
reactions, but he also offers the independent pleasures of his skills as
a solo performer and clown as well as the moral ambiguity of the
morality play vice. The manifest political content of the play may
indeed have made kings fear to be tyrants; for the audience who saw
it performed by a touring company it also offered the subversive
theatrical pleasures of the spectacle of a king's gory end and the
possibility of a dual response of both pathos and laughter.

II

The involvement of a popular audience in the reception of tragic drama
was at the heart of the anxieties about tragedy's political role. The
possibility of a less than solemn response to Cambises is provided in
the scene in Shakespeare's *I Henry IV* when Falstaff and Hal play
impromptu at being kings. Falstaff equips himself with the appropriate
props:

> This chair shall be my state, this dagger my sceptre and this cushion my
> crown;   (II. iv. 368–9)[8]

and promises to perform 'in King Cambyses vein'. The hostess is
overcome with mirth and he reproaches her in a parody of
old-fashioned tragic style:

> For God's sake, lords, convey my tristful Queen;
> For tears do stop the floodgates of her eyes.
>
> (II. iv. 382–3)

She comments:

> O Jesu, he doth it as like one of these harlotry players as ever I did see.
> (II. iv. 385)

Like the prostituted text of *Gorboduc*, the performance of kings is now
associated with players whose relationship with their audience is also
one of harlotry. Commercial relations of production released the high
style of tragedy from its association with high culture and made it
available for any player. When Bottom the weaver in *A Midsummer
Night's Dream* found himself cast as a tragic hero, he was able to offer
not one but two alternative styles in which the speeches could be
performed. He enquires, 'What is Pyramus, a lover or a tyrant?', and
launches straight into a speech in 'ercles vein'. He is equally up to the
performance of a puling lover and can scarcely be restrained by
Quince, the director/writer of the piece.

This impertinent pretension of common players in aping the forms
of tragedy was frequently mocked. Nashe, for example, in spite of his
general support for the stage, deplored 'the servile imitation of
vainglorious Tragedians . . . the Alcumists of eloquence who
(mounted upon the stage of arrogance) think to outbrave better pennes
with the swelling bumbast of a bragging blank verse'.[9] His jibe at
outdated poetic style is partly a restatement of the values of high
culture but his comment, and others like it, indicates the concern of
writers to defend the exclusiveness of their art from mere players and
audiences. The commercial pressure towards innovation encouraged
writers continually to reassert the special character of their art.

This constant pressure for artistic innovation which is characteristic
of commercialized entertainment was evident in the explanatory
prologues and epilogues which accompany so many plays of the

period. It created a degree of self-awareness about the effects of drama which was expressed in the metatheatricality which became a feature of the tragic drama. Metatheatricality, an awareness of the relationship between actor and role, had a moral as well as a theatrical dimension: Hal and Falstaff's performance of a king took place in a play where the political role of king was addressed in theatrical terms. The revenge drama of the age similarly questioned the appropriate relationship between the actor and his action in both the morality and the aesthetics of revenge.

When Hamlet, for example, encounters the players at the court of Elsinore, their demonstration of their playing skills forces him to confront the difference between the player's response to the death of Priam and his own 'motive and cue for passion'. The player's speech recounts, in the high rhetoric of classical tragedy, the death of Priam and Hecuba's grief. His tearful and passionate performance enacts a response to the action of others rather than directly expressing his own suffering. The pleasures it offers are a recognition of rhetorical styles and an invocation of the central tragic action of classical history. However, it is a narrative of terrible events recounted rather than passion shared. Hamlet, as a result, is sceptical about the player's reaction. He contrasts the player's affected passions with the 'reality' of his own situation, which would call forth a much more powerful performance. However, he remains caught in the theatrical metaphor, describing his behaviour as a series of possible roles. He curses Claudius – 'Bloody, bawdy villain! / Remorseless, treacherous, lecherous, kindless villain' – but then breaks off in disgust at the inadequacy, as much artistic as moral, of his words. The formal rehearsal of narrative, characteristic of earlier tragic form, is not appropriate for his revenge, for it separates too clearly the speaker from the action. But the complete spontaneity of anger and contempt will not do either. It is the language of whores and drabs and scullions, lacking the weighty seriousness of a play which would catch the conscience of the king.

The episode with the players and Hamlet's famous speech on finding an appropriate acting style, crystallized the dilemma for the serious writer of tragedy. Like the mechanicals' play in *A Midsummer Night's Dream* Hamlet's speech contrasts the desired acting style with a more old-fashioned theatre in which the clowns spoke more than was set down for them and the tearcat tragic hero tried to 'out-Herod Herod'. He had constantly to assert the authenticity of the action he presented and to distinguish it from the outdated acting style in which convention soon hardened into cliché.[10]

The metaphors of metatheatricality, however, also had dangerous potential for undermining any belief in the action played on stage. Just as Ambidexter and indeed Hamlet himself could perform a variety of roles, serious existential concerns with the nature of action could be expressed through parody and burlesque, particularly in the highly self-conscious and reflexive drama produced by the playwrights who wrote for the boy companies at the turn of the seventeenth century. The boy players' theatre had both to create a repertory for itself and to establish its particular place in the theatrical market. As Reavley Gair has shown,[11] these plays dramatized the question of acting and performance, both as a showcase for all of the skills and styles which the boy actors had at their disposal and as a way of establishing a claim to be the new avant garde theatre. They addressed their audience as an élite group, knowledgeable about theatre and capable of a sophisticated play with that knowledge.

In Marston's *Antonio's Revenge* (1599–1601), for example, the Paul's boys performed a varied series of turns on the format of a revenge play. It combines the plots of both *Hamlet* and *The Spanish Tragedy*: Antonio mourns and eventually revenges the death of his father, Andrugio, and the remarriage of his mother, Maria, to Piero, the murderer; Pandulpho mourns and eventually revenges the death of his son Feliche. Moreover, the revenger's possible reactions, the contest between stoic indifference and rhetorical complaint which Hamlet discussed in soliloquy, are here addressed quite explicitly as possible roles. Alberto urges patience on Antonio who insists that his passion is authentic because physiological:

> Are thy moist entrails crumpled up with grief
> Of parching mischief? Tell me, does thy heart
> With punching anguish spur thy galled ribs?
>
> (I. v. 43–5)

Pandulpho, on the other hand, had responded to the dreadful events with laughter, preferring to avoid the clichéd actions of conventional tragic heroes:

> Wouldst have me cry, run raving up and down
> For my son's loss? Wouldst have me turn rank mad,
> Or wring my face with mimic action,

Stamp, curse, weep, rage, and then my bosom strike?
Away, 'tis apish action, player like.

(I. v. 76–80)

Pandulpho's rejection of a player's passion turns out to be a double bluff. At the end of the play, when Antonio's final revenge is being plotted, he breaks down and admits that

all this while I ha' but played a part,
Like to some boy that acts a tragedy,
Speaks burly words and raves out passion;
But when he thinks upon his infant weakness,
He droops his eye.

(IV. v. 47–51)

The critique of the revenger's style, once incorporated into the plays themselves, rendered any representation of passion unstable. The distinction between 'forced passion' and true passion is constantly being asserted but, since the whole action is playing, it can never be rescued from the infinite regress of the playing metaphor.

III
The domestic solution

At the end of *Antonio's Revenge*, the hero confronts the chaos of his own tragic action and looks forward to a different kind of tragedy being written to celebrate the death of his beloved, Mellida:

And, O, if ever time create a muse
That to th'immortal fame of virgin faith
Dares once engage his pen to write her death,
Presenting it in some black tragedy,
May it prove gracious, may his style be decked
With freshest blooms of purest elegance;
May it have gentle presence, and the scenes sucked up
By calm attention of choice audience;
And when the closing Epilogue appears,
Instead of claps, may it obtain but tears.

(V. vi. 60–9)

In part this conclusion is one of the extra-diegetic gestures which makes the experience of that play so confusing. However, it also expresses the hope that a tragedy with a woman at its centre might be able to draw out the true tears of pathos without the confusing questions about the nature of role playing and the authenticity of passion which afflicted plays on the theme of the revenger. There was some justification for this view in the treatment of women in the tragedies which Marston might have known. The death of the queen in *Cambises* brings the most passionate tears to Ambidexter's eyes, and Ophelia's role and tragic death offers the only unmitigated focus for pathos in *Hamlet*.

The search for a subject which would provide an alternative to the tragedy of revenge was evident in *A Warning for Fair Women*,[12] performed in 1599 by the Chamberlain's Men. The Induction to that play discusses the possibility of including tragedy in the repertory of the commercial theatre. Tragedy dismisses the noisy appeal of History's drum and ensign from the stage and is equally contemptuous of Comedy's 'filthie fiddling trickes / Able to poyson any noble wit'. Comedy, however, is confident of her commercial appeal, reminding Tragedy that

> she may for a day
> Or two perhaps be had in some request,
> But once a weeke if we do not appeere
> She shall find few that will attend her heere.

(lines 35–8)

Tragedy makes it clear that she is making a comeback in commercial terms:

> 'Tis you have kept the Theatres so long,
> Painted in play-bills upon every poast
> That I am scorned of the multitude,
> My name prophande: but now Ile raigne as Queene
> In great *Apollos* name and all the *Muses*.

(lines 74–8)

Comedy's lively objection to Tragedy is on account of the clichés of existing tragic form:

> How some damn'd tyrant to obtain a crown
> Stabs, hangs, impoisons, smothers, cutteth throats:
> And then a Chorus, too, comes howling in
> And tells us of the worrying of a cat:
> Then, too, a filthy whining ghost,
> Lapt in some foul sheet, or a leather pilch,
> Comes screaming like a pig half stick'd,
> And cries, Vindicta! – Revenge, Revenge!

(lines 43–50)

This was no abstract discussion of artistic theory but a contest over theatrical styles in which the new subject matter seemed to offer the opportunity for a pleasing authenticity in tragedy which would provide a new kind of tragic form.

The play presented the true story of how George Browne in 1573 murdered George Saunders to gain the love of his wife Anne. The murder was discovered and, in spite of George Browne's protestations of her innocence, Anne Saunders and he were executed along with Anne Drury and her man Roger who had acted as go-betweens in the affair. The pamphlet account of the story, contemporary with the trial, offered the possibility of reading it as a tragedy. The author compared the scaffold on which the lovers were executed to a theatre in which God is the director of productions:

> when God bringeth such matters upon the stage, unto ye open face of the world, it is not to the intent that men should gaze and wonder at the persons, as byrdes do at an Owle, nor that they should delight themselves & others with the fond and peradventure sinister reporting of them, nor upbrayd the whole stocke and kinred with the fault of the offenders: no surely, God meaneth no such thing. His purpose is that the execution of his judgements, should by the terrour of the outward sight of the example, drive us to the inward consideration of ourselves . . . that we myght both detest wickednesse with perfect hatred and rue the persons with christen modestie.[13]

This account offers a view of tragedy based on a christianized version of Aristotelian *catharsis* in which the pleasure of dwelling on evil is held in balance by horror at the wickedness and pity (rue) for the individuals involved. That balance was rather more difficult to achieve in the theatre. It depended on the deployment of theatrical devices which could set sympathy for the characters against a clear moral attitude to their behaviour.

One such device was to present the authenticity of Browne's love in poetic soliloquy and to develop his character through his anguished recognition of Saunders' rights as a husband. However, the potential sympathy for Browne is reduced by abstracting the personal tragedy into an allegorical action of the conflict between Lust and Chastity. This device holds the moral framework in place but also gives the weight of tragic inevitability to the sometimes trivial and frustrating turns of Browne's attempts to murder Saunders. It also clarifies the action by providing motivation absent from the main plot. Immediately before the murder

> The Music playing, enter Lust, bringing forth BROWNE and ROGER, at one end, Mistress SANDERS and Mistress DRURIE at the other, they offering cheerfully to meet and embrace. Suddenly riseth up a great tree between them. Whereat amazedly they step back. Whereupon Lust bringeth an axe to Mistress SANDERS, showing signs that she should cut it downe: which she refuseth, albeit Mistress DRURIE offers to help her. Then LUST brings the Axe to BROWNE, and shows the like signs to him as before. Whereupon he roughly and suddenly hews down the tree, and then they run together and embrace. With that enters CHASTITY, with her haire dishevelled, and taking Mistress SANDERS by the hand, brings her to her husband's picture hanging on the wall, and, pointing to the tree, seems to tell her, that this is the tree so rashly cut down. Whereupon she, wringing her hands, in tears departs.

This action in effect retells the story, resolving the question of Anne's complicity in the murder.

This slippage between allegory, symbol and metaphor is seen in the trial scene where the stage direction indicates that '*Anne Sanders hath a white Rose in her bosom*'. Anne represents the rose as 'token of my spotless innocence / As free from guilt as is this flower from stain' (lines 1310–11), which could be read as brave defiance. The possibility of moral and dramatic ambiguity is nevertheless closed off at the end of the scene when, after the verdict, as Anne continues to protest her innocence, one of the judges comments:

> It should not seem so by the rose you wear:
> His colour now is of another hue.

As in the flaying of the corrupt judge in *Cambises*, moral symbolism and theatrical trickery combine to simplify the dramatic action.

By the time of their deaths both Browne and Anne accept their guilt and can function much more explicitly as exemplary figures. Browne is given a 'scaffold speech' of great power which separates his character from the rhetorical account of his wickedness, and Anne delivers a lengthy, affecting farewell to her children in which she repents the wrong done to them and bequeaths each of them a book of holy meditations to save them from a similar fate.

The overt manipulation of emotion to a predetermined moral end is all too evident in the final scenes of this play. Nevertheless, it represents an interesting experiment with a different tragic paradigm. In Tragedy's final choric appearance, she explicitly reminds the audience of the change in the formal paradigm, offering reportage as a solution to the problems of authenticity:

> Here Tragedy of force must needs conclude.
> Perhaps it may seem strange unto you all,
> That one hath not revenged another's death
> After the observation of such course:
> The reason is, that now of truth I sing,
> And should I add or else diminish aught,
> Many of these spectators then could say,
> I have committed error in my play.

She bypasses the theoretically vexing problem of conflict between the emotional and the moral, which was at the heart of contemporary discussions of tragedy, by separating the true action which would arouse pity from the exemplary action which would show God's justice. However, the theatrical impact of the hero's self-searching, and the contradictory representations of women seen in Anne's role, indicate possible future developments for a tragedy of feeling based on love rather than revenge.

This potential for a tragedy of love which would bring together the allegorical and mimetic dimensions of adultery and murder is powerfully realized in Heywood's *A Woman Killed with Kindness* (1603). The emotional focus is firmly on the wronged husband, Frankford, in the contrast between the happy and hopeful marriage which opens the action and the miserable loss brought about by the adultery of Wendoll and Anne. The story is fiction, but the sense of authenticity which bypasses considerations of mimesis is created by the realistic details of the setting. At the same time, the moral framework is held in place by Frankford's servant Nicholas, who acts as a choric commentator but is also a fully realized character in the play. Nicholas and the other servants present an idealized version of the life of a country house. Scene viii, for example, is introduced by servants '*one with a voider and a wooden knife to take away all*'. Frankford enters '*as it were brushing the crumbs from his clothes with a napkin*' and is told the dreadful news of his wife's adultery. Anne and Wendoll then play a game of cards with Nicholas and Frankford looking on. Their asides, and Wendoll's dangerously double-edged remarks about being Anne's partner, intertwine with images of playing false, winning and losing. This apparently naturalist action can be used to set up dramatic ironies which generate both the suspense and the sense of loss which are crucial to the tragic conclusion. Heywood, as it were, naturalizes the allegorical banquet of Lust from *The Warning for Fair Women* and integrates its theatrical resonances into the main action.[14]

The scene where Frankford discovers the adulterous lovers once again skilfully balances outrage at the lovers' behaviour with sympathy for Frankford's loss. The lovers are kept off stage, holding the focus on Frankford's point of view, which can then maintain the moral and emotional reaction in tension. He describes how:

> I have found them lying
> Close in each other's arms, and fast asleep.
> But that I would not damn two precious souls
> Bought with my Saviour's blood and send them laden
> With all their scarlet sins upon their backs
> Unto a fearful Judgement, their two lives
> Had met upon my rapier.
>
> (xiii. 42–8)[15]

This speech empasizes the pathos of his situation which is increased by his lament on the inexorable passing of time. The wish

> that I might take her
> As spotless as an angel in my arms
>
> (xiii. 61–2)

invokes the lost happiness of the beginning of the play, insulating the sense of his loss from any consideration of Anne's or Wendoll's feelings.

Having achieved this measure of control over the emotional attention to the scene, the text then packs the remainder of the action into dumbshow:

> *Enter* WENDOLL, *running over the stage in a night gown he* [FRANKFORD] *after him with his sword drawn; the Maid in her smock stays his hand and clasps hold on him. He pauses awhile.*

As Alan Dessen has pointed out,[16] the maid's action is perfectly integrated into the realist mode of the action, but it creates a stage picture which carries all the symbolic meaning of the allegorical actions of psychomachia, inherited from an earlier dramatic tradition.

Frankford makes the connection plain in the speech which acts as the 'word' to this dramatic emblem:

> I thank thee, maid; thou like the angel's hand
> Hast stay'd me from a bloody sacrifice.
> Go villain, and my wrongs sit on thy soul
> As heavy as this grief doth upon mine.

> (xiii. 68–71)

Its integration into the dramatic action allows Frankford's grief and restraint to be part of the dramatic impression as well as the evil of Wendoll's adultery.

From this moment on, however, Anne's role in the play is to act as the emblem on which the tragic action is played out. In the first dialogue with Frankford she is explicitly emptied of all character: as Frankford says, her actions only exist to bring out his reaction:

> Spare thou thy tears, for I will weep for thee
> And keep thy countenance, for I'll blush for thee.

> (xiii. 84–5)

She is instantly remorseful and Frankford's 'kindness' in banishing, rather than killing, her allows the play to draw out the tragedy of his situation in the sorrow of hers. He lists all she has lost, calling for her children only to send them away lest

> Her adult'rous breath may blast their spirits
> With her infectious thoughts.

> (xiii. 126–7)

At this point Anne addresses the women of the audience directly, urging them to see her as exemplary and warning that

> when you tread awry,
> Your sins like mine will on your conscience lie.

> (xiii. 143–4)

The direct debt to the didactic impulse of allegorical dramatic form is evident. However, the emotional impact is far more powerful and, in being linked to Anne's masochistic call for a physical punishment which would redeem her honour, more complex.

The appropriate response to this action, the balance between moral awareness and human sympathy, is made explicit by Anne's neighbour Sir Francis at her deathbed:

> I came to chide you, but my words of hate
> Are turn'd to pity and compassionate grief;
> I came to rate you, but my brawls, you see,
> Melt into tears, and I must weep by thee.   (xvii. 63–6)

The final scene in which Frankford forgives Anne and restores her names and status is the counterpart to the final sequence of *A Warning for Fair Women* in which Anne Saunders takes leave of her children, her forgiveness assured by her Christian faith. The patriarchal politics which transfer that power of forgiveness to Frankford are part of the ideological movements of the time, but they are also the product of a theatrical movement which secularizes the drama and integrates its morality into the emotional dynamic of its narrative. That process of turning allegory into symbol and then playing the symbolic action in a fully realist context creates a potential for the complex dramatic treatments of family and sexual relationships characteristic of Elizabethan and, in particular, Jacobean tragedy.

Domestic tragedies like *A Warning for Fair Women* or *A Woman Killed with Kindness* are sometimes dismissed as a subgenre within Elizabethan/Jacobean drama, linked to popular culture and depending on reportage for their dramatic power. But they were performed by the same companies as the plays of Middleton and Webster and Shakespeare who drew on and adapted the same stock of theatrical structures. The willow scene in *Othello*, the game at chess in *Women Beware Women*, the Duchess of Malfi's affecting farewell to her children are among the many scenes which have obvious structural analogues in domestic drama. Their particular attention to heterosexual love, threatened by the power of courts or the fantasies of corruption in satire, provided the potential for a directness of emotional engagement often absent from other tragic styles.

The roles of women characters were crucial in this development: like the tragic heroes whose complexity was developed in reaction to conventions, so the tragic heroines gained theatrical power when their conventional passivity was explicitly rejected for the unsexing powers of sin or joined to the wit or defiance more usually characteristic of comic figures. For much of Elizabethan and Jacobean tragedy was made up of a process of assembling different theatrical elements, scenes of violence, scenes of pathos, scenes of moral commentary, building them into structures which integrated the different elements into mimetic narrative. Plays like *Cambises* or *A Warning for Fair Women* leave the different elements discrete, revealing most clearly the raw materials of dramatic structures and theatrical effects which were available to other dramatists to accept or react against.

The plays which subsequent critical generations found most powerful were those where the narrative cohered around a poetically articulate individual. Jacobean tragedies undermined that figure and that form even in the moment of its creation. The pressure towards theatrical innovation and the resulting self-consciousness about theatrical form acted as counterweights to the development of naturalist tragedy; on the other hand, the drive towards naturalism, seen in the domestication of tragic passion and the efforts to create authentic protagonists with lives outside the action, offset the attempts to impose didactic theories of tragedy favoured by those who had less faith in the tastes of a paying audience. The need to appease that audience, whether judging or merely weeping, gave a particular slant to the development of tragic drama whether it was directed by Tragedy herself or mocked by the laughter of Ambidexter.

Notes

1. Philip Sidney, *The Defense of Poesie* in *Literary Criticism from Plato to Dryden*, ed. Allan H. Gilbert (New York, 1967) p. 432. See the *Documents* section below, pp. 263–4.
2. See, for example, Franco Moretti, 'The great eclipse: tragic form as the deconsecration of sovereignty', in John Drakakis, *Shakespearean Tragedy* (London, 1992); Leonard Tennenhouse, *Power on Display, The Politics of Shakespeare's Genres* (London, 1986).
3. Sidney, *The Defense of Poesie*, ed. Gilbert, p. 449.
4. Reprinted in Clara Gebert, ed., *An Anthology of Elizabethan Dedications and Prefaces* (New York, 1966). See the *Documents* section below, pp. 264–5.
5. See, for example, Ben Jonson, Preface to the Reader of *Sejanus*; John Webster, Preface to the Reader of *The White Devil*, quoted in the *Documents* section, pp. 265–7. The discourses of art and commerce are discussed in Kathleen McLuskie, 'The poet's royal exchange: patronage and commerce in early modern drama', in Cedric C. Brown, ed., *Patronage, Politics and Literary Traditions in England 1558–1658* (Detroit, Michigan, 1993), pp. 125–34.
6. T. W. Craik, ed., *Minor Elizabethan Tragedies* (London, 1974).
7. As T. W. Craik points out, (edn cit., p. 81 note), the pathos of this scene echoes the presentation of Issac in the miracle play of Abraham and Isaac.

The mother's lament is similar in imagery and conception to Grissil's lament for her children in John Phillips's *Patient and Meek Grissil* (1559).

8. Gary Taylor and Stanley Wells, eds, *The Oxford Shakespeare* (Oxford, 1988).

9. Thomas Nashe, 'Preface to Greene's *Menaphon*', quoted in E. K. Chambers, *The Elizabethan Stage* (Oxford, 1923), 4, pp. 234–5.

10. Compare Beaumont, *The Knight of the Burning Pestle* (V. i. 278–82), or Jonson, Chapman and Marston, *Eastward Ho* (II. i. 122–7). In the Induction to *Bartholomew Fair* (1613), Jonson sarcastically commended the admirer of *The Spanish Tragedy* and Shakespeare's *Titus Andronicus* 'as a man whose judgement shews it is constant, and hath stood still these five and twenty or thirty years'.

11. See W. Reavley Gair, ed., *John Marston: Antonio and Mellida*, (Manchester, 1991).

12. Anon., *A Warning for Fair Women*, ed. C. D. Cannon (The Hague, 1975). See the *Documents* section below, pp. 268–70.

13. Arthur Golding, *A Brief Discourse*, reprinted in Cannon, edn cit. p. 226. See the *Documents* section below, pp. 270–1.

14. The game as an ironic symbol of sexual danger is also used in *Arden of Faversham*, where Arden is murdered as he plays at tables with Mosely, and in *Women Beware Women*, where Bianca is seduced as her chaperone mother-in-law plays a game of chess with Livia, the court procurer. In Ford's *Love's Sacrifice* the irony is doubled back as a game of chess is used to suggest a love affair which, though passionate, is never consummated. Game as metaphor for sexual challenge was used more recently in the television police drama 'Between the Lines', where the hero challenges his mistress's husband to a computer game!

15. Thomas Heywood, *A Woman Killed with Kindness*, ed. R. W. van Fossen (London, 1974).

16. Alan Dessen, *Elizabethan Stage Conventions and Modern Interpreters* (Cambridge, 1984), p. 111.

5 *Identity and ownership: Narratives of land in the English Renaissance*

Melanie Hansen

In his 'Mathematicall Preface' to the *Euclid*, John Dee expounds his views on the function of maps. He writes that 'some, for one purpose, some, for an other, liketh, loveth, getteth, and useth, Mappes, Chartes, and Geographicall Globes. Of whose use, to speake sufficiently, would require a book peculiar'.[1] For all sorts of reasons, it could be argued that investigation of English Renaissance antiquarianism and cartography might require just such 'a book peculiar'. To speak 'sufficiently' on the way in which antiquarian narratives make recourse to the different scholarly disciplines of history, geography and philology to describe the land and landscape necessitates the perhaps peculiar perspective of a literary critic reading and interpreting texts more broadly understood as being 'historical' or 'geographical' documents rather than as 'literary' texts.[2] So, in order to embrace this standpoint, I want to consider this 'peculiarity' from a number of vantage points. The first part of this essay delineates the kinds of narrative descriptions of land that Renaissance antiquarians produced, and the cultural assumptions invested in narratives which attempted to evoke textually 'pictures' of the county and the country. In the second part of this essay, I want to explore the relationship between the social status of the antiquarians and their understanding of antiquarian scholarship as a collective endeavour; for it is that understanding that had a profound effect on the narrative strategies employed by antiquarians to construct 'pictures' of the land as well as upon other 'literary' texts of the period, especially topographical poetry. In this way, despite my engagement with ostensibly 'non-literary' material, my own preoccupations as a literary critic remain with my emphasis upon textual and linguistic analysis. Whilst the focus remains predominantly on antiquarian narratives, I read them not in isolation but as a complex response to and engagement with a changing social and political landscape in which *all* texts are implicated.

So, what exactly were antiquarian narratives? By antiquarian narrative, I am referring to the increasingly prolific and lengthy descriptions of land and landscape, of towns and cities, and of counties and the country as a whole that were written during the Renaissance period. These antiquarian texts varied enormously in their scope, from William Camden's *Britannia* (1610), which ambitiously undertook to describe England, Scotland, Wales and Ireland, to William Lambarde's *Perambulation of Kent* (1576), which was a written description of the county of Kent in which he lived.[3] In constructing these descriptions of the county or country, the antiquarians made recourse to a variety of representational methods: they delineated the history, topography, language, economics and – often – the customs of the inhabitants; they incorporated into their accounts both contemporary maps as well as their own eye-witness narrative descriptions of the landscape; and they included references to chronicle histories and histories of language, lengthy descriptions of the genealogies of the gentry, as well as minute detailings of buildings and sites of interest from castles to local monuments. This eclectic material was gathered together by the antiquarian to produce a written narrative of the county or the nation. Consequently, one might think of English Renaissance antiquarianism itself as interdisciplinary in focus – quite self-consciously consulting and appropriating a range of information from geography, chorography, history, comparative philology and so on. And it is this range of information from which antiquarian narratives are constructed that has culminated in their being understood more as historical or geographical documents than as 'literary' texts.

Reading these antiquarian narratives has generated a number of often interrelating questions. In the first instance, there are the more pragmatic questions such as who were these antiquarians? What motivated their work? What did the antiquarians think they were doing – methodologically, politically, textually – when they were describing the land? What was their relationship to the land they were describing? And what function did these narratives serve during this period? However, there are also a number of critical questions that are raised in the study of this material. These concern, for example, what cultural assumptions are invested in these antiquarian narratives. To what extent might one think about these narratives as formulating some kind of 'antiquarian discourse', a discourse that is articulated through a codified methodology? And if such a discourse and methodology were formulated, what implications did this have for the way in which the Renaissance period as a whole conceptualized the land and the landscape? For perhaps one of the most perplexing and paradoxical questions of all concerns the construction – through narrative – of a sense of county and country, region and nation. Of course, these terms are extremely problematic and they were by no means clearly formulated during this period, as, indeed, they are not today. But the paradoxical nature of this issue manifests itself in these antiquarian narratives by the fact that whilst these terms – county, country, region, nation – are repeatedly employed, their precise referents are never fully disclosed. What I mean by this, is that an antiquarian narrative like that of William Lambarde's *Perambulation of Kent*, for example, can quite self-consciously textually construct a narrative of Kent through its history, its geography, its laws, its administration, its language and even its poets, thereby offering the reader a historical and, simultaneously, a contemporary 'picture' of this county; but at the same time, the engagement with the county in terms of its relationship to the country or nation is never fully confronted; neither is the authorizing status of the narrative itself. The authority that the antiquarian narrative held as an adequate and valid narrative representation of the region or the nation was, in fact, a highly complex and contentious issue during this period, not least because of the social status held by the antiquarians within Renaissance society. In order to address some of these questions, I want to examine who the antiquarians were and what function the Antiquarian Society played in the establishment of antiquarianism as a scholarly pursuit. For it is consideration of the social status of the antiquarians and the understanding of antiquarianism as a collective scholarly endeavour that raises important implications for the kinds of narratives that these antiquarians subsequently produced.

The antiquarians formed a group of individuals who all shared an intense scholarly interest with uncovering and recovering the history and contemporary culture of regional and national society. In formulating models for their narratives, the antiquarians looked back not to the chronicle histories of the medieval period but rather to the work of one particular individual, John Leland. Leland's antiquarian description of England and Wales, entitled *The Laborious Journey and Search of John Leland* (1549), was perceived by the antiquarians of the late sixteenth and early seventeenth centuries to herald the establishment of a new kind of scholarship.[4] Furthermore, Leland's characterization of himself as 'an Antiquarian' brought in being a scholarly status that authorized the production of the antiquarian narrative, a status that had important implications for the function and reception of these texts during this period. Whilst many antiquarians worked independently within their own regions, they consulted – and very often referred to extensively – each other's material. William Lambarde and William Camden, for example, both refer to one another's material in each of their narratives, crediting each other with the uncovering of particular contemporary or historical references. This sharing of information culminated in the antiquarian pursuit being understood as a collective one. As a consequence of this, an Antiquarian Society was founded in London in around 1572, a date that is substantiated by the most important source of the Society, the written records of Henry Spelman.[5] The Society met the most regularly in London between 1590 and 1607; and its primary function was to create a forum for the dissemination of ideas between individuals who shared antiquarian interests. The 200 manuscripts produced by the members of the Society as a whole for discussion are still extant and they represent a significant insight into antiquarian study during this period. Written mainly in English, the manuscripts record membership and discussion of Society business and they include minutes of the various meetings. The manuscripts also illustrate the immense scope of antiquarian endeavour at this time: they range from the discussion of sterling money to the antiquity of the shires, arms in England, dukes, funerals and epitaphs, the antiquity and privilege of heraldry, tombs and monuments, and the antiquity of the laws in England.

With regard to membership of this Antiquarian Society, twentieth-century scholars vary in their identification of the central members; some suggest Sir Robert Cotton as a key figure, whilst others argue for Archbishop Matthew Parker.[6] Despite this debate, however, reference to Henry Spelman's account of the Society illustrates that many of the members who were involved in establishing an institutional basis for antiquarian study were individuals of important social and political standing. Spelman's account of the Society clearly informs his readers of the standing of the Society's members: 'Sir James

Ley Knight, then Attorney of the Court of Wards, since the Earl of Marleborough and Lord Treasurer of England, Sir Robert Cotton Knight and Baronet, Sir John Davies his Majesty's Attorney for Ireland; Sir Richard St George Knt, then Norrey, Mr Hackwell the Queen's Solicitor, Mr Camden, then clarencieux, my self, and some others'.[7] Arthur Ferguson has described these individuals as 'gentlemen scholars', 'members who came to the Society from careers in law, heraldry and the Church'; and Joan Evans confirms that 'many of them owned manorial rights and were interested in the condition of the tenure of land in England'.[8] There are a number of ways of looking at the social and political status of these antiquarians. On the one hand, this list of membership suggests that the focus of antiquarian study upon the antiquity of land, the counties and the law reflected their own specific class preoccupations; and those preoccupations were shared both by the rising gentry as well as the nobility. On the other hand, however, not all antiquarians held such important social and political status: William Lambarde may have owned a manor in Kent and been responsible for administering justice in the county as a member of the rising gentry, but individuals such as William Camden and John Norden had to rely on their own endeavours to gain financial support for their work. William Camden asserted in the *Britannia* that he relied purely on his own financial independence acquired by working at Westminster School; whilst John Norden sought (unsuccessfully) the patronage of Queen Elizabeth. Thus, since the status of the antiquarians was not a clear-cut issue at this time, this necessarily raises the question of why Henry Spelman should emphasize the status of the Society's members. For Spelman was not the only one to emphasize that membership; Richard Carew wrote to Sir Robert Cotton in 1605 to say that: 'I heard by my brother, that in the late Queenes tyme [the Society] was lykelie to have received an establishment and extraordynarie favour from sundrie great personages'.[9]

The stress on the social and political status of the antiquarians by Spelman and Carew implies an attempt to validate and authorize the scholarship of the antiquarians by virtue of that status, rather than to validate that Society through their object of study. And the reason for authorizing antiquarianism in this way was to assert the independence of the Antiquarian Society from the universities, thereby establishing itself as a Society that would explore very different kinds of scholarship. This affirmation of independence and bid for legitimation was further underlined in 1589 by the submission of what is known as the 'Cotton Petition', signed by Sir Robert Cotton, James Ley and Sir John Doddridge.[10] It sought to legitimate their Society and since it was addressed to Queen Elizabeth, the Petition attempted to acquire royal endorsement. Even though the Petition was ultimately unsuccessful in gaining such endorsement, the document remains an important register of the Society's opinion of the universities. The Petition asked:

> . . . for a charter of incorporation, and for some public building where they might assemble and have a library. . . . This Society will not interfere with the Universities, as tending to the preservation of History and Antiquities, whereof the Universities, long buried in the Arts, take regard.[11]

This Petition reveals, then, an attempt to pre-empt an adverse response from the universities by formulating recognition of their work independently; the Petition's request for a public building and a library represents just such a move to create a public site as a means to authorize their study in distinction from that of the universities.

Despite the Cotton Petition's attempt to provide some public recognition for their work, the Antiquarian Society was later to be threatened in its scholarly endeavours not by the universities but by James I. Henry Spelman records how the Society tried to avoid incurring the hostility of James to antiquarianism by alleging that antiquarian scholarship would refrain from encroaching upon politically sensitive material. Spelman claimed that: 'We held it sufficient for that time to revive the meeting, and only conceiv'd some Rules of Government and Limitation to be observ'd amongst us; whereof this was one, that for avoiding offence, we should neither meddle with matters of state, nor of Religion'.[12] Whilst this assertion represents an undertaking to codify antiquarian study, its premise that the antiquarians 'should neither meddle with matters of state nor of Religion' remains unconvincing. This is because Spelman had already placed a great deal of emphasis on the social and political status of the members, members who had included the Lord Treasurer of England and the Attorney for Ireland. In addition, since the manuscripts produced by the Society focused on a whole variety of subjects from sterling money to the antiquity and privilege of heraldry and the laws of England, antiquarian involvement in contemporary political ideologies was implicit. Consequently, regardless of Spelman's claim that the Society refrained from 'meddling in matters of state', James I retained a marked hostility to the meetings. Spelman clearly identifies James's culpability in the demise of the Society through his claim that:

> . . . before our next Meeting, we had notice that his Majesty took a little Mislike of our Society; not being informed, that we had resolv'd to decline all Matters of State. Yet here upon we forbeare to meet again, and so all our labours lost . . .[13]

In fact, the Antiquarian Society was to remain dormant until 1638, with a brief resurrection between 1617 and 1628 via the efforts of Edmund Bolton. It was in the third attempt at forming a Society in 1638 that a far more comprehensive set of regulations concerning the scope of antiquarianism was delineated; and in this, the reformation of the Society looked forward, of course, to the future Royal Society.

This brief outline of the scholarly concerns and ultimate fate of the Antiquarian Society raises a number of issues for the textual and linguistic analysis of antiquarian narratives. That these antiquarians were members of the new professions or landed gentry – or both – necessarily calls into question their motivation for producing narrative descriptions of land. What are the cultural assumptions invested in these narratives and how does the societal status of these antiquarians determine the way in which they selected material for describing the land and the audience to which such descriptions might appeal? For a further point raised by the hostility that the Society generated both in the universities and with James I concerns the function that these texts served during this period, and raises the question whether such hostility may well have derived from the particular kind of representation of the county and nation that these narratives evoked.

I want to address these questions by looking at a number of extracts from Renaissance antiquarian narratives. For these extracts illuminate, through their selection of material and their narrative strategies, the manner in which a 'picture' of the county or nation was constructed. The first extract, printed below, is from *A View of Devonshire (1604–30)*, written by Thomas Westcote, who was a gentry antiquarian describing the county in which he lived. The extract comes from the introduction to his account and it indicates quite clearly the antiquarian negotiation with the selection of material and the appeal to a distinct audience. With his description of Devon, Westcote appeals to his readers that:

> I hope I may intermix a pleasant tale with a serious discourse, and an unwritten tradition with a chronicled history, old ancient armories and epitaphs, well near buried in oblivion, (matters not supervacual nor unworthy to be received and kept living, unless we could be content to have our own name and remembrances to perish with our bodies,) ancient families now extinct, or rather transanimated into others; some etymologies seeming and perchance strange and far fetched; old, new, serious, jovial, curious, trivial: for these and matters of such nature may . . . give recreation to a wearied body and mind (that reads for recreation,) with more delight and content for variety.[14]

In the first instance, this extract illustrates just how wide the range of material considered relevant to antiquarian study was. For Westcote, as with other antiquarians, it included the genealogy of its residents (principally the gentry) together with heraldry and the study of etymology. Furthermore, antiquarian study involved the consultation of different sources, both 'chronicled history' and an 'unwritten tradition'. But in delineating the processes of selection, Westcote also reveals his awareness of the different kinds of perceptual frameworks that were involved in negotiating with this diversity of material: it required the consideration of the 'old, new, serious, jovial, curious, trivial'. It is that awareness of alternative perceptual frameworks that produced, for Westcote, an antiquarian description of land that was both narrative story, 'a pleasent tale' and a learned work, 'a serious discourse'. With regard to readership, this extract indicates that Westcote was appealing to an audience that 'reads for recreation'; and as the full title to this antiquarian narrative suggests, *A View of Devonshire with a Pedigree of Most of its Gentry*, the readers of this text were members of the gentry who wished to read of their own family's history and contemporary status in the county in which they lived. But in producing a 'learned discourse', Westcote also projected an implied scholarly audience that consisted of learned and interested antiquarians. In this reading, then, the cultural assumptions invested in Westcote's description of Devon are explicit. As with many antiquarian narratives of this period, the description of land was determined by the need to register and remember a particular version of cultural history for its contemporary residents. As Westcote claims, the selection of all this diverse material was important because it generated and promoted a sense of historical and regional identity for the gentry families who lived in Devon. Consequently, Westcote's narrative of Devon both registered and appealed to a certain section of the community: the readers of this antiquarian narrative came to 'know' and understand the county of Devon through its gentry. Thus, by presenting knowledge of the land in these terms, the traditional association between monarch and land was disrupted.

Whilst Westcote's *A View of Devonshire* demonstrates the way in which the content of the narrative constructed a particular kind of 'picture' of the county, antiquarian narratives also created that 'picture' through narrative structure. What I mean by this, is that the actual ordering of the antiquarian narrative which described land also culminated in the production of a certain kind of 'picture'. An example of this may be illustrated by an extract from William Lambarde's *Perambulation of Kent* (1576). In this narrative, Lambarde explains to his readers the ordering of material that he will adopt:

> I will observe this order: first to begin at Tanet, and to peruse the East and South Shores, till I come to the limits betweene this Shyre and Sussex: then to ascend Northward, and to visit such places, as lie along the bounds of this Diocese and Rochester, returning by the mouth of Medway to Tanet again, which is the whole circuit of this Bishopricke . . .[15]

Here, Lambarde employs the landscape as an ordering principle for his narrative. And as the title to his antiquarian narrative suggests, the relationship between travelling through the county and the ordering of the narrative of that county were understood by Lambarde as inextricable. By means of this narrative strategy, therefore, Lambarde offers a textual 'map' of the county, a 'map' that presented information about that county through a structure that was predicated on journeys and geography. The model for this structure was John Leland's *Labourious Search and Journey*, which in its emphasis upon structuring his account through travelling, exerted considerable influence in determining antiquarian narrative strategy. In fact, Lambarde's antiquarian narratives present a number of very different kinds of narrative strategy. Whilst Lambarde often exhorted his antiquarian readers to establish antiquarianism as a collective endeavour (a sentiment reflected, of course, in the formation of the Antiquarian Society), at the same time he also argued that the textual representation of land was most adequately undertaken by those who were actually resident in a specific county. For Lambarde, an antiquarian's 'personal' knowledge of a particular place was the only way to construct a 'true' picture of it; and the status of that 'true' picture acquired authority by the status of the antiquarian as resident. And for Lambarde himself, additional authority was conferred upon his *Perambulation of Kent* by dedicating it to the most important member of the gentry in Kent at that time, Henry Wootton. But despite Lambarde's belief in a 'personal' knowledge of the county, he also produced a topographical dictionary of England and Wales, a text that obviously moved beyond personal knowledge of a particular area. In this dictionary, because the towns are listed in alphabetical order, the 'picture' constructed of England and Wales is inherently different from his earlier textual 'map' of Kent or Westcote's narrative of Devon. The implication of Lambarde's use of grammar to structure 'knowledge' of the country through this topographical dictionary was that the alphabet obscured the fragmentary nature of the material selected for the representation of land and the differences in landscapes and cultures of England and Wales. Instead, the dictionary generated a sense of unity. In Lambarde's dictionary, therefore, a 'picture' of the country is produced not so much by the information that is contained within the alphabetical structure but, rather, by the structure itself.

Analysis of the narrative strategies of these antiquarian texts illuminates, then, the importance of selection and structure in producing particular versions of cultural history and knowledge of the county and country. And these strategies were crucial since, in appealing to a gentry readership, they offered that readership a sense of identity through antiquarian narrative. However, because these descriptions of land were written predominantly by the gentry for the gentry, ideological significance is invested within them; and this significance correlates with that of the social and political standing of the Antiquarian Society membership. There has been much critical work on the so-called 'rise of gentry' in this period: with questions ranging from how far one can consider the gentry at this time as a self-consciously socially and politically defined group, to those concerning the formulation of a distinct and authoritative voice that sought to represent the gentry's interests. To a large extent, by including within their narratives accounts of genealogy, heraldry, etymology and so on, the antiquarians registered or recorded – through narrative – a cultural transformation that, from the Reformation onwards, witnessed land changing hands at a prolific rate and which culminated in the creation of new and powerful gentry families. But at the same, whilst recording this cultural transformation within their narratives, antiquarian texts were also profoundly implicated in it. In other words, antiquarian texts can be read as a response to a societal transformation in land ownership and, simultaneously, by virtue of their gentry status, can be understood as taking part in that transformation: their class preoccupations played a significant role in determining the kind of material selected and the version or picture of the county and country that was subsequently produced.

This complex situation can be explored further by considering some textual examples. Edward Worsop, a surveyor, described with some concern in *Sundry Errours Committed by Land Meaters* (1582) the consternation caused by an attempt to survey the land on an estate on which he worked:

> When the lands were parted betweene my Mystress and her three systers, there were certain lawyers, valuers and country measurers, and for three or four days great controversie was among them and such a stir as I never sawe amongst wise men. Some wold have the land measured one way, some another. Some brought long poles, some lines that had a knot at the ende of every perch, some lines that were sodden in rosin and waxe to avoide stretching thereof in the water and shrinking the drought.[16]

Edward Worsop's account is actually one of many that lamented the lack of skill held by many would-be surveyors and cartographers. William Cunningham's *Cosmographicall Glasse* (1559) and Nathanial Carpenter's *Geography Delineated forth in two Bookes* (1625) were two such texts which incorporated definitions of geography and cosmography together with rules and regulations for the surveying of land as a means to encourage the production of adequate cartographic representations. But Worsop's description also testifies to the increasing requirement by the gentry to survey newly acquired land or to divide that land up amongst the family. The crucial issue here, is that it was the gentry who were commissioning these surveys and maps and not the monarch, as had Henry VIII in commissioning military maps of the south-east coast. These surveys, commissioned by the gentry, became primary source material for the antiquarian description of land. For example, the maps of John Norden and Christopher Saxton, who were both surveyors, were included in the 1607 edition of William Camden's *Britannia*. Coupled with these maps and surveys, antiquarian narratives also incorporated often quite extensive lists of genealogies of the gentry, genealogies that presented information about who owned a particular piece of land at any given time. Much of Lambarde's *Perambulation of Kent*, Thomas Westcote's *View of Devonshire*, William Pole's *Description of Devonshire* and Tristram Risdon's *Chorographical Description, or Survey of the County of Devon*, for example, included copious lists which detailed genealogies of the local gentry. Each text begins with a general history and topography of the county, followed by a listing – sometimes in alphabetical order – of towns, villages, estates, and so on. Within these individual descriptions, genealogy features as a narrative method by which knowledge of those towns or estates is conveyed. As a result, the antiquarian narrative explicitly interrelated geography and genealogy.

This interrelationship is especially foregrounded in the representation of 'Yartye' in Devon by the antiquarian narratives of William Pole and Tristram Risdon. In the first extract, from William Pole's *Collection towards a Description, Or Survey of the County of Devon (1603–30)*, the antiquarian depicts Yarty as standing

> . . . in the tithinge of Membiry, and hath borrowed its name from the river of Yartie, which runneth under it. It did first give ye name unto ye dwellers there, which were called de Yartie, which name ceased in King Henry 4 tyme, and sithens yt by ye name and famylye of Frye, and newly builded and augmented by Nicholas Frye, Esquir, whoe is now the owner thereof.[17]

In this description, Pole claims that the name of 'Yarty' was derived from the landscape on which it was situated and he points out that the name was also given to the inhabitants, 'unto ye dwellers there'. This 'geographical significance' is subsequently altered to include the political and social: following the reign of Henry IV, 'Yarty' was known by the family which owned the land, 'whoe is nowe the owner thereof'. In the second description of 'Yartye', by Tristram Risdon in his *The Chorographical Description, Or Survey of the County of Devon*, the transformation from understanding a place through its geography to that of the genealogy of its principle inhabitants is articulated far more explicitly:

> Yartye is in Membury, and standeth under an Hill from the East somewhat advanced above the Water, from whence it borrowed its Name, and gave it again to the Owners, who, by the Names of William and Simon, continued their Dwelling there divers Descents. The last Simon dying issueless, about the Reign of King Richard II, his Sister

brought this Inheritance unto William Fry, Esq.; by her Marriage, which hath continued ever since in that Family. The now Possessor married the Daughter of John Tounge, Esq., his Father, the Daughter of John Brett of Whitstanton, Esq; his Son the Daughter of Sir John Drake.[18]

Again, the etymology of place-name is identified with the name of a geographical site, the river of 'Yartye'. But whilst William Pole in the first excerpt simply described that this name was subsequently given to the inhabitants, the 'dwellers', Risdon suggests that it was the 'Owners' of the land who adopted the name. The place of 'Yartye' is represented, therefore, through the genealogy of the family that owned the land.

Together, these narrative accounts of Devon by William Pole and Tristram Risdon identify the way in which both the historical site and the contemporary place were understood in relation to land ownership; and furthermore, by means of these narratives, naming and land ownership were authorized by reference to the original understanding of the land through the geographical site. Consequently, this interrelationship between history, geography and genealogy as formulated in antiquarian narratives illustrates the way in which land becomes known through its contemporary owners, through the gentry, rather than through the monarch. Antiquarian narratives, then, in their employment and inclusion of surveys of land and genealogies of the gentry, were responding to a changing landscape that followed the radical political upheavals of the sixteenth century. At the same time, because these antiquarians were of gentry status themselves, they were also profoundly implicated in recording and altering the way in which land was understood during this period. The way in which the county or the region, the country or the nation, could be conceptualized and understood by its authors and readers in terms of localized and individual family land ownership, was a conceptualization that antiquarian narratives helped to effect.

In conclusion, there are a number of critical ways in which one can examine the implications of the narrative strategies employed by the antiquarians and the kinds of 'pictures' of the county and the country that they subsequently evoked. In the first instance, that Lambarde, Risdon or Pole described Kent or Devon with reference to the economic and cultural concerns of the gentry suggests the creation of what Roland Barthes might refer to as a 'gentry myth' of land.[19] The readers of these antiquarian narratives came to 'know' Kent or Devon through, say, the genealogies of the gentry resident in the county. The names of these gentry acted as signifiers, not for any aspect of the landscape that the readers might actually see, but of a particular cultural identity. In this way, the antiquarian narrative might be seen to 'mystify', to create the myth of gentry culture, and to act as 'an agent of blindness', one that obscured rather than revealed different kinds of social and political 'realities' of the landscape. However, whilst these antiquarian narratives revealed their own cultural assumptions in the way in which they selected material, their reference to the genealogies of the gentry were by no means unproblematic. In fact, it was the inclusion of these very genealogies that proved to be a particularly contentious issue. Many of these antiquarian narratives also included apologies and disclaimers for not referring to all of the gentry families of any given county. William Camden's *Britannia* is one such narrative that testifies to the consternation caused amongst gentry readers who discovered that their family was not recorded in the description of an area. Camden noted that:

> There are some peradventure which apprehend it disdainfully and offensively that I have not remembered this or that family, when as it was not my purpose to mention any but such as were more notable, nor all them truly (for their names would fill whole volumes) but such as happened in my way according to the methode I proposed to myself.[20]

Camden's response to attacks made against him for omitting certain families was echoed with some frequency in other antiquarian narratives. Thomas Westcote, in his *Description of Devonshire*, included an entire chapter that functioned as an apology to answer the objection that he had 'not noted every ancient house and generous tribe, but purposely neglected some'. Whilst these responses suggested, of course, the assumption that antiquarians were able to discern by some means which particular gentry family were 'such as were more notable' to be included in a description of a county, there is also a perhaps more difficult issue at stake. Camden's note that to include *all* gentry families 'would fill whole volumes' identifies the way in which representing a place through its gentry might actually constitute an impossible narrative project. So, whilst Camden's *Britannia* illustrates the way in which antiquarian narratives sought to represent land textually through its gentry, at the same time, this narrative strategy threatened the entire project. Antiquarian narratives might construct pictures of the county or the nation through its gentry, but at the same time, it is that very reference to the gentry that conflicts, disturbs and threatens any coherent and unified representation. It is for this reason that thinking about the way in which the concepts of county or region, country or nation are formulated in antiquarian narratives is such a problematic and difficult undertaking. Even though antiquarian narratives might appear quite schematic in the way they order their material, the way in which they treat source material from geography, history, philology and so on, and even though the antiquarians attempted to authorize their narratives by conferring upon them scholarly status, the pressure of somehow containing that information was invariably fraught. These antiquarian narratives, then, not only illustrate the struggle to formulate and codify representations of the land and landscape, they also reveal the way in which that very project presents an intricately complex engagement with the possibilities of any kind of narrative representation that sought to produce a narrative 'picture' of the land.

There are, however, further implications in the study of antiquarian narrative strategy and the kinds of 'pictures' of the county and the country that they produced, in that these narratives facilitate readings of the 'literary' texts of this period. Whilst the Antiquarian Society incurred the hostility of James I and thus, according to Spelman, caused its demise; and whilst some gentry families responded adversely to the alleged omission of their names in William Camden's *Britannia* and Thomas Westcote's *A View of Devonshire*, other readers were far from offering such damning criticism. In fact, there were two poets who quite publicly acknowledged their debt to antiquarian study and in particular to Camden's *Britannia*. This antiquarian narrative elicited a dedicatory poem of praise from Ben Jonson as well as becoming the source text for Michael Drayton's long topographical poem, *Poly-Olbion*. This poem, together with Jonson's dedicatory poem 'To William Camden', illuminate just how influential antiquarian 'pictures' of the land were. These narratives were powerful in their influence because their representation of land, towns, families and buildings functioned to raise consciousness about the significance of the county and nation that were textually evoked; furthermore, they foregrounded the relationship between land and the people. This is particularly expressed in Jonson's poem. Because Jonson had been taught by Camden at Westminster School, he would have known directly about the antiquarian's work and his involvement in the Antiquarian Society. In his poem, far from denigrating the *Britannia* as some gentry families had done, Jonson, especially praises the authority of Camden's description of Britain:

> Camden, most reverend head, to whom I owe
> All that I am in arts, all that I know,
> (How nothing's that?) to whom my country owes
> The great renown, and name wherewith she goes;
> Than thee the age sees not that thing more grave,
> More high, more holy, that she more would crave.
> What name, what skill, what faith hast thou in things!
> What sight in searching the most antique springs!
> *What weight, and what authority in thy speech!*
> Man scarce can make that doubt, but thou canst teach.
> Pardon free truth, and let thy modesty,
> Which conquers all, be once overcome by thee.
> Many of thine this better could, than I,
> But for their powers, accept my piety. [21]

(my italics)

Here, Jonson does not just praise Camden's learning and his ability to teach through antiquarian narrative, he also claims that Camden actually gave 'name' to Britain by means of textual account: 'to whom my country owes / The great renown, and name wherewith she goes'. With these lines, Jonson asserts that it is through the process of naming and textual description or 'picturing' that land achieves some kind of identity. But of equal significance in this poem is the fact that Jonson acknowledges Camden's influence on him as a poet: 'to whom I owe / All that I am in arts, all that I know'. Whilst the *Britannia* was initially published in Latin in 1586, its translation into English in 1610 suggests a potential influence exerted on seventeenth-century topographical and country house poetry and, in particular, on Jonson's own 'To Penshurst' as well as Michael Drayton's *Poly-Olbion*. Both of these poetic texts share with antiquarian narratives an explicit concern with the way in which land could be represented in textual form; and both share with those antiquarian narratives an intense preoccupation with the relationship between people and the land, offering thereby a 'picture' of the gentry or noble family, the estate, the county or the country at local and individualized levels.

Perhaps nowhere is this shared preoccupation revealed more explicitly than in Michael Drayton's topographical poem, *Poly-*

Olbion. Drayton, together with his commentator John Seldon, cites Camden's *Britannia* as a source text for the poem. As the full title to *Poly-Olbion* suggests – 'A Chorographicall Description of Tracts, Riuers, Mountaines, Forests, and other Parts of this renowned Isle of Great Britain' – this poem is far more extensive in range than others of the genre. Whilst the poems of Jonson, Lanyer, Carew or Marvell, for example, focus on specific estates, Drayton's poem ranges across all the counties or Britain. It is this range, together with the narrative strategies employed by Drayton, that reveals the influence of antiquarianism. Paralleling Camden's *Britannia*, the poem is divided into chapters, with each chapter concentrating on a particular county and describing its landscape and history; and, imitating Camden's antiquarian narrative again, Drayton prefaces each chapter with an illustration of the county drawn from Christopher Saxton's county maps. But there are further similarities: reflecting other antiquarian narratives of the period, Drayton claims that history is a fundamental constituent of knowledge of the land and, subsequently, of the county or the country. And by history, Drayton includes the political history of Britain as well as that of the 'Nobilitie, or Gentry'. In this way, *Poly-Olbion* contains

> . . . all the Delicacies, Delights, and Rairities of this renowned Isle, interwoven with the Histories of the Britaines, Saxons, Normans, and the later English: And further that there is scarcely any of the Nobilitie, or Gentry of this land, but that he is some way or other, by his Blood interressed therein . . .[22]

Through convergence of the history of nation with the history of families – the gentry and the nobility – Drayton explicitly employs antiquarian methodology. As a result, Drayton directs his poem towards an audience that is comparable to that of antiquarian narratives: that is, the gentry inhabitants of each county who can read of their own family histories and relate them to the history of the county and the nation, just as they would do with Camden's *Britannia*, Lambarde's *Perambulation of Kent*, Westcote's *A View of Devonshire* or Risdon's *The Chorographical Description, Or Survey of the County of Devon*.

Whilst Drayton's *Poly-Olbion* manifests important differences from antiquarian narratives – especially in the kind of ideal and pre-lapsarian landscapes evoked by the poem – its citing of Camden's

Britannia as a source text and its imitation of antiquarian narrative strategy remains crucial. This is because even in its divergence from those antiquarian narratives, there remains the model and function of antiquarian study to which Drayton makes recourse. Camden's narrative provides an important authorizing function for Drayton's poem, a function that legitimates his 'picture' of Britain through reference to antiquarian scholarship. In Jonson's words, Drayton makes clear use of the 'weight' and 'authority' in Camden's 'speech'. Through reference to Camden's *Britannia* in particular, and to antiquarian narratives in general, Drayton allies his *Poly-Olbion* with such narratives of the land, thus projecting a 'picture' of land that is comparable in status and authority. Therefore, whilst the study of antiquarian narratives in their own right remains important, considering their influence on the poetry of Jonson or Drayton, for example, provides us with important information: it illustrates how Renaissance poets made recourse to ostensibly 'non-literary' material at the same time as blurring the boundaries between them; and how scholarship might be employed for literary purposes in order to confer legitimacy and authority. And finally, reading both antiquarian narratives and topographical poetry, and examining the narrative strategies in the selection of material, the structuring of narrative and the emphasis on the relationship between genealogy and geography that they all employ, indicates forcefully the sheer multiplicity of 'pictures' of the county and of the nation that were produced during this period. Both antiquarian narratives and topographical poetry demonstrate that there was no one or homogenous 'picture' by which the county and the nation were understood by its citizens during the Renaissance and that this diversity was registered not so much through maps, but rather through written text.

Notes

1. John Dee, 'Mathematicall Preface', to *The Elements of Geometrie of the most ancient Philosopher Euclide of Megara*, tr. Sir Henry Billingsley, 1570.
2. Research on ostensibly 'non-literary' material has been facilitated by methodological approaches such as new historicism and cultural materialism, approaches which, in Stephen Greenblatt's terms, have questioned 'the literary as a stable ground in the Renaissance' and which have interrogated the relationship between the 'literary text' and the

culture that produced it. Stephen Greenblatt, *Renaissance, Self-Fashioning: From More to Shakespeare* (Chicago, 1980).

3. For an excerpt from Camden's *Britannia* see the *Documents* section below, pp. 271–4.

4. John Leland, *The Itinerary of John Leland In or About the Years 1535–1543*, ed. Lucy Toulmin Smith (London, 1907).

5. Sir Henry Spelman, *The English Works of Sir Henry Spelman*, Part II (Reliquiae Spelmannianae) (London, 1723).

6. For example, Sir Robert Cotton; F. J. Levy, *Tudor Historical Thought* (California, 1967); Archbishop Matthew Parker: Harrison Ross Steeves, *Learned Societies and English Literary Scholarship in Great Britain and the United States* (Columbia, Ohio, 1913).

7. Spelman, *The English Works of Sir Henry Spelman*.

8. Arthur Ferguson, *Clio Unbound: Perception of the Social and Cultural Past in Renaissance England* (Durham, North Carolina, 1979); Joan Evans, *A History of the Society of Antiquaries* (Oxford, 1956).

9. Cited in Ross Steeves, *Learned Societies*, p. 6.

10. Cotton MS *Faustina* EV. 12, fol. 89 (see also a copy in *Titus* BV. 67, fol. 210). The complete petition is printed in Sir Joseph Ayloffe's *Curious Discourses* Vol. II (London, 1771, 1773, 1775).

11. Cited in Rupert Bruce-Mitford, *The Society of Antiquaries of London* (London, 1951), p. 11.

12. Spelman, *The English Works of Sir Henry Spelman*, p. 69.

13. Ibid., p. 70.

14. Thomas Westcote, *A View of Devonshire with a Pedigree of Most of its Gentry (1605–30)*, eds George Olivier and Pitman Jones (Exeter, 1845).

15. William Lambarde, *Perambulation of Kent* (London, 1576).

16. Edward Worsop, *Sundry Errours Committed by Land Meaters* (London, 1582).

17. William Pole, *Collections towards a Description, Or Survey of the County of Devon (1603–30)* (London, 1791).

18. Tristram Risdon, *The Chorographical Description, Or Survey of the County of Devon, with the City and County of Exeter* (London, 1714).

19. See Roland Barthes' reading of the *Blue Guide* in *Mythologies* (London, 1972).

20. William Camden, *Britannia* (London, 1610).

21. 'To William Camden', in *Ben Jonson*, ed. Ian Donaldson (Oxford, 1995), p. 7.

22. Michael Drayton, 'To any that will read it', *Poly-Olbion*, ed. J. William Hebel. Vol. IV (London, 1933).

6 *Popular culture in the English Renaissance*

Mark Thornton Burnett

In any account of popular culture in the English Renaissance, questions of definition must take a prominent place. As investigative terms, both 'popular' and 'culture' have been subjected to an array of conflicting explanations. On the one hand, some historical arguments maintain that popular culture can be seen as the customs and practices enjoyed by the middling and lower sorts, such as feast days, weddings and wakes, games and sports.[1] Broader approaches, however, have stressed that popular culture (defined by Peter Burke, the historian, as an unofficial 'system of shared meanings, attitudes and values, and the symbolic forms . . . in which they are expressed or embodied') should encompass productions as well as practices. In other words, folk narratives, plays, farces, ballads and verses are important indicators of a culture's operations, and can be considered in addition to ritualized events and recreations.[2] Artefacts and festivals, then, offer ways of understanding the period's prevailing activities and ideological preoccupations.

It has also been suggested that popular festivities and literary materials served key social functions. Particularly in the case of ritual, there were regular occasions on which hierarchical distinctions and geographical boundaries could be reinforced. What were called 'ridings' and 'rough music' were opportunities for a community to humiliate in public an erring husband or wife, or to protest against unjust magistrates and enclosers.[3] The 'beating of the bounds' involved villagers walking the perimeters of their parish in a display which established the extent of their land and property.[4] These demonstrations of the community's concerns often had dangerous implications, however: in being strengthened, boundaries and dividing lines could be challenged, while peaceful demonstrations could turn into open revolt.

Taking note of historians' conceptions of popular culture, and of the subversive potential of some cultural manifestations, sociologists have offered wider definitions still. Following the lead of Antonio Gramsci (the marxist philosopher), John Storey holds that popular culture might best be understood as 'a site of struggle between the forces of resistance of subordinate groups in society, and the forces of incorporation of dominant groups in society . . . [or as] a terrain of ideological struggle between dominant and subordinate classes, dominant and subordinate cultures'.[5] In this model of cultural relations, which does not necessarily privilege the practices and artefacts of particular social groupings, issues of gender, race and class receive an obvious emphasis; Storey is concerned to highlight the political inflection of the voices of the underprivileged and to draw attention to attempts made to silence those voices. For Storey, there are (sometimes radical) political meanings that attach themselves to all social exchanges.

In the present essay, I draw upon these definitions in an exploration of a range of what may well be unfamiliar literary materials. Engaging with the view that popular culture represents an unofficial discourse, I mainly refer to treatises, ballads, satires and popular pamphlets and dramas, which form a contrast with traditional courtly forms and private theatrical performances (although there are also numerous points of contact between apparently opposed generic productions). And in assessing representations of marginalized types (women, women in service and apprentices), I endeavour to illuminate both attitudes towards such types and the contradictory meanings that these representations disseminate. While it is illuminating to address constructions of women, women in service and apprentices, I realize that they do not belong to homogeneous categories, and that in all social groupings there are gradations and differences. Bearing in mind the ambivalent effects of some popular festivities, I argue that literary constructions of the subordinate classes were double-edged: they approved virtues of obedience and left open possibilities for criticisms of dominant ideas, they stressed the need for the preservation of hierarchical distinctions even as they foregrounded the changes that a neglect of such distinctions might precipitate. I am, therefore, primarily drawn to Storey's model of popular culture – to the negotiations that cultural transactions initiate and to the ways in which cultural expressions entertain and resist establishment positions.

To maintain that marginalized sections of society may have been empowered by literary representations introduces questions of consumption and audience. Of course, the texts which form the basis of this essay would not always have been read by subordinate groups, which might be seen as recuperating their subversive implications. But reading is not a precondition to the circulation of ideas, and in the English Renaissance textual messages were broadcasted in diverse and powerful ways. In this period many people could read before they could write: an inability to sign a name was not a sure guarantee of illiteracy.[6] Moreover, some texts such as ballads were dramatized by the ballad-seller or posted up on the walls in taverns and private houses.[7] Literacy levels were rising, however: in a sample of shopkeepers in London in the early seventeenth century, 76 per cent could sign their names, and women's literacy rose from 10 per cent in the middle of the century to 48 per cent at the end.[8] Indeed, it is even possible to suggest that some texts were aimed at specific sections of the population with a keen sense of their own cultural importance.

As far as women, women in service and apprentices were concerned, they may have had access to some popular literary forms. Women are in fact addressed as consumers in the 'controversy texts' – defences written by women in opposition to condemnations of their failings in contemporary pamphlets.[9] Among the servant classes, clear signs of literacy are difficult to trace, but in epistles and descriptions in a number of early seventeenth-century moral treatises and jest-books, waiting-women and kitchen-maids are identified as enjoying romances, often in their mistresses' company.[10] Apprentices, as members of the guild system, certainly constituted a discrete sub-culture, and were expected to be able to read and write to be admitted to a livery company: many writers directly appealed to apprentices in their dedications.[11] Similarly, it would be useful to remember recent research pointing to the numbers of women and apprentices attending the London theatres.[12]

Writing women

Perceptions of women in the popular writings of the English Renaissance were profoundly antithetical. Often different views were entertained simultaneously, and contrasting notions vied with each other without being resolved. Although this pattern might appear reductive, there are also ways in which representations were counter-productive, leaving open spaces for an interrogation of established attitudes and privileging varieties of defiance and contest.

At once it would seem that constructions in contemporary satires and moralistic collections were hostile – informed by anxieties about women's ability to upset patriarchal privileges. Views which seek to condemn women for their transgressions are rehearsed in several literary forms, many of which would have been recited or sung aloud in public. Accounts of shrews were common, usually being accompanied by complaints about their plaintive behaviour and uncompromising actions.[13] Even in compendiums of advice women are linked to a range of negative associations: Thomas Gainsford in 1616 held that 'woman is a stinking rose, a pleasing euill, the mous-trap of a mans soule, the thiefe of his life, a flattering wound, a delicate distraction, a sweete death'.[14] In this catalogue of violent opposites is a striking realization of the fear that congress with women entails injury and inevitable entrapment.

In addition to the apparently unmediated character of their ideological inflection, these representations are frustrating in that they are couched in generalities. They offer few specific details about class and place; instead, they tend to gather all women together under similar rhetorical headings. A number of tracts, however, concentrated on women as examples of piety, courage and self-sacrifice, and were precise in identifying matters relating to background and social connections. Taking a cue from classical and continental treatises, some English writers celebrated women's honour and nobility in historical accounts of their admirable cultivation of religion, fidelity and liberal conduct.[15] Condemnations of women and conventional accusations were also demonstrated in verses, apologies and legal publications.[16] Invariably in funeral sermons, furthermore, wives or widows were held up for praise, and their worthy domestic abilities were commemorated.[17] A 1594 rhyming elegy written to remember Lady Helen Branch, wife to Sir John Branch, who had been mayor of London, ran:

> The breathless body of a worthy Dame,
> The Lady Branch, a Nicholson by name,
> A godly, virtuous, and religious Matron:
> For maids, and wives, and widows all a pattern.[18]

Although the mood is laudatory, Lady Branch's virtues are dependent on her social position: her worthiness is predicated on her gentle descent. The eulogy is undercut by the class bias, and other women, it is suggested, can only hope to strive to imitate Lady Branch's memorable qualities.

Contemporary realizations of women's qualities, then, were uneven in the attitudes deployed. Criticisms were offset by pamphlets which defended women against detracting views, and efforts were made to revise entrenched convictions. But those attempts to rescue women from the slur of calumny were themselves informed by inflexibilities. Writings which stressed women's household roles consigned them to a narrow domestic sphere, and classical examples of self-sacrifice similarly discovered wives as essentially subservient to their husbands' interests. Even examples of bravery were bound by the convention that associated masculinity with martial prowess: it was only when women displayed a *'masculine spirit'*, to quote Thomas Heywood in 1640, that they were applauded.[19] Authors may have grappled with divergent arguments, but they chose to reserve praise for specific occasions: when women's behaviour ratified already established ideas about gender and highlighted the superior status of patriarchal standards.

Despite these limitations, I would also like to suggest that some representations discharged subversive functions and threw into confusion theories which equated morality with social stability. In the same way that manifestations of popular festivity granted licence to those not normally in power to question structures of authority, so literary materials could stress the ways in which women were able to undermine contemporary institutions and to use infidelity, clothes and language to articulate a desire for a greater independence. In a jocular rhyme of 1611 the speaker asks:

> Are women wise? Not wise but they be witty,
> Are women witty? Yea, the more the pitty:
> They are so witty, and in wit so wily,
> That be ye ne're so wise, they will beguile ye.[20]

Registered in the invective is the belief that women have the capacity to disempower their husbands: through intellectual and physical deceit they will displace male prerogatives. The theme is taken up in a satirical verse of 1638, in which a husband complains of his wife:

What euer I doe say,
  shee will haue her owne way,
Shee scorneth to obey;
  Shee'll take time while she may:
And if I beate her backe and side,
  In spight I shall be hornify'd.[21]

The lines might be said to represent an epistemological dilemma: conventional punishment has lost its efficacy, and language no longer has the capacity to maintain order or to reflect the husband's primacy in the domestic establishment.

If popular rhymes, the ostensible point of which was to outlaw forms of domestic rebellion, simultaneously devoted attention to the powers that women might assume for themselves, prose descriptions elaborated the suggestion that contemporary gender roles might be extended. In particular, clothes became registers of an unstable authority and an anticipated collapse of sexual discipline. Barnaby Rich berated citizens' wives in 1606:

> What newfangled attires for the heades, what flaring fashions in their garments, what alteration in their ruffes, what painting of shamelesse faces, what audacious boldnes in company, what impudencie, and what immodestie is vsed by them that will needes be reputed honest, when their open breasts, their naked stomackes, their frizled haire, their wanton eie, their shameles countenance, are all the vaunt errours of adulterie.
>
>   With these sleights and shews they haue made Emperours idle, as *Anthonie*, strong men feeble, as *Sampson*, valiant men effeminate, as *Hercules*, wise men dissolute, as *Solomon*, eloquent men lasciuious as *Aurelius*.[22]

What animates the passage is a terror inspired by the wives' attempt to develop their social responsibilities. Their grand fashions are metaphorically analogous to a will to increase the sphere of their influence: the clothes are indicative of a transgressive destabilization of lines of demarcation and gender boundaries. The action is equally the stimulus for a host of related anxieties, centring upon castration, homosexuality and the loss of language.

The concern with the upsetting linguistic capabilities of women is taken up again in accounts of shrewish tendencies. For a number of writers, the figure of the shrew posed the most serious threat to the mechanisms whereby authority was constituted: speaking uncontrollably permits women to carve out opportunities for the expression of criticism and protest. In a 1620 set of essays, Richard Brathwait described the shrew's principal characteristics:

> the volubilitie of an infatigable tongue; her father was a common Barretter, and . . . in her sleepe when shee is barr'd from scolding, shee falls to a terrible vaine of snoring . . . Shee goes weekly to a catterwauling, where shee spoiles their spice-cup'd gossiping with her tart-tongued calletting: shee is a Bee in a box, for she is euer buzzing . . . Silence shee hates as her sexes scandall . . . she . . . wounds with her tongue, terming it her sole defensiue instrument.[23]

In contrast to the ideal woman who is silent and obedient, the shrew is incontinently talkative and fractious, refusing to be tamed by patriarchal dictates: the animal imagery is suggestive. And the metaphor of the instrument is ironically appropriate: rather than the husband using his phallic instrument to exert control, the shrew employs words to usurp norms of female passivity, malleability and weakness.

Women and service

As one instance of popular culture in the English Renaissance, festivals placed boundaries under scrutiny and contributed to a potential rearrangement of hierarchical relations. Turning to popular literary materials, we find a comparable dislodgement of dominant orthodoxies and, in particular, the creation of opportunities for women to speak out against injustice. These representations were not marked by ideological uniformity, and were only intermittently critical, but had a subversive edge in that they contemplated localized kinds of resistance and the possibility of alternative formations. It now remains to discover if modes of empowerment were available to other social groupings usually accorded marginal positions and denied forceful voices.

As far as women in service – kitchen-maids, maidservants and chambermaids – were concerned, the overwhelming impression is that popular writers representing the type either endorsed forms of obedience or found in situations of domestic abuse a cause for entertainment. Ideally the woman as servant was imagined as a reflection of her mistress's chastity and of a smoothly working domestic system. The puritan author of an early seventeenth-century household guide set out the maidservant's duties in terms of a catechetical debate:

> *Quest.* And what properties must a maidservant haue?
> *Ans.* She must be, 1 Carefull. 2 Faithfull. 3 Patient. 4 Neate. 5 Chearefull. 6 Cleanly. 7 Quicke. 8 Honest. 9 Skilfull. And last of all Dumbe.[24]

Although the passage is ostensibly a celebration of virtue, it also harbours inconsistencies, and a shaping assumption is that, unless adequately instructed, the female servant will prove careless, disloyal, impatient, untidy, miserable, dirty, slow, dishonest, unskilful, proud and talkative, resembling her counterpart, the shrew, more powerfully than an idealized domestic.

The conviction that the woman as servant possesses moral shortcomings and is prone to a dereliction of her responsibilities recurs in a number of literary constructions. A repeated scenario situates the maidservant as the innocent but comic victim of sexual manipulations, as the mistreated object of a fellow-servant's intentions or of her master's inclinations.[25] In jest-books and popular satires the maidservant is viewed as insensible to the practice of abuse, the consequences of which are generally not accorded an extended treatment. A collection of jests of 1640 contains the following exchange:

> A Gentleman complained to one of his neighbors that his maid was begot with child by one of his serving-men; whereupon his neighbor asked him whether he himselfe was not a little guilty of it? who answered he did not know of it, but was asleep in his bed when it was done: the other reply'd, it seems you did wink at the fact, which was as bad as if you had done it your selfe.[26]

It might appear as if the master's ignorance is foregrounded rather than the gullibility of his female servant; however, the joke's refusal to answer the paternity question suggests that exploitation can take place without the necessity to dwell on its implications. The gentleman may be able to avoid his responsibilities, but it is clear that the maidservant enjoys no such privilege.

Cumulatively these ideas mark the maidservant as an erring type, as a passive dependant who chooses not to question subordination with counter-argument. In another sense, the maidservant's status allows her a degree of mobility and an opportunity to throw into confusion social distinctions and contemporary norms of rank and degree. For several writers, it is precisely the servant's 'inferior' qualities that become part of her ability to unhinge existing authority structures. An epigrammatic rhyme probably composed in the 1590s proceeds:

> No sooner *Cynus* wife was dead and buried,
> But that with mourning much and sorrows wearied,
> A Maid, a seruant of his wiues he wedded,
> And after he had boorded her, and bedded,
>> And in her Mistris roome had fully plast her,
>> His wiues old seruant waxed his new master.[27]

This verse also turns on the idea of traditional roles and concepts of place, only to invert the anticipated outcome: the elevation of the maidservant brings out a rebellious aptitude, and the attempt to contain her has unexpected results. Paradoxically, therefore, service can be read as an institution that fosters an awareness of inequities and aggravates differences rather than affirming domestic subjects in their assigned locations, a point underscored by Richard Brathwait in *The English gentlewoman* (1631); he notes that 'some of our Chambermaids take vpon them such an vnbeseeming state, when they came to visit their poore friends in the Countrey, as they punctually retain'd both gate and garb of their mincing Mistresses in the City'.[28] Encapsulated in Brathwait's brief statement is the suggestion that the chambermaid's presence endangers conventional separation procedures: city and country merge, maidservant and mistress do not heed the regulations that would keep their social roles intact.

Indeed, representations of the relationship shared by the maidservant and her mistress would seem to introduce the most taxing questions. Mainly in the drama the maidservant appears as outspoken and resilient, advising on suitors and anticipating promotion at her mistress's marriage. While the maidservant herself may agitate for a husband in these scenes, she does not plan to be placed in a subservient position and sees marriage as an opportunity to declare a will to dominance.[29] Even some more exclusive theatrical productions (such as Thomas Randolph's *The Jealous Lovers*, which was staged before the court at Trinity College, Cambridge, in 1632) adapted the idea of the assertive maidservant who flouts proprieties and institutions.

Phronesium, a merry chambermaid, dresses as a knight to fight in the lists and later confronts Simo, an old and doting gentleman whom she agrees to marry, but not until she has set her own conditions:

> Phron.   I will feed high, go rich, have my six horses
>   And my embroider'd coach; ride where I list,
>   Have all the gallants in the town to visit me,
>   Maintain a pair of little legs to go
>   On idle messages to all the madams.
>   You shall deny no gentleman entertainment.
>   And when we kiss and toy, be it your cue
>   To nod and fall asleep.
> Sim.   With all my heart.[30]

Phronesium's speech constitutes a challenge at a range of levels. The catalogue of demands inverts gerontological principles, makes a mockery of theories of service and obedience, and points to a radical revision of ascribed roles within the framework of marriage. Most destabilizing about the play is an interrogation of social taxonomies that places in a critical light perceived ideals of age, gender and class.

Turning back to John Storey's theoretical model of incorporation and resistance, it becomes obvious that anxieties about women in a variety of dependent roles cut across several generic classifications. There are areas of corresponding interest between popular forms and the drama of the private theatres, reminding us that the undermining of dominant meanings was not restricted to unofficial printed materials and languages. In verse satires and prose descriptions, however, could be found more contestatory messages and an emphatic realization of the dangerous powers which women in service might wield. Contemporary literary productions justified a maidservant's appropriation of authority, recalling related popular texts in which women's voices are also granted importance. The maidservant's ambitions are usually confined to marriage, but this does not erase the anxieties – about women's mobility and uncontrollability – which representations of her conduct reflect.

Apprenticeship and revolt

Writers' constructions of apprentices perhaps offer the most powerful points of comparison between literary materials and popular festive traditions. Apprentices were a recognizable political force in the

English Renaissance, rioting on Shrove Tuesday, joining to protest against foreign workers in London, causing disturbances during the economic crisis of the 1590s and banding with parliamentarian groups on the eve of the Civil War. General and specific concerns of relevance to apprentices were examined in prose accounts, ballads and plays, and the messages conveyed were far from consistent – at one and the same time apprentices were urged to cultivate obedience and join in public demonstrations, to remain meek and respectful and to take up arms against foreign insurgences.

Many writers, rather than describing the ideal, concentrated on apprentices as anti-types, as unruly youths who were easily swayed from the path of virtue and quickly corrupted. Foul-mouthed apprentices make regular appearances in moral treatises, while the lack of respect shown by apprentices to their superiors is a favourite area of complaint.[31] Apprentices are encouraged to 'abandon filthy whores, / And dissolute assemblies', to cite from an early seventeenth-century pamphlet, and the effects of such lewd practices are intimately elaborated: the suicidal apprentice is a familiar guest in contemporary religious tracts.[32] Equally popular were ballads in which apprentices lamented the errors of their ways and sued for forgiveness. Of course, such ballads only ventriloquized the apprentice's voice, but the issues they broached carried with them subversive implications. In 'George Barnwell' of 1605, the titular apprentice regrets the way in which he has been entrapped by a prostitute and warns: 'Take heed of harlots then, / And their enticing trains; / For by that means I have been brought / To hang alive in chains'.[33] The problem, however, is that the account fails to contain the criminal tendencies which are its subject; the spectacle of the apprentice's punishment, designed to draw attention to Barnwell's exemplary repentance, is animated by the moral lapses which the ballad as a whole theoretically condemns. From a similar mould is a 1632 ballad in which an apprentice, George Stephens, facing execution for his treasonable offences, urges: 'Children and prentices, [and] old and young, / Serve God in heart, and governe wel your tongue!'[34] But the ballad form allows the speaker access to an impressive eloquence, which would seem to militate against its pleas for a circumspect silence. Although indiscreet speech is arraigned in the ballad, Stephens is permitted to talk at length and to excel in demonstrating the fatal power which words command.

Texts devoted to apprentices worked in opposite directions in the same moment, sustaining criticisms of aberrant behaviour and the formulation of particular needs and frustrations. The unsettling idea behind such representations, therefore, was that structures of authority were at fault and might even be resisted. Certainly this is a reading which could be brought to bear on materials which describe the master's responsibilities. More than one writer sought to explain apprentice infractions in terms of the master's neglect of his primary duties, arguably an interpretive procedure which could license further acts of disobedience. A 1609 collection of prayers contains a set of reflections in which an apprentice asks, 'Take away from him (that is, my master) all thoughts of crueltie', while Thomas Adams in a later seventeenth-century sermon observed: 'There is a difference betwixt apprentices and slaues: they are yours to teach a trade, to direct in the wayes of godlinesse and ciuilitie; not to abuse with ouer-burdenous labours, and inhumane blowes'.[35] As literate adolescents, apprentices consumed such materials as moral pamphlets and were, in addition, regularly enjoined to attend divine service. It is within such a context that we can begin to understand the ambivalent discourses that apprentices experienced: on the one hand, they were instructed to heed their masters' recommendations; on the other, they were made aware of the potential for abuse – sensitized to the dangers accompanying their place and to the system's inevitable imbalances.

The difficulties precipitated by neglectful masters were rehearsed in contemporary apprentice texts; so were the onerous demands of the institution of apprenticeship itself. In airing these preoccupations, writers again reinforced the common interests shared by the fraternity of apprentices and registered feelings of dissatisfaction which may well have been familiar to members of an apprentice audience. Popular dramas are rife with apprentice types who inveigh against the repressive mechanisms which enforce their subjection, and who object to the institutionalized measures that prevent the enjoyment of leisure activities.[36] In a 1642 play, Whatlacke, a citizen's apprentice, complains: 'O that I were but out of my time once! while I am a Prentice I am like seven yeares drunkard, for seven yeares none of mine owne man, but my Masters . . . I must scrape trenchers, make cleane shooes, or scoure the kitchin; and must not pepe forth unlesse of errands'.[37] Whatlacke's protest communicates a sharply experienced sense of humiliation and denial, and the ostracization that his profession necessitates fuels worrying antagonisms: his outburst stands in dangerous opposition to the virtues of honest contentment which the guilds promoted.

A survey of these representations leads to the conclusion that apprenticeship is perceived as an inhibiting structure, one which outlaws youthful impulses and constrains social aspirations. These considerations are voiced in official publications and in materials directed to apprentice readers or spectators, a pertinent illustration of the ways in which meanings are negotiated among dominant and subordinate social groupings. Chiefly for those apprentices from gentle families, the institution was thought to have a demeaning effect, and, responding to this anxiety, writers were quick to point out that entering trade was not reductive or dishonourable.[38] But the perception that apprenticeship was incompatible with noble pretensions continued to circulate, providing further ammunition for those apprentices who thought themselves above the drudgery of their professions. Heywood's *The Fair Maid of the West, Part II* (c. 1630) features Clem, a drawer's apprentice, who, given gold by his newly elevated mistress, exclaims:

> I have gold and
> anon will be as gallant as the proudest of them. Shall I stand
> at the bar to bar any man's casting that drinks hard? No,
> I'll send these pots home by some porter or other, put myself
> into a better habit, and say the case is alter'd. Then will I go
> home to the Bush, where I drew wine, and buy out my time,
> and take up my chamber, be served in pomp by my fellow prentices.[39]

The miraculous ascent to the status of a gallant stages transgressive possibilities. It immediately places in doubt the idealization of hard work as an avenue to material success, but it also refracts escapist fantasies; Clem will now dictate to others rather than himself receiving orders, a situation which must have appealed to those apprentices anxious about the relationship between their gentle qualifications and the stigma of trade.

I have suggested that specific apprentice concerns, which involved questions about moral behaviour, class, identity and individual autonomy, were investigated in contemporary popular literature, and that the arguments forwarded both supported traditional concepts of order and authority and allowed the expression of fears and grievances. In warnings addressed to apprentices and instructions aimed at masters, parallel considerations were aired, which entailed reflections on varieties of oppression and exclusion, and speculation about the extent of the servant's social responsibilities. Protests in literary materials, however, recall associated forms of popular protest, such as the actions of the London crowd and the key role played by apprentices in attacks against alien immigrants, foreign ambassadors and prelates. Apprentices possessed a keen sense of their corporate importance, which was encouraged by the lenient attitude taken up by the city authorities towards their holiday outrages, and it might not be coincidental that many literary texts focused on the apprentice as an avenging soldier, often in ways which were politically resonant. Vagabond pamphlets show apprentices gathering to oust deceiving cony-catchers, while ballads describe knightly apprentices who defeat Turkish foes and perform heroic deeds.[40] An informed assessment of such texts would recognize that they offer a powerful realization of an apprentice solidarity and one manifestation of cultural practices which were part of a continuing political project.

Conclusions

This essay has attempted to extend traditional definitions of popular culture and to broaden its meanings and applications. I have suggested that the experience of popular culture was not always confined to particular sections of society, but that marginalized and privileged groups gained access to a range of written materials in contrasting and indirect ways. Obviously these representations were not univocal in the ideas they addressed; however, they have in common an interrogative attitude towards authority, bringing to mind the role played by popular festivities and the social and political arrangements which they both questioned and supported. The effects of institutionalized rituals were not too far removed from the ambivalent messages which a literary text transmitted.

Inconsistencies in verses, pamphlets and moral tracts were symptomatic of larger cultural changes and developments. Censorship obliged writers to exercise ideological care, although they also ensured that particular concerns, which would have stimulated the interest of some women and servants, were conspicuously visible. Essentially, however, printed productions engaged with social pressures at deeper levels, responding to the ambiguous, shifting status of the subordinate classes. Urban women were taking an increasingly dominant part in the management of the household and beginning to become politically active, notably in sectarian movements; maidservants occupied key positions in the organic culture of the period; and apprentices, many of whom were young adults, were expected to heed regulations designed for children and to bow to the government of a substitute paterfamilias. To account for the discrepancies which a text entertains, we need to attend to the conflicting forces which shape the writer's wider environment.

Other essays in this volume illuminate the political aspects of writing in the English Renaissance, anxieties about sexualities and modes of resistance. They also map the efforts of marginal groups to speak in their own voices, either through the courts or through the practice of radical prophesying. While the important implications of these activities should be heeded, it is also salutary to remember that even official constructions of oppositional gestures are a point of intervention in related debates and arguments. Absences, fissures and contradictions in popular written forms allow us to acknowledge competitions for authority and control, and to appreciate some of the means whereby political subjects could achieve empowerment and advancement.

Notes

1. N. Heard, *Tudor Economy and Society* (London, 1992), p. 124.
2. P. Burke, *Popular Culture in Early Modern Europe* (London, 1978), pp. xi, 24.
3. B. Reay, 'Introduction: Popular culture in early modern england', in B. Reay, ed., *Popular Culture in Seventeenth-Century England* (London, 1988), pp. 8, 21.
4. F. Laroque, *Shakespeare's Festive World: Elizabethan Seasonal Entertainment and the Professional Stage*, tr. Janet Lloyd (Cambridge, 1991), p. 13.
5. J. Storey, *An Introductory Guide to Cultural Theory and Popular Culture* (Hemel Hempstead, 1993), p. 13.
6. J. Barry, 'Popular culture in seventeenth-century Bristol', in Reay, ed., *Popular Culture*, p. 63.
7. T. Watt, *Cheap Print and Popular Piety 1550–1640* (Cambridge, 1991), pp. 12, 14.
8. P. Burke, 'Popular culture in seventeenth-century London', in Reay, ed., *Popular Culture*, p. 49.
9. See K. U. Henderson and B. F. McManus, eds, *Half Humankind: Contexts and Texts of the Controversy about Women in England, 1540–1640* (Urbana and Chicago, 1985).
10. Sir T. Overbury, *The Overburian Characters*, ed. W. J. Paylor (Oxford,

1936), p. 43; H. Peacham, *Thalias banquet* (London, 1620), sigs A3^v–A4^r; A. Stafford, *The guide of honour* (London, 1634), epistle.

11. Burke, 'Popular culture', in Reay, ed., *Popular Culture*, p. 34; Steve Rappaport, *Worlds Within Worlds: Structures of Life in Sixteenth-Century London* (Cambridge, 1989), p. 298.

12. A. Gurr, *Playgoing in Shakespeare's London* (Cambridge, 1987), passim.

13. W. Gamage, *Linsi-woolsie* (London, 1613), sig E3^r; J. Taylor, *Divers crabtree lectures* (London, 1639), pp. 132–49.

14. T. Gainsford, *The rich cabinet furnished with a varietie of excellent discriptions* (London, 1616), fo. 162^v.

15. W. Bercher, *The Nobility of Women* (1559), ed. R.W. Bond (London, 1904), passim; R. Vaughan, *A dyalogue defensyue for women* (London, 1542), passim.

16. N. Breton, *The Wil of Wit* (1599), in *The Works*, ed. A. B. Grosart, 2 vols (London, 1879), II, pp. 57–9; I. G., *An apologie for women-kinde* (London, 1605), sigs B4^v, C1^v; W. Heale, *An apologie for women* (London, 1609), pp. 2, 39, 65.

17. S. Geree, *The ornament of women* (London, 1639), pp. 68–82; J. Ley, *A patterne of pietie* (London, 1640), passim.

18. J. Sylvester, *Monodia* (1594), in Henderson and McManus, eds, *Half Humankind*, p. 330.

19. T. Heywood, *The exemplary lives and memorable acts of nine of the most worthy women of the world* (London, 1640), p. 68. See also Sir T. Elyot, *The Defence of Good Women* (1540), ed. E. J. Howard (Oxford, Ohio, 1940), p. 24; A. Gibson, *A womans woorth* (London, 1599), fos. 5^v, 13^v.

20. F. Davison, *A poetical rapsody* (London, 1611), p. 194.

21. *Cuckolds haven: or the marry'd mans miserie* (London, 1638), unfoliated.

22. B. Rich, *Faultes faults, and nothing else but faultes* (London, 1606), fo. 23^{r-v}. For an extended extract see the *Documents* section below, pp. 000–000.

23. R. Brathwait, *Essaies upon the five senses* (London, 1620), pp. 134–7.

24. R. Hill, *Christs prayer expounded, a christian directed, and a communicant prepared* (London, 1610), p. 181.

25. J. Davies, *Wits Bedlam* (London, 1617), sigs B1^v, F1^r; S. Rowlands, *Good newes and bad newes* (London, 1622), sigs C3^v–C4^v.

26. R. Chamberlain, *Jocabella, or a cabinet of conceits* (London, 1640), no. 141.

27. Sir J. Harington, *The Letters and Epigrams*, ed. N. E. McClure (Philadelphia, 1930), p. 249.

28. R. Brathwait, *The English gentlewoman* (London, 1631), p. 56.

29. See Adriana in L. Barry, *Ram Alley* (1610), ed. P. Corbin and D. Sedge (Nottingham, 1981), II. iii. 728–9, 806–8, IV. i. 1501–2.

30. T. Randolph, *The Jealous Lovers*, in *The Poetical and Dramatic Works*, ed. W. C. Hazlitt, 2 vols (London, 1875), I, V. viii. p. 169.

31. J. Downame, *Foure treatises, tending to disswade all christians from swearing, drunkennesse, whoredome, and briberie* (London, 1609), p. 22; J. White, *The workes* (London, 1624), p. 24.

32. A. Nixon, *A straunge foot-post, with a packet full of strange petitions* (London, 1613), sig. G4^v; Sir W. Denny, *Pelicanicidium: or, the Christian adviser against self-murder* (London, 1653), pp. 4–5.

33. C. Mackay, ed., *A Collection of Songs and Ballads Relative to the London Prentices and Trades*, Percy Society (1841), p. 36.

34. W. Chappell and J. W. Ebsworth, eds, *The Roxburghe Ballads*, 9 vols (London, 1871–97), III, p. 156.

35. T. Dekker, *Foure Birds of Noahs Arke* (1609), ed. F. P. Wilson (Oxford, 1924), p. 9; T. Adams, *The workes* (London, 1629(30)), p. 1111.

36. See T. Heywood, *The Four Prentices of London* (1592), ed. Mary Ann Weber Gasior (New York and London, 1980), lines 113–28.

37. J. L. Murphy, ed., 'A seventeenth-century play from the Essex Record Office', *Collections*, Malone Society 9 (1977), pp. 38–9.

38. T. Nash, *Quaternio or a fourefold way to a happie life* (London, 1633), pp. 57–8.

39. T. Heywood, *The Fair Maid of the West, Part II*, ed. R. K. Turner (London, 1968), V. iii. 16–23.

40. R. Greene, *A Notable Discovery of Cozenage* (1591), in A. F. Kinney, ed., *Rogues, Vagabonds and Sturdy Beggars* (Massachusetts, 1990), p. 175; Mackay, ed., *A Collection*, p. 24.

7 'Demons in female form': representations of women and gender in murder pamphlets of the late sixteenth and early seventeenth centuries

Garthine Walker

Elizabethan and early Stuart pamphlet accounts of criminal trials contain a wealth of material concerning the monstrous deeds of individuals. Yet with the exception of accounts of witchcraft trials, trial pamphlets with female protagonists have only recently come to be subjected to scrutiny as a literary and historical source.[1] In this essay, I shall first examine the ways in which women are portrayed within the conventions of the genre of the murder pamphlet, and question the extent to which women who engaged in activity of this kind are represented differently from their male counterparts. Then, I shall consider the ways in which recent critics have characterized the representation of both female criminality and the nature of patriarchal relations within these texts. By interpreting the murder pamphlets in their historical context, the assumptions which have underlined such characterizations may be questioned. It will be argued here that the primacy often attributed to gender is itself sometimes misplaced; that the ways in which images of women and gender were received by an early modern female readership cannot be understood simply within an essentialist framework in which gender is the sole point of identification; and that the relationship between specific texts and historical actuality is far more complex than is often allowed.

The pamphlet accounts of crime and criminal trials in the Elizabethan and early Stuart periods were written for a popular audience. Sold for a penny or twopence, they contain brief and colourful tales of heinous crimes, by far the most common of which being murder of exceptionally brutal or treacherous form. Many of the accounts were written by clergymen such as the prolific Henry Goodcole, but others were published by literary figures, Thomas Kyd, Anthony Munday and John Taylor being but three. The pamphlets usually begin and end with moral and religious admonitions or polemics. Within this godly framework, the story of the crime and its discovery unfolds, usually along with an account of the state of mind of the criminal both before and after their apprehension and trial, and their confession and/or scaffold speech. Yet the pamphlets are perhaps better described as fictional rather than journalistic texts. The bizarre and gruesome tales were hardly typical of early modern murders. Indeed, whilst the accounts purport to be based upon actual trials, it seems that much of the gruesome detail of the tales was pure fabrication. Although the confession or 'last-dying speech' of the criminal was often presented in the first person, there is little evidence to suggest that the convicted felon had a hand in the composition of either. And, whatever the sensationalist intent and appeal of rehearsing shocking doings, the central organizing theme of the genre was not disquieting titillation or violence, but the restorative and comforting trilogy of sin, divine providence and redemption.[2]

The treatment of women and gender within these pamphlets is representative of the conventions and concerns of the genre, but is not manifestly informative about societal attitudes to criminal women. These representations hinge upon a particular set of notions about order. Gender was, of course, a crucial component of that order and its conceptualization; women were an obvious symbol for both the definition of and the transgression of social, political and religious boundaries.[3] Thus we find godly, virtuous women exemplifying good order, and evil temptresses and murderous women representing the disorderly world of vice in which Satan attempts to rule. Women who kill are often demonized accordingly.

For example, we are told that Mistress Beast, whose servant murdered her husband at her behest, was a 'filthie desirous Woman', a 'harlot', a 'graceless strumpet', a 'most horrible and wicked Womon, a woman, nay a devill', set upon a 'devillish desire'. In contrast, Christopher Tomson, who actually did the dirty deed, had attempted to dissuade his mistress but was unable to deny her for 'she conjured him'. He therefore was not her fellow demon, but her 'sweet dallying friend', 'besotted in his naughtie affection', and 'possessed' by 'the tyranny of love'.[4] It is clear who is held to be the more responsible and culpable. However, such representations do not imply that homicidal women were taken to be more sinful, treacherous and deadly than men. There is, in fact, little difference in the descriptions of male and female criminals. In another pamphlet, Thomas Smith is described in similarly damning terms when he envies and consequently murders his friend: 'the repining at our neighbors prosperity, is not onely monstrous, but a devilish natures. So had this man compassed a monstraous and moste devilish devise . . .'. We are told of Smith's 'unnaturall will' and his 'cruell and monstrous harde heart . . . that could endure this rufull Stratageme', and carry out 'this most bloody and monstrous act'.[5]

Although pamphlet representations of female culprits do indeed depend upon misogynistic stereotypes of feminine vice, the reader is not specifically invited to ponder upon the ill nature of woman. Rather, murderous women and their deeds symbolize the inevitable consequences of the subversion of patriarchal and familial authority – an authority upon which social order itself was seen to rest. What these pamphlets tell us is less about relative societal attitudes toward men and women, and more about the conceptualizations of assaults upon the model of social order which underpinned religious and political hierarchy and control. When a female murderer is the central character in a story, it is her place as a woman *within this schema* which is the axial point, rather than her feminine identity. It is important that we remember that female characters are not the sole bearers of such a message. As Peter Lake has said,

> [T]he message of the pamphlets was that any breakdown of control, any abuse of authority by those on top or dereliction of duty by those underneath threatened to loose the peccant tendencies of fallen human nature with disastrous results.[6]

Positive and negative images of household and familial relations are central to the conceptual and narrative framework of the pamphlets. In *The Most Cruell and Bloody Murther*, the mortally wounded Anthony James begs his male burglar assailants to take pity on his pregnant wife and be merciful to his two children. Whilst this engenders some remorse in the men, the burglars' female accomplice taunts him before killing his wife before his eyes:

> Talkest thou of pittie quoth she, if thy eyes have yet so much sight to be witnes how Ile be pittifull? behould how Ile performe thy peticion. So

drawing out her knife (A act too terrible to report, but the most damnablest that ever was heard of, executed by a woman) she ript her up the belly, making herself a tragicall midwife, or truly a murtheresse, that brought an abortive babe to the world, and murthered the mother.[7]

The particular horror of this passage depends upon the juxtaposition of two alternative stereotypes of woman, describing as it does a deed which would be terrible enough no matter who the perpetrator was, but which seems particularly awful when done at the hands of a woman. The dark image of the 'tragicall midwife' might well be a manipulation of certain popular tensions surrounding the office of midwife; the knowledge and experience associated with childbirth provided a symbol of female power at the point at which that power was most fragile. The unnaturalness of the deed is stressed by the role of woman as midwife causing death rather than facilitating life, as well as by the general image of a pitiless woman. Yet her victim is more than an abstract representation of the good mother. The figure of Elizabeth James is contextualized, located firmly within the structure of the godly household. She and her husband are likened to Abraham and Sarah, 'he loving to her, she obedient to him', and as with that biblical couple, 'it pleased God to enrich them with two children . . . and both contented in so comfortable a blessing'.[8] It is this which the murderous woman destroys. The message is that sin defiles and destroys the unity of the household.

It may appear typical that a woman is held most responsible for this destruction. But if this female murderer is 'more than monstrous', devoid of pity, and presented as more evil and less subject to human responses than her male associates, it must be interpreted in terms of narrative effect rather than merely as yet another misogynist attack on womankind. The misogyny inherent in negative female stereotypes allows the narrative to work, offering a particularly potent set of images and rhetoric with which to titillate and disgust readers. But the male villains here are held equally culpable for both the murders: they too are 'wretches', 'Monsters', and 'devillish'. Whilst the female murderer is described as 'not a woman, but a beast to make a prey' of her 'harmelesse' victim, her male accomplices are 'Nine, I cannot call them men, but villaines'. It was the entire 'hellish Jury' – men and women – who returned the 'damnable . . . verdict' to 'slaughter' Anthony and Elizabeth James, for which they all 'worthily deserved . . . shamefull death'. And two of these men committed the 'most cruell and bloody murther' of the title, an 'inhumane murther', 'on the bodie of a Childe', Anthony James, junior.[9]

Nevertheless, it is significant that the woman is described as 'the most devillish of all' at the point at which the tale turns to the chilling detail of her cruelty to a child. Assaults upon children by women are, along with witchcraft, far more likely than other crimes to be associated with women's propensity to evil and malice in pamphlet literature.[10] The inverse of the romanticization and idealization of the good mother serves as a compelling dramatization of sheer, uncompromising evil, and this pamphlet account maximizes the image by starkly contrasting the purity and innocence of the girl with the 'unnaturalness' of the woman. Whilst the relationship between the boy and his murderers is subject to little discussion, what passes between young Elizabeth and her assailant is detailed. As they walked together, the woman beguiled the child by asking her

> what she walkt upon, what she saw withall, and what she spake withall
> . . . the innocent Child . . . pointing to her foot, her eye, and to her
> tongue, that with those, and by the helpe of those she saw, went and
> spake.

We are told that the girl answered the questions 'so pretyly, that if her leader had left in her any sparke of Womanhood, who by nature are kinder, flexible and remorseable, and not been made up for one to be damned, she would have pitied her'. Yet,

> this bloody Tygris to make her selfe more monstrous, had her put out
> her tongue that she might feele it . . . [and] presently caught it by the
> end, and with her thumbe wresting open the childs jaws to the widest
> she could stretch them, she cut it out even by the root.

This emotive and horrifying picture of female depravity is a particularly potent means of imparting the message that the sinner is utterly corrupted and depraved by his or her sin.[11]

When men are reported to have murdered their own children, they too are described as 'unnatural' and 'monstrous'. Master Caverley, for instance, forgot 'all naturall love'; 'the monstrousnes of the fact' caused his menservants to lament 'a father should be so unnaturall'; and the narrator informs us that Caverley was so devoid of pity that he continued to stab his four-year-old son with his dagger, even though the child gave him 'such a looke, [that] would have driven a hand seaven yeeres prentice unto murther to an ague'. We are told that Caverley committed 'a murder so detestable, that were it not desires record for example sake, Humanitie could with it rather utterly forgot, than any Christian heart shuld trembld with the remembrance of it'.[12]

Nevertheless, the negative exhortations against women in these pamphlets have been interpreted in terms of generalized comments on womankind, which implicitly or explicitly support misogynist attitudes towards women in general.[13] Katherine Henderson and Barbara McManus claim that whilst Margaret Vincent, the 'pitiless mother' of the pamphlet of that name, might have killed her children from religious fanaticism, 'the struggle for supremacy in her marriage was clearly an important underlying motive'.[14] This, I think, is to overstate the case. Margaret Vincent was not simply the mirror image of a positive stereotype of 'good' mother and wife; the strength of the anti-papist argument put forward in the pamphlet depends upon her belief that she *was* behaving as a good mother. Her desire to save her children, however misguided, is presented as the crucial factor for her. The alleged 'struggle for supremacy' is all the more potent because it is in fact a struggle for one religion over another. It is on this level that Vincent's unruliness should be interpreted: the problem was not that she sought to dominate her husband, but that in her heresy she had rejected the protestant God.

The disorder inherent in ungodliness and heresy was analogous with the disorder of the household. Each could be the cause of the other. The circular nature of the rhetoric of this ideology means that we cannot identify the main concern of the author as woman's assertiveness. What we can identify, however, is the centrality of gender in the construction of that ideology. Even when the murderer is male, the interrelation of gender and order retains its rhetorical force in the pamphlets. After he had slaughtered his children, Master Caverley was asked 'the cause that hadde made him so monstrous: He being like a Strumpet, made impudent by her continuance in sinne' did not repent. This negative feminization of Caverley serves to bring our attention back to the cause of the bloodbath: his sin, which emerges through the narrative as the categorical destruction of the godly household. The reference to Caverley as a 'strumpet' forces us to recall the virtuousness of both women with whom he contracted to marry; it specifically contrasts the blamelessness of Caverley's wife, to whom he consistently and unjustly refers as 'strumpet', with the utter culpability of Caverley himself. And, just as with the female robber of

The Most Cruell and Bloody Murther, or Mistress Beast, the whore or strumpet acts as a powerful signifier of the assault upon and defilement of marriage and family values with or without reference to female sexual behaviour.15

The story of Caverley's murderous path begins with his entering a contract to marry the daughter of a Yorkshire gentleman, who 'was by private assurance made Maister Caverleys best beloved wife'; who was 'Maister Caverleys wife, (if vowes may make a wife)', despite the solemnization of the marraige being delayed until Caverley had come into his inheritance. Yet Caverley, 'whether concealing his late contract . . . or forgetting his private and public vowes, or both', went to London and 'made a new bargaine, knit a new marriage knot' before he had untied the old; thus he 'was husband by all matrimoniall rites, to [another] curteous Gentlewoman'. As is characteristic of the murder pamphlets, we are left in no doubt as to the sinful nature and conduct of the murderer. Although Caverley was not technically a bigamist, the language with which his conduct is described implies that he was guilty of spiritual bigamy. And, whilst both women remained virtuous and gentle, forgiving him his faults, and being in word and deed as impeccable as Patient Griselda, Caverley paid dearly for his conduct: 'revenge being alwaies in Gods hand'. Thus it was that preferring vice to virtue, and through 'excesse rioting, as dicing, drinking', Caverley lost his good name and his fortune. Having 'fed one evil with another, and in such continuall use, that his body was not in temper without the exercise of sinne', his remorse for having ruined his family leads only to further evil: he becomes 'overwhelmed by the violence of his passion' and set on murdering his wife and children to save them from the bitterness of dishonour and poverty.[16]
The central importance of the sanctity of marriage is clear throughout. Just as in *A Most Cruell and Bloodie Murther,* the partnership which is ruined by the murderer is described as being like that of the biblical Abraham and Sarah. In the Caverley tale, however, the analogy is made by Caverley's wife in order to defend her husband's name. While she remains true to the comparison with the obedient Sarah, Caverley does not resemble Abraham. Far from being loving towards her, he abuses his wife physically and emotionally. Moreover, at the very time that she is defending his name and honour, he is fighting a duel in which his opponent is defending hers. In this pamphlet we see the consequences of the spiritual, material and physical destruction of marriage, all at Caverley's hands.

In the murder pamphlets, gender usually holds a central place in the construction of the subversion and inversion of good order. In the rare instance of gender being delegated a minor rhetorical role, other forms of household order are subverted instead; gender thus remains a crucial if subtle concomitant of order and disorder in the pamphlet world. In *The cruell murther of Maister Browne*, for example, the victim's wife hovers on the periphery of the unfolding story although she is burnt at the stake for her part in his death. The narrative force of this tale rests with the treachery of the Brownes' servant Peter: a betrayal motivated by covetousness, greed, love and revenge. Thus the 'monstrous fact' is all his. The prerequisite conditions, however, are not restricted to Peter's weaknesses, but exist within the instability and disharmony of the entire household. The significance of Mistress Browne's role is found in the context of her husband's misjudgement and mismanagement of domestic affairs. Mistress Browne shares few characteristics with either Elizabeth Caldwell or Mistress Beast; she is neither virtuous gentlewoman-gone-awry nor lewd harlot, but 'a rich widdow' who appears to be motivated by the love or lust for money. Browne himself is not a wronged godly gentleman comparable to Master Beast, but a man who lives with his wife 'in great unquietnesse togither, for two testie olde folkes have as little agreements when they meete, as two windes'; in fact, 'they lived togither like divided householdes'.[17] Browne's daughter, whom he promised in marriage to the servant Peter, was patently not the 'dutiful and vertuous . . . young Gentlewoman' that she appeared to be: she was illegitimate and disobedient. Browne 'could commaunde her tongue, [but] not . . . her heart', and she 'married her selfe' to a wealthy gentleman instead. Nor was Peter the loyal, trusty, and loving servant he pretended to be; he schemed to gain his master's lands, and when he lost them along with his expected wife, his unrequited love for the girl turned to a desire for revenge against her father. Browne, for his part, did not behave honourably towards Peter either. Having misguidedly raised Peter's expectations from that of servant to son, he betrayed Peter by giving the lands he had formerly promised him to his daughter's new husband. The motif running through this tale is the instability borne of misplaced accountability and obligation; a tale of a world not so much turned upside down as all shook up.[18]

It follows that in this unstable environment, Browne himself is partly responsible for kindling the flames of domestic treachery. This is the most compelling reason for Mistress Browne's role being played down. Gender roles are discordant rather than inverted. Such was the rhetorical force of petty treason committed by a woman, that an emphasis upon Browne's responsibility for his wife's murderous deeds would have undermined rather than reinforced notions of good order. Conversely, in tales where the wife is given a greater responsibility for her husband's death, such as that of Mistress Beast, the husband is introduced as being beyond culpability, directly or indirectly. Beast was 'an honest Husband-man . . . very well reputed among his Neighbours, aswell for his house-keeping, as also for his Godly and honest behaviour'.[19] Whereas Beast is godly, his wife, in stark contrast, is devilish; he honest, she dishonest; and so on. The crucial determinant here is the binary opposition of good and evil. The location of gender on the axis adds rhetorical weight, but when the genders are reversed, the message remains the same. As we have seen, the godliness of the women to whom Master Caverley contracted himself acts as a similar foil to his sinful behaviour as does that of Master Beast to the dreadful conduct of his wife. Given that the language of righteous violence was masculine, along with the ubiquity of dualisms within early modern culture, the ascription of femininity to wrongful violence was not problematic as long as oppositional paradigms were not disrupted.

The majority of pamphlets dealing with spousal murder (and therefore with domestic treachery) focused upon that of husbands by wives. Between 1590 and 1630, two or three such pamphlets were published each decade, whereas the murder of wives featured far more rarely. It has been suggested that murderous husbands appear so rarely in popular representations because wife murder did not seem heinous enough.[20] However, the preoccupation with husband murder was no simple reflection of the double standard, but a reflection of legal and cultural understandings about the nature of violence and order. Spousal murder by wives was characteristic of almost all the conceptual requirements of wrongful violence. In the act of killing one's husband, the product and concomitant of disorder and disobedience were clearly seen; the principles of hierarchial authority were defied; moral law and the King's peace were utterly broken; motive and intent did not easily fit into any category of excusable or justifiable violence; the nature of the act was, by definition, treacherous; and, if it had been planned, it was also aided by deceit, trickery and stealth. In categorizing husband murder as petty treason, the law enshrined the hierarchical context of violence. Whilst the man who murdered his wife was culpable, the degree to which he had offended against the principles listed here was mitigated by his theoretical place within his household. Men who went too far in 'correcting' their wives were neither encouraged nor condoned, but their actions carried a very different implication to those of their female counterparts. The reason why husband murder epitomized 'that radical disobedience to social order which spawned almost all illicit violence', and wife murder did not, is clear. Male violence was sanctioned to uphold social order within the household; female violence within the household was contrarily a subversion of that order.[21]

At its most fundamental, this principle was personified in the murder pamphlets by the likes of Mistress Beast, for whom we are encouraged to feel nothing less than contempt and loathing. More complex, however, are those tales which seek to evoke compassion and pity for the murderous wife. Critics have assumed that the telling of such tales created difficulties for their authors. Frances Dolan argues that 'Once the writers begin to explore motives, they lose control of the moral of the story, for the more the reader engages with the wife, the less simple the lesson becomes'. In other words, delineating plausible motive on the part of the wife introduces the possibility of justification for petty treason.[22] But plausibility and justification are not synonymous. In *A True Discourse, Of the practices of Elizabeth Caldwell,* Caldwell's given motives do not broach justification for her behaviour, but serve to illustrate the ultimate repercussions of tainted domestic relationships. That her husband is held to be culpable for the initial rupture of domestic harmony reinforces the message that the abuse of authority and responsibility creates a rent in social unity which is quickly manipulated by the Devil. Far from being lost, the moral of the story is poignantly inculcated.

From the outset Caldwell is presented as a character with whom the reader can empathize and pity, an identification which is crucial if her subsequent role as religious instructor is to be tenable. The author's expressed purpose is to use the tale 'to plant or to engrase a kind of feare by this way of example, howe murder should herafter beare any braine in sensible creatures . . .'. Caldwell is therefore 'framed and adorned withall the gifts that nature could challenge', from a good family, and well educated. Whilst responsibility for her fault rests in part in her own weakness and susceptibility to sin, full responsibility is always either mediated or displaced, first onto her husband, and then on to her lover, Jeffrey Bownd, and the resourceful widow, Isabel Hall. Bownd attempts 'to withdrawe [Caldwell] to his unlawful desire', but 'she along time withstood their allurements'. Although eventually 'their perswasions did worke with her', she 'was greatly tormented in her conscience, and divers times, earnestlie intreated them to surcease in this practice', so much so that it was not Caldwell's but Bownd and Hall's hearts which were 'so deeply possest by that filthy enemy to all goodnes'. Moreover, the author gives Caldwell only a passive role in the passage in which poison is bought and prepared, and, just before her husband ate the poisoned cakes, 'fear drave such a terror to her hart as she lay in bed, as she even trembled with remorse of conscience, yet wanted the power to call to him'.[23] Until the moment of her repentance, Caldwell thus remains subject rather than agent. Her subjectivity invites empathy, which in turn makes her forgivable; but the characterization and storyline are constructed in such a way as to defy the *positive* identification with Caldwell as husband killer. Once forgiven, Caldwell does assume an active voice and role – as subject, servant and instrument of God.

> Thus the deceitfull devill, who hath sometime permission from GOD to attempt the very righteous . . . was now an instrument to her sorrow, but her feeling faith the more increased, and no doubt to her comfort, though in our eyes terrible: for indeede so it ought, being sent from God as an example to thousands. For where so many live, one or two pickt out by the hand of God, must serve as an example to the rest, to keepe thousands in feare of Gods wrath, and the worlds terror.[24]

The moral of the story is clear; the lesson is surely simple enough.

Representations of women constituted the most accessible images of disorder for pamphleteers to draw upon, yet as we have seen, women were often not the main locus for disorder, nor indeed for evil. The author of the Elizabeth Caldwell pamphlet introduces his account by speaking of 'the strange invasion of Sathan' on Caldwell and her associates, and 'howe that uglie fiende (ever mans fatall oppostite) had made practice, but I hope not purchase, of theyr corruptible lives, and brought them to the last steppe of mortall miserie'.[25] The confession of Anne Saunders similarly states that 'the Devill kindled in my hearte, first the hellish firebrande of unlawfull lust, and afterwarde a murtherous intent'.[26] Even the 'most horrible and wicked' Mistress Beast, over whom 'lust had gotten so much power' that she too resolved to murder her husband, was led astray by 'the wicked instigation and provocation of the Devill'.[27] And Thomas Smith's brutal murder of his prosperous neighbour and friend Robert Greenoll was proof that 'the Devill so farre ruled the course of his envious intent . . . such was the perswasion of the evill spirite'.[28] Satan is often the primary agent for evil, working upon human frailty: the tales instruct us to 'mark how busie the devil is to woork mans utter overthrow'.[29] That frailty might be linked to the female condition, as it is in Elizabeth Caldwell's case. In her scaffold speech, she is reported to have said that the cause of her sin was 'her own filthy flesh, the illutions of the devill, and those hellish instruments which he set on worke'.

> Then said shee, that if the great and tall Ceaders of the Church of God have fallen, as David, Salomon, and Manasses, how then coulde shee stand, being but a bramble, and weake wretched woman.[30]

Likewise, in *A Pitiless Mother*, Margaret Vincent is a woman

> whose life's overthrow may well serve for a clear looking Glass to see a woman's weakness in: how soon and apt she is won unto wickedness, not only to the body's overthrow but [also to] the soul's danger.[31]

But as Joy Wiltenburg points out, 'rhetoric might distinguish women as strangely different, but the actual depictions of their actions tie them firmly to their culture's conceptions of human and criminal nature in general'. Crimes by women and men are thus treated similarly, both sexes being motivated by sin – greed, lust, covetousness. The nature of sin and the power of divine intervention require that in these tales the devil acts more as motivator than adjunct.[32]

We have, moreover, to relocate gendered representations within the genre in which they exist, and not to extrapolate wildly about the influence which such images must have had upon living women of the period. There seem to be no grounds for claiming that Margaret Ferneseede's story 'demonstrates the pervasiveness of these feminine stereotypes in Renaissance England and gives an indication of their power to influence the lives of real women'.[33] When we read these texts we must remain acutely aware that we are not strictly dealing with reports of 'real' events and persons, but with literary constructions. These might be based upon actual incidents, but in the translation from event to narrative, the genre demands that character, motive and detail are subject to a purposeful remoulding. It is anachronistic to suppose, as some commentators have, that the author of *The Arraigment and Burning of Margaret Ferneseede* believed Margaret Ferneseede's denial of complicity in her husband's death to be proof of her shrewish nature rather than a possible indication of her innocence. 'Because', it is argued, 'she fit the stereotype of the unchaste, scolding woman so well, she was immediately believed to be a murderess'.[34] The Margaret Ferneseede of this tale was not a real woman. Whatever the character of the woman who went by that name, and who was executed for petty treason, we must acknowledge that the fictional Ferneseede is just as, if not more, likely to have fitted the stereotype of the unchaste, scolding woman *because* she was a murderess, and not vice versa.

Wiltenburg's assumption that images of female domestic mastery probably encouraged women to perceive themselves as powerful, albeit 'within limits that they may have seen as natural or desirable rather than arbitrarily imposed', is dependent upon another underlying assumption: that a female readership is likely to identify with the text as explicitly and consciously 'female'.[35] The effects of literary representations on actual living women are difficult to gauge, but the relationship between the two is certainly complex. For one thing, the point of identification of a reader (even a female reader) with the text need not necessarily be determined by gender. The world of the pamphlets was one in which the struggle between good and evil prevailed; in which the propensity to sin was manipulated by the devil; and in which providence and divine justice ultimately predominated. The central message was not merely that one sin leads to another, but that all sins lead to hell.[36] As we are told by one pamphlet author,

> mischeife is of that nature, that it can not stand, but by strengthening of one evill with an other, and so multiply in it selfe until it come unto the highest, and then falles with his owne weight.[37]

Given the religious ideology which framed the majority of these texts, it is surely just as likely that the women who had access to the images therein identified as sinners, penitents, or one of the godly as much as they did women: that is, after all, what the rhetoric invites.

In her last-dying speech, the penitent Elizabeth Caldwell 'gave Saint Paules admonition unto every one, Let him that thinketh he stands, take heed of a present fall', before denouncing a catalogue of sins. She informs the crowd that one of her 'chiefe and capitall sinnes' was her neglect of the observation of the Sabbath day,

and although the world did recon and esteeme it a small matter, yet she
knewe it to be one of her greatest sinnes, wishing all people in the feare
of God, to make a reverent account of the Lords glorious Saboth . . .

She 'complained much of adultery, and said it was that filthy sinne
which was the cause of her death'; she spoke out against Roman
Catholicism, saying that 'she ever hated it, knowing it contrary and
flatly opposite against the truth of the great God of heaven'; and
condemned blasphemy, profanity, and the abuse of God's ministers.
'Therefore she desired all to turne from their sinnes, and to turne to
the Lord by true and unfained repentence.'[38] In this way, the author
is displacing Caldwell's femininity as the point of contact with those
for whom her message is intended. The author creates a mechanism
in which even the positive female stereotype does not have
predominance by the end of the text. For whilst the Caldwell who is
introduced at the beginning of the pamphlet was honest and virtuous,
she 'did not know God'. Within the narrative, the personification of
Caldwell as murderous woman shifts to that of Caldwell as sinner.
And it is as redeemed sinner, rather than convicted felon, that Caldwell
and others like her meet their deaths: 'in her might be seene the true
image of a penitent sinner . . . God showing his glory so
aboundantlie, working her penitency . . . '.[39] The glorification here
is not of the actions of criminals, as Wiltenburg supposes, but the
redemptive power and love of God.[40]

However, there is no reason to assume that the early modern
readership was completely undiscerning.[41] Just as Peter Lake has said
with regard to the internalization of the religious message by readers
of either gender, it was surely possible for a female reader to enjoy the
pamphlets 'for the *frisson* of horror or disapproval, the warm glow of
sentimental satisfaction, which such images might induce . . .
without extracting from them any very abstract notions' about the
nature of women and still less without applying such notions to her
own life or experience.[42] The predominance of women who kill in the
texts was in inverse proportion to the incidence of female homicide
which was prosecuted during the period.[43] The pamphlet accounts
were therefore doubly shocking and removed from the lived
experience of the majority of those who read or heard them. If the very
extremity of the tales told in the pamphlets 'mitigated against such an
internalization or personal application of the pamphlet's message' as
regards religion, that same extremity surely could have resulted in a

similar rejection of personal identification with the figures and images along the lines of gender.[44] Life and literature are not the same. All too often, we confuse rhetorical conventions with societal attitudes. Although there is undoubtedly a relationship between the two, that relationship is neither straightforward nor necessarily overtly causal.[45] The worlds of materiality and *mentalité* are at once inseparable and remote.

Notes

1. The most full and recent analyses may be found in Frances E. Dolan, *Dangerous Familiars: Representations of Domestic Crime in England 1550–1700* (Ithaca, 1994), and Joy Wiltenburg, *Disorderly Women and Female Power in the Street Literature of Early Modern England and Germany* (Charlottesville, 1992).
2. Peter Lake, 'Deeds against nature: cheap print, Protestantism and murder in early seventeenth century England', in Kevin Sharpe and Peter Lake, eds, *Culture and Politics in Early Stuart England* (London, 1994), pp. 257–84.
3. Natalie Zemon Davis, *Society and Culture in Early Modern France* (Stanford, 1975), ch. 5; Joad Raymond, ed., *Making the News, An Anthology of the Newsbooks of Revolutionary England, 1641–1660* (Moreton-in-Marsh, 1993), pp. 123–7; Peter Stallybrass, 'Patriarchal territories: the body enclosed', in Margaret W. Ferguson, Maureen Quilligan and Nancy Vicars, eds, *Rewriting the Renaissance: the Discourses of Sexual Difference in Early Modern Europe* (Chicago, 1986).
4. *A Briefe Discourse of Two most cruell and bloudie murthers . . . An other most cruel and bloody murder . . .* (London, 1583), sigs B2^v, B3, B3^v, B4.
5. *A Briefe discourse of Two most cruell and bloudie murthers . . . A most cruel and bloody murder, committed . . . by one Thomas Smith . . .* (London, 1583), sigs A5–A5^v, A7, B1^v.
6. Lake, 'Deeds against nature', pp. 266–7.
7. *The Most Cruell and Bloody Murther committed by an Inkeepers Wife, called Annis Dell . . .* (London, 1606), sig. A3^v.
8. Ibid., sig. A3.
9. Ibid., sigs A3, A3^v, A4, A4^v, A1, B.
10. Wiltenburg, *Disorderly Women*, pp. 232–3.
11. *The Most Cruell and Bloody Murther*, sigs B1^v, B2; Lake, 'Deeds against nature', pp. 259, 266.
12. *Two most unnaturall and bloodie Murthers: The one by Maister Caverely*

. . . (London, 1605), pp. 1, 13, 16. This pamphlet is reprinted in A. C. Cawley and Barry Gaines, eds, *A Yorkshire Tragedy* (Manchester, 1986), pp. 94–110. See also *The Unnaturall Father, Or the Cruell Murther committed by one John Rowse* . . . (London, 1621).

13. Katherine Usher Henderson and Barbara F. McManus, *Half Humankind: Contexts and Texts of the Controversy about Women in England 1540–1640* (Urbana, 1985), p. 67.

14. Ibid., p. 68. *A pitiless Mother* . . . (London, 1616) is reprinted in ibid., pp. 360–7. Religious motivation for parents killing their children is a common theme in early modern sectarian pamphlets. See, for instance, *A Dreadful Relation, of the Cruel, Bloudy, and most Inhumane Massacre and Butchery* . . . (London, 1595).

15. *Two most unnaturall and bloodie Murthers: The one by Maister Caverley*, pp. 17, 5, 6, 8, 9. See also Lake, 'Deeds against nature', p. 264.

16. *Two most unnaturall and bloodie Murthers: The one by Maister Caverley*, pp. 2–3, 4, 7,13.

17. *Two most unnaturall and bloodie Murthers* . . . *The cruell murther of Maister Browne* (London, 1605), p. 22, and passim.

18. This is especially so considering that the Master Browne tale was printed together with the Master Caverley tale in which the dishonour of breaking a marriage contract was given a central place.

19. *A Briefe Discourse* . . . *An other most cruel and bloody Murder*, sig. B2.

20. Wiltenburg, *Disorderly Women*, pp. 214–24.

21. Philippa Maddern, *Violence and Social Order: East Anglia, 1422–1442* (Oxford, 1992), ch. 3, quotation at p. 98; Z. Babington, *Advice to Grand Jurors in Cases of Blood* (London, 1666), pp. 178–9; Garthine Walker, 'Crime, gender and social order in early modern Cheshire', unpublished PhD thesis, University of Liverpool, 1994, ch. 3 passim.

22. Dolan, *Dangerous Familiars*, pp. 32, 37.

23. Gilbert Dugdale, *A True Discourse, Of the practices of Elizabeth Caldwell* (London, 1604), sigs A3, A4, A4^v, B, B1^v. The pamphlet is reproduced in the *Documents* section below, pp. 276–92.

24. Ibid., sigs B2–B2^v.

25. Ibid., sig. A3.

26. *A briefe discourse of the late murther of master George Saunders* (London, 1577), sig. B6^v.

27. *A Briefe Discourse* . . . *An other most cruel and bloody Murder*, sigs B2–B2^v.

28. *A most cruel and bloody murder, committed* . . . *by one Thomas Smith*, sig. A5.

29. *A Briefe Discourse of Two most cruell and bloudie murthers*, 'To the Reader', sig. A3. Lake, 'Deeds Against Nature', pp. 268–9.

30. Dugdale, *A True Discourse*, sigs D, D2ᵛ.
31. *A Pitiless Mother*, reprinted in Henderson and McManus, *Half Humankind*, p. 361.
32. Wiltenburg, *Disorderly Women*, p. 213: cf. p. 212.
33. Henderson and McManus, *Half Humankind*, p. 71.
34. Ibid.
35. Wiltenburg, *Disorderly Women*, p. 4.
36. Lake, 'Deeds against nature', pp. 277, 269.
37. *Two most unnaturall and bloodie Murthers*, p. 7.
38. Dugdale, *A True Discourse*, sigs D, Dᵛ.
39. Ibid., sig. B3ᵛ.
40. Wiltenberg, *Disorderly Women*, pp. 217, 218.
41. Cf. Raymond, *Making the News*, p. 131.
42. Lake, 'Deeds against nature', p. 282.
43. For homicide prosecutions, see J. M. Beattie, *Crime and the Courts in England, 1660–1800* (Oxford, 1986), pp. 74–140; J. S. Cockburn, 'Patterns of violence in English society: homicide in Kent, 1560–1985', *Past and Present* 130 (February 1991), 70–106; J. A. Sharpe, 'Domestic homicide in early modern England', *Historical Journal* 24 (1981), 29–48; Walker, 'Crime, gender and social order', ch. 3.
44. Lake, 'Deeds against nature', pp. 282–3.
45. For ways in which women (and men) manipulated gendered rhetoric and convention to their own ends in constructing narratives recorded by criminal and ecclesiastical courts, see: Natalie Zemon Davis, *Fiction in the Archives: Pardon Tales and their Tellers in Sixteenth-Century France* (Cambridge and Stanford, 1987); Malcolm Gaskill, 'Witchcraft and power in early modern England: the case of Margaret Moore', in Jenny Kermode and Garthine Walker, eds, *Women, Crime and the Courts in Early Modern England* (London, 1994), pp. 125–45; Laura Gowing, 'Language, power and the law: women's slander litigation in early modern London', in idem, pp. 26–47; Garthine Walker, 'Crime, gender and social order', esp. ch. 2.

8 Sixteenth-century women's writing: Mary Sidney's Psalmes and the 'femininity' of translation

Suzanne Trill

In examining the topic of women and fiction in *A Room of One's Own*, Virginia Woolf sought to solve the 'perennial puzzle' of 'why no [Elizabethan] woman wrote a word of that extraordinary literature when every other man, it seemed, was capable of song or sonnet'.[1] Faced with the apparent absence of sixteenth-century women writers, Woolf attempts to fill in the missing pages of history through the powers of her imagination; the tragic tale of 'Shakespeare's Sister' epitomizes the effects of the social construction of gender upon literary creativity and highlights the obstacles that prevented women from writing during this period. Whereas Woolf had to contend with a distinct lack of material about women's lives and writing during the Renaissance, many books on this topic now exist which collectively provide a wealth of information about the tasks that occupied sixteenth-century women 'from eight in the morning till eight at night'; in the process, literary critics and historians have uncovered a number of texts by women writers which prove that they did indeed produce some of 'that extraordinary literature' during the Elizabethan period. One such book is Elaine V. Beilin's *Redeeming Eve*, which rediscovered 34 women writers, twenty of whom were writing between 1521 and 1600; this group produced 33 texts, which corporately span a wide variety of genres and forms (including diaries, letters, prayers and meditations, and original poetry), but perhaps the most striking characteristic of women's writing at this time is the fact that approximately one-third of the texts they produced were translations.[2]

This has led critics to assert that translation was a relatively permissible form of writing for women at this time: one recent critic goes so far as to suggest that 'translations were "defective" and therefore appropriate to women; this low opinion of translation perhaps accounts for why women were allowed to translate at all. A man who labors in this degraded activity must justify himself, "since all translations are reputed femalls" '.[3] The suggestion here is that translations were perceived to be low-status texts precisely because they were 'reputed femalls' and, consequently, that translation was a gender-marked activity which reflected contemporary Renaissance conceptions of male and female social value. Or, as one recent feminist critic explains, 'the opposition between productive and reproductive work organizes the way a culture values work: this paradigm depicts originality or creativity in terms of paternity and authority, relegating the figure of the female to a variety of secondary roles'.[4] From this perspective, translation is a secondary or 'reproductive' activity, which is correspondingly defined as a 'feminine' activity; it is a 'defective' *re*-presentation of an original work, not a creative act in its own right. As such it would appear to be a peculiarly appropriate genre for sixteenth-century women writers, as they were actively discouraged from entering the world of print and particularly dissuaded from producing 'original' texts. But how accurate is this assumed correlation between translation and femininity in the English Renaissance? More specifically, this essay will address the extent to which Mary Sidney's translations of the *Psalmes* can be described as 'feminine'.

1. Theorizing translation

It is often thought that 'translation' and 'writing' represent a binary opposition in which the former is a pale imitation of the latter; this view is founded upon postromantic conceptions of an originary authorial genius in which 'the "original" is a form of self-expression appropriate to the author, a copy true to . . . personality or intention, an image endowed with resemblance, whereas translation can be no more than a copy of a copy, derivative, simulacral, false, an image without resemblance'.[5] In this description, translation appears to be the very antithesis of writing: whereas an 'original' text encapsulates the 'truth' of the author's 'personality or intention', a translation separates the text from its author and can never recapture the fullness of the 'original' text; moreover, the translator's 'personality or intention' is effectively erased from the text s/he produces. However, recent developments in literary theory (most notably poststructuralism) have questioned the nature of the relationship between a text and authorial presence, 'personality or intention'. Critics of a poststructuralist orientation have demonstrated that a text can never be fully explained by reference to the author, arguing instead that a text is understood in relation to other texts and that any piece of writing is, in fact, always a rewriting of pre-existing texts. From this perspective, it can be suggested that *all* writing is a form of translation as no piece of writing is purely the property of a single, originary author: any text contains a variety of discourses which may well conflict with one another and produce meanings that were never 'intended' by the writer; indeed, the text will have many different meanings that arise within the different contexts in which it is reproduced and read. In this sense, translation merely foregrounds processes which occur in any act of communication.

The insights of poststructuralism also facilitate the deconstruction of another familiar binarism that is frequently invoked when discussing translation: that is, the opposition between 'faithful' (word-for-word) and 'free' (sense-for-sense) translations. This opposition suggests that there are two roles that a translator can play in rewriting a text: either s/he can attempt to replicate the 'original' or s/he can actively recreate the text by producing a version that consciously seeks to adapt the 'original' to its new context. However, as poststructuralism proposes that there is no single, unitary meaning neatly contained within a text, this opposition becomes nonsensical; rather, the logic of poststructuralism requires us to recognize that

> a translation is never quite 'faithful,' always somewhat 'free,' it never establishes an identity, always a lack and a supplement, and it can never be a transparent representation, only an interpretative transformation that exposes multiple and divided meanings in the foreign text and displaces it with another set of meanings, equally multiple and divided.[6]

In other words, in both its original linguistic context and in its new linguistic context a given text produces a variety of meanings that cannot be reduced to a single unity: there will always be something missing both from the 'original' text and from the translated text, and there will always be something that is added to both texts by the processes of reading and translation. Consequently, the apparent opposition between 'translation' and 'writing' is brought into question: both are in some sense involved in the rewriting of previous texts, codes and discourses, and in neither case is the writer fully able to control the meaning(s) that the text produces.

Yet this does not mean that there are no limitations to the meaning(s) produced by the text, or that the text is therefore ultimately rendered 'meaningless': both the foreign text and the translation are in some way marked by their moment of production as both can be seen to be grounded within particular social and historical contexts. Moreover, the specific affiliations of the translator, as well as the time and place in which s/he translates, can affect both the choice of the text to be translated and the method by which it is translated. And such factors need to be taken into account when analysing the text. Translation, then, is not simply a passive reflection of a previous text, but a form of writing which, by establishing it within a new context, makes a claim about the status of the translated text; if nothing else it is an indication that it is deemed to be worthy of translation and, therefore, deemed to be of interest to a new audience. If, as the logic of poststructuralism suggests, the oppositions between 'writing' and 'translation', and 'faithful' and 'free' translations are not as static as they might at first appear, to what extent does the opposition between 'male' writing and 'female' translation bear up under scrutiny?

According to the theorist Jacques Derrida, the woman translator is 'not simply subordinated, she is not the author's secretary . . . Translation is writing; that is, it is not translation only in the sense of transcription. It is a productive writing called forth by the original text'.[7] Although Derrida's explanation here does go some way towards redefining the process of translation, one feminist critic points out that his discussion lacks an exploration of the historical and cultural circumstances of specific translations; she argues that in the sixteenth century this is exactly how a woman translator would have been perceived and suggests that 'in some historical periods women were allowed to translate precisely *because* it was defined as a secondary activity'.[8] While it is true to say that the gendering of translation must be understood within its own particular historical and social context, our understanding of that context is itself informed by the questions we ask of the material we examine. In order to place any given translation within its social and historical context, and thus to appreciate its cultural and political function fully, Lawrence Venuti suggests that the critic should examine 'the place and practice of translation in specific cultures, addressing such questions as which foreign texts are selected for translation and which discursive strategies are used to translate them, which texts, strategies, and translations are canonized or marginalized, and which social groups are served by them'.[9] What then was the place of translation during the English Renaissance? Which texts were selected for translation, for what purposes, and by whom? What different kinds of translation were there, and were they equally valued? And, most importantly for my purposes, to what extent is translation represented as a 'feminine' activity?

2. The 'femininity' of translation in the Renaissance

Translation may be fairly described as a central part of English Renaissance culture: one definition of 'Renaissance' is 'the revival of art and literature under the influence of classical models in the fourteenth–sixteenth centuries', and in order to achieve this many writers translated classical texts, famous examples being Chapman's *Homer* and Harington's *Ariosto*. Translation was also an important part of humanist education for men, as is illustrated, for example, in Ascham's *The Scholemaster* (1570). But men did not only produce translations of the classics; as Warren Boutcher has observed, 'the later Elizabethan translator was more likely than his mid-century counterpart to turn to the translation of a modern, French or Italian work dealing with contemporary problems and strategies in morality and politics, and to do so as a conscious bid for a career in law or administration'.[10] Thus, for men, translation could be a means to further their careers and provided them with the opportunity to comment upon political issues.

Yet, apart from the obvious exception of Elizabeth I, women were not eligible for the offices that men might be able to gain via their skills as translators, so what did translation offer them? Current critical opinion holds that women's contribution to the Renaissance translation culture is explained in relation to their exclusion from other forms of expression:

> debarred from original discourse by the absence of rhetorical training, urged to translate for the greater glory of God, women did translate an extensive body of religious work, usually at the prompting of father, brother or husband, and usually works which would be particularly useful to the state or to a political faction.[11]

This last point suggests that women's involvement with translation is perhaps not quite so removed from that of their male contemporaries, for they also translated texts which had a political application. However, rather than a woman achieving direct gain from such an activity, the above representation identifies the woman translator as no more than a site of exchange between a male relative and a political faction.

But there are aspects of the above representation that are potentially misleading: firstly, who were these women translators and, if they did not have any rhetorical training, how were they able to translate at all? In the period 1521–1600 there were eight women who produced translations: Anne Cooke-Bacon, Elizabeth I, Anne Locke, Joanna [Jane] Lumley, Dorcas Martin, Margaret More-Roper, Mary Sidney and Margaret Tyler. The majority of these women were of aristocratic status with protestant connections, whose educational opportunities would have been the best possible for sixteenth-century women; certainly, in order to be able to translate at all, they must of necessity have been able to read and write in more than one language. Collectively, these women produced thirteen translations, four of which are not strictly speaking 'religious': there were, then, only nine specifically religious translations during the sixteenth century, which hardly constitutes an 'extensive' body of texts in this genre.

Furthermore, the suggestion that these women translated such texts at the behest of a 'father, brother or husband' is not entirely accurate. While it is true that the patriarchal organization of Tudor society meant that women were subject to these figures, the circumstances in which their texts were circulated, and their dedications, indicate a rather different picture: Anne Cooke-Bacon dedicated *Fourtene Sermons of Barnadine Ocyne* (1550) to her mother; Elizabeth I translated *The Mirroir of the Godly Soule* (1548) as part of her educational activities, but presented it to her step-mother Catherine Parr; Anne Locke dedicated *Of the Markes of the Children of God* (1590) to the Countess of Warwick; Margaret Tyler produced *The Mirror of Princely Deedes* (1578) at the request of unnamed friends; and Mary Sidney prepared a presentation copy of her *Psalmes* for Elizabeth I. A sizable proportion of the texts translated by women, then, were also dedicated to women. This fact might be taken to reaffirm the secondary status of translation and, indeed, its primary association with women; but these texts were not only of interest to women readers. Some of these translations and other religious works by sixteenth-century women were 'cannonized' by Thomas Bentley in his anthology/conduct book, *The Monument of Matrones* (1582). He claims that these women

> shew themselves woorthie patterns of all pietie, godlinesse, and religion to their sex, and for the common benefit of their countrie, have not ceased, and that with all carefull industrie and earnest indeavour, most painfullie and dilligentlie in great fervencie of the spirit, and zeale of the truth, even from their tender & maidenly yeeres, to spend their time, their wits, their substance, and also their bodies, in the studies of noble and approoved sciences, and in compiling and translating of sundrie most christian and godlie bookes.

(sig. B1^r)

Here, Bentley proffers several crucial points which counteract modern perceptions of the marginality of women's translation: far from being passive regurgitators of other men's texts, these women are 'earnest' and 'dilligent' purveyors of God's word, writing with 'great fervencie of the spirit, and zeale of the truth'. In this description, women are active agents in the writing and promotion of 'sundrie most christian and godlie bookes'; informed by their 'fervencie of spirit' and able to represent the 'truth', these women produce texts which work 'for the common benefit of their countrie'. Elsewhere, John Bale and James Cancellar make similar claims for the importance of Elizabeth I's *A Godly Meditation* and Roger Ascham cites her as an example to shame men for their linguistic inadequacies: 'it is to your shame, (I speake to you all, you yong Gentlemen of England) that one mayd should go beyond you all, in excellencie of learnyng, and knowledge of divers tonges'.[12]

There is perhaps an element of flattery in these comments as the male authors are addressing women of considerably higher social status than their own; moreover, their claims for women's excellence in this area must be tempered by the fact that translations produced by men during this period far outnumber those produced by women. Nevertheless, what should be stressed here is that women are perceived as being successful in an area that *should* be a male activity; a point which questions the idea that translation was held in low regard during this period. Furthermore, whereas modern critics have suggested that the genres in which sixteenth-century women wrote – translations, dedications, epitaphs, letters, private devotional meditations – meant that they were 'relegated to the margins of discourse', the contemporary writers quoted above clearly saw their involvement in these areas as being of central social and religious significance.

The basis of the claim that translation was perceived to be a feminine activity in the Renaissance is founded upon one quotation from John Florio; in one of his prefaces to his translation of Montaigne's *Essays*, he suggests that translations are 'reputed femalls'. But the argument that, therefore, translation is particularly appropriate for women does not explain why there were so few women translators; nor does it take account of the style of Florio's writing and other opinions of translation expressed elsewhere in his prefaces; collectively, Florio's prefaces make it clear that, in fact, he has a very high opinion of translation and, like Ascham, is castigating male scholars who do not share his evaluation of this activity. The main object of Florio's satire is not the innate 'femininity' of translation, but the élitism of those who denigrate it; those who resist translation also resist wider access to learning, fearing that their own power would thereby be wrested from them. Florio's response to this is to suggest mischievously that these scholars should themselves become translators.

A major anxiety about sixteenth-century women's translations seems to be that they are regarded as 'exceedingly literal'.[13] This comment is based upon a comparison of women's religious translations with Chapman's *Homer*, which is hardly a fair comparison. A more accurate 'control' might be to examine, for instance, Sir Philip Sidney's translation of the *Treweness of Christian Religion* or other religious texts translated by male authors; for in such genres authors of either sex understandably display an intense concern for 'literal' translation. In addition to this, the assessment of the 'freeness' of a given translation varies according to different readers, as the fluctuating evaluations of Mary Sidney's texts demonstrate.[14] The question of the 'literal' nature of women's translations, however, betrays deeper concerns about the 'originality' of their work. One of the reasons that translation has been perceived to be an appropriate form of writing for women is precisely because it is deemed to preclude an expression of their own opinions; for example, one critic recently suggested that Mary Sidney speaks from 'behind the curtain' of the male-authored texts she translated, as 'to translate literally is to seek protection in the idea of conveying the author's meaning exactly'.[15] The suspicion that women's translations are too 'literal' reveals an anxiety about their consequent literary value; moreover, it implies that translations can be literal, in contrast to the logic of poststructuralism which indicates that 'a translation is never quite "faithfull," always somewhat "free" '. It also suggests that women writers simply internalized and passively transcribed the ideas and values of the (predominantly) male-authored texts they translated. But is this always the case? In order to address this question, I want now to turn to Mary Sidney's *Psalmes* and to discuss the extent to which they can be characterized as 'feminine'.

3. Mary Sidney's *Psalmes* and the 'femininity' of translation

By translating the Psalms in the late sixteenth century, Mary Sidney appropriated a discourse which was perceived to be pivotal to the construction of Christian subjectivity during this period: for Calvin, the Psalms represented ' "[a]n anatomy of all parts of the Soul"; for there is not an emotion of which anyone can be conscious that is not here represented as in a mirror'; the Reformer Thomas Becon declared that 'the psalmody of David maye well be called the treasure house of the holy Scripture. For it contaynethe what so ever is necessary for a Christen man to know'; and Anthony Gilby announced that 'whereas al other scriptures do teach us what God saith unto us, these praiers . . . do teach us, what we shall saie unto God'.[16] In addition to their relevance to each individual believer, the Psalms had a central role in church services: they were used as communal songs of praise and the psalter was read through monthly. This, plus the sheer volume of commentaries upon and translations of the Psalms, suggests that they represented a discourse that was open to all; that is, open or accessible to both men and women. However, the limitations upon women's education and the stress upon their devotional activities, coupled with the emphasis upon the Psalms in exemplary biographies, meant that this discourse was also one which was peculiarly associated with women during this period. Thus, Mary Sidney was by no means the only woman to demonstrate an interest in, or to be associated with, the Psalms.[17] It is, therefore, possible to situate Mary Sidney's *Psalmes* within a 'female literary tradition', but does this mean that her translations are intrinsically 'feminine'?

On the one hand, the fact that Mary Sidney translated the Psalms could be taken as an indication that she maintained the 'proper' boundaries of female expression, as is illustrated in an often cited quotation from Sir Edward Denny who advised her niece Lady Mary

Wroth to follow the 'pious example of your vertuous and learned Aunt, who translated so many godly bookes and especially the holly psalmes of David'.[18] Much has also been made of Sir John Harington's comment crediting Sidney's *Psalmes* to her chaplain, for 'it was more than a woman's skills to express the sense so right as she hath done in verse'; less often referred to, however, is Harington's description of Sidney as 'that Excellent Countesse, and in Poesie the Mirroir of our Age', or his assertion that her *Psalmes* redeem a subject 'rude and ruinous before'.[19] Moreover, Harington is not alone in identifying her *Psalmes* as a significant literary achievement.

John Donne, for example, argues that Sidney's translation of the Psalms represents 'the highest matter in the noblest forme'.[20] For Donne this is an issue of national honour: he states that the Psalms are '[s]o well atty'rd abroad, so ill at home' (line 38) and declares that the English church cannot truly be called 'reform'd until the English language can encapsulate God's glory. The Sidneian *Psalmes* prove the capacity for the English language to achieve this as they 'teach us how to sing' in words which no longer 'thrust into strait corners of poore wit / Thee, who are cornerlesse and infinite' (lines 22, 23–4). Consequently, Donne proclaims that although 'some have, some may some psalmes translate, / We thy Sydnean Psalmes shall celebrate' (lines 49–50). Similarly, Samuel Daniel specifically situates Mary Sidney as an instructor of both her English contemporaries and foreigners who, 'listening to our Songs another while, / Might learn of thee, their notes to purifie'; in this manner, Mary Sidney elicits praise not only for herself but for her country, as her writing represents

Our accents, and the wonders of our Land,
That they might all admire and honour us.[21]

Both Daniel and Donne praise Mary Sidney's *Psalmes* for their eloquent expression of devotion, but, perhaps even more importantly, they also emphasize their significance for the promotion of the English vernacular.

In her dedicatory poem to Elizabeth I, Mary Sidney makes her own claim for both the national significance of the Psalms in general, and of her and her brother's versions in particular. She asserts that they represent an improvement on previous translations:

Wherein yet well we thought the Psalmist King
Now English denizend, though Hebrue born,

woold to thy musicke undispleased sing
Oft having worse, without repining worne . . .[22]

This point is heightened by the title page of the *Psalmes* which states that the text contains '[t]he Psalmes of David translated into divers and sundrie kinds of verse, more Rare and Excellent for Method and Varietie than ever yet hath been done in English'.[23] Mary Sidney presents the psalms 'in both our names' and suggests that this will 'cause our neighbours [to] see' England's power. The Sidneian *Psalmes*, then, symbolize the capacity of the English vernacular to praise God, and thereby play their part both in substantiating England's claim to be God's chosen nation and in establishing the English vernacular as a language worthy of international respect. This suggests that translating the Psalms was far from a marginal or intrinsically feminine activity: firstly, they were a central discourse in the construction of protestant subjectivity and protestant politics in the sixteenth century; and secondly, while contemporary poetic translations of them were on the whole produced by men, Mary Sidney's versions are represented as exceeding theirs in both form and style. This stresses her ability as a poet and also indicates that, although the subject matter was religious, her translations cannot be seen as unproblematically situating her within the confines of acceptable female expression.

This raises the question of how we are to read her psalms. Mary Sidney altered the context in which women used the Psalms by translating them poetically and, unlike other writers of either sex, she does not provide a framework in which to interpret them. If one takes into account her revision of her brother's versions of Psalms 1–43, Mary Sidney translated all 150 of the Psalms, which means that they, like the biblical versions, can be read in a variety of ways. For these reasons, Mary Sidney's *Psalmes* resist any accurate or straightforward (auto)biographical reading, although there have been attempts to produce one; Beth Wynne Fisken, for example, suggests that one phrase from Sidney's psalms represents 'a poetic equivalent for her own small, personal voice, "my self, my seely self in me" ', and asserts that Sidney's experience of childbirth influences her extension of the image of the embryo in Psalm 58.[24] While these points may have some validity, there is no way of affirming them with any certainty; furthermore, these examples demonstrate a desire to recover a 'feminine' voice in these psalms which is inappropriate. Rather than seeking to find an expression of Sidney's femininity in her *Psalmes*, it is more productive to examine the ways in which the form of her translations self-consciously draws attention to the fact that they are poetic. By emphasizing the role of the speaker and the manner and form of the telling, Mary Sidney situates herself as God's poet-praiser.

That this position falls to Mary Sidney is partly by dint of fate: at least half of the psalms which, due to her brother's death, she translated, are identified by St Augustine as psalms of praise.[25] Moreover, for Calvin, one of the defining characteristics of the Psalms is their capacity to teach the believer how to praise God, as they provide

> an infallible rule for directing us with respect to the right manner of offering to God the sacrifice of praise, which he declares to be most precious in his sight, and of the sweetest odour . . . in short, there is no other book in which we are more perfectly taught the right manner of praising God, or in which we are more powerfully stirred up to the performance of this religious exercise.[26]

On the one hand, then, the fact that Mary Sidney takes upon herself the role of God's praiser is inherent in the text she translates; but, in addition to this, her position as God's *poet*-praiser is accentuated by the way in which her versions draw attention to the 'skill' required to express God's praises. In this, she makes an implicit claim for the literary value of her writing, as she states in Psalm 111:

> At home, abroad most willingly I will
> Bestow on God my praises uttmost skill.[27]

Elsewhere, Sidney's use of the first person constructs an intimate context of direct address, and her inclusion of her audience, through the repetition of the pronouns 'our' and 'your', also highlights the 'skillful' nature of the art of praise:

> Praise, praise our God; praise, praise our King,
>   Kings of the world your judgements sound,
> With Skillful song his praises sing.
>
> (Psalm 47, lines 13–15)

Whether Sidney is consciously drawing attention to herself is a matter of debate, but certainly her translations self-reflexively comment upon the poetic nature of her endeavour. In Psalm 75, whereas the Geneva

Bible version of this psalm, for example, simply exhorts the reader to praise God but says nothing of the manner or mood in which this is to be done, Sidney's version accentuates both:

> And I, secure, shall spend my happie tymes
> In my, though lowly, never-dying rymes,
>> Singing with praise the God that Jacob loveth.

> (lines 25–7)

The expression of praise here is derived from the speaker's security and is the product of 'my happie tymes'; moreover, the form of praise is specifically identified as poetry or 'rymes' and, by emphasizing the lyric 'I', this version simultaneously stresses the speaker's possession of this utterance: they are 'my . . . rymes'. Although these 'rymes' are characterized as 'lowly', they are also eternal, or 'never-dying'; in this, it would seem that Sidney is making her own claim for the immortality of her verse, a point which was underlined in the reception of her *Psalmes* by her contemporaries.

Furthermore, Sidney's version of Psalm 77 reflects upon the process of writing as an aid to memory and as a means of constructing a sense of 'self'; the speaker recalls

> What in my former rimes
>> My self of thee had told.

> (lines 31–2)

The fact that such 'rimes' are themselves constructed is evident in Psalm 96, where the speaker encourages others to praise God with songs that should be reformulated daily: 'Day by day new ditties frame' (line 6). The instruction to 'frame' such 'ditties' on a daily basis perhaps reflects the fact that the Psalms were supposed to be read daily. But it also highlights the fact that these expressions are constantly recreated, they are constructed or framed to the needs of the moment. In the case of Mary Sidney's translations, this also serves to foreground the artistic process involved in framing 'skillful' songs or 'rimes' to God. Additionally, in Psalm 145, Sidney's version explicitly addresses the need to search for an appropriate language in which to express God's praises, and stresses the fact that this is a life-long activity:

> My God, my King, to lift thy praise
>> And thanck thy most thank-worthy name
> I will not end, but all my daies

Will spend in seeking how to frame
Recordes of they deserved fame
Whose praise past-praise, whose greatness such,
The greatest search can never touch.

(lines 1–7)

The search for an appropriate language in which to address God is, of course, a central preoccupation of devotional poets in the Renaissance. Like her contemporaries, Sidney intimates that God's praises are ineffable, they cannot be represented, as they are 'past-praise' and are impossible to 'touch'. But this does not preclude the attempt to do so; rather the speaker promises to '[spend] all my daies' in the search to find an appropriate 'frame' in which to record 'thy deserved fame'. Indeed, the very variety of 'frames' that Sidney uses calls attention to the poetic quality of the psalms, and the versatility of the writer. Accordingly, the Sidney psalter has been termed a compendium of sixteenth-century versification, and is thought to have had an enormous influence upon the poetry of George Herbert.[28] All this suggests that, rather than placing her on the 'margins of discourse', Mary Sidney's *Psalmes* situate her at the centre of the development of the religious lyric.

Significantly, Mary Sidney ends her *Psalmes* by turning the last psalm into a Petrarchan sonnet. According to St Augustine, the last 50 psalms represented the soul when it had achieved grace: in this state the soul was in harmony with its surroundings and, therefore, was able to praise God fully. The final psalm, therefore, represents the culmination of earthly praise, a point which is encapsulated in both the form and the content of Sidney's translation:

O laud the Lord, the God of hosts commend,
   Exault his pow'r, advance his holynesse:
   With all your might lift his allmightinesse:
Your greatest praise upon his greatness spend.

Make Trumpetts noise in shrillest notes ascend:
   Make lute and lyre his loved fame expresse:
   Him lett the pipe, him lett the tabret blesse,
Him organs breath, that windes or waters lend.

Lett ringing Timbrells soe his honor sound,
   Lett sounding Cymbals soe his glory ring,

> That in their tunes such mellody be found,
>   As fitts the pompe of most Triumphant King.
> Conclud: by all that aire, or life enfold,
> Let high Jehova highly be extold.

Playing with assonance, Sidney 'lauds' the 'Lord' and utilizes parallelisms in order to exhort the readers to use 'all your might' to express God's 'allmightinesse'. Once more she stresses the need to employ the full extent of one's skill in the art of praise: '[y]our greatest praise upon his greatness spend'. And she seeks to match the expression to the subject: the words of this translation, like the instruments, must be tuned in a form which 'fitts the pompe of most Triumphant King'. By presenting her praises in the form of a Petrarchan sonnet, Mary Sidney is able self-consciously to conclude not only this psalm but her *Psalmes* as she sums up the purpose of the psalter and her own poetic endeavour in a rhyming couplet:

> Conclud: by all that aire, or life enfold,
> Let high Jehova highly be extold.

The examples I have analysed illustrate the impossibility of locating Mary Sidney's 'own' voice in her *Psalmes*, at least insofar as this is associated with reading them (auto)biographically. Overtly, at least, Sidney seems to follow Calvin's advice upon the use of the Psalms; he states that

> [w]hoever would follow [David] aright, must not allow himself to break forth with reckless and blind impetuosity into the language of imprecation; he must, moreover, repress the turbulent passions of his mind, and, instead of confining his thoughts exclusively to his own private interests, should rather employ his desires and affections in seeking to advance the glory of God.[29]

On one level, Mary Sidney's translations emphasize the desire to employ herself in the advancement of God's glory. However, the stress upon the speaker, or lyric 'I', in these translations, combined with their poetic form and the reception of her *Psalmes* by her contemporaries, indicates that the authorship of these psalms also brought Mary Sidney herself some glory. While an (auto)biographical reading of the psalms is problematic, the author's role in the production of the text is not entirely negated: as John Donne put it, 'though some have, some may some psalmes translate, we they *Sydnean* psalmes shall celebrate' (my emphasis).

While the Psalms do have specific cultural associations with women in the Renaissance and, therefore, could be viewed as an appropriately 'feminine' discourse, Mary Sidney's *Psalmes* cannot easily be said to express her 'femininity'. She does not re-gender the personae of the psalmist or apply the Psalms to particular events in her life; rather, she translates them all and thus, as in the 'original', she expresses the range of emotional states that a Christian could experience. Any attempt to locate a gendered voice in her *Psalmes* is fraught with difficulty and highlights a crucial problem at the centre of feminist reading strategies. In another context, Diane Purkiss notes that feminist critics often set up 'a logocentric cycle . . . whereby a female signature prompts a reading strategy designed to uncover a female consciousness in texts, and this consciousness in turn is held to manifest the presence of a female author'.[30] With regard to Mary Sidney, the issue is slightly different, as she was undeniably a woman and there is no doubt that she produced these translations. Yet, although her translations resist the identification of a specifically 'female consciousness', the fact that she was a woman prompts many critics to seek for it.

Consequently, her *Psalmes* have been taken to represent her desire to remain within the 'proper' boundaries of female expression, because they were religious in nature and because translation has been perceived to be a 'feminine' (and thus marginalized) genre. However, the crucial importance of the art of translation to the Renaissance, and the fact that it was for her *Psalmes* that she was most highly praised, questions the 'marginal' or 'feminine' status of these particular translations. The Psalms were central to the construction of protestant subjectivity during this period and, by translating them poetically, Mary Sidney demonstrates her capacity to write in the (traditionally) most highly valued literary form. Moreover, they circulated in manuscript among her aristocratic contemporaries: in using this method of circulation, Sidney does not display a hesitancy at entering the world of print, but is acting in accordance with protocol for writers of her social status. Add to this the fact that she dedicated her *Psalmes* to the Queen and prepared (although did not deliver) a presentation copy for her, and it would seem that her translations were anything but 'marginal'. Rather, her apparent acceptance of the rules of female expression illustrates the benefit that can be gained from such 'obedience': as Bourdieu puts it, 'quite apart from the direct profit derived from doing what the rule prescribes, perfect conformity to the rule can bring secondary benefits such as *prestige* and *respect* which almost invariably reward an action *apparently motivated by nothing other than pure, disinterested respect for the rule*.[31] She is, after all, the only major English female poet of the sixteenth century, and it is for her achievements as a poet in her *Psalmes* that she obtained prestige and which won her the respect of writers such as Donne and Daniel. The fact that in translating the Psalms she succeeds where many male authors have failed problematizes the assumption that translation was a secondary and 'feminine' activity. Mary Sidney's *Psalmes* are 'never-dying rymes' which both glorify God and immortalize her fame; while they do not directly reflect her 'femininity', they provide an eloquent testimony of her ability to express her faith poetically.

Notes

1. Virginia Woolf, *A Room of One's Own* (London, 1985 [1929]), p. 41.
2. Elaine V. Beilin, *Redeeming Eve: Women Writers of the English Renaissance* (Princeton, 1987). See 'List of Works by Women, 1521–1624', pp. 335–8; there are thirteen texts translated by women c. 1521–1600.
3. Mary Ellen Lamb, 'The Cooke sisters: attitudes toward learned women in the Renaissance', in *Silent but for the Word: Tudor Women as Patrons, Translators, and Writers of Religious Works*, ed. Margaret P. Hannay (Kent, Ohio, 1985), p. 116. Citation is from Montaigne's *Essayes*, tr. John Florio (London, 1603), sig. A2^r.
4. Lori Chamberlain, 'Gender and the metaphorics of translation', in *Rethinking Translation: Discourse, Subjectivity, Ideology*, ed. Lawrence Venuti (London and New York, 1992), p. 57.
5. Venuti, ed., *Rethinking Translation*, p. 3.
6. Ibid., p. 8.
7. Jacques Derrida, *The Ear of the Other: Otobiography, Transference, Translation*, ed. Christie V. McDonald, tr. Peggy Kamuf (New York, 1985), p. 153.
8. Chamberlain, 'Gender and the metaphorics of translation', in Venuti, ed., *Rethinking Translation*, p. 70.
9. Venuti, ed., *Rethinking Translation*, p. 11.
10. Warren Boutcher, 'Florio's Montaigne: translation and pragmatic humanism in the sixteenth century', unpublished PhD dissertation, University of Cambridge, 1991, p. 63. I would like to thank Warren Boutcher for his permission to quote from his thesis and for his assistance in obtaining this material.

11. Hannay, ed., *Silent but for the Word*, p. 9.

12. Roger Ascham, *The Scholemaster* (London, 1570), in *The English Experience*, 15 (Amsterdam and New York, 1968), sig. H1^r. See also prefaces to *A godly medytacyon of the christen sowle*, ed. John Bale (Wesel, 1548), and *A Godly Meditation of the Christian Soule*, ed. James Cancellar (London, 1580).

13. Mary Ellen Lamb, in Hannay, ed., *Silent but for the Word*, p. 124.

14. Compare, for example, Diane Bornstein's comments on Sidney's translations in 'The style of the Countess of Pembroke's translation of Philippe de Mornay's *Discours de la vie et de la mort*', in Hannay, ed. *Silent but for the Word*, with those of Tina Krontiris in *Oppositional Voices: Women as Writers and Translators of Literature in the English Renaissance* (London, 1992).

15. Krontiris, *Oppositional Voices*, p. 66.

16. *Commentary on the book of Psalms by John Calvin*, ed. Rev. James Anderson (Michigan, 1948), I, p. xxxviii; Thomas Becon, *Davids harpe ful of moost delectable armony* (1542), sig. A7^v, cited in Rivkah Zim, *English Metrical Psalms: Poetry as Praise and Prayer 1535–1601* (Cambridge, 1987), p. 30; Anthony Gilby, *The Psalmes of David* (1581), sig. a3^v. For an excerpt from Arthur Golding's 1571 translation of Calvin's *Commentary* see the *Documents* section below, pp. 293–4.

17. For further details about women's association with the Psalms, see Suzanne Trill, ' "Patterns of piety and faith": the role of the Psalms in the construction of the exemplary Renaissance woman', unpublished PhD disertation, University of Liverpool, 1993.

18. Sir Edward Denny to Lady Mary Wroth, Salisbury MSS 130/118–19, Feb. 26, 1621/22, cited in Hannay, ed., *Silent but for the Word*, p. 5.

19. Sir John Harington, cited in H. T. R., 'Lady Mary Sydney and her writings', in *The Gentleman's Magazine* 24 (1845), p. 366, cited in Hannay, ed., *Silent but for the Word*, p. 2; Sir John Harington, 'Letter to the Countess of Bedford', Dec. 19, 1600, in *The Letters and Epigrams of Sir John Harington, Together with the Prayse of Private Life*, ed. Norman Egbert McClure (Philadelphia, 1930), p. 87; Sir John Harington, 'In prayse of two worthy Translations, made by two great Ladies', in ibid., p. 310.

20. John Donne, 'Upon the translation of the Psalmes by Sir Philip Sydney, and the Countesse of Pembroke his Sister', in *Donne: Poetical Works*, ed. Herbert J. C. Grierson (Oxford, 1985), pp. 318–19, line 11.

21. *Samuel Daniel: Complete Works*, ed. Alexander B. Grosart (Private, 1885), III, p. 26, lines 79–80, 87–8.

22. Mary Sidney, 'Even Now that Care', in *The Triumph of Death and other unpublished and uncollected poems by Mary Sidney, Countess of Pembroke, 1561–1621*, ed. Gary F. Waller, *Elizabethan and Renaissance Studies* 65 (Salzburg, 1977), pp. 88–91, lines 29–32.

23. Ibid., p. 87.
24. Beth Wynne Fisken, 'Mary Sidney's *Psalmes*: education and wisdom', in Hannay, ed., *Silent but for the Word*, pp. 169, 177.
25. See discussion of St Augustine in Barbara K. Lewalski, *Protestant Poetics and the Seventeenth Century Religious Lyric* (Princeton, 1979), pp. 49–50.
26. Anderson, ed., *Commentary*, I, pp. xxxviii–xxxix.
27. *The Psalms of Sir Philip Sidney and the Countess of Pembroke*, ed. J. C. A. Rathmell (New York, 1963), Psalm 111, lines 1–2. All further quotations from Mary Sidney's *Psalmes* are taken from this edition.
28. Hallett Smith, 'English metrical psalms in the sixteenth century and their literary significance', *Huntingdon Library Quarterly* 9 (1946), 249–71.
29. Anderson, ed., *Commentary*, III, pp. 167–8.
30. Diane Purkiss, 'Material girls: the seventeenth-century woman debate', in *Women, Texts, Histories 1575–1760*, ed. Clare Brant and Diane Purkiss (London, 1992), p. 71.
31. *Pierre Bourdieu: Outline of a Theory of Practice*, tr. Richard Nice (Cambridge, 1977), p. 22 (my emphasis).

9 'A grain of glorie': George Herbert and seventeenth-century devotional lyrics

Helen Wilcox

The English Renaissance – if we may stretch this notoriously vague term to encompass at least the first half of the seventeenth century as well as the late sixteenth century – witnessed the greatest flourishing of the religious lyric in the history of English literature. Poems on the individual's relationship with God were conceived, written, circulated, read, published, quoted, sung, copied out and imitated, with an excitement and fervour which it may be hard for us today to imagine. Some of the authors of these devotional poems will already be familiar – George Herbert, John Donne, Henry Vaughan, Richard Crashaw, Andrew Marvell – but there are many more names to add to even a selective list: Robert Southwell, Thomas Campion, Francis Quarles, An Collins, Henry Colman, John Abbot Rivers, Elizabeth Major, Cardell Goodman, Mary Carey, Thomas Washbourne, Vavasor Powell, and a woman called 'Eliza' known only from the title of her book of poems, *Eliza's Babes*.[1] Using evidence as wide-ranging as the titles on publishers' lists and the jottings in private commonplace-books, we can build up a picture of a thriving culture of holy verse. The purpose of this essay is to examine the poetry of the leading figure in this culture, George Herbert, in the wider context offered by contemplation of the phenomenon as a whole.

1. 'Gods own portion'

We may begin to understand the prominence of devotional lyrics when we recall that religion, though often treated with scholastic seriousness and the subject of great learning and formal dispute at the time, was in fact one of the fundamental elements of day-to-day life and popular culture in the English Renaissance. Jeremy Taylor summed up the prevailing, basically spiritual, understanding of the function of life when he wrote in 1650 that

> as every man is wholly Gods own portion by the title of creation: so all our labours and care, all our powers and faculties must be wholly imployed in the service of God, even all the dayes of our life . . .[2]

Although it is likely that only a pious few lived up to this ideal, it provides a salutary reminder of the routinely religious ideology of the period. In more practical terms, attendance at church on Sundays was required by law, and thus, whether they liked it or not, the great British public of the late sixteenth and early seventeenth centuries became familiar with the doctrines, language and rituals of the Church of England. In addition, sermons, often delivered out of doors, could be classed as a form of public entertainment and were liable to draw huge crowds. The Bible in English, available from the Reformation onwards but published in the 'Authorised Version' with the blessing of the King in 1611, was undoubtedly the most widely read (or listened to) book at the time. The sixteenth-century Reformation, turning the established church in England into a national protestant church rather than a part of that international phenomenon, Roman catholicism, had ostensibly made more room for the religious needs and local experiences of ordinary people. It led to the introduction of a more accessible vernacular church liturgy, collected together in the *Book of Common Prayer*,[3] and its theology laid greater stress on the individuality of redemption. Not only was a human being 'a little world made cunningly',[4] in which a world's-worth of spiritual and other activities took place, but Christians at this time were advised to keep close watch on the microcosm of their own selves, as Herbert wrote in his 'Church-porch':

> Summe up at night, what thou hast done by day;
> And in the morning, what thou hast to do.
> Dresse and undresse thy soul: mark the decay
> And growth of it . . .[5]

Thus the general context in England, in theological and practical terms, was marked by a heightened consciousness of personal religion. This led to a newly intense stress upon private discourse with the divine, by means of meditation, personal dialogue with God, prophetic and other visionary inspirations, and poetical expression of intimate relationships between God and the individual believer.

However, Christian thinking and practices were not only part of the everyday experience of social, moral and inner life at this time, but also essential to the political structures of Renaissance England. A clear example of this is the *Book of Homilies* which provided sermons to be read by ordinary ministers of the church Sunday by Sunday. During the reign of Elizabeth I these clearly functioned as instruments of social control, a fascinating mixture of moral instruction and political manipulation.[6] As religion was so close to the heart of both the nation and its individual subjects, expressions of political unrest and social tensions tended to emerge in the form of religious dissidence. The process worked both ways: critics of the established church, sometimes labelled 'puritans', also became associated with political radicalism. This complex interplay of theology and politics can be seen at its most extreme in the years leading up to the Civil War in the mid-seventeenth century, when it is difficult, and perhaps unwise, to attempt to disentangle secular and religious motivation in the affiliation of Royalist and Parliamentarian groupings.

As religion played such a prominent role in people's lives at this time, it is perhaps no surprise that many of them wrote about it – in doctrinal studies, polemical pamphlets, devotional manuals, published sermons and, of course, collections of poems. But given this context of religious tension and uncertainty, why is it that lyrical poetry[7] appealed to so many writers and readers during the English Renaissance? One possible explanation is that this short and apparently private poetic form offered a quiet, contemplative space in which to depict the conversations between God and the human soul, both for those who wrote and for those who entered this space by reading. This is to suggest that such poetry represented a sort of escape from the polemical, a retreat from the tension of argument and doctrinal controversy. There is surely some truth in this,[8] but there is also a danger that this theory allows us to distinguish too easily between the 'political' and 'personal' aspects of religion, which were in fact closely interwoven. This tendency is also present in the temptation for us, as literary historians, neatly to separate 'religion', in its formal and doctrinal mode, from the more personal 'devotion', and to say that the lyric expresses the second of these. For we have to realize that private devotion, spiritual meditation, and the expression of personal doubts and triumphs of faith, were all in themselves also theological positions. When a poet sought to explore and express his or her own individuality in a devotional lyric, this was in itself a statement that religious experience can be validly analysed in personal terms, and the language chosen betrayed some of the very same theological assumptions which were being formally and heatedly debated in contemporary pamphlets.

We are dealing here, therefore, with a polemic of the personal, which might be seen as the theological parallel to the literary phenomenon of a rhetoric of privacy. Both phrases contain within them the apparent contradiction that a private mood can be formally or publicly constructed; and both may be appropriately applied to the religious lyric in the English Renaissance. We should add here one further possible contradiction in the nature of the early seventeenth-century religious lyric which was also supplied by the contemporary theological context. In addition to the focus on spiritual selfhood which was intensified by the post-Reformation debates, there was increasing stress on the plainness of the language which should be used to address, and speak about, God. The activity surrounding newly translated vernacular prayer books and Bibles brought the issue of language itself to the fore, and raised the profile of simplicity as a linguistic virtue. This, naturally, introduced paradoxical elements into poems and sermons which consciously attempted to give expression to elaborate heavenly subjects in plain earthly language. However, to do otherwise, the argument went, would be to intrude the writer's or preacher's own art and skill into the process of praising the infinitely greater art of God. Any but the plainest human words would tamper with, or even dangerously mystify, the divine Word itself.

The religious context is, for these and many other reasons, vital to our understanding of the English Renaissance devotional lyric. The pervasive presence and influence of Christian traditions, structures and controversies must never be forgotten in our readings of the poems, however private the texts may seem. A recognition of the complex interplay of the political and devotional, or polemical and personal, in religious experience can help us to understand the role of the lyric in this period. The spiritual significance of questions of literary style in the English Renaissance must also form a starting point for our reading of this group of texts.

2. 'Who aimeth at the sky'

A poet has to have a peculiar mixture of ambition and humility to decide to write a religious lyric at any time, but particularly, as has been hinted above, to choose to do so in the 1620s, with controversy raging over so many of the ingredients of such a lyric: God, worship, individuality, words. In his sequence of poems posthumously published in 1633 as *The Temple*, George Herbert found a winning combination of modesty, vocation and skill, as his many readers in the seventeenth century and since have testified. The appeal of these lyrics seems to derive largely from a judicious balance of conflicting elements: personal and communal, plain and artful, and – perhaps most important of all – earthly and heavenly. One stanza in his introductory poem, 'The Church-porch', may help to interpret Herbert's attitude to the problem of the audacious poet on earth who is called to write about things above the sky. These lines are not themselves part of a discussion on how to write devotional verse, but, like most of 'The Church-porch', constitute advice to a 'sweet youth' trying to find his way in the world:

> Pitch thy behaviour low, thy projects high;
> So shalt thou humble and magnanimous be:
> Sink not in spirit: who aimeth at the sky,
> Shoots higher much then he that means a tree.
> A grain of glorie mixt with humblenesse
> Cures both a fever and lethargicknesse.
>
> (lines 331–6)

Herbert's words of encouragement to the ambitious worldly reader of 'The Church-porch' would appear also to anticipate the mood of the main body of Herbert's lyrics, 'The Church'; the stanza may be read as a blueprint for the work of a religious lyricist. The 'project' to address God in verse is 'high' – as high as a Christian poet could hope to reach – and does indeed 'aim at the sky'. But the extremes of 'feverish' overeagerness and 'sinking' lethargy, to which the self-conscious lyricist is prone, are countered by a double awareness: of the humility of the supplicant's position, yet also of the 'glorie' towards which he is bold enough 'to shoot'. The medical metaphor of the last couplet is typical of Herbert in its familiarity and accuracy; if a tiny dose of the hope of salvation is mixed, as in a homely recipe for a herbal cure, with the properly 'low' humility of a sinner, then it is indeed possible to reach the 'sky'. This is both the epitome of Herbert's spiritual attitude and an image of his stylistic aesthetics.

Herbert and his contemporaries well knew the difficulties of 'aiming at the sky'. It was all too easy to overreach and think that knowing the 'wayes of learning', as Herbert summed them up in 'The Pearl', would open the way to heaven. But aiming upwards without the humility of devotion would prove futile, as An Collins wrote in her *Divine Songs and Meditations* of 1653:

> He that hath studied astronomy,
> Though his meditation ascend to the sky
> He may miss of heaven and heavenly bliss
> If he can practise no study but this.[9]

The falseness of human vanity, in assuming that learned 'study' could take the place of faith, is here indicated by the deliberate ambiguity in Collins' use of the word 'meditation', which is both likened to 'study' and yet implicitly contrasted with it. 'Meditation' was a key term in the practice of devotion at this time, defined by Joseph Hall in 1606 as a 'bending of the mind upon some spiritual object', a concentrated and imaginative devotional act which would 'find out some hidden truth' or help with 'the enkindling of our love of God'.[10] In Collins' lines, then, ordinary human 'study' of the stars is set against a holy 'meditation' on the spiritual significance of the 'sky' beyond the stars. Many of the religious lyrics of the early seventeenth century derive from this practice of meditation, whether in formal terms or in a more generalized sense of creative concentration of devotional thoughts.[11] This did not mean that religious lyrics ignored the immediate human context; as Hall commented, the contemplation of 'inferior things'[12] in everyday life can inspire humans to a sense of God's presence and purpose. Herbert underlined this outlook when he wrote in *The Country Parson* that 'things of ordinary use', such as 'a plough, a hatchet, a bushell, leaven, boyes piping and dancing', were not only available for 'drudgery' but, metaphorically 'washed, and cleansed', could be used in meditations, sermons and poems to 'serve for lights even of Heavenly Truths'.[13]

In the strange paradox of faith, the way to 'reach heav'n, and much more thee',[14] was to recognize, as Herbert noted in his poem 'Coloss. 3.3', the 'double motion' of earthly and heavenly side by side:

My words & thoughts do both expresse this notion,
That *Life* hath with the sun a double motion.
The first *Is* straight, and our diurnall friend,
The other *Hid* and doth obliquely bend.
One life is wrapt *In* flesh, and tends to earth.
The other winds towards *Him*, whose happie birth
Taught me to live here so, *That* still one eye
Should aim and shoot at that which *Is* on high:
Quitting with daily labour all *My* pleasure,
To gain at harvest an eternall *Treasure*.

The poem enacts the process of planting a 'grain of glorie' in the humble soil of earthly language. The context of the poem, its own 'words & thoughts' as identified in the opening line, offers a framework into which the biblical quotation from Colossians 3, 'Our life is hid with Christ in God', can be embedded. While daily life is 'straight' and regular, the 'hidden' presence of an 'oblique' heavenly trajectory can be discerned within it, countering it but nevertheless expressed through it. The 'double motion' is not only that of 'flesh' and spirit, but also the double reading that the poem invites: horizontal, and diagonal. While one eye is on the familiar pattern of a poem's progress, the other 'can aim and shoot at that which *Is* on high' – a devotional attitude which is also a fascinating account of the reading process of this very visual poem. The same metaphor as in the more secular, 'Church-porch' passage discussed earlier, 'aiming' towards the sky, is here employed in an overtly spiritual way, looking to Christ, as well as with conscious overtones of the way Herbert's poem itself works. The technique is witty and skilful, to be sure, but the fundamental idea is supremely simple and consistent: we work simultaneously with humility and high aims, in poetic art as in life. The intention is that both 'motions' end up at the same goal, the '*Treasure*' which is both the last word of the poem and Christ, the original and ultimate 'Word'.

3. 'King of Glorie'

Once the devotional poet had set his or her eye firmly on the 'sky', one of the major purposes of writing was to express praise of God. To 'languish' in a 'drooping and dull' state, Herbert wrote in 'Dulnesse', is to imply that we are 'all earth':

> O give me quicknesse, that I may with mirth
> Praise thee brim-full!

As Herbert wisely advised the 'Country Parson', 'nature will not bear
everlasting droopings'.[15] To achieve the balance of the 'double
motion' as depicted in 'Coloss. 3.3', the believer must ensure plenty of
upward lifting of the heart in praise, to counter the inevitable lowering
of the spirit through sin and misery. Typically, much devotional poetry
expends its energy in wringing praise out of a gloomy sense of personal
failure and impending judgement, as in the fearful 'Holy Sonnets' of
Donne. But if a lyric begins rather than ends with a 'turning' of the
'face' to God,[16] the chances of mirthful praise are so much the greater.
Herbert's 'The Odour' opens with an almost sensual contemplation of
the title of Christ as his 'master':

> How sweetly doth *My Master* sound! *My Master!*
> As Amber-greese leaves a rich sent
> Unto the taster:
> So do these words a sweet content,
> An orientall fragrancie, *My Master.*

Here the poetic meditation is on something at once earthly and
spiritual: a phrase in language, but also one of the names of Christ. In
this linguistically conscious era, one way of finding a 'grain of glorie'
in the plainness of the everyday was to draw out the heavenly
implications of an ordinary phrase, letting the scriptural overtones be
heard. The power of the name of Christ, evoked in the title 'Master'
which asserts a bond of service on the part of the speaker, is here
rendered as immediate and as 'sweet' as the scent of an eastern
perfume, suggestive of the enormous significance accorded to mere
words. As Jeremy Taylor observed, the negative impact of this was to
call individuals to account for 'every idle word', making 'idle talking
and unprofitable discoursings' a cause of major concern.[17]

As an antidote to 'idle' words, devotional poets turned to the divine
word, the text of scripture, as the source of their own inspiration, the
starting point for their meditation, or (as we have already seen in
Herbert's 'Coloss. 3.3') words actually to be incorporated in their own
texts. The poets writing religious verse at this time claimed that they
needed no other muse than Christ, no other word than the Word, in
order to 'sing his praise'.[18] The 'Invocation' to Henry Colman's *Divine
Meditations* (1640) makes this abundantly clear:

I invoke noe Nymph, noe Grace, noe Muse
To helpe my wit, I vtterly refuse
All such fond aides, and call vpon thy name
Alone, O God t'inspire me with a flame
Terse, and sublime; that whatsoe'r I write
May season'd be by thy diviner Sp'rite;
Inspire my barren fancy, and distill
Such sacred matter through my feeble quill
That ev'ry line I write thy name may raise
And every leafe may celebrate thy praise.[19]

Traditional secular 'aides' to poetic inspiration are 'vtterly refused' here, peremptorily dismissed as 'fond', foolish and powerless; the only muse called upon, as in the opening of Herbert's 'The Odour', is the 'name' of God. This contrasting of secular and sacred muses is a familiar trope in spiritual writing, but in this instance we are reminded of how personal the process of religious inspiration was deemed to be. Unlike the 'nymphs' and 'graces' mentioned in the first line (only to be rejected), the influence of the holy spirit is not expressed as an external force or figure; it is internalized as a 'flame' which will in alchemical fashion 'distill' some 'sacred matter' through the writer's own pen. The poet is a vessel through which God is felt to work; the aesthetic is both intimately individual, and yet strangely impersonal in its apparent passivity. The aim of the devotional poet here is, ultimately, circular, as the final couplet makes clear: the 'name' which caused the poems to be written, and not the believer who held the pen, is then to be their subject, too. The paradox of the devotional writer's act is highlighted here: it is private yet not one's own, and it is physical and linguistic yet attempts to renounce the things of earth. With intriguingly material references to 'ev'ry line' of verse and 'every leafe' of his book, Colman consolidates the purpose of his writing, which is not material at all but the upward spiritual motion of 'praise'.

Herbert wrote three lyrics entitled simply 'Praise', and the second of these encapsulates the justification, and the joy, of praising God in verse:

King of Glorie, King of Peace,
        I will love thee;
And that love may never cease,
        I will move thee.

Thou hast granted my request,
      Thou hast heard me:
Thou didst note my working breast,
      Thou hast spar'd me.

Wherefore with my utmost art
      I will sing thee,
And the cream of all my heart
      I will bring thee.

Though my sinnes against me cried,
      Thou didst cleare me;
And alone, when they replied,
      Thou didst heare me.

Sev'n whole dayes, not one in seven,
      I will praise thee.
In my heart, though not in heaven,
      I can raise thee.

Thou grew'st soft and moist with tears,
      Thou relentedst:
And when Justice call'd for fears,
      Thou dissentedst.

Small it is, in this poore sort
      To enroll thee:
Ev'n eternitie is too short
      To extoll thee.

As the stanza form with its rhythmic refrain pattern suggests, this poem is conceived, like so may of Herbert's lyrics, as a *song* of praise: with 'utmost art' he will 'sing' God's 'Glorie'. The third stanza is the central statement of the poem's function, beginning with its very telling 'Wherefore'. The poem is written because of what God is and does, not just out of human whim. The song opens with a reminder that God's 'Glorie' and 'Peace' are the cause of the poet's response, and during the poem the qualities of noticing, listening, showing mercy and granting forgiveness are added to the list of divine attributes. So praise, in Herbert's view at least, is a reciprocal act, with its logic of 'wherefore'. The third stanza then introduces the possible clash of skill and sincerity: the poet sings with high 'art', but what he wishes to express is love, 'the cream of all my heart'. As in Colman's 'Invocation', there is an implicit sense that love and divine inspiration will be sufficient, a view also expressed by Herbert in 'A true Hymne'; but against this is set the striving for 'utmost art', the best, the most skilful poetic music which it is possible for the human writer to create. The attempt to reconcile the rhyming pair, 'heart' and 'art', is fundamental to the project undertaken by devotional poets, and was particularly controversial in the early seventeenth century when the whole question of art and faith, ritual grandeur versus 'true beauty',[20] was a cause of religious and political division. But the limit of both aspects of the human – the loving and the artful – is precisely that they are earthly; the only place where the poet can 'raise' God is in the 'heart' and not 'in heaven'. Again we are reminded of the 'grain of glorie', here the praise of the 'King of Glorie' which must be confined to 'this poore sort' and will always, the poet knows, fall short of its heavenly objective.

4. 'Then was my heart broken'

Much devotional poetry focuses on the human capacity repeatedly to 'fall short' – whether in art or in life – and takes as its subject the recurring phenomena of sin and inadequacy, the sufferings of earthly existence and the misery of being out of tune with God's harmony. In the early seventeenth century these were, as at any time, deeply personal experiences, but also continually formed the topics of heated theological debate. Was human distress the sign of a divine judgement on the individual concerned, or an unavoidable factor of human existence which had nevertheless been shared and overcome by Christ's death on the cross? Was the natural condition of humankind one of unalterable total depravity, as Calvinists argued, or could devotional 'zeal and desire', as Jeremy Taylor put it, lead individuals into 'the wayes of grace'?[21] In the century or so after the Reformation, these were matters of, quite literally, life and death to the devotional poets and their contemporaries.

Mary Carey was one of several seventeenth-century women poets who approached the issue of death and judgement through the bitter experience of the loss of a baby. In 1650 she wrote 'On the Death of my 4th, & only child, Robert Payler':

My lord hath called for my sonne
   my hart bre[a]th's forth; thy will be done:

my all; that mercy hath made mine
   frely's surrendered to be thine:

> But if I give my all to the[e]
> lett me not pyne for poverty:
>
> Change wth me; doe, as I have done
> give me thy all; Even thy deare sonne:
>
> Tis Jesus Christ; lord I would have;
> he's thine, mine all; 'tis him I crave:
>
> Give him to me; and I'le reply
> Enoughe my lord; now lett me dye.[22]

The poem begins with an attitude of humble acceptance of the mother's sorrowful lot, made all the more striking by its poignant simplicity. Her newborn child has been 'called for' by God, and she submits with her 'hart' to God's 'will', in a direct echo of the Lord's Prayer as well as the words of Christ the night before his crucifixion.[23] The free 'surrendering' of her son is expressed by Carey as a logical response to the original 'mercy' and generosity of God, an acceptance that human lives are in the hands of a greater power whose right it is to take as well as to give. However, at this point in the poem comes a resounding 'But', by which Carey makes it clear that she does not regard her distress as a judgement on her sinfulness, but rather a bargaining point in the larger scheme of redemption. As she has given her 'all' by losing her '4th, & only Child', so God must make an exchange and give his 'all' in the form of his only son, Jesus Christ. She 'craves' him, a startlingly urgent statement suggesting not only the mother's desire but the feminized soul's almost physical longing for her 'lord'. The final lines recall the ever-insistent threat of judgement: she will not die until she is sure of Christ by her side as her 'mediator and advocate', as the *Book of Common Prayer* puts it,[24] to plead for her salvation.

The ambivalent last line of Carey's elegiac poem raises the issue of how devotional poets close their poems of sorrow and protest. 'Enoughe my lord; now lett me die' could be interpreted as an unresolved ending, simply a cry that she has suffered 'enoughe' and seeks release from misery, whatever the consequences. But the preceding lines suggest that she hopes the words may imply otherwise: that the gift of Christ to her is 'enoughe' to secure her redemption and therefore she can die with confidence. The uneasy uncertainty of Carey's conclusion epitomizes the difficulty of reconciling suffering and faith, particularly in an era when the interpretation of life's events was enacted with such theological precision. What could such misery mean? Sometimes the consequent spiritual crises were worse even than their physical suffering or loss. Many of Herbert's poems express the agony of frustration that, however hard he tries, he cannot get into a right relationship with God. And for a writer whose poetic and theological focus was on endings, this raised the dilemma of how to find words and verse forms to express and, more importantly, escape from spiritual discontentedness.

Perhaps the finest example of this mood in *The Temple* is 'Deniall':

> When my devotions could not pierce
> Thy silent eares;
> Then was my heart broken, as was my verse:
> My breast was full of fears
> And disorder:
>
> My bent thoughts, like a brittle bow,
> Did fly asunder:
> Each took his way; some would to pleasures go,
> Some to the warres and thunder
> Of alarms.
>
> As good go any where, they say,
> As to benumme
> Both knees and heart, in crying night and day,
> *Come, come, my God, O come,*
> But no hearing.
>
> O that thou shouldst give dust a tongue
> To crie to thee,
> And then not heare it crying! all day long
> My heart was in my knee,
> But no hearing.
>
> Therefore my soul lay out of sight,
> Untun'd, unstrung:
> My feeble spirit, unable to look right,
> Like a nipt blossome, hung
> Discontented.
>
> O cheer and tune my heartlesse breast,
> Deferre no time;
> That so thy favours granting my request,
> They and my minde may chime,
> And mend my rhyme.

As its title implies, this is a poem wracked by the idea that the speaker is denied access to God. His maker, having given him a 'tongue' with which to express himself, now denies him a 'hearing'. In its vocabulary, as well as its 'broken' verse form, the lyric suggests a sense of utter and almost surreal dislocation. There is a 'broken' heart but also strangely 'silent' ears, which would not normally be expected to speak; 'bent thoughts' fly around, and 'dust', material of the body but here oddly disembodied, has a 'tongue'; there is a 'heart' in a 'knee', and a soul lying 'unstrung' like a dismembered musical instrument. The 'disorder' in the body, the spirit and the verse builds up to an image of chaos, the opposite of a created world in divine control. God will not respond to the call '*Come*'; has he abandoned his world and, in it, the miserable poet? Perhaps this sense of isolation, or Godforsaken-ness, is worse than any other spiritual despair; even the threat of judgement, perversely, may mean that God is taking some notice. But at this point, the other meaning of the title must come into play. Who is doing the denying? The idea that the speaker's spirit is 'unable to look right' becomes important; is it the speaker's outlook which is denying the possibility of contact with God, an attitude produced by 'fears' as when St Peter denied Christ?[25] The poem certainly seems to change direction, not when God is seen to alter in any way, but when the tone of the lyric voice itself changes from angry narrative to desperate prayer at the beginning of the last stanza. The poet asks for a speedy solution – 'deferre no time' – and expresses it in terms of the structure of his own verse: if the speaker and God are in renewed harmony, then instead of the previous 'untun'd' sounds there will be 'chime' and 'ryme' again. As this quotation reminds us, by the end of the lyric the formerly unrhymed last lines are indeed 'chiming', an emblem of recreated harmony in spiritual as well as poetic terms. Before the despairing speaker can even conclude the prayer which has emerged out of his suffering, that very prayer has, so the poem's form reassures us, been answered. The poet's wit, with its embedded metaphor of a divine poet at work with words which 'mend', closes the poem with an implicit theology of divine intervention: 'Deniall' concludes with a resounding denial of God's distance from human suffering.

Herbert's brief lyric, 'Bitter-sweet', sums up the activities of a devotional poet:

Ah my deare angrie Lord,
Since thou doast love, yet strike;
Cast down, yet help afford;
Sure I will do the like.

I will complain, yet praise;
I will bewail, approve;
And all my sowre-sweet dayes
I will lament, and love.

The poet is a respondent rather than an initiator; God's acts precede his or her own, which are then an imitation, an attempt to 'do the like'. In Herbert's ironic tit-for-tat, the 'like' consists of the mixture of praise and complaint which we have seen are the fundamental attitudes of the religious lyricist. The language may well be simple, and the mood is intimate; but as we have also noted, these are not straightforwardly personal poems. In a context of sensitivity to the individuality of belief, of controversy over how to interpret human experience, the polemic over the truthful beauty of plain words, the lyric offered a very public privacy. After all, no 'humblenesse' could be allowed totally to veil the presence of 'glorie'.

Notes

1. *Eliza's Babes: or The Virgins-Offering* (London, 1652).
2. Jeremy Taylor, *Holy Living* (1650), ch. I, ed. P. G. Stanwood (Oxford, 1989), p. 17. See also the *Documents* section below, pp. 294–6.
3. See, for example, the *Documents* section below, pp. 258–9.
4. John Donne, 'Holy Sonnet' V, in *The Complete English Poems of John Donne*, ed. C. A. Patrides (London, 1985), p. 437.
5. George Herbert, 'The Church-porch', lines 451–4, in *The English Poems of George Herbert*, ed. C. A. Patrides (London, 1974), p. 45. All further references to Herbert's poems are taken from this edition and are cited by title only.
6. See the extract in the *Documents* section below, pp. 257–8.
7. For a discussion of what defines the religious lyric in this period, see my ' "Curious Frame": the seventeenth-century religious lyric as genre', in *New Perspectives on the Seventeenth-Century Religious Lyric*, ed. J. R. Roberts (Columbia, Missouri, 1994), pp. 9–27.
8. I considered the idea of the religious lyric as retreat from controversy in 'Exploring the language of devotion in the English Revolution', in *Literature and the English Civil War*, ed. Thomas Healy and Jonathan Sawday (Cambridge, 1990), pp. 75–88.

9. An Collins, from 'A Song demonstrating the vanities of earthly things', in *Her Own Life: Autobiographical writings by seventeenth-century Englishwomen*, ed. Elspeth Graham, Hilary Hinds, Elaine Hobby and Helen Wilcox (London, 1989), p. 67.

10. Joseph Hall, *The Art of Divine Meditation* (1606), ch. II, in F. L. Huntley, *Bishop Joseph Hall and Protestant Meditation in Seventeenth-Century England* (Binghamton, New York; 1981), p. 72. See the *Documents* section below, pp. 296–301.

11. See, for example, Louis L. Martz, *The Poetry of Meditation* (New Haven, 1954), and Barbara K. Lewalkski, *Protestant Poetics and the Seventeenth-Century Religious Lyric* (Princeton, 1979).

12. Hall, *The Art of Divine Meditation*, ch. III, in Huntley, *Bishop Joseph Hall*, p. 73.

13. Herbert, *A Priest to the Temple, or, The Country Parson his Character and Rule of Holy Life*, ch. XXI, in *The Works of George Herbert*, ed. F. E. Hutchinson (Oxford, 1941), p. 257.

14. Herbert, 'Affliction' (IV).

15. Herbert, *A Priest to the Temple*, ch. XXVII, in *Works*, ed. Hutchinson, p. 268.

16. Donne, 'Good Friday, 1613. Riding Westward', in *The Complete English Poems*, ed. Patrides, p. 456.

17. Taylor, *Holy Living*, ch. I section I, p. 19.

18. Herbert, 'Easter'.

19. Henry Colman, *Divine Meditations (1640)*, ed. Karen E. Steanson (New Haven, 1979), p. 69.

20. Herbert, 'The Forerunners'.

21. Taylor *Holy Living*, ch. I, p. 17. For a discussion of Calvinist doctrine in relation to the lyrics of Herbert, see Richard Strier, *Love Known: Theology and Experience in George Herbert's Poetry* (Chicago, 1983).

22. Mary Carey, *My Lady Carey's Meditation and Poetry*, Bodleian Rawl. MS D.1308, p. 149, in *Kissing the Rod: An Anthology of Seventeenth-Century Women's Verse*, ed. Germaine Greer, Jeslyn Medoff, Melinda Sansone and Susan Hastings (London, 1988), pp. 156–7. I have added letters in square brackets where the meaning is otherwise unclear from the original spelling.

23. Matthew 26.42 'O my Father, if this cup may not pass away from me, except I drink it, thy will be done'.

24. 'Grant this, O Father, for Jesus Christ's sake, our only mediator and advocate', the closing words of the prayer for the church during the Communion Service, in *The Book of Common Prayer, 1559: The Elizabethan Prayer Book*, ed. John E. Booty (Charlottesville, Virginia, 1976), p. 254.

25. Matthew 26.75: 'And Peter remembered the word of Jesus, which said unto him, Before the cock crow, thou shalt deny me thrice. And he went out, and wept bitterly'.

10 Marvell's news from nowhere

John Hoyles

Marvell's writings from the 1640s to the 1670s both engage with, and disengage from, the burning issues of his day. The twin themes of political and sexual commitment are causes too good to be fought for by a poet and satirist who never lost sight of his ironic utopia as both the best place and nowhere.

To flesh out this argument I have divided the body of my text into the following sections: 1. An introductory meditation on Marvell's unique brand of poetic utterance in which the green freedom of poetry feeds off a knowledge of the red necessity of politics (including sexual politics). Texts addressed include 'The Mower Against Gardens', *The Rehearsal Transprosed*, 'A Dialogue between the Resolved Soul and Created Pleasure' and 'A Dialogue between the Soul and Body'. 2. An investigation of sexual commitment in Marvell's work, with special reference to the Pastoral Dialogues, 'The Picture of Little T.C.' and 'The Unfortunate Lover', the Mower Poems, and the 'Coy Mistress'. 3. An investigation of political commitment in Marvell's work, with special reference to his early Royalist tendencies, to the 'Horatian Ode', and to 'Bermudas' and 'The First Anniversary'. 4. A meditation on the green dream of utopian detachment which underpins Marvell's sexual and political attachments, with special reference to 'The Garden', 'Upon Appleton House' and 'The Mower Against Gardens'.

Readers are advised to have the texts of poems by their side when following my commentary.[1]

1. 'That famous flower the Marvell of Peru'

Another world was searched, through oceans new,
To find the *Marvel of Peru*.
And yet these rarities might be allowed
To man, that sovereign thing and proud.
('The Mower Against Gardens')

. . . those various accidents which perplex our actions and make them
like that famous flower the Marvell of Peru, which changes the colour
of its leaves every day. (Anthony Ascham, *The Bounds and Bonds of
Public Obedience*, 1649)

The Marvel of Peru may be a fortuitous trope but it tells us that
Andrew Marvell (1621–78) was a rare plant in English letters and that
the garden he grew in was both public and private, political and lyrical.
In 'The Mower Against Gardens', Marvell is, amongst other things,
protesting against horticultural imperialism. The sin of pride can allow
sovereignty to get out of hand and reduce the human condition to a
thing. Charles I, King of England by divine right, allowed his
sovereignty to get so out of hand that on 30 January 1649 he found
himself (a very special sovereign thing) on the scaffold, victim of the
mower's revenge. The trial and execution of the English sovereign is
certainly the chief among 'those various accidents which perplex our
actions and make us like that famous flower the Marvell of Peru'. And,
we are invited to assume, no-one was more perplexed than that famous
flower's namesake, poet, puritan and patriot, Andrew Marvell.

The Marvel of Peru is a fitting emblem for a writer whose rarity
was to have been both a famous flower in the garden of English poetry
(albeit barely discovered until the twentieth century) and a consistent
defender of English constitutional liberties. Botanically the Marvel of
Peru is *Mirabilis Jalapa*, otherwise known as the four o'clock, a
tropical American plant with yellow, red or white flowers that open
in the late afternoon. Though Marvell (unlike his junior contemporary
Dryden) was no Vicar of Bray, it could be argued that he enjoyed that
cast of mind praised by Keats as essential in the true poet, that negative
capability of the chameleon, which like Ascham's famous flower
'changes the colour of its leaves everyday' precisely because it grows
in troubled climes and times and is subject to those 'various accidents
which perplex our actions'.

But what is good for poetry is not necessarily good for politics. One of the issues perplexing men's minds following the execution of their king was the so-called Engagement Controversy. One of the principal contributors to the debate as to whether people should sign an oath of allegiance to the new regime in the years 1649–52 was Anthony Ascham (c. 1618–50). In his pamphlets *Of the Confusions and Revolutions of Governments* (1648) and *The Bounds and Bonds of Public Obedience* (1649) Ascham took a principled secular approach to politics (akin to that of Hobbes) and argued for the Engagement. Unlike Marvell, who was still a bit of a Royalist, Ascham played a part in drawing up charges against Charles and in 1650 was sent to Spain as ambassador of the new regime. He was assassinated in Madrid by *émigré* Royalists before he had time to present his credentials. Marvell eventually came round to Ascham's position, but by 1653 when Milton first tried to get Marvell a job, and certainly by 1657 when Marvell became Latin Secretary to the Council of State under Cromwell, the Engagement Controversy was no longer an issue. Marvell thus avoided having to commit himself until circumstances made him a servant of the new powers-that-be.

Taking a government job at £200 a year engaged Marvell politically, though never so deeply as Ascham or Milton. Perhaps his more symptomatic engagement was as tutor to Lord Fairfax's daughter Mary at Nun Appleton House in Yorkshire. This was a disengaged engagement during which time (1650–52) he wrote his great lyrics, vexed and perplexed in his cool green manner with the relative values of commitment and withdrawal, as befited an employee of that commander of the parliamentary army who so resembled Fabius Cunctor that he turned the moderate's tendency to delay into a fine art of virtual retreat. From 1659 until his death Marvell assiduously performed his engagements as MP for Hull. He became one of the leading lights in the emerging opposition to Charles II's personal rule and defended the constitutional rights of the English Parliament and people in a series of outspoken satires against absolutism in the 1670s.

Just as Milton's work suffered from the ideological dissociation of sensibility whereby prose and poetry are declared separate spheres of influence (in Milton's case as defined by Dr Johnson, the prose was republican and evil, the poetry sublime and good), so was Marvell's work divided between his Restoration political satire and his Nun Appleton lyrics. The former gave him the long-lasting reputation as a constitutional patriot as celebrated in William Mason's 1756 'Ode to

Independency'; the latter was rescued from oblivion by Grierson and Eliot in 1921, though a minor critic writing in 1901 (in preparation perhaps of the Georgian movement) acclaimed Marvell as 'the laureate of grass and greenery'. It took the impact of modernism to recognize Marvell as a great poet, textually edited by Margoliouth in 1927 and critically surveyed by Legouis in 1928. But in spite of Grosart's antiquarian Victorian edition of the complete works, it is only recently that Marvell's poetry and prose have been put back together again for the general reader.[2]

What has the laureate of grass and greenery got to do with English liberties? My own approach to Marvell picks out as his most interesting writings 'To His Coy Mistress', the 'Horatian Ode' (1650) and 'The Garden' from the Nun Appleton period together with *The Rehearsal Transprosed* (1672–73). From the later prose satire I pick out Marvell's luminous but enigmatic description of the Puritan Revolution as 'a cause too good to be fought for' and apply this back from the prose to the poetry.

It is often asked of Marvell's work, 'what side is it on?'. In my view his work in verse and prose is marked by a fascinating combination of engagement and disengagement which is not so much a sign of vacillation or even moderation as a dialectic of opposites inscribed in the texts themselves. Thus in the love poems, sexual engagement is a cause too good to be fought for and the 'Coy Mistress' poem pursues this paradox to the climax of the sexual act itself. Thus in the public poems, political engagement is a cause too good to be fought for and the 'Horatian Ode' pursues this paradox to the climax of Cromwell's revolutionary activity. And thus in the green poems, sexual and political disengagement are ironically celebrated as the narrator of 'The Garden' indulges his own fantastic dream of escaping the rigours of a world full of sex and politics.

Finally it should be noted that although Marvell clearly takes sides in his Restoration pamphlets, there is a sense in which the finest prose passages in *The Rehearsal Transprosed* transcend their party political function. As Swift pointed out in that astounding manifesto of the English Enlightenment, the Preface to *A Tale of a Tub*, we read Marvell against Parker not so much because Marvell was on the right side and Parker on the wrong side (indeed from Swift's point of view Marvell was on the wrong side), but because of Marvell's wit. Wit may be engaged in party political struggle, it may be Whig or Tory, but to be engaged (and engaging) as literature which enlightens the human spirit, it must sparkle. Whether he operates in the genre of metaphysical verse or satirical prose, Marvell sparkles as a writer committed to the cause that is too good to be fought for. As Christopher Hill has pointed out, Marvell's irony is made possible only by deep conviction. His irony is not a defence mechanism to hide a lack of commitment, but rather a device or persona whereby the riddling paradox of the human condition may be scrutinized with a view to understanding and improvement.

The dialectic between engagement and disengagement in Marvell's work finds its most succinct expression in the two 'Body and Soul' poems. As its title indicates, 'A Dialogue between the Resolved Soul and Created Pleasure' is a committed poem in which there is a clear surplus of conviction beyond the play of irony. In the manner of Milton's 'Comus', the poem's dialogue is subject to the ideological programme of platonic and Puritan armed struggle against Cavalier temptation. The Soul, like Bunyan's Christian, has put its armour on and is ready to fight the good fight. The temptations of created pleasure (taste, touch, smell, sight, sound, beauty, riches, glory, knowledge) are successfully resisted. The soul is particularly brave when it resists the hyperbolic ironic utopia of the sybaritic rosebed ('roses strewed so plain / Lest one leaf thy side should strain', lines 21–2).

Or is it? 'Conscious of doing what I ought' (line 24), the soul cannot escape the implications of its own rather hollow priggishness. And this sense that the resolved soul is too ridiculously resolved is accentuated by the mechanical piety of the chorus. And yet, even if the conviction is subject to some ironical disturbance, the engagement controversy is clearly defined and the poem may be taken to represent Marvell's transparent understanding of the need to know what side he is on. As in Milton's great prose tracts, the body belongs to the Cavaliers, the soul to the Puritans. Marvell is on the side of the Puritans (later the Whigs). He knows that consciousness equals conscience and that the Creator is greater than the creation. He has written a poem in the tradition of Herbert's 'Pearl' in which the powerful attractions of Renaissance culture are evoked only to be abandoned in the interests of a higher moral and spiritual principle.

In 'A Dialogue between the Soul and Body' there is no resolution. This poem is marvellously opaque, schizophrenic and caught up in its own perplex. There is civil war and Cartesian dualism at the heart of the human condition. The body and the soul have equally convicing arguments and complaints about having to live together.

It is, however, significant that the body has the last word, and an extra four lines, in which the soul is blamed for sin and for messing about with nature ('So architects do square and hew, / Green trees that in the forest grew', lines 43–4). Here Marvell is moving into his green dreamworld. The cause of humanity is too good to be fought for. Civil war rends not only the body politic but also the little world of man. Here the soul gains no victory, and the narrator slips away from civilization and its discontents to become a green thought in a green shade as far away from the architects of this world as possible.

2. Sexual commitment

This Ecstasy doth unperplex . . .
We see by this, it was not sex,
We see, we saw not what did move.

(John Donne, 'The Ecstasy')

No wars unless our rams well fed
Butt at each other's curled head;
No work unless perhaps you find
Bees dig in king-cups golden mine;
No fold to keep one lamb from harms,
Only, Dorinda, thee mine arms.

('A Dialogue between Thyrsis and Dorinda')

Donne's sexual utopia lies in a negatively defined transcendent ecstasy. For Marvell love's mysteries are dialectically presented in terms of a fantastic green disengagement at odds with the red bloody warfare of sexual engagement. The key to the expressive power of 'To His Coy Mistress' is that love, like political revolution, is a cause too good to be fought for. And yet love, like history, has its own red necessity. Thus sexual activity is forced to a conclusion in the 'Coy Mistress' just as political activity is forced to a conclusion in the 'Horatian Ode'. The green love of Marvell's ironic utopia is always predicated within his male fantasy on the threat of red female sexuality. These two drives (one green, the other red) are dramatically juxtaposed in the 'Coy Mistress', but elsewhere the green dream prevails.

In the pastoral dialogues the well-worn motifs of Theocritus are given a marvellous millenarian shape. The poet enters into an engagement controversy with eros in a search for that sexual utopia beyond flesh and death. In 'A Dialogue between Thyrsis and Dorinda' the lovers' death-wish is fulfilled in an abandonment of work and an orgy of poppies and wine: 'So shall we smoothly pass away in sleep' (line 48). The sexual utopia is also a socio-economic utopia as the extra six lines quoted above and absent from some editions indicate: 'No wars . . . No work . . . No fold . . . Only, Dorinda, thee mine arms.'[3]

The abolition of war, work and property is a tall order indeed. This utopia is both marvellous and absurd. When Dorinda says to Thyrsis: 'Let us spend our time to come / In talking of Elysium' (lines 29–30), the reader is pulled beyond the conventional discourse of nymphs and shepherds into a world where the intertextual echoes include the marvellous (Wesker's 'I'm talking about Jerusalem') and the absurd (Eliot's 'The women come and go talking of Michelangelo'). When Marvell's nymphs and shepherds spend their time talking about Elysium, the irony does not shatter the conviction, indeed (as in the 'Coy Mistress') the irony heightens the conviction.

All the correct pastoral furniture is in place (rams, bees, buttercups and lambs) but the poem is profoundly engaged in its fantasy vision of a world without war or work, a world where there is not even one lost sheep, a religious and erotic paradise where in the syntactically collapsed 'thee mine arms', the lovers' intertwined arms are the only form of defence required in a demilitarized world. Marvell knows it's impossible, and so do we; but he wants the impossible and so do we. Talking about Elysium, Michelangelo, Jerusalem – that is to speak of the fatuous and the sublime, the marvellous and the absurd in the same breath – and that's what poets are for.

Marvell's variations on Greek pastoral are investigations into green sex, sex without war, property or work. Clorinda and Damon in the poem of that name debate the issues. The male soul appears resolved to resist the temptation of the female body. What Clorinda calls 'that unfrequented cave', Damon calls 'that den'; what Clorinda calls 'Love's Shrine', Damon calls 'virtue's grave' (lines 9–10). That cool sex which for Clorinda is 'safe from the sun' is for Damon not safe from 'heaven's eye' (line 12). Pastoral sex is safe sex but Damon is not convinced. Clorinda carries on her cool tease, waxing clinical in her detached description of the sexual landscape around love's shrine: 'Near this, a fountain's liquid bell / Tinkles within the concave shell.' To which Damon in the pastoral mode of polite innocence responds: 'Might a soul bathe there and be clean, / Or slake its drought?' (lines 13–15).

Damon's problem is that he is under the influence of the great god Pan. Clorinda's sexual challenge must be diverted, sublimated into a pantheism of green sex, removed from female seduction. Damon is now safe from the dangerous distractions of Clorinda's liquid bell and concave shell. He has transferred his affections to the great god Pan: 'And his name swells my slender oat' (line 23).

Since Marvell is disarmingly bland and enigmatic about all this, he's not going to tell us what he means. And so as modern readers we say: Ah, the binary sexual division is transcended by self-embowered auto-eroticism; or, Damon's fragile penis (that slender oat emblematic of the limits of masculinity) proving impotent before the shrine of female sexuality is turned into a pan-pipe, thus demonstrating that unsuccessful sexual energies can be sublimated into successful artistic energies; or, we might even plump for the idea that Pan is typologically Christ, so that Damon becomes the psalm-singing born-again Puritan who can no longer cavort with Clorinda, Amaryllis and all those other Cavalier lasses in the shade.

Take all that on board, and what is left is Marvell's tone, at once opaque and translucent, serious and tongue-in-cheek, passionate and ironic, engaged and disengaged, semi-detached. When the Chorus concludes that 'all the world is our Pan's choir' (line 30), Marvell puts us in touch (as he so often does) with that lightly sketched green utopia (never quite coterminous with any actual sexual or political activity) which lies at the core of his poetic vision.

In a third pastoral dialogue, 'Ametas and Thestylis Making Hay-ropes', rope is the manufactured hay produced by the two agricultural labourers. The poem enacts an escape from rope to hay, from work to play, from labour to love, from laboured love to casual sex. This sexual utopia bypasses or cuts through the tangled knot of unrequited love. Male phallocentric tropes (stand = erection; disband = unpaid soldiers deserting the army) are countered by the female argument that twist and twine (i.e. the battle of the sexes) are necessary both to make love out of desire and rope out of hay. The male complains that woman's love is looser than ropes of hay. The woman counters the impossible male hope of constancy with a definition of love as contingent and occasional. This comes across as both a tease and as female pragmatism ('taken as you may', line 14). And in the logic of the carefully measured intellectual dialogue, it allows the male to check-mate with 'Then let's both lay by our rope, / And go kiss within the hay' (lines 15–16).

The game is over thanks to the device whereby the hay-ropes perform the role of a dialogic trope enabling the sexual partners to twist and twine in the hay. The poet has removed his pastoral players from the social world of agricultural labour into the fantasy world of sexual bliss. It is also possible that ropes (which bind) stand for courtly love and civilized values, whereas the hay stands for a prelapsarian undifferentiated nature unworked by surplus labour. Within the larger context of Marvell's work, where sex and politics are fraught with danger and where sometimes engagement is forced on the would-be disengager, these pastoral dialogues are meditations hung upon the maypole of life, green thoughts in a green shade.

The threat of adult female sexuality and the thought that love may be a cause too good to be fought for are motifs which inform all of Marvell's investigations into the nature of eros. Only in the 'Coy Mistress' is the battle fought and won. Elsewhere his poetic persona conjures up spectacles of blood (as in 'The Unfortunate Lover'), of a world scorched by sex (as in the Mower poems), or a voyeuristic retreat into a world of little girls (as in 'Little T.C.' and 'Young Love'). Indeed, in 'Mourning' there is the suggestion that the highest form of love is onanistic narcissism, or as Camille Paglia would put it, self-embowered autoeroticism. In that poem a bereaved young woman in a 'solitary bower' 'courts herself in amorous rain . . . herself both Danae and the shower' (lines 18–20). And in 'Definition of Love' Marvell appears to place an impossible, divine, platonic love above anything that might be possible in this world.

Marvell's unfortunate lover in the poem of that name has been expelled from his green utopia where 'infant Love yet plays' in 'shadows green' (lines 2–4). His fate, which resembles that of England in the civil wars, is evoked in phrases such as being 'split . . . in a Caesarian section' (lines 15–16), being subject to a 'tyrant Love' with 'winged artillery' (lines 45–6), being 'dressed / In his own blood' (lines 55–6), being 'forced to live in storms and wars' (line 60), the whole 'spectacle of blood' (line 42) being summed up in the heraldic device of 'a lover gules . . . in a field sable' (line 64). Gules, from the French *gueule* meaning throat and more technically red-dyed fur neck ornaments, creates an emblem of sexuality viewed as red and bloody against the black backcloth of 'the funeral of the world' (line 24). Sex equals warfare and death.

In 'Young Love' Marvell lightly touches on a utopian alternative where he will love a 'little infant' whose 'fair blossoms are too green

/ Yet for lust, but not for love' (lines 11–12). In a world before Freud and *Lolita* these 'sportings' are declared to be 'as free / As the nurse's with the child' (lines 7–8). But in 'The Picture of Little T.C. in a Prospect of Flowers' the world of 'Young Love' is juxtaposed with the world of 'The Unfortunate Lover'.

Little T.C., possibly a real little girl called Theophila Cornewall born in 1644, is associated with 'green grass' (line 3) and only plays with the roses. Marvell fantasizes that she will stay a violet for as long as possible and manage to disarm the roses of their thorns. But he knows what fate awaits this Alice once she grows up and out of her wonderland. She will have to confront the adult world of 'wanton Love' (line 12). If her chastity resists under the severe command of Puritan generalship she will still cause havoc, war and bloodshed among her suitors, perhaps Cavalier beaux who will be defeated ('bow broke and ensigns torn', line 14) in battle. In any case she will be a fierce power in the land, and, like Cromwell, her 'conquering eyes' with their 'glancing wheels' will have enough 'force to wound' (lines 18–20). Against this threat of triumphal female sexuality, Marvell sets his green dream of detached voyeurism: 'Let me be laid, / Where I may see thy glories from some shade' (lines 23–4). These variations on the theme of infant love are part and parcel of Marvell's dialectic of sex. They contribute to the rich texture of the 'Coy Mistress' where green and red fight it out to the finish.

The Mower poems add another dimension, but some of their thoughts can be aligned with the theme of sexual commitment. Damon the Mower in the poem of that name has been stung by Juliana's 'scorching beams' (line 24). He is feverish with 'unusual heats' (line 9) and 'hot desires' (line 26). Love is a snake which 'glitters in its second skin' (line 16) and his attempt to disarm it 'of its teeth and sting' (line 36) utterly fails. He has received his death-wound from Juliana's eyes, but he knows that in reality he is responsible for his own downfall. All flesh is grass (Isaiah 40.6). Damon has scythed himself. Falling on grass, he is 'the Mower mown' (line 80). In 'The Mower to the Glow-worms' Juliana is blamed for the mower's distraction, alienation and lunacy: 'For she my mind hath so displaced / That I shall never find my home' (lines 15–16). And in 'The Mower's Song', with its mesmerized incantatory refrain ('Juliana comes, and she / What I do to the grass, does to my thoughts and me', lines 23–4), the 'greenness of the grass' (line 3) is no protection from the sexual death-wish as the protagonist's 'thoughts more green' end up as 'heraldry' for his 'tomb' (lines 26–8).

This motif in the Mower poems finds an echo in 'The Nymph Complaining for the Death of her Fawn', where the nymph, having seen her pet shot by 'wanton troopers riding by' (line 1) (a random casualty of some Civil War skirmish?), remembers that utopian period in her life before sex and politics reared their ugly heads, a time when she had 'a garden of her own' (line 71) in which she could 'play' her 'solitary time away' (lines 37–8) with only her fawn whose love was so much 'better than / The love of false and cruel men' (lines 53–4). Neither the mower nor the nymph can escape the cruel rigours of sex and politics. The green dream is doomed.

In the 'Coy Mistress' a green dream of vegetable love is indulged in with some seriousness. The passion and irony underscore each other on a knife-edge between utopia and reality. Courtly love of the platonic variety has its attractions. Marvell can play the game by the rules. Those *blasonneurs* whose poems meticulously divide up the woman's body into heraldic devices reminiscent of the butcher's cuts of meat are referred to in homage as well as pastiche: 'For, Lady, you deserve this state; / Nor would I love at lower rate' (lines 19–20).

By 1649, however, that which is 'vaster than empires, and more slow' (line 12) was in some peril. History has split the body politic; civil war has effected a Caesarian section before the fruit of any vegetable love can come to full term. Revolutionary politics has accelerated the normal course of history. Love, like reform, is too good a cause to be fought for, but it is being fought for and so the lover, like the politician, must join the fray. Within the genre of the *carpe diem* convention this means that we must act before time runs out. 'That long-preserved virginity' (line 28) must not be left for the worms. Love must act in the bodily matter of the here and now, otherwise the sexual organs of male lust and female 'quaint honour' (line 29) will end up under the ground: 'The grave's a fine and private place, / But none, I think, do there embrace' (lines 31–2).

The green dream has to be fought for in the three-dimensional world of history and the senses. In this poem the mower will not be mown. The old *Liebestod* of western culture and the new-fangled Cartesian dualism which threatened a dissociation of sensibility by separating body from soul will be transcended in a sexual commitment braver by far than those easy Cavalier lays. And so the soul is extended through the pores of the skin with its glue/dew/hue (lines 33–4) (whichever variant you fancy) and the lovers become 'amorous birds of prey' (line 38), not, as in 'The Unfortunate Lover' and elsewhere, to tear each other apart, but, like Cromwell, to ruin the work of vegetable time, fit only for vast slow monarchies, to join the cause that was too good to be fought for, to 'tear our pleasures with rough strife, / Thorough the iron gates (or grates) of life' (lines 43–4), to transcend subjection to love as tyrant, to forge through mutual activity a commonwealth of love, to triumph over the powers-that-be, political, sexual, metaphysical: 'Thus, though we cannot make our sun / Stand still, yet we will make him run' (lines 45–6).

The green dream of disengagement has incarnated itself in sexual commitment. The cause too good to be fought for has been joined.

3. Political commitment

> I do declare and promise that I will be true and faithful to the Commonwealth of England as it is now established, without a king or House of Lords.
>
> (An Act for Subscribing the Engagement, 2 January 1650)

> Whether it were a War of Religion, or of Liberty, is not worth the labour to enquire. Which-soever was at the top, the other was at the bottom; but upon considering all, I think the Cause was too good to have been fought for. Men ought to have trusted God; they ought and might have trusted the King with that whole matter . . . For men may spare their pains where Nature is at work, and the world will not go the faster for our driving.
>
> (*The Rehearsal Transprosed*, 1672)[4]

Writing against ecclesiastical tyranny under Charles II, Marvell has the benefit of hindsight. And yet the Puritan Revolution under Cromwell had made the world go faster, and in the 1650s Marvell joined the good old cause and, like the lovers in the 'Coy Mistress', helped to speed up history and make the sun run. Marvell may not have had to subscribe to the Engagement of 2 January 1650, but in the summer of that year he composed 'An Horatian Ode upon Cromwell's Return from Ireland', a poem which matches Yeats's 'Easter 1916' as a passionate and critical investigation into the pros and cons of political commitment.

The 'Horatian Ode' is Marvell's special contribution to the Engagement Controversy and the place where he most succinctly expresses the dramatic situation in which the English people found themselves following the execution of Charles I. The 'Ode' was such a hot potato that it was cancelled in most copies of the 1681 Folio and not printed again until 1776.

Just as the 'Coy Mistress' gains some of its power from Marvell's ironic hankering after the slow progress of courtly vegetable love, so the 'Ode' is enhanced by the traces of Marvell's residual Royalism. In 1639, aged eighteen, he had run away from Cambridge and briefly converted to Roman Catholicism. His father found him in London and sent him back to university. In a tribute to the imprisoned Cavalier poet Lovelace (1649?) he had complained that 'our Civil Wars have lost the civic crown' (line 12) and that wit was now corrupted by the 'reforming eye' of the Presbyterians (characterized as both 'young' and 'grim', lines 22–4). In an elegy on the death in a Royalist uprising of the son of the first Duke of Buckingham (1648), he referred to 'heavy Cromwell' (line 14) and 'long-deceived Fairfax' (line 16). Part of his complaint in his elegy on Lord Hastings (1649) is that 'the democratic stars did rise' (line 25). And in his 1650 attack on the presbyterian hack-poet Tom May, he once again (in private) parades his anti-republican sentiments. Cromwell is no better than Spartacus (line 74). Faction prevails ('Must we Guelphs and Ghibillines be?', lines 61–2). And all the poet can do is to sing of 'ancient rights and better times' (line 69).

The 'Horatian Ode' carries this baggage in its text, but now (after 1649 as after 1916) all is changed and a terrible beauty is born. The poet is forced by events out of his green dream into the red world of political commitment.

The adjectives are ambiguous ('forward youth', line 1, 'restless Cromwell', line 9), but the verbs ('breaking', line 14, 'burning', line 21, 'rent', line 22, 'blast', line 24) cut through the sensitive habits of the detached spectator: 'So much one man can do, / That does both act and know' (lines 75–6). Cromwell is God's instrument in history. The cameo of Charles's execution, though it has been interpreted as a tribute of the kind Burke paid Marie Antoinette, is in fact a sideshow within the poem. Charles quite clearly does not both act and know. He is merely the 'royal actor' adorning the 'tragic scaffold' (lines 53–4). Success on the stage is no substitute for failure in the world of politics and history (as Shakespeare's poetic Richard II discovered). The only applause Charles deserves is what he gets when Cromwell's soldiers 'clap their bloody hands' (line 56).

Marvell is coming round to the position of the Engagers, but not without thinking the matter through. Cromwell is praised for leaving 'his private gardens' (line 29) to save the country from chaos, and if he is the falcon who devours Irish rebels as efficiently as the lovers in the 'Coy Mistress' devour their time, he is nonetheless a falcon who can hear the falconer. Unlike the anarchic-cum-totalitarian political landscape evoked in Yeats's apocalyptic 'Second Coming', Cromwell is not yet a dictator out of control but, like the falcon, 'still in the Republic's hand' (line 82). In a splendid image of the revolution armed and not yet betrayed, Cromwell is likened to a bird of prey who 'having killed, no more does search / But on the next green bough to perch' (lines 93–4).

Marvell's soul in the interior landscape of his garden takes up a similar perch (line 53). But in this poem, unlike 'The Garden', there is important work to be done by Cromwell and the English Republic on behalf of the international protestant liberation movement, and Marvell, a new recruit to the cause, rejoices (as Milton did in his defence of the English people) that England has sent such a clear and powerful message 'to all states not free' (line 103), i.e. those under the yoke of Roman Catholic ecclesiastical tyranny.

Marvell consolidates his new-found commitment in 'Bermudas' (1653) and 'The First Anniversary' (1655). In 'Bermudas' the green and the red are fused in a Puritan utopia where a succession of refugees from ecclesiastical tyranny end up as pilgrims 'on a grassy stage, / Safe from the storms, and prelate's rage' (lines 11–12). In this poem Marvell nicely combines his fantasy of escape into a tropical prelapsarian landscape with a sense of committed solidarity with generations of Puritans whose strategic retreat was to found a new world. The 'English boat' symbolizes the new commonwealth full of 'holy' and 'cheerful' pilgrims whose progress is as measured and harmonious as the oars they work (lines 37–8).

In 'The First Anniversary of Government under his Highness the Lord Protector', Cromwell is seen as the architect of a New Jerusalem whose citizens are 'all composed by his attractive song / Into the animated city throng' (lines 85–6). He alone 'the force of scattered time contracts, / And in one year the work of ages acts'; whereas 'heavy monarchs . . . though they all Platonic years should reign, / In the same posture would be found again' (lines 13–18). Marvell thus continues to identify monarchies with the vast slowness of vegetable love and Cromwell's regime with the accelerated activism of his engaged lovers.

4. The green dream

> No white nor red was ever seen
> So amorous as this lovely green.

(The Garden)

> How safe, methinks, and strong, behind
> These trees have I encamped my mind.

(Appleton House)

The quintessence of Marvell's poetic alchemy boils down to those two enigmatic phrases: 'a cause too good to be fought for' and 'a green thought in a green shade'. 'The Garden' gives us that third element in the trinity of which the 'Coy Mistress' and the 'Horatian Ode' are the other two. 'The Garden' enacts a profound and ironic disengagement from the twin distractions of sexual and political commitment. It gives us the green dream, disengaged from the white and red of woman's love, disengaged from the entrenched encampments of political activism.

In 'The Garden' Marvell's escape from the world of sex and politics is both ironic and utopian. The retreat is carefully stage-managed as the narrator goes about the business of 'Annihilating all that's made / To a green thought in a green shade' (lines 47–8). The 'uncessant labours' (line 3) of men in society, military (palm), political (oak) and aesthetic (bays), are alchemically reduced to 'garlands of repose' (line 8). The white and red of 'passion's heat' (line 25) are sublimated into the prelapsarian landscape where the protagonist is seduced, not by the fleshly Eve, but by a cornucopia of luscious fruit. The fall of man is metamorphosed into a jouissance of vegetable love: 'Stumbling on melons, as I pass, / Ensnared with flowers, I fall on grass' (lines 39–40). Not only is woman removed from 'that happy garden-state' (line 52), but, in the last stanza, the narrator himself vanishes from his own fantasy, leaving the garden to God the 'skilful gardener' (line 65) and to 'the industrious bee' who 'Computes its time as well as we' (lines 69–70).

Time's winged chariot which pressurizes the busy world of sex and politics is, by the subtle device of a metaphysical pun, transformed into a herb (thyme). In ludic vein Marvell has disengaged himself from his own garden leaving the reader to contemplate in close-up a world of busy men and women annihilated to a green thought in a green shade, to an industrious bee sucking a herb.

The raw materials both biographical and aesthetic for this amazing tour de force can be gathered from 'Upon Appleton House' dedicated 'To my Lord Fairfax'. Through the prism of the Fabian Fairfax's country house and garden Marvell concocts an epic series of lyrical tropes. In a parody of Milton's 'cloistered and fugitive virtue' (*Areopagitica*, 1644), the ghosts of 'subtle nuns' (line 94) from before the dissolution of the monasteries are imagined 'chaste in bed, / As pearls together billeted, / All night embracing arm in arm / Like crystal pure and cotton warm' (lines 189–92). Horticultural and military tropes are extensively interchanged, raising the spectre of bloody civil war at the heart of the garden retreat (lines 281–368). And Marvell, the poet-tutor, muses himself into this fanciful fabric, clinging to his vision as if it were Noah's ark: 'But I, retiring from the flood, / Take sanctuary in the wood, / And, while it lasts, myself embark / In this yet green, yet growing ark' (lines 481–4).

Fairfax had his reasons for withdrawing. Marvell's withdrawal takes on an increasingly crazy, surrealist, pathological colour. Caterpillars crawl all over him, ivy licks and clasps him (lines 588–90); brambles and briars chain him, nail him and stake him down so that he 'may never leave this place' (lines 609–24). And having invoked the young Mary Fairfax to metamorphose 'loose Nature' (line 657) into a nature 'wholly vitrified' (line 688), and praised her as 'heaven's centre, Nature's lap, / And paradise's only map' (lines 767–8), the poet's deranged fancy conjures up one last image of 'salmon-fishers' who 'like Antipodes in shoes, / Have shod their heads in their canoes' (lines 771–2).

Readers will make of all this what they will. There is something Swiftian about Marvell's persona in this poem, as if, Gulliver-like, he was perplexed and crazed by life's experiences. Perhaps Marvell is struggling with the problem of civilization and its discontents.

In 'The Mower Against Gardens' Marvell inveighs against 'luxurious man' (line 1), 'that sovereign thing and proud' (line 20), who 'first enclosed within the gardens square / A dead and standing pool of air' (lines 5–6). Gardens can be, like a 'green seraglio' (line 27), 'all enforced' (line 31). And yet, at the same time, Marvell cannot abandon his green dream. Or, as he puts it in his translation from Seneca: 'Climb at court for me that will / Giddy favour's slippery hill [variant: Tottering favour's pinnacle]; / All I seek is to lie still, / Settled in some secret nest' (lines 1–4).[5] That is the measure of Marvell's dilemma and he makes it the measure of ours.

Notes

1. I have used Andrew Marvell, *The Complete Poems*, ed. E. S. Donno (Harmondsworth, 1972). All quotations from and references to Marvell are taken from this edition.
2. See *Andrew Marvell: Selected Poetry and Prose*, ed. Robert Wilcher (London, 1986).
3. Donno, ed., *The Complete Poems*, p. 222.
4. For an extended extract, see the *Documents* section below, pp. 301–5.
5. Donno, ed., *The Complete Poems*, p. 274.

11 'The meaning, not the name': Milton and gender

Tony Davies

Not, let's be quite clear, 'Milton and sex'. Edward le Comte, among others, has already written about that, in a book of the same name. By focusing on gender, I want to attempt to unravel the way behavioural characteristics ('feminine'/'masculine') are mapped onto the biological facts of sexual difference (female/male) and discursively organized into a system of gendered roles, functions and personalities. Gender belongs, that is to say, not to 'nature' but to 'culture'. But by calling it a 'system' I don't mean to imply that it is commonly experienced as such; for most people, on the contrary, it is simply and self-evidently a fact of life, a basic piece of 'common sense' grounded in biology and therefore, unanswerably, in 'nature' to the extent that any challenge to its inexorable prescriptions can be dismissed as perverse and unnatural. The first question about every newborn – 'Is it a boy or a girl?' – immediately sets in train a ritual of gendered expectations and acknowledgements symbolized by the infant's first clothes (pink or blue) and toys and – even more elusively pervasive – by the very ways in which she or he is held, addressed and manipulated by adults. That such ideological expectations of the feminine and masculine only very imperfectly express, and sometimes actively mutilate, the potential variety of biological and psychic sexualities they seek so powerfully to determine is well known. Gendered subjectivity is, for most people most of the time, contradictory, frustrating, often oppressive. It is nonetheless an inescapable condition of existence, not least because it presents itself not as an externally imposed tyranny, an alien taxonomy of sexual orders, but as our immediate experience of ourselves and others, in a world steeped, from birth to death and beyond, in gendered meanings. At the same time, precisely because the linkage between sexual difference and gender, the genital signifier and the cultural signified, is itself culturally constructed rather than biologically given, there will always be a gap, a slippage, a moment of excess and indeterminacy that even the most ruthless ideological surveillance can never fully contain.[1]

It is reasonable to assume that sexual difference has always played an important part in human identity and in the symbolic and social systems of human communities. But the saturation of culture and personality with the prescriptive codings of gender is also identifiably historical. Specifically, I shall argue, it emerges (to use a convenient, later shorthand) with the Renaissance, in the early formation of capitalist society, and in particular in the bourgeois discourses of humanism and reformation. In England, though its traces are everywhere in his immediate predecessors (Philip Sidney, Jonson, Shakespeare, Donne) and contemporaries, its most striking literary exemplar is Milton, in whose writings the polemical sexual politics of the reformers and the gendered neoplatonic allegories of the Florentine humanists collide and mingle to often spectacular effect. I stress those antecedents and intertextualities because I don't want to seem to be claiming a unique canonical status (not even that of chief patriarchal 'bogy'[2]) for Milton, whose texts, like any writer's, are always 'already written', and nowhere more so than when they engage with the problematics of gender; but especially because I don't want to fall into the trap (as, for example, Le Comte does) of reducing the abundant complexity of texts to the pathology of the individual author, and ascribing all the richly suggestive genderings of the writings to Milton's (supposed) sexual timidity, misogyny or matrimonial disappointments. But I do believe that something decisively important is happening in Milton, and the pages that follow are an attempt to explore the implications of Mary Nyquist's suggestive comment, in a study of the divorce pamphlets, that 'by specifying a desire that only "woman" can satisfy, and by associating that desire with a transcendence of sexual difference as vulgarly understood', Milton's writings 'seem almost to open up a space for the category of "gender" '.[3]

First, then, to glance briefly at one or two of those humanist and protestant antecedents, by way of suggesting some discursive reference points for the discussion of Milton. One of the most widely influential ideas in the sixteenth and seventeenth centuries is the Machiavellian opposition, central to the symbolic repertoire of European humanism, between *virtù* and *fortuna*. *Virtù*, the defining quality of the active citizen and the successful ruler, which we must translate not as 'virtue' but as something more like 'prowess' or 'mastery', is engaged, in *The Prince* (1532) and Machiavelli's other political writings, in an endless struggle to impose its will upon the unpredictable interplay of danger and opportunity within which it must operate, and which Machiavelli personifies as the capricious goddess Fortuna. 'Men make their own history', Marx was to write, more than three centuries later, 'but not of their own free will; not under circumstances they themselves have chosen but under the given and inherited circumstances with which they are directly confronted';[4] and the allegorized figures of *Virtù* and *Fortuna* represent the Florentine's attempt to articulate the central problem for a secular and historical understanding of the world, the relationship between human agency ('free will') and the already-given and unpredictable circumstances into which it is thrust and which it must attempt to shape to its desires and needs. For Machiavelli that relationship, as words like 'mastery' imply, is gendered: the masculine *virtù* (the word is cognate with 'virility', both deriving from the Latin *vir*, 'man') pitted against the feminine blandishments and treacheries of a fickle fortune:

> I conclude, therefore, that fortune being fickle, and men being stubborn in their ways, they can be successful so long as the two are in agreement, and unsuccessful when they disagree. My own considered view is this: that it is better to be decisive than cautious, because fortune is a woman, and if you want to keep her under it is necessary to beat her and abuse her. And it is evident that she allows herself to be mastered by a man of that kind, rather than by those who go coldly about their work. Like a woman, therefore, she is always a lover of young men, because they are less cautious, more fiery, and command her with greater audacity.[5]

But for all its stress on mastery, on the resolute masculinity of the aspiring *virtuoso*, Machiavelli's treatment of fortune betrays a deep ambivalence, a troubled recognition not only of the capriciousness of human affairs but of the power of the feminine. As Hannah Pitkin notes in her study of the sexual politics of *The Prince*,

> When the focus is primarily on the sexual conquest of fortune, Machiavelli's image seems to be neither of an outright rape nor of romantic courtship. There is a certain mutuality between fortune and the man of *virtù*, but they are not equals . . . If he succeeds in conquering her, it is a matter of her deciding to grant her favours, to "let him master her".[6]

In this interpenetration of the vocabularies of politics and gender, it is not possible to say which has priority, which is merely the metaphorical or allegorical figure through which the other is illustratively elaborated. Rather, it looks as if each is the condition of emergence of the other, as if the discourses of secular political theory and of gendered difference, like Milton's good and evil, 'as two twins cleaving together, leapt forth into the world'.[7] Of course, great shifts in social meaning like this don't really 'leap forth', fully formed. They emerge over decades, perhaps centuries, across a range of knowledges and ways of thinking. That the genderings of discourse, and the discourses of gendering, are not limited to or by either the private preoccupations of Niccolò Machiavelli or the political agenda of Florentine republicanism is demonstrated by another greatly influential humanist polemic, one closer still to Milton in style and ethos, Desiderius Erasmus's anti-clerical satire *The Praise of Folly* (1511). Writing in Latin (a language, like Machiavelli's Tuscan, in which all the nouns are grammatically gendered), Erasmus weaves a comic mythology around the central figure of *Moria* (Greek for 'foolishness', with a punning allusion to his friend Thomas More), providing her with a mock-heroic ancestry and a train of allegorical companions:

> Neither the first Chaos, Zeus, Saturn or Japhet, nor any of those thred-bare, musty Gods, were my Father, but Plutus, Riches . . . Nor did he produce me from his brain, as Jupiter that sowre and ill-look'd Pallas; but of that lovely Nymph call'd Youth, the most beautiful and galliard of all the rest . . . This here, which you observe with that proud cast of her eye, is Philautia, Self-love; she with the smiling countenance, that is ever and anon clapping her hands, is Kolasia, Flattery . . . and, as to the two Gods that you see with them, the one is Komos, Intemperance, the other Negretos Hypnos, Dead Sleep.[8]

That Erasmus is fully conscious of the social as well as the mythological implications of his allegory is clear throughout the text:

> As it doubles the crime if any one should put a diguise upon Nature, or endeavour to bring her to that she will in no wise bear, according to that proverb of the Greeks, 'An Ape is an Ape, though clad in scarlet'; so a woman is a woman still, that is to say foolish, let her put on whatever Vizard she please. But, by the way, I hope that Sexe is not so foolish as to take offence at this, that I myself, being a woman, and Folly too, have attributed Folly to them.[9]

Another humanist text whose allegorical genderings call forth a tactical apology ('O lovely, graceful nymphs of England! / Not in repugnance nor in scorn / Our spirit holds you, / Nor would our pen abase you / More than it must – to call you feminine!') is Giordano Bruno's extraordinary sequence of moralized Petrarchan conceits, *Gli Eroici Furori* (1585), whose strenuous sublimation of sexual passion into the 'heroic frenzies' of philosophy is haunted, like so much neoplatonic writing, by a neurotic terror of the physical and (what comes to be seen as virtually synonymous with it) the female:

> "Now this active and most noble number, which is the soul, in what way do you understand that it may be severed from the ignoble number, which is the body?" ". . . those powers which are not comprehended and imprisoned in the womb of matter, sometimes as if inebriated and stupefied, find that they also are occupied in the formation of matter and in the vivification of the body; then, as if awakened and brought to themselves . . . they turn towards superior things . . .
>
>> That god who shakes the sounding thunder,
>> Asteria as a furtive eagle saw;
>> Mnemosyne as shepherd; Danae gold;
>> Alcmene as a fish; Antiope a goat;
>> Cadmus and his sister a white bull;
>> Leda as swan . . .".[10]

These anxious assertions of masculine authority, always on its guard against the blandishments of a castrating effeminacy, have numerous parallels in Milton. 'Laws are Masculin Births', he declared in the *History of Britain* (1670), ridiculing the supposed legislative achievements of the legendary British queen Martia (*CPW*, V, p. 32), and echoing Bacon's description of science as 'temporis partus masculus', 'the masculine offspring of time'.[11] Instructing Adam in the causes of human misery and political thraldom, the archangel Michael ascribes them to 'man's effeminate slackness' (*Paradise Lost*, XI, line 634),[12] recalling the denunciation in *Eikonoklastes* (1649) of 'effeminate and uxorious magistrates' under whose government 'great mischiefs and dishonour hath befallen to nations' (*CPW*, III, p. 421). Here the link between a gendered metaphorization (effeminate = weak, indecisive, susceptible) and the institution of sexual regulation is close, since the effeminacy of the magistrates is explained – a common Miltonic topic, this – by their domestic arrangements: 'who being themselves govern'd and overswaid at home under a Feminine usurpation, cannot but be farr short of spirit and autority without dores, to govern a whole Nation' (*CPW*, III, p. 421). The royalist propagandist Claude de Saumaise, savagely portrayed as a hen-pecked ninny, is berated in the same vein in the *Defence of the English People* (1651): 'No wonder then that you endeavour to obtrude absolute regal government upon others, who are yourself grown accustomed to bear female rule so slavishly at home' (*CPW*, IV, p. 518).

But the metaphors constantly threaten to break loose of institutional anchorage and take on a discursive life of their own. Charles I, the uxorious absolutist, seeks to impose his (male) will on a reluctant commons, 'so that the Parliament, it seems, is but a Female, and without his procreative reason, the Laws which they can produce are but wind-eggs. Wisdom, it seems, to a King is natural, to a Parlament not natural, but by conjunction with the King' (*CPW*, III, p. 467); a good example, this passage from *Eikonoklastes*, of the instability of these gendered discourses of power and sexuality, since we can read its sarcastic mockery of Charles's procreative (and legislative) *virtù* as an implied critique of the misogyny of Milton's own *History*. But the king's folly is worse than this, for the 'female' parliament is not his wife or concubine but, since 'it was a Parlament that first created Kings', his mother:

> He ought then to have so thought of a Parlament, if he count it not Male, as of his Mother . . . And if it hath bin anciently interpreted the presaging signe of a future Tyrant, but to dream of copulation with his Mother, what can it be less then [than] actual Tyranny to affirme waking, that the Parlament, which is his Mother, can neither conceive or bring forth *any autoritative Act* without his Masculine coition.
>
> (*CPW*, III, p. 467)

So Charles's crime is not only the tyranny of Julius Caesar, who dreamt of sleeping with his mother, but the pestilential pollution of Oedipus, who actually did.

This incestuous coupling, productive of tyranny and death, recalls the account of the birth of Death, and his rape of his mother Sin, in Book Two of *Paradise Lost*:

> 'Pensive here I sat
> Alone, but long I sat not, till my womb
> Pregnant by thee, and now excessive grown

Prodigious motion felt and rueful throes.
At last this odious offspring whom thou seest
Thine own begotten, breaking violent way
Tore through my entrails, that with fear and pain
Distorted, all my nether shape thus grew
Transformd: but he my inbred enemie
Forth issu'd, brandishing his fatal Dart
Made to destroy: I fled, and cri'd out Death;
Hell trembl'd at the hideous name, and sigh'd
From all her Caves, and back resounded Death.
I fled, but he persu'd (though more, it seems,
Inflam'd with lust than rage) and swifter far,
Mee overtook his mother all dismayd,
And in embraces forcible and foule
Ingendring with me, of that rape begot
These yelling Monsters.'

(lines 777–95)

This gruesome 'ingendring' is also a gendering – the very first, in fact, since Sin is, cosmologically as well as narratively, the first woman. Angels, we learn later, can 'assume what shape they choose' for sexual purposes. The birth of Sin requires an obstetrically novel method of delivery, from her father Satan's head (like the 'sowre and ill-look'd Pallas' from Zeus's); but she is conventionally sexed, and the arrival of her son Death, though hardly edifying, is anatomically familiar. Like Eve, taken from Adam's side, she is a literal instance of those 'masculine births' Milton had earlier attributed to law and, in a famous passage, to truth:

> For Truth is as impossible to be soil'd by any outward touch, as the Sun beam. Though this ill hap wait on her nativity, that shee never comes into the world, but like a Bastard, to the ignominy of him that brought her forth: till Time the Midwife rather than the mother of Truth, have washed and salted the Infant, declar'd her legitimat, and Churcht the father of his young Minerva, from the needlesse causes of his purgation.
>
> (*CPW*, II, p. 225)

Many commentators have noted the baroque grotesquerie of this accouchement from *The Doctrine and Discipline of Divorce* (1643), in which a male author usurps the solitary parenthood of female Truth, demoting Time from parent to midwife (not necessarily, by the way, a demotion from 'male father' to 'female midwife', as Annabel

Patterson argues;[13] Time retains his traditional (and grammatical) gender even as a midwife, and achieves here figuratively what the College of Physicians was attempting to do actually in this period, to supplant the customary functions of midwives and 'gossips' with an all-male obstetric monopoly).[14] Some, too, have gone on to relate this scene, in which a male mother and a male midwife preside at the birth of a female child, to the tendency, elsewhere in Milton, to resolve the miseries and contradictions of sexual difference by resort to the platonic fantasy of a world without women:

> O why did God,
> Creator wise, that peopled highest heaven
> With spirits masculine, create at last
> This novelty on earth, this fair defect
> Of nature, and not fill the world at once
> With men as angels without feminine,
> Or find some other way to generate
> Mankind?
>
> (*PL*, X, lines 888–95)

a wish endorsed more succinctly by Milton's friend Andrew Marvell:

> Such was that happy garden-state,
> While man there walked without a mate . . .
> Two paradises 'twere in one
> To live in paradise alone.[15]

We can feel in passages like these the intense ideological and psychological pressure that is forcing the generic nouns, 'Man', 'Mankind', towards an exclusive gendered specification, *vir* rather than *homo*; the same pressures, in the wider society and polity as well as in Milton's own painfully fraught engagement with sex and marriage, that enforce a reading of the crucial early verses of Genesis as the inscription of male authority rather than sexual equality.[16] But while I don't discount the force of personal and social fantasy, the masculine will-to-power, in these passages, I would want to emphasize the importance of language in the construction out of the materials of sexual difference of the cultural categories of gender. Gender, in Milton, is certainly a question of ideology, psychology, culture; but it is also a matter of philology. His writings reveal a remarkable awareness, a sometimes disconcerting precision in usage, of language as a gendered activity.

I suspect that there's something specifically English about this preoccupation, reflecting, paradoxically, the fact that, alone among the major European languages, English nouns have no grammatical gender, in contrast to its pronouns, which do. Not for the English the heroic glamour of 'La République',[17] the chaste allurements of 'La Vérité'. In everyday use, this causes no problems with abstractions, for which the neuter pronoun 'it' serves. Unlike the speakers of romance or germanic languages, we don't have to remember whether words like truth, time, virtue, freedom or error are masculine or feminine, since they are neither. But for Milton, with his Spenserian love of prosopopoeia and his deeply classical and European imagination, it is precisely those abstractions, capitalized and personified as the protagonists of a platonic drama, that carry the full burden, and the contradictions, of gender. Consider the pronouns in the following:

Love Virtue, she alone is free.   (*Comus*, line 1019)

He that can apprehend and consider vice with all her baits and seeming pleasures, and yet abstain, and yet distinguish, and yet prefer that which is truly better, he is the true warfaring Christian. I cannot praise a fugitive and cloister'd vertue, unexercis'd & unbreath'd, that never sallies out and sees her adversary.
                    (*Areopagitica* (1644); *CPW* II, pp. 514–15)

Methinks I see in my mind a noble and puissant Nation rousing herself like a strong man after sleep, and shaking her invincible locks: Methinks I see her as an Eagle muing her mighty youth, and kindling her undazl'd eyes at the full midday beam.
                    (*CPW*, II, pp. 557–8)

[The licensing ordinance] was the immediat image of a Star-chamber decree to that purpose made in those very times when that Court did the rest of those her pious works, for which she is now fall'n from the Starres with Lucifer.
                    (*CPW*, II, pp. 569–70)

In these instances, as in others quoted earlier, the gendering of the noun, given by etymological derivation or association, generates its own drama, and sometimes its own apparent contradictions. The insistence that Virtue, boldly active, uncloistered and alone worthy of love, is female challenges the humanist emphasis on the word's inherent masculinity (an implication perhaps supported by Milton's preferred spelling, 'vertue', which seems to associate it with *veritas* (truth) rather than *virtus*). And the female nation (*natio, respublica*) shaking her invincible locks sets up a rich and disturbing figurative dissonance with the Samson-qualities the text attributes to her, recalling the massively muscled female figures of the Sistine frescoes. Similarly, though the midwife Time (*tempus, chronos*)[18] and the author-parent (*auctor*) must be male, the child Truth herself (*veritas, aletheia*) cannot be anything but female. The text has referred, a few lines earlier, to the 'womb of teeming Truth' (*CPW*, II, p. 224); so the imperatives of masculine creativity require her demotion, too, from mother to child, creator to created. And the same process of gendered allegorical prosopopoeia can be turned to satirical use, as in the mockery of the Anglican liturgy (*leitourgia*) of the 1630s, which 'hath run up and downe the world like an English gallopping Nun, proffering her selfe, but wee heare of none yet that bids money for her', and which now, in 1642, 'pranks her selfe in the weeds of a Popish Masse . . . no otherwise then [than] a wife affecting whorish attire kindles a disturbance in the eye of her discerning husband' (*CPW*, I, pp. 680, 687).

What is it, discursively and historically, that is so urgently pressing the meaning of gender, and the gender of meaning, into the writing here? Why is it that the figures of sexual difference are proliferating in the language, saturating its utterances, insisting that all difference and thus all signification is ultimately referrable to the sexual? The last phrase quoted, from the *Animadversions Upon the Remonstrant's Defence* (1642), suggests a way of approaching the question: 'a wife affecting whorish attire kindles a disturbance in the eye of her discerning husband'. The woman's body, attired (but also, as we shall see, unattired), is not immediate, self-evident, transparently meaningful to the man. It has to be 'discerned' (the word means both 'seen' and 'critically evaluated'): read, interpreted; and because all reading, all interpretation is equivocal, distanced from the body/text it reads by a gap that can never be closed, it inevitably 'kindles a disturbance' in the eye of the reader. Here is an elaborately rhetorical example from *Samson Agonistes* (1671), a poem with a close intertextual relationship with the divorce pamphlets. The chorus has spotted the approach of Samson's wife, Dalila:

> But who is this, what thing of sea or land?
> Female of sex it seems,
> That so bedecked, ornate and gay,
> Comes this way sailing
> Like a stately ship

Of Tarsus, bound for th'isles
Of Javan or Gadier
With all her bravery on, and tackle trim,
Sails filled, and streamers waving,
Courted by all the winds that hold them play,
An amber scent of odorous perfume
Her harbinger, a damsel train behind;
Some rich Philistian matron she may seem,
And now at nearer view, no other certain
Than Dalila thy wife.

(lines 710–24)

This piece of inference, almost comically laborious in its exposition of
the process of interpretative 'discernment', certainly kindles the most
violent disturbance in her unfortunate husband ('Out, out, hyena;
these are thy wonted arts, / And arts of every woman false like thee
. . .'). Another example, tragic and complex, is the wonderful account
in Book Nine of *Paradise Lost* of the effect on Adam of eating the fruit.
Here again the emphasis is on the eye, on seeing as interpretation, in
this case reinterpretation; and again a powerful disturbance is
produced, first of desire, then of shame:

he on Eve
Began to cast lascivious eyes, she him
As wantonly repaid; in lust they burn,
Till Adam thus 'gan Eve to dalliance move.
'Eve, now I see thou art exact of taste
And elegant, of sapience no small part,
Since to each meaning savour we apply,
And palate call judicious . . .
For never did thy beauty since the day
I saw thee first and wedded thee, adorned
With all perfections, so enflame my sense
With ardour to enjoy thee, fairer now
Than ever, bountie of this virtuous tree.'
So said he, and forbore not glance or toy
Of amorous intent, well understood
Of Eve, whose eye darted contagious fire [cf. *kindles* a disturbance]
. . . up they rose
As from unrest, and each the other viewing
Soon found their eyes how open'd and their minds
How darken'd;

(IX, lines 1013–54)

and the passage goes on to compare them to 'the Danite strong /
Herculean Samson' rising 'from the Harlot-lap / Of Philistean Dalila'
(lines 1059–61).

It is clear from these passages that we cannot, in Milton, oppose
the plurality and indeterminacy of language to the presence,
immediacy and transparency of the body, as though the latter
incarnated an irreducible reality (like D. H. Lawrence's notion of
woman as 'the inexpressible which man must ceaselessly strive to
utter'). The body is itself a text, not a privileged source of meaning but
a provocation to discernment and so to disturbance. The body exists
only within language, within the order of representation and hence of
uncertainty and displacement. My third example of the body-as-text
is also from *Paradise Lost*, a passage that has become canonical in
accounts of Milton's patriarchal belief in male superiority. Satan has
entered Paradise, and among all the other 'living creatures new to sight
and strange'

> Two of far nobler shape erect and tall,
> Godlike erect, with native honour clad
> In naked majesty seem'd lords of all,
> And worthy seem'd, for in their looks divine
> The image of their glorious maker shone,
> Truth, wisdom, sanctitude severe and pure,
> Severe, but in true filial freedom plac'd;
> Whence true authority in men; though both
> Not equal, as their sex not equal seem'd;
> For contemplation he and valour form'd,
> For softness she and sweet attractive grace,
> He for God only, she for God in him.
>
> (IV, lines 288–99)

Milton's early editors treated this passage, approvingly, as the
definitive enunciation of a Miltonic, indeed a universal commonplace.
Later critics, including most recently J. A. Wittreich in *Feminist Milton*
(1987), have noticed that the whole passage, far from offering an
'authorial' commentary of unquestionable authority, is presented from
Satan's point of view; but none, I think, has drawn the right kind of
conclusion from that, a conclusion irresistibly suggested by the
repetition of 'seem'd' (which must, though it doesn't seem to have been
noticed, qualify the last three lines too): that Satan is here 'discerning'
(reading, distinguishing) the meaning of these new creatures, on the

basis of their physical features and differences, in terms drawn from his own experience and priorities. He (who else?) recognizes 'the image of their glorious maker'. He attributes to Adam the Satanic qualities of contemplation and valour. Above all, he can read the woman's body as the signifier of 'sweet attractive grace' because he has himself been recently reminded by his daughter Sin of the 'attractive graces' he once found in her (II, line 762), and now extends to women in general. Of course Satan's 'discerning' is also Milton's, and our own, since we are not offered an alternative. But precisely because the meaning of sexual difference is placed under the sign of interpretation, not of absolute ontological authority, we are alerted to its contingent, historical, provisional status, its potential for 'disturbance': not nature but culture, not being but meaning. We could certainly apply to these lines what Nyquist says of the divorce writings, that in their 'transcendence of sexual difference as vulgarly understood . . . [they] open up a space for the category of "gender" '.[19]

The examples given so far, particularly the last, might prompt you to suggest, even supposing that you agree with my reading of them, that the world of gendered representation is a Satanic, fallen world. We have scriptural authority, after all, for the idea that in this vale of tears we see 'through a glass, darkly', our understanding always mediated and disturbed by the mists of *différance*,[20] the incoherence of the sign. Before and after, we are assured, unfallen or redeemed, we did and shall see the meaning of things shining refulgently from and through the things themselves, their names already inscribed, like the incarnate Logos, in their bodily form. This view has been attributed to Milton, but his writings will not sustain it, as one last passage from *Paradise Lost* can show. Asked by Adam to describe the war in heaven that resulted in the defeat and damnation of Satan and the other rebel angels, Raphael wonders 'how shall I relate / To human sense th'invisible exploits / Of warring spirits . . . ?', but agrees that 'what surmounts the reach / Of human sense, I shall delineate so, / By likening spiritual to corporeal forms, / As may express them best, though what if Earth / Be but the shadow of heaven, and things therein / Each to other like, more than on Earth is thought?' (V, lines 564–76). The relation between reality and consciousness is one of correspondence (what Milton would have called 'accommodation'), not of identity, and Raphael's account of it is fraught with uncertainty ('how shall I? . . . what if?') and anxiety ('how last unfold / The secrets of another world, perhaps / Not lawful to reveal?'). When he comes, on Adam's prompting, to narrate the creation of the world, he starts by warning him once again that human understanding, limited as it is by the sequential temporality of language, can never possess the truth, and must be content with a copy, a representation opaque to the original:

> Immediate are the acts of God, more swift
> Than time or motion, but to human ears
> Cannot without process of speech be told,
> So told as earthly notion can receive.

(VII, lines 176–9)

Thus the story of the six-day creation is not to be taken as literal, an account that claims the status of transparent authenticity, but as an allegory, forever displaced from the unutterable real by the nature of language and consciousness itself. And the important thing about that allegory, which for human purposes corresponds to the only reality we can ever know, is that it exhibits everywhere the codes of socio-sexual differentiation, of gender:

> Let there be light, said God, and forthwith light
> Ethereal, first of things, quintessence pure
> Sprung from the deep, and from her native east
> To journey through the airy gloom began,
> Spher'd in a radiant cloud, for yet the sun
> Was not; she in a cloudy tabernacle
> Sojourn'd the while . . .
> The earth was form'd, but in the womb as yet
> Of waters, embryon immature involv'd,
> Appear'd not: over all the face of earth
> Main ocean flow'd, not idle, but with warm
> Prolific humour softening all her globe,
> Fermented the great mother to conceive,
> Satiate with genial moisture . . .
> First in his east with glorious lamp was seen,
> Regent of day . . . less bright the moon,
> But opposite in levell'd west was set
> His mirror, with full face borrowing her light
> From him, for other light she needed none
>   . . . swarming next appear'd
> The female bee that feeds her husband drone
> Deliciously.

(VII, lines 243–491)

The whole extraordinary rewriting of the creation narrative in Genesis can be read, in fact, as an inscription of the inescapability of gender, as a cultural and discursive fact not only about this human earth and its inhabitants but, speculatively, about the rest of the universe, where, Adam is told, 'other suns perhaps / With their attendant moons thou wilt descry / Communicating male and female light, / Which two great sexes animate the world' (VIII, lines 148–51). This shift from biology to culture, from sex to gender, is a great historical step. In Milton's case it starts in the divorce writings; and to understand it properly we would need to look closely at the social and psychic economy of 'companionate marriage', the bourgeois 'wedded love' of which *Paradise Lost* is one of the founding documents.[21] But I'm concerned here only with Milton; and his texts remind us, in case we're in any danger of falling into sentimental collusion with their own idealization of wedded love, that the ascription of gender is also the inscription of power. None of Milton's reworkings of Genesis is more significant than his rewriting of 1.27: 'So God created man in his own image; in the image of God he created him; male and female he created them'. Here, most biblical commentators agree, the words of the 'Priestly' writer must imply that, in spite of the translators' genderings of the singular pronoun, 'man' is generic, containing both man and woman.[22] But in the Miltonic version (which conflates the verse with the later words of the more obviously patriarchal 'Jahwist' author), 'man' is singular, primary and male:

> This said, he form'd thee, Adam, thee O man,
> Dust of the ground, and in thy nostrils breath'd
> The breath of life; in his own image he
> Created thee, in the image of God
> Express, and thou becam'st a living soul.
> Male he created thee, but thy consort
> Female for race.
>
> (*PL*, VII, lines 524–30)

In case there is any doubt here about the purposiveness of the rewriting, and its relevance to my argument, the third of the divorce pamphlets, *Tetrachordon* (1645), provides the commentary:

> It might be doubted why he saith, In the image of God created he him, not them, as well as male and female them; especially since that Image

> might be common to them both, but male and female could not, however the Jewes fable, and please themselves with the accidentall concurrence of Plato's wit, as if man at first had bin created Hermaphrodite; but then it must have bin male and female created he him. So had the image of God bin equally common to them both, it had no doubt bin said, In the image of God created he them. But St. Paul ends the controversie by explaining that the woman is not primarily and immediatly the image of God, but in reference to the man. (*CPW*, II, p. 589)

For all its obsessive attention to verbal detail, there is nothing dryly pedantic about this ruthless *explication de texte*. The battle of the sexes is being fought with all the scholarly and controversial energy the writer can command, as the dangerously multiplying ambiguities and polysemies of the Genesis verses are pruned back and tied in to conform with the ideological imperatives of patriarchal wedded love. The hierarchy inaugurated here decrees that the power of the interpreting gaze belongs to the man: he discerns, she is discerned. Milton's liberal-feminist critics, like Joan Webber and Stevie Davies,[23] intent on defending him against the charge of misogyny, have not always given enough consideration to the possibility that his celebrations of the creative power of the feminine may be conducted nonetheless in the name, and the interest, of the masculine; may be, indeed, a kind of male appropriation of femininity. Truth is female, but her only parent is male; virtue is a 'she', but only he, the 'true warfaring Christian', can possess and embody her. Femininity, released from the biologically female into the free economy of representation, becomes, like women themselves, an object of exchange, a token, a commodity. Authority, like authorship, remains firmly in the hands of men. Christine Froula[24] has noted how in the opening of *Paradise Lost* the 'heavenly muse' mutates from observer to creator, from female inspirer to male progenitor:

> Thou O Spirit . . . Thou from the first
> Wast present, and with mighty wings outspread
> Dove-like sat'st brooding on the vast abyss
> And mad'st it pregnant.
>
> (I, lines 17–22)

Here is a paradigm of Milton's 'masculine births': the spirit (*spiritus*, m.) both 'brooding' mother and inseminating father, female dove and (in a powerful evocation of the story of Leda) male bird-god, the archetype of those masculine incarnations that had inspired Bruno's heroic frenzies.

Directly parallel to this is the invocation to the muse Urania at the beginning of Book Seven of the poem. Here, in a turn that exposes the metaphoricity underlying all the poem's multitudinous namings, the name is no sooner uttered than it is disowned:

> Descend from heaven Urania, by that name
> If rightly thou art called, whose voice divine
> Following, above the Olympian hill I soar,
> Above the flight of Pegasean wing.
> The meaning, not the name I call: for thou
> Nor of the Muses nine, nor on the top
> Of old Olympus dwell'st, but heavenly born.
>
> (PL, VII, lines 1–7)

The point is that Urania 'means' heavenly; and the exclusively masculine character of the poem's depiction of heaven suggests that the disavowal of the name in favour of the meaning may go for the figure's gender too, the 'goddess' (VII, line 40) standing as an allegorical surrogate for a male inspirer. The text remains equivocal; but where Milton declines to specify, his editors can be trusted, like officious midwives, to deliver him of the reluctant meanings he can't quite manage for himself. 'It seems far more likely', declares Alastair Fowler, after reviewing the alternatives, 'that Milton's Muse is the Logos, the agency of creation and the Son of God'.[25] *Logos*, need I say, is (grammatically, figuratively) masculine.

This myth of a male incarnation and creation, in which woman and the feminine is always secondary, created by and for the uses of man, returns me to the distinction I started with. For if you ask me about the sexual politics of Milton's writings, I can only reply that they constitute a myth of origins that inscribes patriarchy and the subordination of women unalterably in the fundamental order of things. But – and this is the crucial and saving contradiction – in the very process of doing so they are obliged to uncouple the meaning from the name, to break the link between sexual difference and its cultural representations, to inaugurate the categories of gender as a shifting and transferable signifier, and so to make it possible for later readers to interrogate, redefine, indeed refuse those categories, to practise new kinds of discernment and produce new forms of disturbance even, whether they like it or not, in Milton's writings themselves.

Notes

1. For an accessible and provocative summary of recent debates about gender, sex and sexuality, see Judith Butler, *Gender Trouble* (London, 1990), pp. 6–34.
2. 'Milton's bogy' is Virginia Woolf's phrase, in *A Room of One's Own* (1923; reprinted Harmondsworth, 1945), p. 112.
3. 'The genesis of gendered subjectivity in the divorce tracts and in *Paradise Lost*', in *Re-Membering Milton: Essays on the Texts and Traditions*, ed. M. Nyquist and M. W. Ferguson (London, 1987), pp. 99–127.
4. Karl Marx, *The Eighteenth Brumaire of Louis Bonaparte* (1852), in *Political Writings, Volume 2: Surveys from Exile* (Harmondsworth, 1973), p. 146.
5. Niccolò Machiavelli, *Tutte le Opere*, ed. M. Martelli (Florence, 1971), pp. 295–6. The best modern edition of *The Prince* is by Quentin Skinner (Cambridge, 1988); but Skinner uses a translation by Russell Price that eccentrically neuters the personal pronoun in ch. 25, referring to fortune as 'it' until the last paragraph, where he switches awkwardly to 'she', so disrupting the figurative continuity of the chapter. This translation is my own. For an excerpt from the anonymous 1640 translation of *The Prince*, see the *Documents* section below, pp. 308–11.
6. Hannah Pitkin, *Fortune is a Woman: Gender and Politics in the Thought of Niccolò Machiavelli* (Berkeley, 1984), p. 156.
7. Quoted from John Milton, *Complete Prose Works*, 8 vols (New Haven, 1953–82), III, p. 514. Hereinafter referred to as *CPW*.
8. Desiderius Erasmus, *The Praise of Folly*, tr. John Wilson (1688), pp. 13–16. A fuller extract from Thomas Chaloner's version of 1559 can be found in the *Documents* section below, pp. 305–8.
9. Ibid., p. 33.
10 Giordano Bruno, *The Heroic Enthusiasts*, tr. L. Williams (London, 1887), p. 87.
11. See Bacon's *Works*, ed. J. Spedding, R. L. Ellis and D. D. Heath (London, 1887), 3, pp. 527–39. Bacon promises the young man to whom the essay is addressed 'sanctum, castum et legitimum connubium cum rebus istis . . . Ex qua consuetudine (supra omnia epithalamiorum vota) beatissimam prolem vere Heroum . . . suscipies' ('a holy, chaste and lawful marriage with things themselves . . . From which cohabitation (surpassing all the prayers of the marriage bed) you will indeed acquire the most blessed offspring of Heroes'). There is a helpful discussion of this text, and of Bacon's other writings, in Genevieve Lloyd, *The Man of Reason* (London, 1993), pp. 10–17. Lloyd's argument, which is concerned with the gendering of knowledge in western philosophy from Plato to Sartre, is relevant in its entirety to the theme of this essay.

12. Quotation of *Paradise Lost (PL)* is from *John Milton: The complete Poems*, ed. B. A. Wright (London, 1980).

13. 'But still more unsettling is Milton's distortion of the familial structure of several stories at once, so that Time becomes not Truth's male father, a commonplace of Renaissance thought, but her female midwife': Annabel Patterson, ' "No Meer Amatorious Novel" ', in *John Milton* ed. A. Patterson (London, 1992), p. 97.

14. For an account of seventeenth-century disputes about midwifery, see Jean Donnison, *Midwives and Medical Men*, 2nd edn (New Barnet, 1988), and Audrey Eccles, *Obstetrics and Gynaecology in Tudor and Stuart England* (London, 1982).

15. 'The Garden', lines 57–8, 63–4, in *Andrew Marvell*, ed. Frank Kermode and Keith Walker (Oxford, 1994), p. 46.

16. The opening chapters of Genesis contain two accounts of the creation of humankind, attributed by Old Testament scholars to different compilers, the (historically later) Priestly writer (who uses the feminine plural *elohim* for the creator), responsible for 1.26–27, and the earlier Jahwist (who prefers the name *jahweh*), responsible for 2.7–25. In the Priestly version, 'Adam' (the word means something like 'the earth-creature') is created simultaneously male and female; while in the orthodox (Pauline) interpretation of the Jahwist narrative Adam is created first, Eve being formed later, from his rib, as a 'help meet'. The implications of the two narratives have been explored by feminist theologians: see, for example, Elaine Pagels, *The Gnostic Gospels* (New York, 1979). For a reading that challenges the orthodox reading of 2.7–25 and argues for the compatibility of the two versions, see Mieke Bal, 'Sexuality, sin and sorrow: the emergence of female character (a reading of *Genesis* 1–3)', in *The Female Body in Western Culture*, ed. Susan R. Suleiman (Cambridge, Massachusetts), pp. 317–38; a position that is itself criticized as unhistorical by Nyquist, *Re-Membering Milton*, pp. 100–1.

17. The active symbolic gendering is even more evident in the personification of the French republic as 'Marianne', most recently incarnated, on postage stamps and elsewhere, by the actress Catherine Deneuve.

18. The Latin *tempus* is grammatically neuter, becoming, like other neuter nouns, masculine in low Latin and the romance languages that developed from it. The frequent conflation of Greek *chronos* (time) with Kronos (father of Zeus, corresponding to the Roman Saturn) must have helped to reinforce the strongly gendered and patriarchal associations of 'Old Father Time'.

19. Nyquist, *Re-Membering Milton*, p. 111.

20. *Différance* is a Derridean coinage denoting both the 'difference' intrinsic to all sign systems and the constant 'deferral' of semiotic closure resulting

from the incapacity of the signifier to exhaust the meaning of the signified, and vice versa.

21. For discussion of 'companionate marriage' see Lawrence Stone, *The Family, Sex and Marriage in England 1500–1800* (London, 1977), and Roberta Hamilton, *The Liberation of Women* (London, 1978).

22. See note 16 above.

23. Joan Malory Webber, *Milton and His Epic Tradition* (Seattle, 1979); Stevie Davies, *The Idea of Woman in Renaissance Literature* (Brighton, 1986) (published in America as *The Feminine Reclaimed*, Lexington, 1986), and *Milton* (1991).

24. Christine Froula, 'When Eve reads Milton', *Critical Inquiry* 10 (1983); reprinted in *John Milton*, ed. Patterson, pp. 158–61.

25. *PL*, ed. Fowler, p. 357.

12 *Preaching common grounds: Winstanley and the Diggers as concrete utopians*

Christopher Kendrick

I

Winstanley is remembered today because he was the chief spokesman and ideologue for the Diggers, a group of religious communists who attempted to institutionalize their beliefs in the first year after the establishment of the Commonwealth. Claiming that rural common and waste lands ought rightly to belong to the common people – by which they mainly meant the poor and dispossessed – the Diggers materialized in the form of a number of small groups attempting to cultivate such 'common' sites. Formulating a brief, yet non-reductive description of these groups' activity is not easy. It is fruitless to try to decide whether they were mostly charity organizations run by the poor for themselves; collective economic enterprises; or so many conventicles of a radical protestant church. For the commonly accepted truth is that they were all three: a principal aim of the Digger groups was no doubt simply to feed themselves, and at a time when the poverty endemic to the countryside had been exacerbated by the wars, when hunger was widespread and a climate of emergency reigned, their settlements necessarily appeared partly as self-help ventures. Yet hunger and emergency were in a sense pretexts: in claiming the commons for themselves, the Diggers also explicitly presented themselves as combating private land ownership, as introducing collectivist social relations which were to be the germ of a whole new society. But in planting the common lands together the Digger groups were also practising a new form of worship; or, better – at least if Winstanley's pamphlets accurately represent their consciousness – they were attempting to reduce Christianity to its true basis, to locate and practise the essence of the Christian cult: 'True

Religion, and undefiled, is to let everyone quietly have earth to manure, that they may live in freedome by their labours'.[1]

In the body of this paper, I want to consider why the Digger enterprise took the precise form it did, and to enquire into the logic of that form. This will entail close analysis of various of Winstanley's justifications for the Digger occupation of common lands. But first, the Digger story needs, at least briefly, to be told.[2]

II

Winstanley's chosen name for his group seems to have been the *true levellers*. The metaphorical implications of *true-levelling* are less profound perhaps than those of *digging*,[3] but the term does have the virtue of directing one to the Diggers' main 'source' or model. Even a story limited to the bare facts about the Diggers should probably begin with the Levellers, or rather with the defeat of this diffuse, democratic party as a powerful military and political force. The Levellers are usually presented, and for good reason, as a more political, less religious group than the Diggers: they agitated for an extension of the franchise and of the political and legal rights of the 'freeborn Englishman'; their religious principles, which were not prominent in their programmes, were undogmatic, unelaborate, and primarily ethical in focus ('golden-rulish').[4] However radical their programme was in relation to the *status quo* before the Civil War, it stopped short at *political* democracy; the Levellers did not develop a critique of property, and were evidently divided among themselves as to whether the franchise should be extended to dependents.[5] Their core support seems to have come from the urban, small-propertied classes.[6] Nonetheless, the Levellers routinely claimed to be for the poor, and not only for the people, against the rich; and as has often been noted, one can find tendencies to a critique of property in some later Leveller pamphlets – of which *Light Shining in Buckinghamshire*, a savagely satirical pamphlet by rural Levellers, is the chief case in point.[7] The Leveller spectrum of opinion about the rights attaching to property possibly correlates to a general distinction between rural and urban small property (especially to the relative security thereof);[8] and if this was so, then one readily understands how Cromwell and Fairfax's effective defeat of the Levellers in early 1649 would have freed such incipient communal sentiment as existed to seek out its appropriate constituency and fuller formulation.[9]

On a Sunday, 1 April 1649, a small group of men and women announced that they were occupying George Hill, in the parish of Walton-on-Thames in Surrey, just outside London, and proceeded to plant carrots, parsnips, and beans.[10] Just what passed among these people – the internal history of what is sometimes called the Digger colony – remains vague. According to Winstanley, the Digger action was prompted by a revelation given to him, in which he heard a voice declaring: 'Live together, eat bread together, declare this all abroad'. One thus imagines a pooling of members' resources; from the fact that Diggers were soon laying claim to common lumber (a fact for which they were of course prosecuted), one knows in any case that a common stock was essential to the plan. One also imagines that they shared meals together. And since, when the Diggers' operation was attacked, there were always at least a few people there to be harassed and beaten, it seems clear that some of the party were actually camping on the commons between April of 1649 and April of 1650, tending and guarding the crops and staking a claim to the ground. One may speak, then, of an actual Digger settlement. But it is not clear how much of a communal living experiment the Diggers managed or even intended. If there was a specifically Digger 'romance of the communal', it seems largely to have had to do with (economic) property and with food; while there was a general ethic of sharing, enthusiastic religious experience, for example, does not seem to have been among the things that were supposed to be shared; nor certainly, again if Winstanley be taken as the authority, did the ethic lead to a critique of personal property or of the family form.[11] The Diggers were naturally accused – in accordance with what seems a transhistorical requirement of propertarian consciousness – of practising community of women, but there is no evidence that they did so.[12]

The story of the Diggers' internal dynamics as a group, then, is not one that can be told in any detail. It is otherwise with their external relations. Common and waste land belonged to no single proprietor, but codified rights of usufruct lay dense on their soil. In occupying common ground, the Diggers were trespassing against the law, according to which it ordinarily belonged to some manor or manors. In claiming that they had an exclusive, quasi-legal right to it, they were also trespassing against the collective custom so closely related both in principle and fact to land law. It is thus no wonder that they were prosecuted and harassed, attacked both legally and extralegally, from the first day of their endeavour.

The assembled army at least spared them. Having received conflicting reports about the occupation, Fairfax went out of his way back to London after quashing the Leveller mutiny at Burford to see the Surrey Diggers' works for himself.[13] Fairfax's decision to give the Diggers a sporting chance was likely complexly motivated:[14] if the general whose mild and moderate wisdom Marvell was shortly to celebrate had not known that the Diggers had little chance to sustain themselves he almost surely would have thrown them off George Hill himself. Nonetheless, Winstanley was perhaps not entirely unjustified in claiming army sanction for Digging on the basis of Fairfax's refusal to destroy the colony. The army's peaceful visit may have given the local authorities some pause.

Still, Fairfax of course knew the lay of the law and the land. Very soon, Winstanley is printing a pamphlet in which he denounces a pair of local freeholders for leading a violent attack on the Diggers. This was only among the most violent in a series of vigilante actions: the Diggers' crops were pulled up, their sheds pulled down, their persons beaten.[15] Soon after the freeholder pamphlet, the head Diggers were indicted for trespassing and taken to the nearby town of Kingston to be tried, and Winstanley is addressing a tract to the House of Commons, by his argument the only remaining legal court in the land, in which he can be seen working out the legal and historical basis for the common people's occupation of common lands.[16] After the Diggers were found guilty, and fined, for trespassing, they moved to a nearby common at Cobham. Gradually the main tenant of Cobham manor, one Parson Plattes, emerges as a somewhat special oppressor, becoming a low-keyed type of the whole English social order in its covetous and hypocritical aspects. Parson Plattes promises to let the Diggers be on their (his) common if Winstanley can prove their right from Scripture; Winstanley supplies him with several texts, to the parson's evident satisfaction; but soon thereafter Plattes' men are back at the game of intimidation.[17] On Good Friday 1650, they beat the Diggers off their land and then stake a guard over it, evidently to see to it that the Diggers' Christ remains this time in the tomb, and that the Parson's Easter Sunday isn't ruined. The Diggers never tried to reappropriate that common or tried their luck with another. It seems that their economic plight had grown increasingly desperate during the winter. Probably it was clear by the spring that they would be less able to grow crops than they had been in the previous year.

III

Robert Brenner has recently observed that the English Revolution went no further than it did, and could not consolidate itself, because of the political conservatism and apathy of the rural lower classes.[18] I say 'observes', because Brenner presents rural conservatism and apathy as an obvious thing, indeed as more or less a commonplace. Yet Brenner's construction of the revolution leaves one in a position to appreciate this commonplace anew, to grasp it as something of a paradox. For Brenner perhaps more than anyone else has made the case for the economic and political precocity, and for the comparative unity, of the English landed class as a whole, which he presents as having made the transition to capitalism, and as having become a – variegated, to be sure, and multiply interested – rural bourgeoisie, well before the 1640s. But if the English landholding class was both remarkably 'advanced' economically and remarkably class-conscious, then one is led to consider why the rural labouring classes were not equally advanced and acute. In a certain (economic) sense, of course, the English rural labouring class *was* advanced: it is axiomatic that if the landholding class was capitalist, then they were extracting surplus in the form of surplus value; in other words, they were exploiting wage-labour, which means that the rural labouring class was in an economic sense proletarianized. Why then could the rural proletariat not become aware of its real interests as against those of the landed classes? Why could it not attain to a comparable level of class-consciousness? The answers to these questions are largely historical and political in kind, and are fairly well known; I do not intend to canvas them here, but rather to highlight those respects in which the Digger venture did indeed embody an emergent proletarian consciousness. The analysis offered will not be intended to call the commonplace about rural apathy and conservatism in question, exactly; instead I mean to heighten one's appreciation of the significance of the commonplace by exposing what we might call its deep limits.

One will not appreciate either the Diggers' strategy, or their tenacity in holding together for a whole year, unless one has a sense of what they were up against. Let us begin, then, with one of Winstanley's more vivid depictions of, and responses to, rural conservatism in action. The following paragraph opens *A declaration of the bloudy and unchristian acting of William Star and John Taylor of Walton, with divers men in womens aparell, in opposition to those that dig upon George-hill in Surrey, &c.* It is perhaps worth noting that while the attack here described was not the first against the Diggers, it seems to have been the most violent. No other attack elicited its own pamphlet, or such graphic description:

> Upon the 11. day of June 1649, foure men only being fitting and preparing the ground for a winter season, upon that Common called George-hill, there came to them, *William Starr* of *Walton*, and *John Taylor*, two free-holders, being on horseback, having at their heels some men in womens apparell on foot, with every one a staffe or club, and as soon as they came to the diggers, would not speak like men, but like bruit beasts that have no understanding, they fell furiously upon them, beating and striking those foure naked men, beating them to the ground, breaking their heads, and sore bruising their bodies, whereof one is so sore bruised, that it is feared he will not escape with life.[19]

Star, Taylor and company may seem to have been making a statement here that requires little analysis: they wanted to beat the Diggers badly enough, at least, that they would not come back; this was evidently meant to be the final attack on the Diggers' camp. Yet their introduction of the cross-dressing motif strikes an odd note, and draws our attention to the symbolic strategies inherent in the action, which we can recover only from Winstanley's account. Why did the vigilantes attack in just this way, with most of the men dressed as women and the leaders Taylor and Star in proper person on horseback?

Reluctance to take sides openly, it should be stressed, is unlikely to have been a principal motive for the disguises. Well into the eighteenth century, male cross-dressing was marked as traditional symbolic practice, one of several sorts of symbolic reversal associated with festive occasions and activities. For our purposes here, what is important about cross-dressing is that it was thus associated with the popular morality, the 'true public opinion', which was supposed to be celebrated on holidays; and what is important to remember about festive or holiday practices in general is that they were sometimes used, on occasions of communal disorder or crisis, to *enforce* popular morality, or at least to make it known, to *signify* it.[20] This last is what the cross-dressing must be doing here. A more vital motive than simple disguise on the vigilantes' part would have been to claim a frighteningly impersonal, yet collective sanction for the force they applied. The transvestism of Taylor and Star's troop must have been intended to impress upon the Diggers – this group that claimed popular support for their actions – that their beating expressed the judgement of 'the collective' upon them.

That would have been the most important aspect of the message implicit in the cross-dressing; but there are at least two further nuances which would have sharpened considerably the effect of this symbolic blow. The first of these depends on our (and on the Diggers') consciousness of the opposition between two popular-cultural traditions, the traditional festive and the radical protestant, and more precisely between the practice of festive reversal and the sort of radical protestant reversal that the Diggers have 'invented'.[21] It might seem that the Diggers' focus on the here and now has driven sectarian millennialism to the point where it can almost make fruitful contact with the more secular, socially oriented festive culture, where it might draw somehow on the explosive energies that that culture both disciplined and put on display. The men dressed as women are there to make the point that this won't be; and they do it by drawing a sarcastic *equation* between Digger and festive culture. If the Diggers want a holiday, if they want to turn the world upside down, that is very well with the men dressed as women, they will join the party – so we might read them as saying. But *this* holiday reversal will only last for a day, as it should, and afterwards everything will be as normal.

The second nuance inherent in this collective message resides in the distinction – sharply pointed though unmoralized by Winstanley – between the freeholders, who come in stark and brazen person on horseback, and their footsoldiers in drag. The effect of this distinction is to put the 'collective' part of the judgement rendered upon the Diggers in their beating in quotation marks: it is not 'really' the people who have decided to smash the Digger colony, but the freeholding masters; or at least one cannot be sure it is not the freeholders who act through them. By *staging* this bitter festive reversal on the Diggers' waste land, the freeholders are saying that there *is* no popular will really, and that such practices as continue to bear a popular stamp – like the land itself which the Diggers hope to control – are the freeholders' to do with as they wish. If the Diggers had hoped to tap the 'immemorial' collective resources conventionally brought into play, and signalized, by popular festive modes, they will fail – so the brazen presence of Star and Taylor tells them – not because the people are against them, but because the people *have* no will of their own.

In both these dimensions, then, the cross-dressing served as symbolic intimidation; it was intended to hurt the Diggers in places that physical blows could not touch, and if it did not do the desired damage that of course would not have been because of the implicit contradiction between the two nuances just rehearsed. One might argue that popular festivity exercised a conservative function here, or was deployed to a conservative end, and one would not be wrong: the 'festive' crew was clearly out to teach the Diggers a conservative lesson about the social order. But if one recalls that this, the only cross-dressed attack, was the last in the initial series of such actions, it will not seem implausible that the festive motif served an exploratory, unconsciously cognitive, purpose as well; like a blow delivered in the dark, it must have been meant to *discover* the Diggers' symbolic habitation as well as to hurt them in it.[22]

There is some evidence in Winstanley's printed rejoinder to suggest that the freeholders did indeed hit a sensitive spot. But this is by no means easy to see at a glance; and it should be emphasized, before turning to this evidence, that what first strikes the reader is how readily and easily Winstanley can turn the attack against the freeholders. For what are perhaps obvious reasons, Winstanley tends to hold specifically Digger tenets in reserve. Instead the brutality of the attack is stressed, the better to represent it as an episode in a larger narrative of victorious suffering: it is the Foxean tradition of apocalyptic national martyrdom that is activated. Though in Winstanley's version this tradition is more collectivized and secularized than was ordinary – the Digger martyrs suffer anonymously, and simply for insisting on the right to subsistence which the taxes they have paid to Parliament should have bought them – still the invocation of Foxe's legacy would seem calculated to appeal even to more respectable Puritans.[23]

But if he can handle Taylor and Star easily enough by casting them as anti-Christ's agents, Winstanley seems less certain how to treat the men dressed as women. What one does not find in *A declaration of the unchristian acting* is any reference to the hidden or heartfelt sentiments of the freeholders' retinue. When Winstanley tells in a later pamphlet, for example, of yet another treacherous assault, in which some servants destroy the Diggers' makeshift dwellings at the command of their lords, he suggests that the servants' smiles, on receiving a reward of ten shillings to drink, conceal seditious feelings: 'they durst not laugh out, lest their Lords should hear they jeer'd them openly; for in their hearts they are Diggers'.[24] Such a reference testifies to Winstanley's faith in the social resources available for tapping by a project such as his. But in the earlier *A declaration of the unchristian acting*, Winstanley does not make the women's apparel into the sign of a Digger unconscious, nor does he even acknowledge its festive significance.[25] And it seems plausible that he shies away from doing these things because he feels the apparel to be already too strongly charged with collective meaning, too closely identified with a group of traditional practices expressive of the popular will. If this is so, it helps to explain the uncommonly paranoid note present in this short pamphlet's closing movement, in which Winstanley declares that while England's 'striving' in the civil war before now had involved Dragon against Dragon, one oppressing power against another, the war has now entered a new, decisive phase, and England 'begins to fight against the Lamb, the Dove, the meek Spirit, the power of Love', which is represented by the Digger sufferers and which will soon 'grind thee [England] to powder'.[26] England does not only figure as the Diggers' opponent in this final passage; it retains its status as privileged witness of reformation – but only barely: and I would suggest that it is especially the spectre of the women's apparel – that repressed sign of secular hostility to Winstanley's project – that threatens to break his millennialism free of its national framework.

However this last may be, the chief points to be stressed here seem unassailable enough. On the one hand, the freeholders' festive attack, in its adoption and its failure, testifies not only to perdurable rural conservatism, but also to the uncertainty that the novelty of the Digger project inspired, and the difficulty of locating them symbolically. On the other hand, while Winstanley's part in the 'dialogue', his Foxean dodge and counterattack, does much to convince one of the symbolic elasticity and strength of his project, questions are raised, as the martyr-code comes to the fore, as to the ultimate social and symbolic resources of the Digger programme.

IV

To consider the Diggers' resources entails specifying the essential elements of their political strategy, since the most consequent Digger propaganda crystallized in the George Hill venture, and since it was really this venture that defined their identity and gave them their notoriety as a political faction and sect. The question I wish to answer in this section, then, is: How and why did Winstanley's experimental and materialistic religion lead him, after his communist revelation, to George Hill? Why did the Digger venture take the form of a claim to common land, and what were the strategic ends of this claim? My argument will be that the Diggers had a deep (we would say a 'structural') justification for their action all along; but that this, the real cause of their action, paradoxically became more legible when, in the course and as a consequence of their struggle, they were forced to generate more 'superficial' or politically viable justifications. As Digger discourse became more political and secular, their project came to appear at once more integrally socio-economic and more irreducibly religious or millennial, more dependent on 'outside assistance'. When the Diggers first occupied George Hill, Winstanley's pamphlets were fairly clearly calling for a massive rural strike; as their occupation continued, it tended to devolve into a demonstration whose aims, if increasingly trenchant and far-reaching, were in the same measure increasingly symbolic.

Because it is the form of the Digger enterprise that is in question here, I will be taking more or less for granted, as an ideological precondition of Digger strategy, Winstanley's religious materialism – the notion that God is immanent in, spreads himself through, creation, and knows perhaps no other mode of existence. As Hill has shown, such materialism was far from being peculiar to Winstanley, but came to be marked, once the censorship went out if not before, as a discursive medium especially characteristic of the sectarian left, associated as it was with sundry varieties of egalitarianism and a proto-sociological critique of 'respectable Protestant' sin (and accordingly of heaven and hell).[27] The mystical materialism of Winstanley's early pamphlets placed him on the left wing of the revolutionary forces even before it led him to preach communist social doctrines and before he took up a spade at George Hill. And it did *lead* him, I would suggest, though I do not have the space to argue it here: an implicit case will be that Winstanley's tracts reveal the remarkable social-epistemological potential of religious materialism; Winstanley's spreading God served as a revolutionary divining rod, leading him to those places and discourses of justice in the body politic which were indeed as likely as any to issue in a radical breakthrough.

Sabine, in his introduction to his edition of Winstanley's writings, noted that 'it was natural' for Winstanley to hit upon the common and Crown lands as a source of support for the poor in the situation prevailing in 1649.[28] We do not need to dispute this statement. With near famine conditions prevailing in London and elsewhere in the country, Parliament had especially vigorous recourse to the traditional extraordinary measures of ordering the authorities to provide the poor with corn and coal, and of devising plans to put the poor on work. Several people suggested that Crown lands might be used to remedy the plight of the poor and the national economy; Peter Chamberlen, most notably, proposed a radical scheme in which Crown and common lands would be run as a joint stock company and worked by the poor.[29] What would have made proposals such as Chamberlen's more 'natural' and plausible was the association set up between the rural poor and common/Crown lands by the practice of squatting on these lands, a practice approximately as perennial as the depopulation that accompanied primitive agrarian accumulation. Keith Thomas was the first to have observed that the Diggers' colony on George Hill ought to be thought of as fashioning the fugitive collectivism of the burgeoning class of rural dispossessed into a programmatic project.[30] But while the existence of the tradition of squatting helps to explain why the Diggers occupied the common land – they did so for the same reason squatters did: because there was nowhere else to go, and then also because the tradition existed – it obviously is not sufficient to explain their justifying the common people's collective appropriation of the common lands, and turning the tradition into a programme. It may have been natural for the Diggers to turn to the common lands, but it was not so for them to preach what they practised – to try to *legitimate* squatters' collective rights to these lands.

Winstanley's most general justification for taking the commons was religious, as should already be clear. But to say that the earth was, and ought to be, a common treasure house, was not enough. To defend the Digger occupation over the course of the year, he was more or less forced to come up with supplementary justifications, more concrete and practical than his initial ones. The evidence of the pamphlets suggests that it was particularly the legal action taken against the Diggers that prompted such supplementation, and which thus helped to crystallize the true Digger 'position'.[31]

In his later pamphlets Winstanley routinely forwards several arguments, which habitually flow together, so that it would take a good deal of patience to separate out all the logical strands. The mixing of arguments ought not to be seen as a flaw: his intention, a time-honoured rhetorical one, is evidently that the arguments combine to project a general position which will seem all the more like common sense for being irreducible to any one argument. While I believe he is successful in attaining this effect, my explanation as to why this is so cannot be exhaustive (there are simply too many arguments for that), but will focus on what I take to be the two main practical lines of argument in Winstanley's pamphlets. This procedure, while it misses some of the polemical richness of Winstanley's position, has the virtue of directing one to the deepest and most strategic, if more or less unspoken, argument for the Digger occupation.

The first argument is explicit in the texts of several pamphlets. It might be called an argument from constitutional emergency. With the victory over the king and abolition of monarchy, so this argument runs, the legal status of common and waste land has become a question. For the lords of manors had possessed superior rights to this land only on the king's donation, and now that the chain of monarchy has been broken, so is their claim to common land without legal standing.[32] But why should the poor have a valid claim to this land? Chiefly because they ought to have *something*, and there is no better solution at the moment to the question of what that something should be. They should have something, Winstanley argues, because they made a tacit deal with the House of Commons to assist them in their war against the king, and the time has come for Parliament to deliver on its part of the bargain.[33] But even if a contract were not at least tacitly agreed to, still the people have fought with and for Parliament to defeat the king, and now equity demands that as part of the victorious party they should receive part of the spoils – the category into which common lands along with Crown and delinquent lands are now fitted.[34] The gentry and lords of manors who fought for Parliament now hold their lands independently of the king's tenure; the House of Commons is free to represent the freeholding element unchecked by king or lords; the common or poor people should enjoy collective rights to the common lands, and to at least a large part of the forfeited (Crown and delinquent) lands: that is the deal that should be struck, according to Winstanley; that is the outline of the new constitution that was really being fought for all along. According to this first, perfectly explicit argument, then, squatting happens to be justified in light of current events, the victory over the king. Squatting happens now to know its day.

Now this may seem an aggressive enough argument for Winstanley to make.[35] Yet from the point of view of Digger first principles, according to which the earth is rightfully a common treasury, the new constitution for which Winstanley argues is of course not satisfactory: under the new regime, the well-affected gentry, who fought to have their enclosures free from kingly encumbrance, will become the new agents of self-interest, of kingly power. However aggressive the proposal might seem, it represents a compromise on Winstanley's part, and presumably derives partly from his recognition that it would be absurd to expect any freeholders to agree that they had been fighting against the King all along in order that they might hold things in common with the poor. It is politic of Winstanley then, it's politics, to limit himself to the formula – which can give one pause when it is placed in close proximity to the 'common treasury' principle – that the younger brother (i.e., the poor) has as much right to the commons and wastes as the elder brother (i.e., the gentry and freeholding class) has to his enclosures.

But there is more to it than this; or rather, this particular compromise is supported by a second, unemphatic but strongly implicit, justification from squatting: what we might call a deep-constitutionalist, or post-Norman Yoke, argument. Winstanley cedes the elder brother his enclosure partly because, in the Digger version of the Norman Yoke theory,[36] a significant level of oppression and enclosure reigned in England before the bastard William's conquest. Winstanley never spells out exactly how he envisages pre-Norman society, but it is clear that the freeholding element was already in place, and that the 'spirit of enclosure' which it represented was so to speak extended and elaborated, was given a ruling, systemic character, by the Conquest. The common people, it is implied, enjoyed the commons to themselves before William, though Winstanley is silent on how they held these lands (whether 'privately' or 'commonly').

Given the Digger reading of the Norman Yoke, the formula about the younger brother's right to the commons being equal to the elder brother's right to his enclosures makes sense as an indication of what the revolution's current minimal programme should be. With the expulsion of William's heir and the abolition of monarchy, property relations ought to return to what they had been before the Conquest, and the dispossessed common people to re-inherit their old possessions: and what lands would be more likely candidates for 'old possessions' than the common lands? According to this justification of the squatters' activity, squatting is not read simply as a practice that happens to be useful at the moment; rather, the squatters who camped on common ground before the Diggers are implicitly recognized to have been doing so on the basis of the old constitution, to have been agitating all along for the return that can now be effected.

The justifications just rehearsed are of course tactically, even strategically, crucial to the Digger programme. But neither goes to the heart of the logic put in play by the Digger occupation – not even the deep-constitutional argument, though this argument shades off almost imperceptibly, I think, into the one that the Diggers are 'really' making, and helps to make it more legible than it otherwise would be. It shades off into this deeper, rather symbolic than discursive, argument especially because, by implying that vagrant settlement was agitating for a return to the pre-Norman constitution all along, it ascribes to this activity a *hermeneutic* character: past squatters were actually indicating the solution to the problem of monarchy, attempting to reconstruct the pre-Norman state of affairs. But then if this was what the squatters were about, Digger *communism* may be taken to indicate the pre-Norman constitution's merely provisional, expedient status. It points, in other words, toward a deeper, more collective, return, back behind the original fall, in which the earth of current-day England will again, but in a more developed sense, be a common treasury.

This indication made by squatting/Digging is corroborated by the affinity between common land and people harboured in linguistic usage itself. Winstanley only rarely disposes individual sentences so as to make the argument that the common people should hold the commons in common because language itself says it should be so. More often the word 'common' is simply used often enough in different senses in close proximity to suggest an underlying natural connection between people and land. And perhaps the argument from language is stronger for usually only being alluded to, since in this way the proof of the argument tends to be left to the future and to action: if the Diggers succeed in establishing the poor on the common lands across the nation, then the commons will be common in a new sense; the signified will have shifted under the signifier to produce a new meaning, and the simple-minded Digger etymology will prove true. The sense that the affinity between land and people is an emergent, contemporary phenomenon is underscored, I think, by the parallelism between two phrases that Winstanley frequently uses to designate land and people: to match the *waste* and *common* land, we have the *poor* and *common* people.[37] Since, in late sixteenth- to mid-seventeenth-century England, common land was increasingly seen as waste by improving landlords, and since the category of common people was coming to be increasingly indistinguishable from the poor, it seems legitimate to read the chime of *waste* and *common* with *poor* and *common* as linking these two contemporary problems, and thus as semi-consciously suggesting that they are part of a (single) process to which the Diggers stand as the providential, but logical solution.

Here, then, we arrive at a third argument for Digging, a third justification and interpretation of squatting. This argument is certainly not articulated as such anywhere in Winstanley's pamphlets. At most it is only hinted at in details, or broadly, gesturally indicated in the form taken by the Digger venture and the motion of Winstanley's practical arguments. Nonetheless, I believe it is the strongest of the three arguments, in the sense of being the most historical and truly strategic. If it were plainly spoken, it would consist in the claim that English agrarian space is now divided into two kinds of land, the enclosed and the common; and that this opposition is properly one between private and collective tenancy spaces. It would offer as evidence for the propriety of this division the increasingly stark division between rich and poor, between those who can live off the land they freely hold and those who are dispossessed in fact or in tendency. And, as evidence for the propriety of the collective cultivation of the commons, it would allude to the spontaneously collective nature of previous squatting forays.

We might call this root argument the *utopian* one. I do not mean *utopian* mainly in a comparative sense – though certainly, relative to other schemes for improving agricultural efficiency or handling the problem of the poor, Winstanley's programme stands apart for the way in which it thoroughly redefines the terms of the problem(s). Rather, Winstanley's argument is utopian in a more literal, and literary, sense. Digger strategy depends, like literary utopias, on the perceived emergence of real possibilities, of quasi-hypothetical new social space or spaces, from within the shifting and decoded space of the nation. But Winstanley's Utopia, unlike at least More's and Bacon's literary utopias, does not exist in *parallel*, either to the (English) nation or to the city. Instead it has fallen into the world, where it takes the form of a locale, or rather of a vaguely defined network of locales. This collective other space remains abstract, but it is really there, embedded in the land. The land cries out to be free, and the Digger goal is to populate it, to incarnate the communality it cries for. Or better, since only a part of English social space is utopian, the Digger goal is, by setting up a commune network, to activate the implicit struggle between opposed tenancy spaces coming ever more visibly to be inscribed across the face of the English countryside.[38]

If we stand back from this strategy, we can see that it is based upon an accidental, and to some extent illusory, but nonetheless structural consequence of agrarian uneven development, of the hardening of agrarian property rights within the old manorial framework; the strategy assumes that enclosure is rendering not just private property, but also common (and waste) land, 'absolute', and attempts to put an end to the process by extraditing the new pockets of communal space from the exclusive, enclosing space of 'kingly power' (i.e., capitalist property). Registering the long-term or structural contemporaneity of the Digger project in this way helps one to appreciate its deep ingenuity, and helps to explain the sources of their confidence and moral courage. For the specific virtue of Winstanley's 'strategic utopia' would seem to be that it affords a way, a place, of thinking the unity of the (primarily agrarian) poor and dispossessed.

At the same time, even if the explicit Leveller-inspired justifications work to make the more truly strategic, utopian one more visible, this last argument for Digging remains largely symbolic – implicit in the practice of Digging rather than explicit in Winstanley's discourse. And in truth, the discursive register that most nearly in itself conveys the dynamic of manorial capitalism, hence the Diggers' strongest argument, remains the generally conditioning one of materialist religion. The spirit of self-preservation (Satan) having ramified and extended its enclosing tentacles since its original conquest in the fall to the point where it is now weak from overdevelopment, the spirit of common preservation (God) now begins to grow strong, and to reassume his original form. So speaks Winstanley, throughout the Digger venture. When the Diggers took George Hill, they were doing millennial work, they were the spreading God returning to Paradise. This does not mean that all the Diggers needed to do, according to Winstanley's conception, was to stay on their hill and praise God by planting vegetables. Rather, as I have been arguing, the Diggers' millennial utopianism paved the way for strategic, political thinking. It conditioned the appearance of the problem how to organize the rural poor and dispossessed – even as it set limits, finally, whose specific nature I will now go on to show, to that problem's lucid elaboration.

The Digger plan was consciously a plan of the moment, aiming to exploit the crisis and indecision in the ranks of the ruling class. Their first goal, conceivable by virtue of this crisis, was to set up a *network* of Digging communities: the George Hill venture, as described in Winstanley's pamphlets, was expressly exemplary, one among many other imagined communal experiments. As this network established itself, Digging was to take on the character of an agrarian strike. The first two Digging pamphlets make it abundantly plain that this was an integral part of the original Digger vision; the voice proclaiming 'Live together, eat bread together, declare this all abroad' goes on to warn Winstanley's readership, in decidedly threatening tones, that no-one should work for a master.[39] After the Diggers had weathered attacks on their common, this particular strain is not heard anymore; it is a paradox that with the sharpening of Digger ideology and the increasing symbolic clarity of their utopian strategy, the sect's overt politics became less militant, more *strictly* symbolic or millennial. Nonetheless, the plan throughout was evidently to create a solidary ethic of masterlessness, and to use the lure of freedom to draw off the landholding class's wage-labour force. The Diggers would then be in a position to make the ruling class understand from within 'the cry of necessity' that Winstanley describes, in *The Law of Freedom*, as constituting the origins of good government when and as long as it is heard.[40] Thereafter the old powers would perhaps be willing to negotiate new social arrangements.

Such was the general plan. But the question remains, how was the strike actually to materialize? How was the Digger network to be set up and maintained against the inevitable opposition? The content of Winstanley's pamphlets is not terribly informative on the matter of Digger *tactics*. It seems that the network was to establish itself more or less by contagion, to use a favourite ruling-class metaphor for the spread of lower-class religion and revolt:[41] to put it less figuratively, one's impression is that a diffuse proselytization was to be set in motion by the Digger action and by Winstanley's pamphlets proclaiming and justifying the venture. One would like to know more about oral forms of proselytization. But I am tempted to suggest that the relative lack of evidence on this score may amount to evidence for the relative difficulty, and marginality, of oral propaganda for the Diggers. I would propose, accordingly, that Winstanley's pamphlets were tactically crucial to the Digger programme *in their very form*, and that the Diggers relied on achieving critical mass through writing and the printed word.

The pamphlets were to serve three main tactical aims. First, and most crucially, in a play for a broad popular following, they aimed to publish and protect the Digger story – to see that it was not only known through the deformations bound to occur to such a story in oral transmission, or through the crucified versions the newspapers saw fit to print. In publishing the story, the pamphlets would also be circulating the new popular wisdom, the Digger common sense, that made their version true. Winstanley's pamphlets were of course published in London (by the famous radical printer Giles Calvert) and addressed to some central institution, to London itself, or to the whole nation. If you imagine the dissemination of these pamphlets outwards, I believe you will be composing a figure for the rural expansion/extension of the Leveller project that Digging was meant to be: true-levelling politics was much more a politics of the pamphlet than the Levellers' ever was. This tactical context has implications, incidentally, and should be recalled when considering such an apparently independent feature of the pamphlets as their frequent reiteration of themes and 'mythemes'. Given the novelty of Digger ideology, such repetition, as well as other of the characteristics of lay preaching, would have been justified even when transcribed in print; for it would have helped to secure new Diggers in the truth, to harden collective common rights.[42]

Second, the pamphlets must have been intended to secure, not just lower-class members, but also a few ruling-class sponsors. The Diggers needed above all to accredit themselves, whether as harmless or as well-intentioned, with the army. They needed some time if they were to activate the common lands, to free their utopia. To have a hope of staging their strike, they had to make an initial appeal to authority. The sweet reason of the Digger pamphlets, their pacifism and openness, would seem calculated to win just the sort of equivocal patronage that Fairfax did bestow on them.

Now this initial appeal for sponsorship would seem coherent with the Digger programme. The logic of institutions is not reducible to the logic of classes, and individuals do not necessarily act in their manifest class interest. But neither army neutrality nor the individual assistance from benevolent aristocrats which was never forthcoming could be expected to enable the Diggers to succeed against the secular power of the landholding class, once this class, as a class, had had the opportunity to register the Digger threat for what it was. Thus it seems to me that the pamphlets cannot be denied to have a third tactical aim – an aim that is also beyond doubt utterly *strategic*, and which thus casts confusion on the Digger experiment in its origins. This aim is that of appealing to the diffuse millennialism shared by ruling as well as subaltern English classes. Now, though it proved to be one of the principal functions of the Interregnum to exorcize this demon from the ranks of the respectable once and for all, millennialism was still somewhat of a national possession in England,[43] so one ought not to pronounce this appeal 'unrealistic' too quickly. As a way of thinking the political demoralization of the gentry at the end of a war of position, or in other words as a way of conceiving the effect of the Diggers' ultimate 'negotiations' should they have attained a position from which to conduct them, the millennial claim makes good sense. But if one reads the 'tactic' thus, Winstanley is getting ahead of himself, for the pamphlets are of course not published in an endgame situation, and Winstanley knows this. It is one thing that the English gentry possessed a millennial ideology; it was quite another to expect their millennial beliefs to lead them in anything approaching critical mass to side with the heretical communes who aimed at stripping them of their labour and their privileges. The Winstanley who could state matter of factly that the revolution against the King had been on behalf of the gentry who now held their lands free of royal encumbrance surely possessed the political and sociological acuteness to recognize this difference. This final appeal, then, does indeed introduce incoherence into the Digger programme. In the artificial order in which we have been reconstructing it, if the initial, universal-millennial, appeal is successful, then the appeal made by the agrarian strike will be unnecessary; if the first appeal goes unheard, then the second appeal will never be made. I would not be taken to be arguing that Winstanley's millennialism is a shackle or a limit on his thought in any simple sense – I have already argued that millennialism paves the way to political thought by helping to locate the space in which the unity of the dispossessed might be conceived. Nonetheless, because, at least in the circumstances of 1649–52, it must involve an irreducibly primary appeal to the whole nation, Winstanley's millennialism does seem to me to be symptomatic of an underdevelopment in Digger thought as politically representative thought, as the thought of a class.

Even as its deep, class logic became more unmistakable, then, the Digger project was doomed to turn with time and in practice into something like a self-help venture dependent on the charitable permission of the landholding classes. Brenner's assertion that these classes' ideological dominance prevented the extension or confirmation of the revolution is if anything corroborated, for what we have just seen is that the most advanced agrarian element was not able to break utterly with them even in thought.

Yet what I would underscore in conclusion here is, not the limits imposed by the unevenness of Digger political thought and strategy, but the remarkable sociological sensitivity that enabled Winstanley to 'discover' the unity of the dispossessed as a class, its collective form, before the development of manufacture and the emergence of the factory system had provided it with its socio-economic underpinnings. The main 'object' to which this sensitivity is (at least indirectly) attuned must be the specifically capitalist dynamic of accumulation, which the Digger plantations have it as their deep aim both to develop and to terminate, to explode to its logical conclusion, so to speak. One could argue, indeed, that Winstanley was an economist thinker before the fact – before economism became, with the autonomization of the market, an engrained ideological tendency and constant temptation to political strategists. But if Winstanley was economist, he was religiously so. The best and most direct 'medium' of Winstanley's (economic or long-term) sensitivity is not an economic or specifically sociological language: Winstanley can hardly claim to have participated in any way in the invention of political economy or anthropology, and though he was remarkable as a constitutional 'thinker' – witness *The Law of Freedom* (1653), Winstanley's utopian last word on the Digger experiment, in which he can be seen attempting to redress the political deficiencies uncovered in its course – this was not the sphere of his greatest achievement. Rather, the really moving idiom, as I have suggested before, was the peculiar one in which his millennialism is expressed. One can see it happening in the pamphlets of early 1649, in which Winstanley's impersonal spreading God, the Christ rising in us all, stakes a special claim to the common lands. This would seem to be a case of one discourse interacting with, and replacing another: the tendentially 'poor' and 'absolute' character accorded to common lands in enclosure debates provides Winstanley's God with a natural point of access back into the enclosed Eden of England, and Winstanley's God gives the poor a political purchase, ascribes to them a de facto autonomy, almost certainly undreamt of in the manorial courts where these debates were presumably mostly focused, and whence they stemmed.[44] However this may be, millennialism provides the most vivid and direct, though not the exclusive, register of the dynamic of rural accumulation and depopulation that seems to have reached a temporary apogee at mid-century.

The Diggers seem to have been wrenched from historical memory soon after the Restoration, and were rather notoriously without direct impact within subsequent political history, having to wait till the modern communist movement to be rediscovered. Yet who is to say that they were not influential even as repressed? In his *Memorials of English Affairs* (1682), after recounting the meeting between Winstanley and Fairfax at Whitehall in which Winstanley and his fellow Digger leader Everard failed to doff their hats and were assured that they would be left to the law and the country gentlemen to take care of them, Bulstrode Whitelock concludes his journal entry with the following remark: 'I have set down this the more largely, because it was the beginning of the appearance of this opinion, and that we might the better understand and avoid these weak persuasions'.[45] Context makes it fairly clear that the weak persuasions are communistic in kind, though communism had of course been heard of long before the Diggers, and was hardly a threat in the later seventeenth century. Whitelock, one imagines, must have been thinking in the late '70s of the widespread lower-class nonconformity, especially Quakerism, which was one of the great social legacies of the revolution, and exaggerating its threat (while at the same time oddly registering its appeal) in time-honoured conservative fashion. Yet the connection, if slightly hysterical, is an interesting one. It suggests that the Diggers had turned into the token, in at least one ruling-class mind, of a new, or newly massive, kind of political danger, coming to be associated now especially with lower-class religion, but also perhaps with the category of the people in general. The Diggers are made to signify the transition to a political epoch in which the character of class relations has become more fraught than previously, and communism has become a deep, but permanent and objective, threat.

Notes

1. *The Works of Gerrard Winstanley*, ed. George H. Sabine (Ithaca, 1944), p. 428. This will be the edition in which Winstanley is quoted throughout. For a complete text of *The True Levellers' Standard Advanced*, see the *Documents* section below, pp. 311–25.
2. For fuller versions of the Diggers' story, and for stimulating discussion of Winstanley's pamphlets, see Sabine's introduction to his edition of Winstanley's works (n. 1 above); Robert W. Kenney's introduction to his edition of *The Law of Freedom in a Platform* (New York, 1973 (orig.

pub. 1940)); Christopher Hill, *The World Turned Upside Down* (Harmondsworth, 1972); Olivier Lutaud, *Winstanley: Socialisme et Christianisme sous Cromwell* (Paris, 1976); and D. W. Petegorsky, *Left-Wing Democracy in the English Civil War* (London, 1940). A caveat should be registered here: because there was only one Winstanley – i. e., because there was only one known Digger ideologue, who was associated with a particular Digger group in the parish of Walton-on-Thames, in Surrey – this story, like most histories of the Diggers, will be Surrey-centred. It should be kept in mind that there were several other Digger communities, each no doubt with its own specific history of struggle and ultimate failure; and that, though it seems probable that the Surrey Diggers were the leading group, this is not certain. It is a noteworthy fact that the Digger movement was finally suppressed shortly after evidence of communication among groups came to light and was publicized. This suggests that a comprehensive history of the Diggers would take the network of communities, or the emergence thereof, as its focus.

3. It is not entirely clear how *Diggers* came to be the sobriquet of record; evidently, though, the name was applied from outside and accepted by the group itself. The term was used to refer to some of those who reclaimed common lands in the Midland riots (1607), and so tends to set the Diggers in the tradition of rural revolt (see Kenney, *The Law of Freedom*, p. 27). But it also surely took on a weighty metaphorical sense: the Diggers dug down and exposed the basic truths about society, they intended to plant its institutions anew, or to return to the time when Adam delved and Eve span, and so on. See Lutaud, *Winstanley*, pp. 14–15, for this latter sense.

4. For Leveller religion, see the informative article by Brian Manning, 'The Levellers and Religion', in *Radical Religion in the English Revolution*, ed. J. F. McGregor and B. Reay (Oxford, 1984), pp. 65–90. For good brief discussions of Leveller politics, see Hill, *The World Turned Upside Down*, ch. 4, and A. L. Morton's introduction to his selection of Leveller writings, *Freedom in Arms* (New York, 1975).

5. For an interesting and controversial treatment of the Levellers and the question of the franchise, see C. B. Macpherson's chapter on the Levellers in *The Theory of Possessive Individualism* (Oxford, 1962).

6. See especially Morton, *Freedom in Arms*, pp. 27–30.

7. For the indefinite border between Levellers and Diggers, see especially Hill, *The World Turned Upside Down*, ch. 7. *Light Shining in Buckinghamshire* is printed in Sabine, ed., *The Works*, pp. 611–26.

8. My assumption is that rural small property tended to be either one or the other, either less or more secure than urban (less if copyhold, more if not). But it should be remembered that Winstanley himself had failed as a small clothier in London before moving to Surrey.

9. Hill makes it clear that public opinion usually didn't draw a distinction between Levellers and Diggers (see *The World Turned Upside Down*, pp. 118–23). This was doubtless in good part tactical (i. e., it was intended to embarrass the Levellers); but it was perhaps also partly 'honest', and thus might be taken to indicate real perceived continuity between the two 'parties'. If Winstanley's term *true-levelling* is of course somewhat invidious at the Levellers' expense, it also, as I have already implied, suggests that he saw the Diggers as extending and deepening the Levellers' project.

10. See Sabine, ed., *The Works*, pp. 257–66, for Winstanley's first description, and defence, of what the Diggers were doing at George Hill.

11. See Kenney, ed., *The Law of Freedom*, for evidence that Winstanley did not envisage doing away with the household as the basic social unit of consumption (p. 515): 'Every Family shall live apart, as now they do; every man shall enjoy his own wife, and every woman her own husband, as now they do . . . '.

12. When, late in 1649, the Ranters appeared on the scene, making the accusation more plausible, Winstanley adamantly attacked what he saw as their libertinism. See Sabine, ed., *The Works*, pp. 399–403.

13. Fairfax had already spoken to the Digger leaders (Winstanley and John Everard) before he paid this visit, having called them before the Army Council on first hearing of their existence. See Lutaud, *Winstanley*, pp. 169–72, 206.

14. Winstanley later reminds Fairfax that 'you promised me in *Whitehal Gallerie*, that you would not meddle with us, but leave us to the Law of the Land, and the Country Gentlemen to deal with us' (Sabine, ed., *The Works*, p. 395).

15. For Winstanley's recapitulation of the Digger sufferings see the appendix to *A New Year's Gift*, in Sabine, ed., *The Works*, pp. 392–3.

16. Ibid., pp. 301–12.

17 Ibid., pp. 433–7.

18. Robert Brenner, *Merchants and Revolution* (Princeton, 1993), p. 539: 'As almost all sections of the alliance of forces that made the revolution of 1648 were aware, any fully democratic settlement would have restored the conservative gentry to power. This was simply because, with the important exception of London (and of course the army), relatively few areas in the nation had experienced significant radicalization during the Civil War years. In fact, in view of the ideological hegemony exercised by local landlords over most of the countryside and the relative immunity of agricultural laborers to radical politics in this epoch, relatively little mass radicalization could have been expected at this time from rural England'.

19. Sabine, ed., *The Works*, p. 295.

20. For an authoritative general treatment of festive practices see Peter Burke,

Popular Culture in Early Modern Europe (New York, 1978). For their use on occasions of communal disorder or crisis see Natalie Zemon Davis, *Society and Culture in Early Modern France* (Stanford, 1975); and, with focus on England, for a later period, E. P. Thompson, *Customs in Common* (London, 1991).

21. David Underdown has argued that some such popular-cultural division is what made the Civil War possible; see *Revel, Riot, and Rebellion* (New York, 1985). In his great book on the Civil War sects, *The World Turned Upside Down*, Hill suggests that radical sectarians' symbolic activity drew on traditions of festive reversal (see, e.g., pp. 16–17); but he devotes little space to this theme.

22. Cf. Zemon Davis's influential argument for the exploratory character of festive practices, in *Society and Culture.*

23. For the influence of Foxe's *Book of Martyrs* see William Haller, *Foxe's Book of Martyrs and the Elect Nation* (London, 1963), ch.7.

24. Sabine, ed., *The Works*, p. 368.

25. The cross-dressing is either simply noted, or it is made into the sign of *brutishness*, a move that would smack simply of the classically puritanical if it were not then read as a telling metaphor for the arrogance and unreason of the freeholders' mentality and methods. In the former case, the festive motif stands out as a symbolically indeterminate element (do the men dressed as women carry long staves too, and what does that mean if they do?). In the latter case, the reading seems somewhat forced, even if the association that leads to it is clear enough. In both cases, Winstanley fails directly to confront the fairly obvious festive meaning of the cross-dressing.

26. Sabine, ed., *The Works*, p. 297.

27. Hill, *The World Turned Upside Down*, esp. pp. 139–83.

28. Sabine, ed., *The Works*, pp. 11–14.

29. Ibid., pp. 13–14.

30. Keith Thomas, 'Another Digger Broadside', *Past and Present* 42 (Feb. 1969), 57–68.

31. See particularly 'An Appeal to the House of Commons' and 'A Watchword to the City of London and the Armie' in Sabine, ed., *The Works*.

32. See, e.g., ibid., p. 112. Note, though, that Winstanley never lays such stress on the king's role in the establishment of lordly property as does the author of *Light Shining in Buckinghamshire* (ibid., p. 613).

33. Ibid., pp. 115, 182–5.

34. Ibid., p. 173.

35. For the theory of the Norman Yoke and the use the Levellers made of it see Christopher Hill, *Puritanism and Revolution* (London, 1962), pp. 75–82.

36. E.g., Sabine, ed., *The Works*, p. 115.

37. For the impoverishment of the common people see Keith Wrightson, *English Society 1580–1680* (London, 1982). For the changing attitude to common land, see, e.g., J. A. Yelling, *Common Field and Enclosure in England, 1450–1850* (Hamden, 1977).

38. It is worth underscoring the lack of complete agreement between the two preceding, more political and short-term arguments for Digging, and this third, utopian, more socio-economic and long-term one: the two Leveller-inspired arguments are confined to answering the question as to what the war has been fought for, and what would be a just settlement to the struggle that has come to an end with the king's beheading; the utopian interpretation can hardly be so confined, once it is perceived for what it is, but looks frankly behind the king's literal deposition to the abolition of kingly power, arguing for the initiation of a 'quiet', pacific struggle between private and collective tenancy spaces.

39. Sabine, ed., *The Works*, p. 262.

40. Ibid., pp. 538–9.

41. Consider this striking figure from *The New Law of Righteousness*: 'everyone is to wait, till the Lord Christ do spread himself in multiplicities of bodies, making them all of one heart and one mind' (Sabine, ed., *The Works*, pp. 182–3).

42. For a stimulating discussion of 'mythemes' in Winstanley's work see Lutaud, *Winstanley*, pp. 387–412.

43. See J. G. A. Pocock, *The Machiavellian Moment: Florentine Political Thought and the Atlantic Republican Tradition* (Princeton, 1975), ch. 4.

44. For debates on enclosure in manorial courts see Yelling, *Common Field and Enclosure.*

45. I quote from Lutaud, *Winstanley*, p. 171.

13 *Female prophecy in the seventeenth century: the instance of Anna Trapnel*

Kate Chedgzoy

In the mid-seventeenth century, as increasing numbers of women began to seek a public voice and to write with publication in mind, one of the key forms they turned to was prophecy: according to one study, in the years from 1649 to 1688, more than half the texts published by women were prophecies.[1] These prophetic texts bring together political and religious concerns, constituting a form of literary expression which allowed women to engage with the public sphere and address some of the key issues of the turbulent and unpredictable times in which they found themselves living. In this essay, I shall locate the phenomenon of female prophecy in its seventeenth-century context, considering its contemporary significance with reference to questions of religion, politics and gender. But I also want to argue that the questions it raises remain relevant today; I shall therefore indicate some of the ways in which a modern reader of women's prophetic writing can make sense of it across the gulf of time and assumptions which separate us from women like Anna Trapnel, the prophet whose writing will serve as a 'case-study'. I will focus primarily on Trapnel's *The Cry of a Stone* (1654), briefly referring also to her *Report and Plea* (1654), and to a thousand-page folio volume of poetry held in the Bodleian Library, Oxford; the title page of this work is missing, but it has been attributed to Trapnel.[2] I have chosen to focus on these texts partly because of their relatively ready (though still limited) availability, in contrast to Trapnel's other works, and partly because they offer us insights into a wide range of issues concerning female prophecy, and examples of the form and content which typified Trapnel's own prophecy.

Trapnel was a member of the Fifth Monarchist movement which took its name from the biblical prophecies of Daniel, who had a vision of an everlasting kingdom which would follow the four great world monarchies. As we shall see, the period 1653–54 was a crucial one for this radical group, and so it is no coincidence that *Anna Trapnel's Report and Plea* and *The Cry of a Stone* were both published in 1654, a year which saw the publication of four of Trapnel's six works.[3] She first came to public attention in January 1654, when she went to Whitehall to attend the legal examination of the writer and preacher Vavasor Powell. While there, she fell into a trance which lasted twelve days, and which took the form of periods of unconsciousness punctuated by outbursts of prayer and prophesying which were recorded by a friend. Two accounts of this trance and reports of the circumstances surrounding it were soon published: one of these was *The Cry of a Stone*, the other *Strange and Wonderful News from Whitehall*. Trapnel then set out to Cornwall, where a further episode of prophesying led to her arrest. The *Report and Plea* is an account of this journey, her experiences in Cornwall, and her return to London where she was imprisoned in Bridewell.

The *Cry of a Stone* begins with an anonymous preface addressed to 'all the wise Virgins in Sion, who are for the work of the day, and wait for the Bride-grooms coming'.[4] It goes on to state that 'it was the desire of this Maid to present this her Testimony to you, though it is not for you only, but for all'. The address to 'wise Virgins' by a woman who is described as a 'Maid' may appear to locate the text within a gender-specific, exclusively feminine context. But while, as I said before, women were sometimes seen as having a special relationship to prophecy, I think that we need to proceed cautiously before making such assumptions. The 'wise Virgins' who await the Bridegroom are drawn from the biblical parable about the wise virgins who kept oil for their lamps for the wedding, in contrast to the foolish ones who let them burn down and were caught out. It is a story about being ready for the coming of the Kingdom, and thus one which is as apt in the context of English radical religion of the mid-seventeenth century, as in the millenarian world of the New Testament. The metaphor of Christ as bridegroom and the Church as his bride is a frequently used one, and clearly does not imply that all members of the Church are female – in the early seventeenth century, King James had used the same analogy to present himself as husband and his realm as wife. We need therefore to be careful to locate seventeenth-century religious language in its own context, and not leap to possibly anachronistic conclusions about its significance.

The document is presented as defensive and justificatory, it is a 'true and faithful Relation' intended to counterbalance the numerous false reports which circulated of Trapnel, as of many other prophets – accounts which had been falsified by 'the pervertings and depravings of the Reporters'. The text has an inbuilt screening mechanism; only those who 'know what it is to be filled with the Spirit, to be in the Mount with God, to be gathered up into the visions of God', will be in a position to understand it and to judge Trapnel's words and actions. Others should keep silent, because their criticisms will only serve to betray their lack of grace.

The Cry of a Stone is thus introduced to the reader by a preface which stresses Trapnel's divine inspiration and the truth of the account. It is significant that these assertions are not made in her own voice, but are mediated by the anonymous author of the preface. This is the pattern throughout the text, which is characterized by the interplay of Trapnel's reported voice with that of the anonymous reporter/commentator/editor. This is in part a matter of practical necessity, of course; Trapnel was supposed to be unconscious when she prophesied, so she was not in a position to remember or record what she said herself. But it is also a question of the need to authorize her speech by testifying to the authenticity of the prophetic moment, witnessed by a diverse company of onlookers – 'Members of the late Parliament' are singled out, and a number of captains, colonels and 'Ladies' are mentioned by name. To this end, the text of *The Cry of a Stone* itself begins by setting a scene. In January 1654, Trapnel came to London to attend the examination of the Baptist/Fifth Monarchist Vavasor Powell. When he met her on the seventh day of that month, she was already slipping into an ecstatic state:

> She was beyond and besides her thoughts or intentions, having much trouble in her heart, and being seized upon by the Lord: she was carried forth in a spirit of prayer and singing, from noon till night.
>
> (p. 1)

Becoming weak, Trapnel took to her bed for twelve days. She lay motionless with her eyes shut, and for the first five days she neither ate nor drank; thereafter she occasionally took 'a very little toast in small beer' (p. 1), often spitting it out after holding it in her mouth for a moment. Transcription of her utterances began on the fifth day, and the relation of what she said in her prophetic trance is preceded by a biographical account, 'taken from her own mouth' (p. 2).

Anna Trapnel was the daughter of a shipwright and grew up in Poplar; she describes both her parents as 'living and dying in the profession of the Lord Jesus', and implicitly attributes her endowment with prophetic gifts to her mother's dying words, significantly uttered three times, 'Lord! Double thy spirit upon my child' (p. 3). The other details that Trapnel thinks it necessary to mention are that she is literate – 'brought up in my book and writing' – and that she had 'walked in fellowship' with her church for four years. The account then goes on to relate how she had become a servant of the Lord, seven years previously. She had been close to death with a fever when the Lord gave her faith to believe that she would recover on the third day; she did, and for the following year 'the Lord made use of me for the refreshing of afflicted and tempted ones' (p. 3). At the end of that year, her prophetic vocation was revealed to her in these words:

> in that thou hast been faithful in a little, I will make thee an instrument of much more; for particular souls shall not only have benefit by thee, but the universality of saints shall have discoveries of God through thee.
>
> (p. 3)

Again, the language used here is essentially biblical, recalling the New Testament parable of the good and faithful servant, and the statement that God will be revealed through her emphasis that she is a passive tool of the divine purpose. It was soon after this, Trapnel says, that she began having visions and embarked on her career as a prophet, which eventually brought her to Whitehall in January 1654, and thus to the intense prophetic experience which is recorded in *The Cry of a Stone*.

What, though, does it mean to speak of Anna Trapnel as a prophet? In the late twentieth century, prophecy tends to be equated with mystical knowledge of what is to come and prediction of future events. On those rare occasions when an individual woman claims to have prophetic authority, she is usually asserting that she has been granted an exceptional insight into the future – insights which are perceived as the gift of some divine or supernatural force – and that this empowers her to tell people how they should act, even though her orders may seem to contravene the norms of behaviour to which they are accustomed. Although such a woman may attract a band of devoted followers to her, by most people she will be seen as a marginal, eccentric figure, both pathetic and laughable, as in the case of the young Ukrainian woman who in late 1993 was carted off to prison when the end of the world did not occur as she had foretold. Explanations advanced by journalists and 'experts' to account for her peculiar behaviour centred on two themes: the traumatic effect of recent social and political upheavals in the Ukraine; and the prophet's own personal history of emotional trauma – in other words, that she was a crazy woman who suddenly found herself in tune with crazy times.

In many ways, female prophets in the seventeenth century would have been perceived similarly: as eccentric, transgressive, even comical individuals, who took advantage of a moment of social disruption and cultural change to make claims for themselves which would not have been heard at other times. Yet they were clearly also perceived as threatening – the intensity of the ridicule and punishment directed at seventeenth-century women prophets, compared with their modern counterparts, suggests that their activities were genuinely challenging and anxiety-producing. If women like Anna Trapnel had been universally perceived as merely eccentric and ludicrous, there would have been no need for the authorities to harass and imprison her. It was precisely because so many people in the mid-seventeenth century took women prophets seriously, and engaged with the extremely radical social and religious implications of their utterances, that ridicule of their imputed eccentricities and transgressions was called into play as a strategy for defusing the serious challenge to the accepted order which was entailed by both their public role as prophets, and the content of their prophecies. It may not be entirely coincidental that, just as the phenomenon of women prophets came to prominence in England during the upheavals of the Civil War period, especially during the 1650s, so it re-emerged in the modern Ukraine at a moment when the long-established order of the USSR was disintegrating, releasing religious and social tensions and diversity which had long been held in check by an oppressive regime. But there are, of course, many historically specific factors which are of crucial significance in understanding the way that prophecy functioned in the social, religious and historical context of the seventeenth century. I therefore want now to define prophecy and locate it with reference to the specific context in which it emerged in mid-seventeenth-century England.

Firstly, it is important to establish a definition of prophecy as it was used in the seventeenth century, and which was rather different from the sense in which we commonly use the word today. Prophecy, in general, was speech or writing which was directly inspired and authorized by God; more specifically, it was a form of inspired discourse which took commentary on a passage from the Bible as its starting point, taking off from there to hold forth on a whole range of spiritual issues, which were more often than not of contemporary social and religious significance. Women prophets of the seventeenth century frequently use scriptural references to present themselves as the modern counterparts of Old Testament prophets such as Daniel, divinely sanctioned messengers whose task is to convey and interpret the Word of God to his chosen people, even in the face of resistance and opposition. In her *Report and Plea*, for example, Trapnel repeatedly uses biblical quotations to testify to her sense that she is doing the Lord's work, and will be guided and protected by him in this task. Recounting her legal examination at the Truro sessions house, for example, she states, 'I related the scriptures, as that in the Psalms, and in the prophet Isaiah, how the presence and spirit of the Lord should be with me, and he would uphold me and strengthen me with the right hand of his righteousness'.[5] But Trapnel does not merely use biblical citations to support her claims to be the vessel of a divine message; in the language of her texts, there is often a strong sense that she feels herself to have been overcome by the Word of God – that a force more powerful than she is working through her and using her. This sense is clearly expressed in her ecstatic address to the Lord, in one passage from *The Cry of a Stone*:

> This that thou hast now done upon thy servant, they will not understand that it is an intimation to them of the pouring out of thy Spirit upon thine own, wherein they shall go forth against the world: thy servant was one that was simple, an Idiot, and did not study in such things as these, and must thy servant now float upon the mighty and broad waters [of the Spirit]? . . . Oh thy servant knows it [i.e. her prophetic utterance] is from the Spirit; let them [i.e. disbelievers] know that it is so too, by the language of it, by the rule through which it comes: how is the written Word carried forth in it! thy Spirit takes the Scripture all along, and sets the soul a-swimming therein.   (p. 67)

Rather than using the Scripture to support her assertions, the prophet is used by it; Trapnel presents herself here as quite passive, scarcely conscious or in control of what she says. This is a notion which recurs frequently in seventeenth-century prophetic writing: the prophet operates by abandoning control of the self to God. Whereas here

Trapnel images her soul swimming along in a tide of the Spirit, elsewhere in her writings the process is often represented by the image of an empty vessel being filled up by God: 'the Lord filled me with many spiritual hymns', she says, or 'thou pourest forth by a vessel that is altogether unlikely that any such liquor should enter into it' (*Cry of a Stone*, pp. 10, 74); or again, 'Then the Lord made his rivers flow, which soon broke down the banks of an ordinary capacity, and extraordinarily mounted my spirits into a praying and singing frame' (*Report and Plea*, p. 75). Equally, the periods of silence which were interspersed with Trapnel's visions are represented as being under divine control; she says that when she fell silent she felt as if 'the clouds did open and receive me into them; and I was as swallowed up of the glory of the Lord and could speak no more' (*Cry of a Stone*, p. 15). The phrasing here is ecstatic and mystical; but Anna Trapnel was also capable of taking a much more pragmatic view of the divine authorization of both her speech and her silence. When she is required to appear before judges at the Truro sessions, her initial anxiety about what she should say is quickly replaced by a faith that the Lord will instruct her both what to say, and when to remain silent:

> And though I had heard how the form of bills run, and of that word 'Not guilty', according to the form of the bill, yet I said, 'I shall not remember to say thus, if the Lord don't bid me say so; and if he bids me, I will say it.' And this I thought, I would be nothing, the Lord should have all the praise, it being his due.[6]

Trapnel thus constructs herself as a medium by which the word of the Lord may be uttered in secular contexts, in order to bring credit not on the speaker, but on the Spirit which animates her.

In the seventeenth-century sense, then, prophecy was primarily concerned with the relations between the individual, society, and the Scriptures, and it did not directly foretell what was to happen in the future. But the content of prophetic visions might offer an image of how the godly future should be, and inspiration and exhortation to God's people to work to bring this about. For example, Trapnel uses the biblical notion of the redemption of the natural world to hold out to the faithful the promise of a peaceful and prosperous future, depicted in the image of a pleasant landscape:

> we have hankered from mountains to hill, we have said salvation is in this hill and in that but let us say so no longer, when we shall thus be

drawn up to thee, then we shall prosper, and thou wilt give us vineyards
and gardens, and trees of thine own, which shall abide.

(*Cry of a Stone*, p. 18)

Trapnel's picture of the redeemed future is a double-edged one,
though, since she represents it both, as here, by celebrating images of
abundance and contentment, and by showing how this Edenic state
will be achieved by means of the overthrow of oppressive powers, in
a sort of divine revolution. In one of the passages of poetic prophecy
recorded in *The Cry of a Stone*, for example, she begins by depicting
the longed-for moment of Jesus's glorious return, before enumerating,
at some length, the processes of social and spiritual transformation by
which this will be achieved:

> Oh King Jesus thou art longed for,
> Oh take thy power and reign,
> And let thy children see thy face,
> Which with them shall remain.
>
> Thy lovely looks will be so bright,
> They will make them to sing.
> They shall bring offerings unto thee,
> And myrrh unto their King.
>
> For they know that thou dost delight
> To hear their panting soul;
> They do rejoice in thy marrow,
> And esteem it more than gold.
>
> Therefore thou hearing their hearts cry,
> Thou sayest, Oh wait a while!
> And suddenly thou wilt draw near,
> The world's glory to spoil.

(*Cry of a Stone*, p. 19)

There follow some twenty stanzas, which explain precisely how this
apocalyptic return of 'King Jesus' will destroy the 'world's glory' –
glory which, in Trapnel's view, consists largely of injustice,
self-interest, dishonesty and wrong-doing. Interestingly, images of the
natural world recur here as images of waste and sterility; powers,
counsellors, protectors, captains and colonels are among those who
must be overthrown,

Because they have not honoured God,
They have not paid their vows:
But only blustering oaks have been,
Great tall branches and boughs.

Which have no spirit or moisture, then,
How can they longer stand,
Though a while they have active been:
Yet they must out o'th'land.

The Lord will reckon with them all,
And set their words before:
They have not brought forth righteousness,
Nor relief to the poor.

Which they said they would chiefly eye,
But their words do not speak:
But all unto their own nets, they
Do stretch themselves and creep.

Pen down how all their gallantry,
Shall crumble into dust:
For the Lord he hath spoken, that
To dust they vanish must.

(*Cry of a Stone*, p. 20)

The extravagant, apocalyptic tone of these stanzas is characteristic of much prophetic writing produced in the 1640s and 1650s. It was a period of intense social, religious and political ferment, and the upheavals of the 1640s in particular prompted many people to believe that they were witnessing the dramatic events, foretold in the Bible, which would herald the end of the world and its transformation into the kingdom of heaven with the return of Christ. The precise form which these transformations were expected to take varied widely across social classes, and political and religious groupings: millenarian hopes and beliefs had been circulating in English culture, in one form or another, for many years before the disarray associated with the Civil War seemed to signal that the millennium might at last be at hand. But there is no doubt that the events of the 1640s gave added impetus to the more radical forms of millenarianism, including the Fifth Monarchists, the group with which Anna Trapnel was affiliated. As I noted above, the Fifth Monarchy movement took its name from the biblical prophet Daniel's vision of an everlasting kingdom of divine justice and egalitarianism which would follow the four great world monarchies – a notion to which Trapnel refers directly in *The Cry of a Stone*, in an exultant passage which vividly expresses the excitement of the millenarian groups who believed, for a time in the 1640s and early 1650s, that the last days of the world were at hand:

> The Lord is gone forth mightily,
> He all might doth appear;
> Oh come, oh come you enemies,
> The great God for to fear.
>
> Oh tremble and astonished be,
> To hear that he draws on,
> Against you he comes forth apace,
> The oppressors of the land.
>
> Oh he hath said that he will reign,
> Therefore rulers shall fly,
> Oh he hath said that he'll cast out
> The fourth great Monarchy.

(p. 72)

The Fifth Monarchist movement emerged at the beginning of the 1650s, maintaining a steadfast commitment to political and religious radicalism at a time when such extreme hopes as those which are voiced in these verses were being dimmed and it appeared that the impetus for radical change was being lost, as the more moderate groups were preparing to settle for limited gains – for example in freedom of worship – rather than total social transformation. The Rump Parliament was cautious, even conservative, and Cromwell's commitment to millenarian ideals appeared to be wavering; the radicals 'felt themselves thwarted at the very threshold of the new Jerusalem'.[7] And then hope seemed to dawn again when, in April 1653, Cromwell staged a military coup and as a result the Rump Parliament was dissolved. In July, Cromwell bypassed the electoral process and gathered together, under the name of the Barebones Parliament, an assembly of men chosen for their religious and moral credentials, including a dozen Fifth Monarchists and many other radicals. In his inaugural speech, he seemed to signal the triumph of the millenarian groups by drawing heavily on the biblical prophecies which, as we have seen in the case of Anna Trapnel, underpinned their world-view. Some of the reforms demanded by the radicals seemed to be closer to realization than ever before. However, it soon emerged that Parliament was divided on almost every issue, and that Cromwell's commitment to the millenarian view was stronger in rhetoric than reality. In December 1653 the assembly dissolved itself, and Cromwell was left to rule directly as Protector; the Fifth Monarchists were marginalized as a party of opposition.

It was in this context that Anna Trapnel came to prominence as a prophet, asserting the continued significance of the Fifth Monarchist cause at a time when it was under severe pressure. Thus her writings are a topical response to and intervention in current events; she uses the prophetic mode to express her views on the political situation. In *The Cry of a Stone*, she recalls

> a vision I had concerning the dissolution of the parliament about four days before it was . . . Nine weeks after this, coming up to London, Mr. Smith, a linen-draper in Newgate market . . . asked me what I thought of the new representatives that was then in choice? I answered that I had faith to believe that little good should be done to the Nation by their sitting.
>
> (p. 10)

Another vision allegorizes the political events I have just described, depicting them as a bloody fight amongst 'a great company of cattle, some like bulls and others like oxen, their faces and heads like men . . . For the foremost, his countenance was perfectly like unto Oliver Cromwell' (p. 13). An apocalyptic description of the fight and its consequences ensues, and then the voice of the transcriber/commentator abruptly intervenes to emphasize the authenticity and importance of Trapnel's prophetic commentary on current affairs, which seeks to reveal the truth despite 'that cloud of unchristian condemnings, odious censures, and black defamations of unsatisfied, interested, envious, and unbelieving persons which are gone forth' (p. 14). Is it significant that this male voice apparently finds itself obliged to intervene in order to authorize Trapnel's remarks on political matters? I suggested earlier that prophecy was an important form for early modern women writers; but is there anything about her subject matter here which is marked or determined by her gender? Both men and women produced prophetic writings in the mid-seventeenth century; but recently, female prophets have become a particular focus of interest, as a result of the feminist endeavour to reclaim women writers who have been ignored or marginalized by history. Women prophets do, of course, need to be seen in the context of the radical religious movements in which they worked alongside men, but there are also issues which are specific to female prophecy. I noted above that more than half of the surviving texts published by women in the mid-century can be defined as prophetic: this indicates both that it was a form which was in some way significant and useful for women, and that these texts were considered to be worth preserving. Why, then, was there a special association between women and prophecy, and what was the significance of the form for women?

These questions have been hotly contested in recent years, and numerous different explanations have been advanced. The radical sects which burgeoned during the revolutionary decades appear to have offered women the opportunity of a public role and voice which was otherwise denied them; yet paradoxically, this opportunity may have been facilitated by precisely those aspects of the mid-seventeenth-century ideology of femininity which held them back in other areas of life. The historian Phyllis Mack has argued that women were thought to be naturally predisposed to prophecy because of their tendency to be emotional, irrational, and easily influenced by powerful exterior forces. In the context of prophecy, their lowly and insignificant social status became an advantage, both because it would presumably make them less likely to be sinfully proud of being singled out as the bearers of divine inspiration, and because it graphically illustrated the belief, crucial to seventeenth-century radical religion, that God's purpose was to reverse unjust social hierarchy and create a new, egalitarian order in which the weak would be strong, and the last first:

> The combination of her despised status and her ecstatic, yet authoritative, behaviour made the female prophet a perfect symbol of a world turned upside down . . . She represents a spiritual and political authority which was inappropriate, even monstrous, by conventional standards, but conforming to a more profound and more radical vision of human equality, on earth and in heaven.[8]

In the seventeenth century, this argument was advanced by the prominent early Quaker Margaret Fell. No prophet herself, Fell was less radical than a figure like Anna Trapnel in relation to both religious and political matters; although it is important to put the differences between them in the context of the fact that Fell was active in the 1660s, after the restoration of the monarchy had foreclosed on many of the more utopian dreams of the 1650s. Nevertheless, she did advocate women's right to speak on religious matters, claiming that the choice of such an insignificant creature as a woman to bear a divine message was itself a sign of God's power and grace, as well as of the utopian equality which would characterize God's kingdom when it was finally established:

> And such hath the Lord chosen, even the weak things of the world, to confound the things which are mighty; and things which are despised, hath God chosen to bring to nought things that are, I Cor[inthians], 1. And God hath put no such difference between the Male and Female as men would make.[9]

We have already seen that Anna Trapnel constantly insists on her own insignificance and passivity, representing herself as merely the transmitter of God's message; yet she is also empowered by the social status that being a prophet gives her. A passage from the untitled volume of her writings held in the Bodleian illustrates the ambiguity of her position, and the sense of self associated with it, very vividly:

> That voice which is mine, is very dross,
> It is filthy dregs also:
> But what is of the Lord Christ, is that
> For which the Spirit do blow.
> Voice that is mine, throw to the pit,
> It's worthy to have no other place:
> But what is of the Lord shall be advanced
> In its most lovely grace.[10]

Trapnel continues in similar vein at some length, contrasting the foulness and insignificance of her own voice with the purity and glory of 'the Lord Christ'. Yet there is a curious irony here, in that it is her own poetic voice which encloses and oscillates between statements both of her own supposed degradation and of the 'royal grace' of her divine master. It is the prophet's very self-abnegation which enables her to celebrate that which is holy, as these lines neatly encapsulate:

> Voice which is mine, bury under ground,
> And let it no more come:
> But what is of the Lord, let it run forth
> With a mighty discovering tongue.

Here, both the subterranean voice and the 'mighty discovering tongue' are Trapnel's. These lines illustrate the extent to which prophecy constructs an ambiguous position for women, in which weakness becomes a kind of strength, and a public voice with which to make pronouncements on the key social and religious issues of the day is attained, albeit at the cost of reaffirming conventional views of female weakness and irrationality. Anna Trapnel's *Report and Plea* manifests this tension very clearly. The text repeatedly insists on Trapnel's self-abnegation and insignificance; yet at the same time, she often seems to delight in the fact that her passive submission to the divine gift of prophecy makes her the centre of attention – the self is most flagrantly displayed at the very moment of its greatest humility and humiliation. For example, Trapnel recounts how she was mocked and taunted by the crowds of people who followed her to court; but she consoles herself, in a remarkably paradoxical moment of simultaneous self-abasement and self-glorification, by comparing her sufferings to those of Christ:

> But I was never in such a blessed self-denying lamb-like frame of spirit in my life as then; I had such lovely apprehensions of Christ's sufferings, and of that scripture which saith, 'He went as a sheep, dumb before the shearers, he opened not his mouth; and when reviled, he reviled not again' [Isaiah 53.7; 1 Peter 2.23] . . . So that I was a gazing-stock for all sorts of people, but I praise the Lord, this did not daunt me.[11]

Trapnel's description and vindication of her activities in the *Report and Plea* is thus characterized by an ambiguous strategy of self-representation in which humility is flaunted, and her claims to be passive and insignificant are cast into question by the very fact of their utterance in contexts which proclaim them to be signs of the Lord's grace.

This ambiguity, which permeates the ways in which the woman who speaks in a prophetic text constructs her own voice, means that women's prophetic writing has been interpreted by historians and literary critics in a wide variety of ways. English social historians such as Christopher Hill and Keith Thomas have seen the women within the context of the male-dominated sectarian groups to which they belonged, and have interpreted their utterances within the framework of a general challenge to social hierarchy.[12] Thus they do not believe either that women had a distinctive contribution to make to sectarian politics, or that female prophecy might have had any special significance for women themselves. Elaine Hobby, in contrast, argues that women prophets can be seen in some sense as 'proto-feminists', because they actively and deliberately used the discourse of prophecy and the identity/social role of prophet to 'transcend the bonds of true feminine self-effacement, using the ideas and structures of contemporary thought to negotiate some space and autonomy'.[13] However, Hilda Smith denies that the prophets were concerned with 'feminist issues' such as family structure and the uses of male power, and did not assert a political identity as women, and so were less feminist than the royalist women who, despite their religious and political conservatism, did, in her view, seek to challenge patriarchal structures.[14] Sociologists, anthropologists, and psychoanalytic critics have also had their say; Phyllis Mack sums up the variety of lenses through which modern scholars have viewed women like Anna Trapnel:

> depending on her (or his) own theoretical and political predispositions, the modern observer might view the woman prophet of the seventeenth century as a symbol of undiluted, charismatic energy; as a proto-feminist embarked on a meteoric public career; as the struggling victim of a repressive childhood; or, perhaps, as one of a reserve army of female spiritual labour, brought in to affirm egalitarian principles and accomplish dangerous ascetic practices and missionary work during a period of radical social change and laid off when these activities were no longer timely.[15]

Mack goes on to express an anxiety that these analyses tell us more about the preoccupations of the scholars than about the prophets, and that most of them insist on viewing women's spirituality as a metaphor for something else, refusing to focus on the religious content of the prophecies. And yet her insistence that these texts should be read exclusively as religious documents itself falsifies them, for the religious radicals of the seventeenth century acknowledged no such separation between the spiritual and the secular.

In reading the works of women like Anna Trapnel, our task is in part to attempt an historically grounded reconstruction of the contexts which shaped their writing and their reading during the turbulent decades of the mid-seventeenth century, and in this essay I have tried to suggest some of the issues which need to be taken into consideration in doing so. Nevertheless, it remains inevitable and legitimate that we should explore the past in terms of what matters to us in the present. Without the impact of feminism on literary studies, for example, hardly anyone would be reading women's prophecy today. We cannot wish away the huge cultural gap which separates us from Anna Trapnel and her contemporaries; what matters is that we should be aware of it, and aware of the preconceptions which we bring to a study of the subject.

Notes

1. Elaine Hobby, *Virtue of Necessity: English Women's Writing 1646–88* (London, 1988), p. 26.
2. Portions of the *Report and Plea* have been reprinted in Elspeth Graham, Hilary Hinds, Elaine Hobby and Helen Wilcox, eds, *Her Own Life: Autobiographical Writings by Seventeenth-Century Englishwomen* (London, 1989), pp. 71–86; a brief passage from *The Cry of a Stone* is included in Germaine Greer, Jeslyn Medoff, Melinda Sansome and Susan Hastings, eds, *Kissing the Rod: An Anthology of Seventeeth-Century Women's Verse* (London, 1988), pp. 175–9. A students' edition of *The Cry of a Stone* is currently being prepared by Hilary Hinds, and selections from the untitled folio will feature in the forthcoming anthology of Civil War verse edited by Peter Davidson. Throughout this essay, quotations from *Anna Trapnel's Report and Plea* are taken from *Her Own Life*; quotations from *The Cry of a Stone* are taken from the original text. Further extracts can be found in the *Documents* section below, pp. 325–31.
3. The others are *Strange and Wonderful News from Whitehall* (1654), *A Legacy for Saints* (1654) and *A Voice for the King of Saints* (1658); plus a 1000-page volume of poetry, held in the Bodleian Library in Oxford, from which the title page is missing but which has been attributed to Trapnel.
4. This preface is unpaginated.
5. Graham *et. al.*, eds, *Her Own Life*, p. 83; the precise references here are to Psalms 139.7–10 and Isaiah 29.21.
6. Graham *et al.*, *Her Own Life*, p. 78.
7 Bernard Capp, 'The Fifth Monarchists and popular millenarianism', in J. F. McGregor and B. Reay, eds, *Radical Religion in the English Revolution* (Oxford, 1984), pp. 165–89 (p. 170).
8. Phyllis Mack, 'Women as prophets during the English Civil War', in Margaret C. Jacob and James Jacob, eds, *The Origins of Anglo-American Radicalism* (London, 1984), p. 219.
9 Margaret Fell, *Women's Speaking Justified*, 2nd edn (1667), p. 3.
10. Quoted from a section headed 'From the 29th day of the 10th month, 1657', p. 257. I am very grateful to Peter Davidson for providing me with

a transcript of this and other extracts from the Bodleian volume (shelfmark 5. 1. 42 Th).

11. Graham *et al.*, *Her Own Life*, p. 79.

12. Christopher Hill, *The World Turned Upside Down* (Harmondsworth, 1975); Keith Thomas, 'Women and the Civil War sects', *Past and Present* 13, (1955).

13. Hobby, *Virtue of Necessity*, p. 27.

14. Hilda Smith, *Reason's Disciples: Seventeenth-Century English Feminists* (Urbana, Illinois, 1982). My comments on Hill, Thomas and Smith are indebted to Elaine Hobby's account in *Virtue of Necessity*.

15. Phyllis Mack, *Visionary Women: Ecstatic Prophecy in Seventeenth-Century England* (Berkeley, California, 1992), p. 3.

Part II
Selected Documents

Most of the texts discussed in this volume are readily available in the standard editions referred to in the notes to each essay. Some, however, are not, and they are reproduced in this section either in their entirety or in extract. Each text has been freshly edited. Spelling has been modernized, but punctuation has generally been left unaltered. Obvious errors have been silently emended.

1. From 'An Exhortation Concerning Good Order and Obedience to Rulers and Magistrates' in *Certain Sermons, or Homilies* (1547). The extract is from the version of 1559:

Almighty God hath created and appointed all things, in heaven, earth, and waters, in a most excellent and perfect order. In heaven he hath appointed distinct (or several) orders and states of archangels and angels. In earth he hath assigned and appointed kings, princes, with other governors under them, all in good and necessary order. The water above is kept, and raineth down in due time and season. The sun, moon, stars, rainbow, thunder, lightning, clouds, and all birds of the air, do keep their order. All the parts of the whole year, as winter, summer, months, nights, and days, continue in their order. All kinds of fishes in the sea, rivers and waters, with all fountains, springs, yea, the seas themselves, keep their comely course and order. And man himself also hath all his parts both within and without, as soul, heart, mind, memory, understanding, reason, speech, with all and singular corporal members of his body, in a profitable, necessary, and pleasant order. Every degree of people, in their vocation, calling, and office, hath appointed to them their duty and order. Some are in high degree, some in low; some kings and princes, some inferiors and subjects; priests and laymen, masters and servants, fathers and children, husbands and wives, rich and poor; and every one have need of other. So that in all things is to be lauded and praised the goodly order of God: without the which no house, no city, no commonwealth can continue and endure (or last); for, where there is no right order, there reigneth all abuse, carnal liberty, enormity, sin and Babylonical confusion. Take away kings, princes, rulers, magistrates, judges, and such estates of God's order, no man shall ride or go by the highway unrobbed; no man shall sleep in his own house or bed unkilled; no man shall keep his wife, children, and possessions in quietness; all things shall be common; and there must needs follow all mischief and utter destruction both of souls, bodies, goods, and commonwealths.

But blessed be God that we in this realm of England feel not the horrible calamities, miseries, and wretchedness which all they undoubtedly feel and suffer that lack this godly order. And praised be God that we know the great excellent benefit of God showed towards us in this behalf. God hath sent us his high gift, our most dear sovereign lady Queen Elizabeth, with godly, wise, and honourable council, with other superiors and inferiors, in a beautiful order and goodly. Wherefore let us subjects do our bounden duties, giving hearty thanks to God, and praying for the preservation of this godly order. Let us all obey, even from the bottom of our hearts, all their godly proceedings, laws, statutes, proclamations, and injunctions, with all other godly orders. Let us consider the scriptures of the Holy Ghost, which persuade and command us all obediently to be subject, first and chiefly to the Queen's majesty, supreme head over all, and next to her honourable council, and to all other noblemen, magistrates, and officers, which by God's goodness be placed and ordered.

2. From 'The Form of Solemnisation of Matrimony' in *The Book of Common Prayer* (1549). The extract is from the version of 1552:

The priest shall thus say: Dearly beloved friends, we are gathered together here in the sight of God, and in the face of his congregation, to join together this man and this woman in holy matrimony, which is an honourable estate instituted of God in paradise, in the time of man's innocency: signifying unto us the mystical union, that is betwixt Christ and his church: which holy estate Christ adorned and beautified with his presence and first miracle that he wrought in Cana of Galilee, and is commended of St Paul to be honourable among all men, and therefore is not to be enterprised, nor taken in hand unadvisedly, lightly or wantonly, to satisfy men's carnal lusts, and appetites, like brute beasts that have no understanding: but reverently, discreetly, advisedly, soberly, and in the fear of God: duly considering the causes for which matrimony was ordained.

One was the procreation of children, to be brought up in the fear and nurture of the Lord, and praise of God.

Secondly, it was ordained for a remedy against sin, and to avoid fornication, that such persons as have not the gift of continency, might marry, and keep themselves undefiled members of Christ's body.

Thirdly, for the mutual society, help and comfort, that the one ought to have of the other, both in prosperity and adversity, into the which holy estate these two persons present, come now to be joined. Therefore, if any man can show any just cause, why they may not lawfully be joined together: let him now speak, or else hereafter for ever hold his peace . . .

If no impediment be alleged, then shall the curate say unto the man: . . . Wilt thou have this woman to thy wedded wife, to live together after God's ordinance in the holy estate of matrimony? Wilt thou love her, comfort her, honour, and keep her, in sickness, and in health? And forsaking all other, keep thee only to her so long as you both shall live? . . .

Then shall the priest say to the woman: . . . Wilt thou have this man to thy wedded husband, to live together after God's ordinance, in the holy estate of matrimony? Wilt thou obey him and serve him, love, honour and keep him, in sickness and in health, and forsaking all other keep thee only unto him, so long as you both shall live? . . .

Then shall the minister speak unto the people: Forasmuch as N[ame] and N[ame] have consented together in holy wedlock, and have witnessed the same before God and this company, and thereto have given and pledged their troth either to other, and have declared the same, by giving and receiving of a ring, and by joining of hands: I pronounce that they be man and wife together. In the name of the Father, of the Son, and of the Holy Ghost. Amen.

3. Thomas Carew, 'A Rapture', from *Poems by Thomas Carew* (1640):

I will enjoy thee now, my Celia, come
And fly with me to love's Elysium:
The giant, honour, that keeps cowards out,
Is but a masquer, and the servile rout
Of baser subjects only bend in vain   5
To the vast idol; whilst the nobler train
Of valiant soldiers, daily sail between
The huge Colossus' legs, and pass unseen
Unto the blissful shore; be bold, and wise,
And we shall enter, the grim Swiss denies   10
Only to tame fools a passage, that not know

He is but form, and only frights in show
The duller eyes that look from far; draw near,
And thou shalt scorn, what we were wont to fear.
We shall see how the stalking pageant goes   15
With borrowed legs, a heavy load to those
That made, and bear him; not as we once thought
The seed of Gods, but a weak model wrought
By greedy men, that seek to enclose the common,
And within private arms empale free woman.   20
     Come then, and mounted on the wings of love
We'll cut the flitting air, and soar above
The monster's head, and in the noblest seats
Of those blest shades, quench and renew our heats.
There shall the queens of love, and innocence,   25
Beauty and nature, banish all offence
From our close ivy twines; there I'll behold
Thy bared snow, and thy unbraided gold;
There, my enfranchised hand, on every side
Shall o'er thy naked polished ivory slide.   30
No curtain there, though of transparent lawn,
Shall be before thy virgin-treasure drawn;
But the rich mine, to the enquiring eye
Exposed, shall ready still for mintage lie,
And we will coin young Cupids. There, a bed   35
Of roses, and fresh myrtles shall be spread,
Under the cooler shade of cypress groves:
Our pillows, of the down of Venus' doves,
Whereon our panting limbs we'll gently lay
In the faint respites of our active play;   40
That so our slumbers, may in dreams have leisure,
To tell the nimble fancy our past pleasure;
And so our souls that cannot be embraced,
Shall the embraces of our bodies taste.
Meanwhile the bubbling stream shall court the shore,   45
Th'enamoured chirping wood-choir shall adore
In varied tunes the deity of love;
The gentle blasts of western winds, shall move
The trembling leaves, and through their close boughs breathe
Still music, whilst we rest ourselves beneath   50
Their dancing shade; till a soft murmur, sent
From souls entranced in amorous languishment,
Rouse us, and shoot into our veins fresh fire,
Till we, in their sweet ecstasy expire.

Then, as the empty bee, that lately bore   55
Into the common treasure, all her store,
Flies 'bout the painted field with nimble wing,
Deflowering the fresh virgins of the spring;
So will I rifle all the sweets, that dwell
In my delicious paradise, and swell   60
My bag with honey, drawn forth by the power
Of fervent kisses, from each spicy flower.
I'll seize the rose-buds in their perfumed bed,
The violet knots, like curious mazes spread
O'er all the garden, taste the ripened cherry,   65
The warm, firm apple, tipped with coral berry:
Then will I visit, with a wandering kiss,
The vale of lilies and the bower of bliss;
And where the beauteous region doth divide
Into two milky ways, my lips shall slide   70
Down those smooth alleys, wearing as they go
A tract for lovers on the printed snow;
Thence climbing o'er the swelling Apennine,
Retire into thy grove of eglantine;
Where I will all those ravished sweets distill   75
Through love's alembic, and with chemic skill
From the mixed mass, one sovereign balm derive,
Then bring that great elixir to thy hive.
    Now in more subtle wreathes I will entwine
My sinewy thighs, my legs and arms with thine: 80
Thou like a sea of milk shalt lie displayed,
Whilst I the smooth, calm ocean invade
With such a tempest, as when Jove of old
Fell down on Danae in a storm of gold;
Yet my tall pine shall in the Cyprian strait   85
Ride safe at anchor and unlade her freight:
My rudder, with thy bold hand, like a tried
And skilful pilot, thou shalt steer, and guide
My bark into love's channel, where it shall
Dance, as the bounding waves do rise or fall: 90
Then shall thy circling arms, embrace and clip
My willing body, and thy balmy lip
Bathe me in juice of kisses, whose perfume
Like a religious incense shall consume,
And send up holy vapours to those powers   95
That bless our loves, and crown our sportful hours,
That with such halcyon calmness fix our souls

In steadfast peace, as no affright controls.
There, no rude sounds shake us with sudden starts;
No jealous ears, when we unrip our hearts   100
Suck our discourse in; no observing spies
This blush, that glance traduce; no envious eyes
Watch our close meetings; nor are we betrayed
To rivals by the bribed chambermaid.
No wedlock bonds unwreathes our twisted loves;   105
We seek no midnight arbour, no dark groves
To hide our kisses; there, the hated name
Of husband, wife, lust, modest, chaste or shame,
Are vain and empty words, whose very sound
Was never heard in the Elysian ground.   110
All things are lawful there, that may delight
Nature or unrestrained appetite;
Like and enjoy, to will and act is one,
We only sin, when love's rites are not done.
      The Roman Lucrece there reads the divine   115
Lectures of love's great master, Aretine,
And knows as well as Lais, how to move
Her pliant body in the act of love.
To quench the burning ravisher, she hurls
Her limbs into a thousand winding curls,   120
And studies artful postures, such as be
Carved on the bark of every neighbouring tree
By learned hands, that so adorned the rind,
Of those fair plants, which, as they lay entwined,
Have fanned their glowing fires. The Grecian dame,   125
That in her endless web, toiled for a name
As fruitless as her work, doth there display
Herself before the youth of Ithaca,
And th'amorous sport of gamesome nights prefer,
Before dull dreams of the lost traveller.   130
Daphne hath broke her bark, and that swift foot
Which th'angry Gods had fastened with a root
To the fixed earth, doth now unfettered run,
To meet th'embraces of the youthful sun:
She hangs upon him like his Delphic lyre,   135
Her kisses blow the old, and breathe new fire:
Full of her God, she sings inspired lays,
Sweet odes of love, such as deserve the bays,
Which she herself was. Next her, Laura lies
In Petrarch's learned arms, drying those eyes   140

That did in such sweet smooth-paced numbers flow,
As made the world enamoured of his woe.
These, and ten thousand beauties more, that died
Slave to the tyrant, now enlarged deride
His cancelled laws, and for their time misspent,   145
Pay into love's exchequer double rent.
    Come then, my Celia, we'll no more forbear
To taste our joys, struck with a panic fear,
But will depose from his imperious sway
This proud usurper, and walk free as they,   150
With necks unyoked; nor is it just that he
Should fetter your soft sex with chastity,
Which nature made unapt for abstinence;
When yet this false impostor can dispense
With human justice and with sacred right,   155
And maugre both their laws, command me fight
With rivals or with emulous loves, that dare
Equal with thine, their mistress' eyes or hair:
If thou complain of wrong, and call my sword
To carve out thy revenge, upon that word   160
He bids me fight and kill; or else he brands
With marks of infamy my coward hands.
And yet religion bids from bloodshed fly,
And damns me for that act. Then tell me why
This goblin honour which the world adores,   165
Should make men atheists, and not women whores?

4. From Sir Philip Sidney, *The Defence of Poesy* (1595):

So that the right use of comedy, will I think, by nobody be blamed;
and much less of the high and excellent tragedy, that openeth the
greatest wounds, and showeth forth the ulcers that are covered with
tissue, that maketh kings fear to be tyrants, and tyrants manifest their
tyrannical humours, that with stirring the affects of admiration and
commiseration, teacheth the uncertainty of this world, and upon how
weak foundations gilden roofs are builded: that maketh us know,

> Qui sceptra saevus duro imperio regit,
> Timet timentes, metus in auctorem redit.
> [The cruel ruler who governs his dominions harshly fears those who fear him:
> fear returns to its author.]

But how much it can move, Plutarch yieldeth a notable testimony of the abominable tyrant Alexander Phereaus, from whose eyes a tragedy well made and represented, drew abundance of tears, who without all pity had murdered infinite numbers, and some of his own blood: so as he that was not ashamed to make matters for tragedies, yet could not resist the sweet violence of a tragedy. And if it wrought no further good in him, it was that he in despite of himself, withdrew himself from hearkening to that which might mollify his hardened heart.

5. From Thomas Norton and Thomas Sackville, *Gorboduc* (1570):

The Printer to the Reader.

Where this tragedy was for furniture of part of the grand Christmas in the Inner Temple first written about nine years ago by the right honourable Thomas now Lord Buckhurst and by Thomas Norton, and after showed before her majesty, and never intended by the authors thereof to be published: yet one W. G. getting a copy thereof at some youngman's hand that lacked little money and much discretion in the last great plague, anno. 1565. about v. years past, while the said lord was out of England and Thomas Norton far out of London, and neither of them both made privy, put it forth exceedingly corrupted: even as if by means of a broker for hire, he should have enticed into his house a fair maid and done her villainy, and after all to bescratched her face, torn her apparel, bewrayed and disfigured her, and then thrust her out of doors dishonested. In such plight after long wandering she came at length home to the sight of her friends who scant knew her but by a few tokens and marks remaining. They, the authors I mean, though they were very much displeased that she so ran abroad without leave, whereby she caught her shame, as many wantons do; yet seeing the case as it is remediless, have for common honesty and shamefastness new apparelled, trimmed, and attired her in such form as she was before. In which better form since she hath come to me, I have harboured her for her friends' sake and her own, and I do not doubt her parents, the authors, will not now be discontent that she go abroad among you good readers, so it be in honest company. For she is by my encouragement and others somewhat less ashamed of the dishonesty done to her because it was by fraud and force. If she be welcome among you and gently entertained, in favour of the house from whence she is descended, and of her own nature courteously disposed to offend no man, her friends will thank you for it. If not, but that she shall be still reproached with her former mishap, or quarrelled at by envious persons, she poor gentlewoman will surely play Lucrece's part, and of herself die for shame, and I shall wish that she had tarried still at home with me, where she was welcome: for she did never put me to more charge, but this one poor black gown lined with white that I have now given her to go abroad among you withal.

6. From Ben Jonson, *Sejanus, His Fall* (1605):

To the Readers.

The following and voluntary labours of my friends, prefixed to my book, have relieved me in much, whereat (without them) I should necessarily have touched; now, I will only use three or four short and needful notes, and so rest.

First, if it be objected that what I publish is no true poem; in the strict laws of time, I confess it; as also in the want of a proper chorus, whose habit and moods are such, and so difficult, as not any whom I have seen since the ancients, (no, not they who have most presently affected laws) have yet come in the way of. Nor is it needful, or almost possible, in these our times, and to such auditors as commonly things are presented, to observe the old state and splendour of dramatic poems, with preservation of any popular delight. But of this I shall take more seasonable cause to speak; in my observations upon Horace his *Art of Poetry*, which (with the text translated) I intend shortly to publish. In the meantime, if in truth of argument, dignity of persons, gravity and height of elocution, fullness and frequency of sentence, I have discharged the other offices of a tragic writer, let not the absence of these forms be imputed to me, wherein I shall give you occasion hereafter (and without my boast) to think I could better prescribe, than omit the due use for want of a convenient knowledge.

The next is, lest in some nice nostril the quotations might savour affected, I do let you know that I abhor nothing more; and have only done it to show my integrity in the story, and save myself in those common torturers that bring all wit to the rack: whose noses are ever like swine spoiling and rooting up the muses' gardens, and their whole bodies, like moles, as blindly working under earth to cast any the least hills upon virtue.

Whereas they are in Latin and the work in English, it was presupposed, none but the learned would take the pains to confer them, the authors themselves being all in the learned tongues, save one, with whose English side I have had little to do: to which it may be required, since I have quoted the page, to name what editions I followed. *Tacitus*. Lipsius. in quarto. Antwerp edition. 1600. *Dio Cassius*. Folio. Henricus Stephanus. 1592. For the rest, as Suetonius. Seneca. etc., the chapter doth sufficiently direct, or the edition is not varied.

Lastly, I would inform you that this book in all numbers is not the same with that which was acted on the public stage, wherein a second pen had good share; in place of which I have rather chosen to put weaker (and no doubt less pleasing) of mine own, than to defraud so happy a genius of his right by my loathed usurpation.

Fare you well. And if you read farther of me, and like, I shall not be afraid of it though you praise me out: *Neque enim mihi cornea fibra est* [For my heart is not made of horn].

But that I should plant my felicity in your general saying *Good* or *Well*, etc., were a weakness which the better sort of you might worthily contemn, if not absolutely hate me for.

BEN. JONSON. and no such.
Quem palma negata macrum, donata reducit opimum.
[The refusal of the palm sends a man home lean; the award of the palm sends him home plump.]

7. From John Webster, *The White Devil* (1612):

To the Reader.

In publishing this tragedy, I do but challenge to myself that liberty, which other men have taken before me; not that I affect praise by it, for *nos haec novimus esse nihil* [we know these things are nothing], only, since it was acted, in so dull a time of winter, presented in so open and black a theatre, that it wanted (that which is the only grace and setting out of a tragedy) a full and understanding auditory: and that since that time I have noted most of the people that come to that playhouse, resemble those ignorant asses (who visiting stationers' shops their use is not to enquire for good books, but new books) I present it to the general view with this confidence:

Nec rhonchos metues, maligniorum,
Nec scombris tunicas, dabis molestas.
[You – my book – will not fear the sneers of the malicious, nor be used for
wrapping mackerel.]

If it be objected this is no true dramatic poem, I shall easily confess
it, *non potes in nugas dicere plura meas: ipse ego quam dixi* [you
cannot say more against my trifling works than I have said myself],
willingly, and not ignorantly, in this kind have I faulted: for should a
man present to such an auditory the most sententious tragedy that ever
was written, observing all the critical laws, as heighth of style and
gravity of person; enrich it with the sententious chorus and as it were
life'n death in the passionate and weighty *nuntius* [messenger]; yet,
after all this divine rapture, *O dura messorum ilia* [O strong stomachs
of harvesters], the breath that comes from the incapable multitude is
able to poison it, and ere it be acted, let the author resolve to fix every
scene, this of Horace: *Haec hodie porcis comedenda relinques* [You
will leave these today for the pigs to eat].

To those who report I was a long time in finishing this tragedy, I
confess I do not write with a goose-quill, winged with two feathers,
and if they will needs make it my fault, I must answer them with that
of Euripides to Alcestides, a tragic writer: Alcestides objecting that
Euripides had only in three days composed three verses, whereas
himself had written three hundred: Thou tellest truth, (quoth he) but
here's the difference, thine shall only be read for three days, whereas
mine shall continue three ages.

Detraction is the sworn friend to ignorance: for mine own part I
have ever truly cherished my good opinion of other men's worthy
labours, especially of that full and heightened style of Master
Chapman; the laboured and understanding works of Master Jonson;
the no less worthy composures of the both worthily excellent Master
Beaumont, and Master Fletcher; and lastly (without wrong last to be
named), the right happy and copious industry of Master Shakespeare,
Master Dekker, and Master Heywood, wishing what I write may be
read by their light: protesting that, in the strength of mine own
judgment, I know them so worthy that though I rest silent in my own
work, yet to most of theirs I dare (without flattery) fix that of Martial:
non norunt haec monumenta mori [these monuments do not know
how to die].

8. From Anon., *A Warning for Fair Women* (1599):

Induction.
*Enter at one door, History with drum and ensign:
Tragedy at another, in her one hand a whip, in
the other hand a knife.*

Tragedy:	Whither away so fast? peace with that drum:	5
	Down with that ensign which disturbs our stage	
	Out with this luggage, with this foppery,	
	This brawling sheepskin is intolerable.	
History:	Indeed no marvel though we should give place	
	Unto a common executioner:	10
	Room, room for God's sake, let us stand away,	
	Oh we shall have some doughty stuff today.	

Enter Comedy at the other end.

Tragedy:	What yet more cat's guts? O this filthy sound	
	Stifles mine ears:	15
	More cartwheels cracking yet?	
	A plague upon't, I'll cut your fiddle strings,	
	If you stand scraping thus to anger me.	
Comedy:	Gup mistress buskins with a whirligig, are you so touchy?	
	Madam Melpomene, whose mare is dead	20
	That you are going to take off her skin?	
Tragedy:	A plague upon these filthy fiddling tricks,	
	Able to poison any noble wit:	
	Avoid the stage or I'll whip you hence.	
Comedy:	Indeed thou mayest, for thou art murder's beadle,	25
	The common hangman unto tyranny.	
	But History, what all three met at once?	
	What wonder's towards that we are got together?	
History:	My meaning was to have been here today,	
	But meeting with my Lady Tragedy,	30
	She scolds me off:	
	And Comedy, except thou canst prevail,	
	I think she means to banish us the stage.	
Comedy:	Tut, tut, she cannot; she may for a day	
	Or two perhaps be had in some request,	35
	But once a week if we do not appear,	
	She shall find few that will attend her here.	

Tragedy: I must confess you have some sparks of wit,
      Some odd ends of old jests scraped up together,
      To tickle shallow injudicial ears,   40
      Perhaps some puling passion of a lover, but slight and
         childish,
      What is this to me?
      I must have passions that move the soul,
      Make the heart heavy, and throb within the bosom,
      Extorting tears out of the strictest eyes,   45
      To rack a thought and strain it to his form,
      Until I rap the senses from their course,
      This is my office.
Comedy: How some damned tyrant, to obtain a crown,
      Stabs, hangs, empoisons, smothers, cutteth throats,   50
      And then a chorus too comes howling in,
      And tells us of the worrying of a cat,
      Then of a filthy whining ghost,
      Lapped in some foul sheet, or a leather pelch,
      Comes screaming like a pig half sticked,   55
      And cries *Vindicta*, revenge, revenge:
      With that a little rosen flasheth forth,
      Like smoke out of a tobacco pipe, or a boy's squib:
      Then comes in two or three like to drovers,
      With tailors' bodkins, stabbing one another,   60
      Is not this trim? Is not here goodly things?
      That you should be so much accounted of,
      I would not else.
History: Now before God thou'lt make her mad anon,
      Thy jests are like a wisp unto a scold.   65
Comedy: Why say I could? what care I History?
      Then shall we have a tragedy indeed:
      Pure purple buskin, blood and murder right.
Tragedy: Thus with your loose and idle similes,
      You have abused me: but I'll whip you hence,   70
      [*She whips them.*]
      I'll scourge and lash you both from off the stage,
      Tis you have kept the theatres so long,
      Painted in playbills, upon every post,
      That I am scorned of the multitude,
      My name profaned: but now I'll reign as queen   75
      In great Apollo's name and all the Muses',
      By virtue of whose godhead I am sent,
      I charge you to be gone and leave this place.

History:	Look Comedy, I marked it not till now,	
	The stage is hung with black; and I perceive	80
	The auditors prepared for Tragedy.	
Comedy:	Nay then I see she shall be entertained,	
	These ornaments beseem not thee and me,	
	Then Tragedy, kill them today with sorrow,	
	We'll make them laugh with mirthful jests tomorrow. 85	
History:	And Tragedy although today thou reign,	
	Tomorrow here I'll domineer again. [*Exeunt.*]	
Tragedy:	Are you both gone so soon? why then I see	
	[*Turning to the people.*]	
	All this fair circuit here is left to me:	
	All you spectators, turn your cheerful eye,	90
	Give entertainment unto Tragedy,	
	My scene is London, native and your own,	
	I sigh to think, my subject too well known,	
	I am not feigned: many now in this round,	
	Once to behold me in sad tears were drowned,	95
	Yet what I am, I will not let you know,	
	Until my next ensuing scene shall show.	

9. From Arthur Golding, *A Brief Discourse of the Late Murder of Master George Sanders* (1577):

Now remaineth to show what is to be gathered of this terrible example, and how we ought to apply the same to our own behoof. First I note with St Paul, that when men regard not to know God, or not to honour him when they know him; God giveth them over to their own lusts so as they run on from sin to sin, and from mischief to mischief, to do such things as are shameful and odious, even in the sight of the world, to their own unavoidable perils. And when the measure of their iniquity is filled up, there is no way for them to escape the justice of God, which they have provoked. Insomuch that if they might eschew all bodily punishment, yet the very hell of their own conscience would prosecute them, and the sting of their mind would be a continual prison, torment and torture to them, wheresoever they went. Again on the other side, we must mark the infinite greatness of God's wisdom and mercy, who perceiving the perverse wilfulness of man's froward nature to sinning, suffereth men sometimes to run so long upon the bridle, till it seem to themselves that they may safely do what they list, and to the world that they be past recovery unto goodness: and yet in the end catching them in their chief pride, he raiseth them by their overthrow, amendeth them by their wickedness, and reviveth them by their death, in such wise blotting out the stain of their former filth that their darkness is turned into light, and their terror to their comfort. Moreover, when God bringeth such matters upon the stage, unto the open face of the world, it is not to the intent that men should gaze and wonder at the persons, as birds do at an owl, not that they should delight themselves and others with the fond and peradventure sinister reporting of them, nor upbraid the whole stock and kindred with the fault of the offenders: no surely, God meaneth no such thing. His purpose is that the execution of his judgments, should by the terror of the outward sight of the example, drive us to the inward consideration of ourselves. Behold, we be all made of the same mould, printed with the same stamp, and endued with the same nature that the offenders are. We be the imps of the old Adam, and the venom of sin which he received from the old Serpent is shed into us all, and worketh effectually in us all. Such as the root is, such are the branches, and twigs of a thorn or bramble can bear no grapes. That we stand, it is the benefit of God's grace, and not the goodness of our nature, nor the strength of our own will. That they are fallen, it was of frailty: wherefrom we be no more privileged than they: and that should we oversoon perceive by experience, if we were left to ourselves. He that looketh severely into other men's faults, is lightly blind in his own: and he that either upbraideth the repentant that hath received punishment, or reproacheth the kindred or offspring with the fault of the ancestor or ally, how great soever the same hath been; showeth himself not to have any remorse of his own sins, nor to remember that he himself also is a man: but (which thing he would little think) he fully matcheth the crime of the misdoer, if he do not surmount it by his presumptuousness.

10. From William Camden, *Britannia, or A Chorographical Description of the Most Flourishing Kingdoms, England, Scotland, and Ireland*, translated by Philemon Holland (1637):

But who were the most ancient and the very first inhabitants of this isle, as also, from whence this word *Britain* had the original derivation, sundry opinions one after another have risen; and many we have seen, who being uncertain in this point have seemed to put down the certain resolution thereof. Neither can we hope to attain unto any certainty herein, more than all other nations, which (setting those aside that have their original avouched unto them out of holy scripture) as well as we, touching their point, abide in great darkness, error and ignorance. And how, to speak truly, can it otherwise be? considering that the truth, after so many revolutions of ages and times, could not choose but be deeply hidden. For the first inhabitors of countries had other cares and thoughts to busy and trouble their heads than to deliver their beginnings unto posterity. And say they had been most willing so to do, yet possibly could they not, seeing their life was so uncivil, so rude, so full of wars, and therefore void of all literature; which keeping company with a civil life, by peace and repose, is only able to preserve the memory of things and to make over the same to the succeeding ages. Moreover, the *Druidae*, who being in the old time the priests of the Britons and Gauls, were supposed to have known all that was past; and the *Bardi*, that used to resound in song all valours and noble acts, thought it not lawful to write and book anything . . . Howbeit, in the ages soon after following, there wanted not such as desired gladly to supply these defects; and when they could not declare the truth indeed, yet at least way for delectation, they laboured to bring forth narrations, devised of purpose, with certain pleasant variety to give contentment, and delivered their several opinions, each one after his own conceit and capacity, touching the original of nations and their names . . . [Geoffrey of Monmouth's theory about the origins of the name Britain was that it was derived from Brutus, a Trojan who conquered the land and named it after himself.] Sir Thomas Eliot, by degree a worshipful knight and a man of singular learning, draweth it from the Greek fountain . . . [from] a term that the Athenians gave to their public finances or revenues. Humfrey Lhuyd, reputed by our countrymen for knowledge of antiquity, to carry, after a sort, with him all the credit and authority, referreth it confidently to the British word *Prid-cain*, that is to say, *a pure white form*. Pomponius Laetus reporteth that the Britons out of Armorica in France, gave it that name. Goropius Becanus saith that the Danes fought here to plant themselves, and so named it Bridania, that is, *Free Dania*. Others derive it from *Prutenia*, a region in Germany. Bodine supposeth that it took the name of *Bretta* the Spanish word which signifieth *Earth*; and Forcatulus, of *Brithin*, which as we read in Athenaeus, the Greeks used for drink. Others bring it from the *Brutti* in Italy . . . As for those smatterers in grammar, who keep a-babbling and prating that Britain should carry that name, of British manners, let them be packing.

These are all the opinions (to my knowledge) that have been received touching the name of Britain. But herein as we cannot but smile at the fictions of strangers, so the devices coined by our own countrymen pass not current with general allowance. And verily, in these and such like cases, an easier matter it is to impeach the false, than to teach and maintain a truth . . .

Forasmuch then as all writers are not of one and the same mind as touching the very name and the first inhabitants of Britain, and I fear me greatly that no man is able to fetch out the truth, so deeply plunged within the winding revolutions of so many ages, let the reader of his candour and humanity, pardon me also among others, if modestly and without the prejudice of any man, I likewise interpose my conjecture; not upon any mind I have contentiously to wrangle (be that far from me), but in my desire to search out the truth; which hath wholly possessed me and brought to this point, that in the question now in hand, I had rather ask forgiveness for my fault (if there be any) than commit no fault at all . . . Although these things so far remote from memory, are overcast with such mists and darkness that the truth seems rather to be wished than hoped for; yet, for all that will I do my best to trace out the truth and declare as briefly as I can, what my judgment is: not minding to put down ought prejudicial to any man, but most willing, if anyone shall bring more probable matter to welcome and embrace the same. For I affect and love the truth not in myself more than in another, and in whomsoever I shall see it, I will most willingly and gladly entertain it.

First, by the reader's good leave, I will take this for granted and proved; that ancient nations in the beginning had names of their own and that afterwards, from these, the Greeks and Latins, by wresting them to the analogy or proportion of their speech, imposed names upon regions and countries; to speak more plainly, that people were known by their names, before regions and places, and that the said regions had their denominations of the people . . .

We must of necessity think that this our island Britain took denomination from the inhabitants, or from the Gauls their neighbours; that these first inhabitants were called *Brit* or *Brith*, some things induce me to think: first and foremost that verse which goeth about under the name of Sybilla:

Twixt Brits and Gauls their neighbours rich, in gold that much abound,
The roaring ocean sea with blood full filled shall resound . . .

The Saxons also themselves called the Britons in their language *Brith* . . .
Considering now that nations devised their names of that wherein they
either excelled others or were known from others . . . the most
sufficient authors that be, as Caesar, Mela, Pliny and the rest do show
that the Britons coloured themselves with woad . . . What if I should
conjecture, that they were called Britons of their depainted bodies?
For, whatsoever is thus painted and coloured, in their ancient country
speech, they call *Brith* . . .

Now, as *Brito* came of *Brith*, so did *Britannia* also in my opinion.
Britannia, saith Isidore, *took that name from a word of their own
nation.* For what time as the most ancient Greeks (and these were they
that first gave the island that name) sailing still along the shore, as
Eratosthenes saith, either as rovers, or as merchants, travelled unto
nations most remote and disjointed far asunder, and learned either
from the inhabitants themselves, or else of the Gauls, who spake the
same tongue, that this nation was called *Brith* and *Brithon*; then they
unto the word *Brith* added *Tania*: which, as we find in the Greek
glossaries, betokeneth in Greek, a region . . .

Thus have you, as touching the original and name of Britain, mine
error or conjecture, whether you will, which if it swerve from the truth,
I wish it were by truth itself reformed. In this intricate and obscure study
of antiquity, it is thought praiseworthy somewhat to err: and
remember we should withal that such things as at first sight being
slightly thought upon are deemed false, after a better review and
further consideration oftentimes seem true. Now if any man should
summon me to appear before the tribunal of verity, I have no other
answer at all to make. And as our countrymen the Britons, such as be
of the learneder sort, I do most earnestly beseech and desire them to
employ all their labour, industry, wit, and understanding in the searching
out hereof so long; until at last, the truth with her own clear bright beams
may scatter and dissolve all mists of conjectures whatsoever.

11. From Barnabe Rich, *Faults, Faults And Nothing Else But Faults* (1606):

We have hitherto spent the time in delivering of those faults and follies
that are conversant amongst men. And I think if a man were made all

of eyes, as Argus was, he could not look into the one half of those vices that now do infect the world, but is there any escape to be found amongst women? Men you see are full of faults, but amongst women (some will say) there is but two faults and those are, they can neither do nor say well. But this (as I take it) is rather to be objected in the way of merriment than to be received for a truth. But this is true, there hath been both good and bad women from the beginning; but for those that have been accounted ill, they were never half so detestable in times past as they be at this hour; nay, those women that now would be accounted good, and would be angry if there should be any exceptions taken to their honesty, are more courtesan-like (to the shrew of the world) than ever was Lais of Corinth, or Trine the famous courtesan of Thebes.

What newfangled attires for the heads, what flaring fashions in their garments, what alteration in their ruffs, what painting of shameless faces, what audacious boldness in company, what impudency, and what immodesty is used by those that will needs be reputed honest, when their open breasts, their naked stomachs, their frizzled hair, their wanton eye, their shameless countenance are all the vaunt errors of adultery.

With these sleights and shows they have made emperors idle, as Anthony; strong men feeble, as Samson; valiant men effeminate, as Hercules; wise men dissolute, as Solomon; eloquent men lascivious, as Aurelius.

What is become of that age when the simple beauty was best beseeming an honest woman; when bashful modesty enclosed in a virtuous breast was their best lure, whereby to induce an honourable reputation? They were then beloved by the virtuous, by the wise, by the learned; but now most commonly by the lascivious, by the idle, and by those hermaphrodites that are not worthy the name of men.

Thucydides will needs approve that woman to be most honest that is least known, and in whose praise or dispraise there is no report at all; but it is not possible for any woman so to behave herself, but she shall be misreported; and the more honest in life, so much the sooner infamed, when it is the common practice of every known strumpet to scandalise and slander that woman, which she in her own conscience thinks to be most honest because it helpeth to cover her own abominations (as she thinketh); and the more to blaze it forth, she shall not want the assistance of her Russians, her apple-squires, and of those brothel queens that lodge, that harbour, and that retain her, and such as she is, in their houses for commodity and gain.

Nay, they have the sleight, even then most devilishly to inflame when they will make show most honestly to excuse. And under the pretence of flying reports, which they will say hath been told them by others, they will spread their own venom, complotting and devising those untruths, that never were heard nor thought on.

12. Gilbert Dugdale, *A True Discourse of the Practices of Elizabeth Caldwell* (1604):

To the right virtuous, the Lady Mary Cholmsly, and the right worshipful these knights . . . and all the rest, as well knights as gentlemen then at the assizes present, the true witnesses of this following history: your kind poor countryman Gilbert Dugdale, engaged to you all in debt and duty, committeth this discourse with true and due commends, with continual prayers for your good healths, and successful fortunes.

Most endeared and right virtuous lady, and you the rest of the right worshipful these kind Cheshire knights; after my long being at Chester, in the time of this reported trouble, I in my melancholy walks bethought me of the strange invasion of Satan, lately on the persons of Elizabeth Caldwell and her bloody lover Jeffrey Bownd, together with that untimely actor Isabel Hall widow, how that ugly fiend (ever man's fatal opposite) had made practice, but I hope not purchase, of their corruptible lives and brought them to the last step of mortal misery. And then revolving with myself the great goodness of God in calling sinners to repentance, and withal admiring his gifts in the penitent, I could no less than write my heart's trouble, as well to partake the world with my meditation, as to make them wonder at this Cheshire chance; and thereby to plant or to engraft a kind of fear by this way of example, how murder should hereafter bear any brain in sensible creatures, considering how the very stones shall bewray the inward thoughts of massacre. All these considered, when I had coted this wonder, thinking how incredulous our nation is in things true and how uncertain they are to believe fopperies feigned, I could no less for the certainty hereof but call you to witness of the proof because sith such an example was preferred unto us that others, not eyewitness thereunto, might the rather assure themselves of the same. First, I knowing your general griefs for the fall of so good a gentlewoman, and when no remedy could be, to comfort such a godly soul, as well in her time of imprisonment as at the hour of her death, my own occasions also for that time considered, and being your true and natural countryman, I could do no less but ostend my duteous love to you all in this kind, desiring you to accept my poor mite, only considering this, the poor man's plenty is prayer to regrate your worthy loves, and as truly as I live, that shall be no niggard; for that night wherein I lie me down and pray not for you all, let my rest be broad-waking slumbers, and my quiet, waking dreams; and that will be punishment more than I would enjoy for so regardless a good as I so late and so happily received. True it is that diverse reports passed up and down the streets of London as touching this last act of murder, but how scandalously, as five murdered, three murdered by the means of six persons, which your worships know is false, only three murdered one; marry the intent was to him that now lives. Therefore being an ear-witness to this false alarm, it made me more diligent in the setting forth the truth, whereby God in his power might be known, Satan in his meaning no doubt overthrown, and the world's idle fabling by a contrary meaning known. For as it was, it was, and no otherwise, and thus it was, as your presences both at the examination, arraignment, and execution can justify; and how odious it is to hear any truth racked by slandering tongues, judge or imagine; only this, pardon my boldness, witness the right, accept my good will in the publishing; and so I commit you to God's protection.

Your poor countryman, ever
yours, Gilbert Dugdale.

The practice of Elizabeth Caldwell, against the life of her own husband.

I purpose, God willing, to describe in brief the life and death of Elizabeth Caldwell, late wife of Thomas Caldwell in the county of Chester, and daughter to one Master Duncalfe of the said county; a gentleman of very good sort, who fatherly and carefully trained up his daughter from her infancy, she being framed and adorned with all the gifts that nature could challenge, and wanting no good education, did in her tender infant years bestow her in marriage to the said Thomas Caldwell; giving her a good dower to her better preferring in the said marriage; with a yearly nuity of ten pounds, to extend to her said husband and his heiress for ever. And as the like matches do not often prove well, so this Caldwell, being young and not experienced in the world, gave his mind to travel and see foreign countries, which tended rather to his loss than profit, as also to the great discontentment of his wife, and other his friends, leaving her oftentimes very bare, without provision of such means as was fitting for her, that by these courses he did withdraw her affection from him. So that in the continuance of his absence, a young man named Jeffrey Bownd, a neighbour unto the said Elizabeth Caldwell, and she as I said before, enjoying all the excellent gifts of nature, set his affections abroad, and being a man of good wealth, spared neither cost nor industry both by himself and others to withdraw her to his unlawful desire, and omitting no opportunity in this suit; though she a long time withstood their allurements, insomuch that he feed an old woman named Isabel Hall, late wife of John Hall, and preferred as an instrument to work her to an unlawful reformation, so that in process of time, with many earnest persuasions, they won this silly soul to their will. And having so done, the said Bownd's insatiable desire could not be so satisfied, but persuaded her of himself, and also by the said Isabel Hall, to yield her consent by some means to murder her said husband; the which she was, though drawn to the other, yet very unwilling to agree unto that. But by many and often assaults and encouragements, their persuasions did work with her and took effect; the which being obtained, then were they as busy as before, devising which way to set their devilish and most hellish practices awork, preferring many devices for the accomplishment thereof. And she oftentimes entering into consideration with herself what a damnable part it was, first to abuse her husband's bed and then in seeking to deprive him of his life, was greatly tormented in her conscience, and diverse times earnestly entreated them to surcease in this practice, laying before them the great and heavy punishments provided for such offenders both in this world, and in the world to come. But their hearts being so deeply possessed by that filthy enemy to all goodness, that there was nothing to them more odious than such persuasions, still persevered in their former wicked inventions and drew her to associate them in this villainy, laying many plots for the performing of it. Amongst which Isabel Hall, as she was very expert in such like actions, being an ancient motherly woman and to all men's judgments in her outward habit was far from harbouring such a thought; yet, as I was about to say, she advised Bownd to give a brother of hers, namely George Fernley, five pounds and she would persuade him that he should use some means to murder Caldwell; the which Bownd agreed unto, being that to him all her motions were medicines and for that her house was the place that Bownd and Elizabeth Caldwell did resort for their meeting place. And he having an intent to further this matter caused this Fernley to be sent for and conferred with him; and he being a man slenderly furnished with means, agreed to this their motion, affirming that he would delay no time till he had effected their desire. Though in my conscience he pretended nothing less but only to soothe them with fair words, for lucre of the money, made a show to Bownd as if he were very diligent about the execution thereof, but still was prevented; insomuch that Bownd entered into a great rage with the poor fellow, and swore most terribly if he did not dispatch his business with all expedition, he would lay him by the heels for his five pounds.

Notwithstanding, he made delays so many, that the old fox, I mean Hall's wife, devised with herself of another course and willed Bownd to buy some ratsbane, and she would minister it in oaten cakes for that she knew that Caldwell much affected them; and they being made, his wife should give them unto him and so procure his speedy dispatch. Which device he very willingly consented unto and used no delay in the matter but presently repaired to a town in Cheshire called Knutsforth, there bought the poison and brought it to Elizabeth Caldwell, and wished her to send it to Isabel Hall with all speed. Whereupon she received it, and instantly upon the receipt thereof, Hall's wife sent her maid to Elizabeth, and willed her to send the spice she spoke to her for: so the maid innocently went as her dame commanded her and received the poison, and brought it to the said Isabel Hall her dame, who presently did take it and minister it, as I said before, in oaten cakes. The which being done, she sent them to Elizabeth Caldwell, where she and her husband did sojourn; whereupon, being in the evening, she laid them in her chamber window. In the morning next ensuing, Caldwell, as his accustomed manner was, rose very early, and his wife still keeping her bed, he spied the cakes lie in the window, and demanded of her if he might take any of them; she answered, yea, all if he would, and thereupon he took some three or four of them, and went into the house and called for some butter to eat them with, the which was brought him.

But let me tell you by the way, so soon as he was departed the chamber with the cakes, fear drave such a terror to her heart as she lay in bed, as she even trembled with remorse of conscience; yet wanted she the power to call to him to refrain them, insomuch as he himself did not only eat of them but the most part of the folks in the house, children and all. Yet God bestowed his blessing so bountifully on them, as they were all preserved from danger, saving one little girl which could not so well digest them, which was a neighbour's child of six or seven years old, and coming in by chance for fire: to the which master Caldwell gave a piece of a cake and she ate it, and by reason she had been long before visited with sickness, she went home and died presently, while the rest by way of vomit were saved. But that which master Caldwell did vomit up again, two dogs and a cat did eat, and they died presently also. Whether upon the force of that poison or no the child died I cannot say, but well I know they were all three brought within the compass of murder for the death of it, and were all executed at Chester for the same fact, as you shall hereafter understand.

Upon the death of this child, Elizabeth Caldwell was apprehended, and brought before three justices of the peace; namely, Sir John Savage, Sir Thomas Aston and Master Brooke of Norton, where before them she truly confessed all their practices and proceedings from the beginning, even till that day. Upon which confession, Bownd and Isabel Hall were apprehended and brought before the same justices, and examined as touching the murder; and they very stoutly denied all, affirming that they were not guilty to any such action, although her confession in her examination did manifest against them, being laid to their charge: all which would not move them to acknowledge their fault, the devil having so great a command over them. Notwithstanding, they were all committed to the castle of Chester, there to remain without bail or mainprize, till they should be delivered by due course of law, according to the tenure of warrants directed in such a case.

So the assize approaching within few days after their commitment, their causes and trial for that time was rejourned, till the next great assizes holden there. And whether it was by special means of Bownd made to the judge, or for that Elizabeth Caldwell was with child, I cannot truly say, but there they continued from that time, being a sennight after Easter, till Michaelmas following: during which time they were not admitted one to speak to another. And for Elizabeth Caldwell, from her first entrance into prison till the time of her death, there was never heard by any so much as an idle word to proceed out of her mouth; neither did she omit any time, during her imprisonment, in serving of God, and seeking pardon for her sins, with great zeal and industry, continually meditating on the bible, excluding herself from all company, saving such as might yield her spiritual comforts, as learned divines, and such, the faithful servants of God. There was many of all sorts resorted to see her, as no fewer some days than three hundred persons: and such as she thought were viciously given, she gave them good admonitions, wishing that her fall might be an example unto them.

Thus the deceitful devil, who hath sometime permission from God to attempt the very righteous, as Job, was now an instrument to her sorrow, but her feeling faith the more increased, and no doubt her comfort, though in our eyes terrible: for indeed so it ought, being sent from God as an example to thousands. For where so many live, one or two picked out by the hand of God must serve as an example to the rest, to keep thousands in fear of God's wrath and the world's terror. But see her constancy. All the time of her imprisonment, she used all possible means, both of herself and by those good members that did visit her, to convert all the rest of the prisoners, which good work begun in her did take good effect, for she sent some days a dozen letters to several preachers to be resolved touching her faith, and the want of a sound resolution that God had pardoned her offences. Where the Lady Mary Cholmsly of Cholmsly amongst others, together with the comfortable relief of one Master John Battie (no doubt both God's children) so relieved, as want never grieved her conscience, but that she continued in zeal, without grief of the world's offences both in soul and body: nay, not only her, but also to the rest of the prisoners. For note, that death never feared or daunted her, but only fearing she was not fully purged from her sins, till at the end, as by her words at her execution appeareth.

This foresaid Master Battie well deserves a due remembrance for his clemency and charity showed to that distressed and deceased poor soul, by whose good means, which in mere compassion by him extended, did not only receive comforts for her bodily relief, but also great satisfaction for her soul. He oft employed such industry to the learned, both to repair unto her themselves, as likewise daily in sending unto her good and learned instructions. Surely, he deserves to be registered in the hearts of all well-disposed persons, and his demerits (no doubt) will find restitution at the hands of him, who is the paymaster for all such charitable deserts.

It is also to be noted that after these three aforenamed persons had remained in prison all the whole summer, at Michaelmas then ensuing the assizes were holden. And Elizabeth Caldwell had her trial, where she openly before the judges, and the rest of the worshipful audience, acknowledged her offence; for the which she first demanded pardon at the hands of God, then of her husband, lastly of all the world; and desiring, as it was ever her prayer, that she might be as a looking-glass to all that either did see or hear of her fall, that by her they might see into their own frailness, and the infirmities which are subject to the flesh: and having, as I said, acknowledged her guiltiness, was condemned. And by reason she was not then delivered of child, still reprieved. And at the same assize Bownd was indicted; and whether by evil counsel given him or for his own obstinacy, I cannot truly report, but he would not answer the articles objected against him, nor refer his cause to God and the country, but stood mute. Though the judges very earnestly moved him to put his cause to trial, all which would not persuade him and, therefore, according to the law, he was adjudged to be pressed, receiving his judgment on the Saturday, to be executed on Monday following. And for Isabel Hall, her matter that assize was not called in question, which yielded her such encouragement that she was altogether regardless of the good of her soul.

But Bownd, ever before he perceived how he should speed, pleaded to every one whom he had any communion with of his innocency, till he saw no hope of life; then he, before two or three preachers, and others, did manifest the whole truth, and affirmed that flesh and blood was not able to endure the often assaults that Elizabeth Caldwell had of him and Isabel Hall, and upon the Monday about nine of the clock was pressed: where to every man's judgment there present, he made a very penitent end; being heartily sorrowful for his offences, and very devoutly craved pardon of God and all the world, and so died (I trust) the true servant of Jesus Christ.

Then that night next after his death, Elizabeth Caldwell was delivered of a boy, which child is yet as I take it still living with another boy she had before her imprisonment: the which are at the keeping of Caldwell their father. And as it was generally reported, he made suit to the judge to procure a warrant to have his wife executed within a certain time after her delivery; but how true it was that he made such means, I cannot truly affirm, but sure I am, a warrant was granted and sent the keeper for to have her executed within thirteen days or thereabouts after she was delivered; the which was convented by reason the constable of the castle did mistake the delivery of the warrant to the sheriff till the date was out. Though she a sennight before the time had prepared herself, only to receive the mercy of God and terror of death, yet it pleased God otherwise a while to prolong her days, which time given her, she did not vainly spend, but employ her uttermost endeavours to obtain mercy and forgiveness in such rare sort, as if I should describe the particulars thereof, it would not only be endless and tedious but, I doubt, to the hearers and readers, it would be thought incredible; for in her might be seen the true image of a penitent sinner, as the like hath not often in these days been seen, God showing his glory so abundantly, working her penitency, as to me, and many more, was most admirable. For if she espied in anyone, of what calling or degree soever, that they wilfully or carelessly abused God's holy ordinances, she would reprove them for it and courteously entreat them to amend such and such abuses; though some disdained she should seem so to do, in regard of her own former offence, though indeed none might better do it than she, having smarted even at her soul for her sins. This is the frailness of our flesh, we only disdain not our afflicted brethren, but also their good admonitions: God of his mercy I beseech him give us grace, that we may see into our fickle estates and receive willingly any reproof that may tend to the good of our poor souls.

So by this means, as I showed you before, this Elizabeth Caldwell was still detained in prison till the next assize following, at what time Isabel Hall was indicted as an actor in this murder, and found guilty by the jury, condemned and executed. And Elizabeth Caldwell also received the death of execution at the same instant, though my Lady Cholmsly very worshipful and lovingly made earnest suit unto the judge for her reprieve till the assize following: that which by no means would be granted. And she seeing her suit would not take effect, being very sorrowful, like a kind lady, went unto Elizabeth Caldwell herself, and showed her she could not therein prevail for her.

Indeed my lady and others had an intent, if they could have got her reprieve, to have used means to the king for a petition, but seeing it would not be, Elizabeth dutifully yielded thanks unto her ladyship; and said she was very content to receive the death ordained for her. My lady departed, and she practising her former exercises, I mean prayer, until such time as the keeper came and told her the sheriff was come to the Glovers' Stone to receive her and the rest of the prisoners appointed for death: and she very cheerfully answered: I trust in my God I am ready, and farewell to the law, too long have I been in thy subjection. And so departing the castle, taking leave with everyone, and from hence to the place of execution, she sometimes sung Psalms, and used other godly meditations, as was thought fitting for her, by those divines and godly preachers, which accompanied her even to her death.

A letter written by Elizabeth Caldwell to her husband, during the time of her imprisonment.

Although the greatness of my offence deserves neither pity nor regard, yet give leave unto your poor sorrowful wife to speak unto you what out of her own woeful experience, with abundance of grief and tears, she hath learned in the school of affliction; it is the last favour that I shall ever beg at your hands, and the last office that ever I shall perform unto you. And therefore dear husband, if you have any hope or desire to be partaker of the joys of heaven, let my speeches find acceptance and do not slightly esteem what I write unto you, but read these lines again and again, and lay them up in your heart, where I beseech almighty God they may take deep root and impression. For my witness is in heaven, that my heart's desire and earnest prayer to God is that your soul may be saved. And if the loss of my blood or life, or to endure any torments that the world can inflict upon me might procure your true conversion, I should esteem it purchased at an easy rate. But sith none can have salvation without true reformation, both inward and outward, amendment in changing the affection, words, and works from evil to good, which till you feel in your soul and conscience to be effectually wrought, you have not repented; defer not time, but call to God for grace of true repentance, which may be found even in this accepted time, when the doors of God's mercy are open, that so he may have mercy on you; lest he give you over to hardness of heart, that you cannot repent: and so you knock with the foolish virgins, when the date of God's mercies are out and then nothing but woe, woe, and vengeance. Therefore, the longer you defer, the harder it will be for you to repent: and delays are most dangerous, for what know you how suddenly, death may strike you, and then, as the tree falls, so it lies; that is, as you die, so shall you have, if in true repentance, joy, if in your sins, sorrow. Therefore, saith Solomon, All that thy hand shall find to do, do it with all thy power, for there is neither work, nor knowledge, invention, nor wisdom in the grave whither thou goest.

O husband, be not deceived with the world and think that it is in your power to repent when you will, or that to say a few prayers from the mouth outward a little before death, or to cry God mercy for fashion sake is true repentance. No, no, not everyone that saith Lord, Lord, shall enter into the kingdom of heaven, but he that doth the will of my Father which is in heaven, saith our Saviour. Late repentance is seldom true and true repentance is not so easy a matter to come by as the world doth judge. Do not presume on it, and so run on in your sinful course of life and think to repent when you list; you cannot do it, for repentance is the rare gift of God, which is given but to a very few, even to those that seek it, with many tears and very earnestly with fervent prayers. None can better speak of it, for none better knows it than myself; my sorrowful heart hath smarted for it, and my soul hath been sick to the gates of hell and of death to find it; and to have it, is more precious than all the world. Therefore, cease not to pray day and night with the prophet, Turn thou us unto thee, O Lord, and we shall be turned, and with Ephraim, Convert thou me, O Lord, and I shall be converted: for except you be converted, you shall not enter into the kingdom of heaven.

And because none can be converted, nor come unto Christ except the Father draw him, never leave to solicit the Father of mercy to create a new heart and renew a right spirit within you, and call to remembrance the dissoluteness of your life. I speak it not to lay anything to your charge, for I do love you more dearly than I do myself, but remember in what case you have lived; how poor you have many times left me; how long you have been absent from me, all which advantage the devil took to subvert me. And to further his purpose, he set his hellish instruments awork, even the practice of wicked people, who continually wrought upon my weakness, my poverty and your absence, until they made me yield to conspire with them the destruction of your body by a violent and sudden death, which God in his great mercy prevented. And on the knees of my heart, in the abundance of his compassion, I beseech him to forgive us all, and wash our souls in the blood of his Christ, and to open the eyes of your understanding that you may see by my example, which the providence of God for some secret cause best known to himself hath appointed to come to pass. How weak and wretched we are and how unable to stand of ourselves, when it shall please him to take his grace from us and to leave us to ourselves. Therefore good husband, as you tender the welfare of your soul, go no further on in your sinful race, but turn unto the Lord and so shall you save your soul alive. If you continue in your abominations and shut your ears against the word of exhortation, you cannot have any hope of salvation; for the book of God is full of judgments against wilful sinners, and mercy is to them that repent and turn.

Therefore, I beseech you use no delay, defer no time, but presently be acquainted with the scriptures, for they will lead you to eternal life: make haste, even before your hands part with this paper to search therein, that so you may truly understand the wretched estate and condition of those, who following the lusts of their eyes, wallow in all sensuality and so heap up vengeance against the day of wrath: even heavy judgments, no less than condemnation both of soul and body. As Solomon saith, *Rejoice O young man in thy youth, and let thy heart cheer thee, in the days of thy youth, and walk in the ways of thy heart, and in the sight of thine eyes, but know that for all things God will bring thee to judgment.* Remember he spared not the angels when they sinned, but cast them down into hell; nor of the old world but eight only escaped, the rest were drowned in their sins because they would not be warned. Balthazar, saith Daniel, expounding the fearful vision of the hand's writing, when he was banqueting with his concubines, thou art weighed in the balance and are found light.

These and many more are written for our admonition, upon whom the ends of the world are come; search for them, and I pray God you may be warned by them, and that you may seek the Lord now while he may be found and call upon him while he is near. Behold now the day of salvation, even now, when he in mercy offereth himself unto us by preaching of his word; receive not these graces in vain, but redeem your time and run unto the house of God, and there in the great congregation, pour forth your plaint; with obedience hear the word of God, and endeavour to practise what you hear in your conversation, for the doers only shall be justified at the last day. The word must judge us, in this life it worketh effect for which it was sent: it either converts or hardens; it is the favour of life unto life, or of death unto death. It is offered to all; to those that embrace it, it brings life; to those that will not be reformed by it, it brings death, to those that love and desire it, it is the quicking spirit; to those that refuse it, it is the killing letter; it is no special argument of God his favour unto any, unless they feel the power thereof working reformation in them, then it is the power of his spirit, the pledge of his blessing. Ignorance must not excuse you, for the prophet saith, My people languish for want of knowledge, and knowledge without practice, leaves all men without excuse; for he that knoweth his master's will, and doth it not, shall be beaten with many strips: therefore make more conscience of the word of God, than you have done, and love his messengers, the preachers that brings that glad tidings; for to love them is to love Christ, and to hate them, is to hate Christ, as our Saviour saith, *He that despiseth you, despiseth me*, and it is hard to kick against the prick. And love the children of God that profess Christ Jesus, for hereby shall men know that you are my disciples, if you love one another saith our Saviour. And for the sabbath day, be ye assured that the Lord of heaven hath not in vain chosen it to himself, commanding us to sanctify it unto his holy name; no, no, if ever we desire to be partakers of the spiritual sabbath in heaven, whereof ours on earth is but a type and a figure, then must we strive to keep the same sabbath on earth as much as in us lies, which the saints keep in heaven. They are at rest from those labours that mortality is subject unto and uncessantly sing praises unto the Lamb; so should we rest that day from the labours of our calling, and spend the whole day in the hearing of the word preached, praising the Lord publicly in the great congregation, privately at home with our families, preferring such other holy exercises as may tend to the glory of God, the comfort of our souls and the good of others, which we are bound to perform so straightly, as that we may not that day be allowed to speak such words as concern of vocations. And howsoever it please the world to think of the great God of heaven and of the sanctifying of the sabbaths, yet be you assured he is a jealous God, and will visit sinners, and one seed of his word shall not be lost; but he will be glorified by it either in the salvation of those who in a good conscience willingly endeavour to sanctify them, or in the condemnation of those who wilfully oppose themselves against his blessed ordinance to profane them: which is one of the crying sins of this land, wherewith the whole kingdom is infected: and if there were not some few to stand in the gap, for whose sake the Lord doth spare the rest, it had not been possible we should so long have escaped his heavy judgments.

O dear husband, the Lord hath long since taken his sword in his hand to execute his vengeance against all disobedient wretches who turn the sabbath of the Lord into a day of wantonness, liberty and licentiousness; and although in his great mercy he doth yet forbear to proceed to judgment, as it were in great mercy, waiting our repentance, yet there will suddenly come a day of reckoning, all together. And the wicked make the patience of our God an occasion to commit sin and profaneness; yet let them know, the Lord will take vengeance of his adversaries and reserve wrath for his enemies, and though he be slow to anger, yet is he great in power, and will not surely clear the wicked: though he defer the sessions, yet they will come; and though he have leaden feet, yet hath he iron hands; though the fire light not upon Sodom all the evening, yet it came. Do not therefore provoke the Lord any longer by your profaneness, for he is strong, ready to punish, and hath promised that the person that despiseth his words shall be cut off. Did he not command a man to be stoned to death for gathering a few sticks on the sabbath day, and is he not still the same God? Yes certain, his arm is not shortened if we wilfully persist in our disobedience.

Six market days he hath given us to provide us necessaries for our bodies, and but one hath he chosen for himself to be a day of holiness, which is the market day for the soul, wherein we should provide us comforts for the whole week. The excellency and worth of this day is unspeakable to those that sanctify it. It is the badge and livery whereby they are known to be the servants of God: to those that profane it, in spending the day in worldly pleasures, drunkenness and filthiness, it is the certain badge and livery whereby they are known to be the servants of the devil, according to the sayings of the apostle, *Know you not unto whomsoever ye give your selves as servants to obey, his servants ye are, to whom ye obey, whether it be of sin unto death, or of obedience unto righteousness.*

If my people will sanctify my sabbath, saith the Lord, it shall be a sign between me and them that they may know that I am the Lord their God; and blessed are they who have the Lord for their God. So that to those that profane the sabbath, the Lord is not their God, but the devil: and cursed are the people that are in such a case. Therefore dear husband, defer no time, put not off from day to day, to turn unto the Lord, neither be you deceived, for God is not mocked, the longer you run on, the more you set on the score, and such as you sow, such shall you reap: for the Lord hath said, He that heareth my words, and doth bless himself in heart, saying, I shall have peace, although I walk according to the stubbornness of my heart, thus adding drunkenness to thirst, the Lord will not be merciful unto him; but the wrath of the Lord, and his jealousy, shall smoke against that man, and every curse that is written in this book shall light upon him, and the Lord shall put out his name from under heaven: but unto them that repent, the Lord hath said, when the wicked turneth away from his wickedness that he hath committed, and doth that which is lawful and right, he shall save his soul alive. You see the judgments of God are begun already in your house, happy shall you be if you make a holy use of them, otherwise heavier may be expected, especially if you persist. In his mercy he hath spared you, and doth yet wait for your repentance, do not you abuse his patience any longer, lest thereby you provoke him to proceed to execution against you, but embrace his mercy which is yet offered unto you: for which, that you may so do, I shall not cease to pray whilst I live to him who only is able to effect it, even the Lord of heaven, who send us joyful meeting at the day of our resurrection.

Your poor wife
Elizabeth Caldwell.

The words of Elizabeth Caldwell at the time of her death.

First she desired that the Lord would give a blessing unto the speeches that she delivered that they might tend to the converting of many of the hearers, and also she said that the word of God did not give her any privilege and authority to sin, but that it was her own filthy flesh, the illusions of the devil and those hellish instruments which he set on to work. Yet notwithstanding, she ever had a detestation to those sins that she lived in, but she affirmed that she wanted grace to avoid them; therefore, as she had given a great scandal to the word of God by professing and not practising the same, even so she desired the great mercy of God to forgive her that sin, acknowledging that she stood too presumptuously upon her own conceit, and grew too proud, vowing and swearing that she would never do such and such things, but suddenly fell into the like again.

Therefore she gave St Paul's admonition unto everyone, *Let him that thinketh he stands, take heed of a present fall*: likewise she exhorted all to the diligent observation of the sabbath day, saying that one of her chief and capital sins was the neglect thereof, and although the world did reckon and esteem it a small matter, yet she knew it to be one of her greatest sins. Wishing all people in the fear of God to make a reverent account of the Lord's glorious sabbath, she complained much of adultery and said it was that filthy sin which was the cause of her death, and was persuaded in her conscience that her afflictions was rather for that than any murder she ever committed. Notwithstanding, she yielded herself culpable in concealing of it, manifesting that in regard of her sins and iniquities, she deserved a thousand deaths; praying most earnestly unto God that herself might be a warning and example unto all there present; wishing them most earnestly to serve the Lord, of what degree soever they were, if they were never so poor, but were forced to crave their living from door to door, which done then they were happy creatures.

Then again, she admonished all to keep the sabbath, to go to the church and hear the word of God preached, for that was the only truth and able to save their souls. But as touching papistry, she ever hated it, knowing it contrary and flatly opposite against the truth of the great

God of heaven and his holy word, praying for the confusion and desolation of the great whore of Babylon, but most devoutly and sincerely, praying for the current passage of the gospel of Christ Jesus throughout the whole world, to the converting of thousands, desiring that the very stones of the street might set forth the glory of God. And withal, most religiously she prayed for the king's most excellent majesty, and said she might call him her king while she lived, that his sacred and royal person might be a bright shining lamp of God's glory in the advancement of the gospel of Christ, and the overthrow of popery and superstition in these his kingdoms and dominions. Then made known that she could teach as the preachers, for they taught as they found it in the word, and she was able to speak from a feeling heart, very confidently affirming that her sins were the greatest reason of the dulness and hardness of her heart, and the separation of God's mercies from her: and therefore she carefully advised all to beware of sin because it was hateful and odious in the sight of God and all reasonable creatures.

Concerning repentance, she spake thus; that it was not in the power of man to repent when he list, but the only gift of God, protesting before the Lord of heaven and earth that during the time of her imprisonment, being a full year and a quarter, she had sought the Lord with many bitter tears, with broken and contrite heart, to see if his majesty would be entreated, and yet she found not such assurance as she had desired: but avouched what she did was done in simplicity of heart, whatsoever the world did other was censure. Moreover, saying that in the mercies and merits of Christ Jesus, she hoped her sins were pardoned, and said I believe Lord, help my unbelief. Also she said that in the time of her imprisonment the Lord had been very gracious and merciful unto her, for many the faithful ministers and dear servants of Jesus Christ had recourse unto her, by whose means she had recovered great comfort, praising the Lord for the same. Yet notwithstanding, the world most injuriously did deride, scoff and mock them, which was most wicked and abominable: saying, that if there were forty and two children devoured for mocking the prophet Elijah, what then shall befall of them that do blaspheme the name of the great God of heaven, profane his holy sabbath, speak evil of his word and abuse his faithful ministers. Therefore, she desired all to turn from their sins, and to turn to the Lord by true and unfeigned repentance, praying very earnestly for her husband's conversion, and that her two children might have the fear of God before their eyes, and that the glory of God might appear in the conversion of prisoners, though it were with the loss of her own life, so infinite was her zeal.

Then she prayed the Lord, that he would pardon all her grievous and heinous sins in the bloodshed of Christ Jesus, beseeching him to cleanse her from her secret sins: praying that she might be a doorkeeper in the house of God and receive the meanest place of glory. Then said she, that if the great and tall cedars of the church of God have fallen, as David, Solomon, and Manasseh, how then could she stand being but a bramble and a weak, wretched woman. Therefore she exhorted everyone to depend only upon the Lord, and not to stand upon their own strength as she had done. And greatly then desiring all the people to pray unto God for her, she called for her prayer book, reading and praying zealously and devoutly to almighty God with her eyes lift up towards heaven; which done, she requested that they would sing a Psalm, reading it herself and singing with a good spirit, that afterwards she uttered that she felt the mercies of God and her soul was much comforted: and hoped that in the blood of Christ Jesus her sins were pardoned; and said she could not amend that which was past, but was most heartily sorrowful for her former sins; saying, that if she should live yet many years, her desire would be in serving the Lord. Therefore, she desired him upon the knees of her heart that he would respect the will for the deed and accept her poor desires; saying, O suffer me yet once to recover my strength, before I go hence and be seen no more. Praying likewise for all those that ministered comforts unto her in her misery and distresses, that the Lord would bless them and continue them faithful unto the end.

Then forgiving, and asking forgiveness of all, making herself ready, saying her bodily death did not dismay her, concluding with these her last words, Lord Jesus receive my spirit; and so she left this miserable world, and died the true servant of Jesus Christ, the xviii. day of June, 1603.

Now yet again remember our old beldame aforenamed, that uncharitable creature Isabel Hall, widow, being the only instrument of this timeless action: who standing on the ladder, and ready to suffer for her fact, did notwithstanding very stoutly deny everything that had been done in their late proceedings, nay and abjured it, had not Elizabeth Caldwell with affirmation of all inserted her confession in that behalf: who with an easy repentance to the world's eye, ended her life. Whereby may be seen how strong the devil in some actions is, that she by whose instigation all was done, both in the adultery and murder, would so impudently deny every particular, notwithstanding the trial of the cause both manifested by judge and jury. But thus we see the boldness of sin, and the coldness of the truth, till God in mercy makes plain the truth of the one and the wonder of the other. All which tending to the example of others may move us to lively repentance, which not done, salvation cannot come, but truly effected, breeds both the comfort of the soul and body. To which comfort, God in mercy bring us for his son Jesus Christ his sake.

FINIS.

To the right honourable, and his singular good lady, the Lady Mary Chandois, R. A. wisheth health and everlasting happiness.

My honourable and very good lady, considering my duty to your kind ladyship, and remembering the virtues of your prepared mind, I could do no less but dedicate this strange work to your view, being both matter of moment and truth. And to the whole world it may seem strange that a gentlewoman so well brought up in God's fear, so well married, so virtuous ever, so suddenly wrought to this act of murder; that when your ladyship doth read as well the letter as the book, of her own inditing, you will the more wonder that her virtues could so aptly taste the follies of vice and villainy. But so it was, and for the better proof that it was so, I have placed my kinsman's name to it, who was present at all her troubles, at her coming to prison, her being in prison, and her going out of prison to execution. That those gentlemen to whom he dedicates his work witnessed, may also be partakers in that kind, for the proof thereof, that your ladyship and the world so satisfied, may admire the deed, and hold it as strange as it is true.

We have many giddy-pated poets that could have published this report with more eloquence, but truth in plain attire is the easier known: let fiction mask in Kendal green. It is my quality to add to the truth, truth, and not leasings to lies. Your good honour knows Pink's poor heart, who in all my services to your late deceased kind lord, never savoured of flattery, or fiction: and therefore am now the bolder to present to your virtues, the view of this late truth, desiring you to think of it, that you may be an honourable mourner at these obsequies, and you shall no more do than many have done. So with my tendered duty, my true ensuing story, and my ever wishing well, I do humbly commit your ladyship to the prison of heaven wherein is perfect freedom.

Your Ladyship's ever
in duty and service,
Robert Armin.

13. From *The Psalms of David and Others*. *With Mr John Calvin's Commentaries*, translated by Arthur Golding (1571):

Not without cause am I wont to term [the Psalms] the anatomy of all the parts of the soul, inasmuch as a man shall not find any affection in himself, whereof the image appeareth not in this glass. Yea rather, the Holy Ghost hath here lively set out before our eyes, all the griefs, sorrows, fears, doubts, hopes, cares, anguishes, and finally all the troublesome motions wherewith men's minds are wont to be turmoiled. The rest of the scripture containeth what commandments God hath enjoined to his servants to be brought unto us. But in this book, the prophets themselves talking with God, because they discover all the inner thoughts, do call or draw every one of us to the peculiar examination of himself, so as no whit of all the infirmities to which we are subject, and of so many vices wherewith we are fraughted, may abide hidden. It is a rare and singular profit when by searching out all the lurking holes, the heart is cleansed from the most noisome infection of hypocrisy and laid open to the light. Again if the calling upon God be the greatest defence of our welfare: inasmuch as a better and more certain rule thereof cannot be fetched from elsewhere than out of this book . . .

Here shall the readers as well be wakened to feel throughly their own evils, as also put in mind to seek remedies . . . If at any time sundry doubts do disquiet us, we may learn to wrestle with them until the mind mount up free unto God. And not this only, but also let us wade even through doubtings, fearfulness and trembling unto prayer, until we be glad of it for the comfort that we receive . . . in this book (than which nothing is more to be wished) there is brought to pass for us, not only how we may have familiar access unto God, but also how we may lawfully and freely utter before him the infirmities which shame forbiddeth us to be aknown unto men. Moreover, in what sort the sacrifice of thanksgiving is to be offered aright, the which God avoucheth to be most precious and of most sweet scent unto him, it is here also prescribed most exactly. Nowhere are read more evident commendations as well of God's singular bounty towards his church, as also of all his works. Nowhere are showed so many deliveries or proofs of his fatherly providence and care towards us so beautifully set out; to be short, nowhere is there either a more full and perfect manner of praising God taught us, or a sharper spur put to us for the performance of this duty of godliness. Besides this, albeit that this book be replenished with all manner of precepts, whatsoever may avail to frame the life after a holy, godly, and rightful sort: yet will it chiefly instruct us to the sufferance of the cross, which is the true trial of obedience, when utterly forsaking our own affections, we submit ourselves to God, and suffer our life to be so governed at his pleasure that the miseries which are to us most bitter do wax sweet because they come from him. Last of all, not only the general commendations of God's goodness are here recited, which may teach us to stay upon him only that the godly minds may look for assured help at his hand in all their necessities; but also the free remission of sins (which alone both maketh God at one with us and purchaseth us quiet peace with him) is so set out, that there wanteth nothing at all toward the knowledge of everlasting salvation.

14. From Jeremy Taylor, *The Rule and Exercises of Holy Living* (1654):

CHAPTER I. Section I. The first general instrument of holy living: care of our time.

He that is choice of his time will also be choice of his company, and choice of his actions, lest the first engage him in vanity and loss, and the latter by being criminal be a throwing his time and himself away, and a going back in the accounts of eternity.

God hath given to man a short time here upon earth, and yet upon this short time eternity depends: but so, that for every hour of our life (after we are persons capable of laws, and know good from evil) we must give account to the great judge of men and angels. And this is it which our blessed Saviour told us, that we must account for every idle word; not meaning, that every word which is not designed to edification, or is less prudent, shall be reckoned for a sin, but that the time which we spend in our idle talking and unprofitable discoursings, that time which we might and ought to have been employed to spiritual and useful purposes, that is to be accounted for.

For we must remember, that we have a great work to do, many enemies to conquer, many evils to prevent, much danger to run through, many difficulties to be mastered, many necessities to serve, and much good to do, many children to provide for, or many friends to support, or many poor to relieve, or many diseases to cure, besides the needs of nature, and of relation, our private and our public cares, and duties of the world, which necessity and the providence of God hath adopted into the family of religion.

And that we need not fear this instrument to be a snare to us, or that the duty must end in scruple, vexation, and eternal fears, we must remember, that the life of every man may be so ordered (and indeed must) that it may be a perpetual serving of God: the greatest trouble and most busy trade, and worldly encumbrances, when they are necessary, or charitable, or profitable in order to any of those ends, which we are bound to serve, whether public or private, being a doing God's work. For God provides the good things of the world to serve the needs of nature, by the labours of the ploughman, the skill and pains of the artisan, and the dangers and traffic of the merchant: these men are in their callings the ministers of the divine providence, and the stewards of the creation, and servants of the great family of God, the world, in the employment of procuring necessaries for food and clothing, ornament and physic. In their proportions also, a king and a priest, and a prophet, a judge and an advocate, doing the works of their employment according to their proper rules, are doing the work of God, because they serve those necessities which God hath made, and yet made no provisions for them but by their ministry. So that no man can complain, that his calling takes him off religion, his calling itself and his very worldly employment, in honest trades and offices, is a serving of God, and if it be moderately pursued, and according to the rules of Christian prudence, will leave void spaces enough for prayers and retirements of a more spiritual religion.

God hath given every man work enough to do, that there shall be no room for idleness, and yet hath so ordered the world, that there shall be space for devotion. He that hath the fewest businesses of the world, is called upon to spend more time in the dressing of his soul, and he that hath the most affairs, may so order them, that they shall be a service of God; whilst at certain periods they are blessed with prayers and actions of religion, and all day long are hallowed by a holy intention.

However, so long as idleness is quite shut out from our lives, all the sins of wantonness, softness and effeminacy are prevented, and there is but little room left for temptation: and therefore to a busy man temptation is fain to climb up together with his businesses, and sins creep upon him only by accidents and occasions; whereas to an idle person they come in a full body, and with open violence, and the impudence of a restless importunity.

Idleness is called the sin of Sodom and her daughters, and indeed is the burial of a living man, an idle person being so useless to any purposes of God and man, that he is like one that is dead, unconcerned in the changes and necessities of the world: and he only lives to spend his time, and eat the fruits of the earth, like vermin or a wolf, when their time comes they die and perish, and in the meantime do no good; they neither plough nor carry burdens: all that they do, either is unprofitable, or mischievous.

Idleness is the greatest prodigality in the world: it throws away that, which is invaluable in respect of its present use, and irreparable when it is past, being to be recovered by no power of art or nature. But the way to secure and improve our time we may practise in the following rules.

Rules for employing our time:

1. In the morning, when you awake, accustom yourself to think first upon God, or something in order to his service; and at night also, let him close thine eyes; and let your sleep be necessary and healthful, not idle and expensive of time, beyond the needs and conveniences of nature; and sometimes be curious to see the preparation which the sun makes, when he is coming forth from his chambers of the east.

2. Let every man that hath a calling, be diligent in pursuance of its employment, so as not lightly, or without reasonable occasion to neglect it in any of those times, which are usually and by the customs of prudent persons and good husbands employed in it.

3. Let all the intervals, or void spaces of time be employed in prayers, reading, meditating, works of nature, recreation, charity, friendliness and neighbourhood, and means of spiritual and corporal health: ever remembering, so to work in our calling, as not to neglect the work of our high calling; but to begin and end the day with God, with such forms of devotion, as shall be proper to our necessities.

15. From Joseph Hall, *The Art of Divine Meditation* (1607):

Chapter. I. The benefit and uses of meditation.

It is not, I suppose, a more bold than profitable labour, after the endeavours of so many contemplative men, to teach the art of meditation. An heavenly business, as any belongs either to man or Christian; and such as whereby the soul doth unspeakably benefit itself. For by this do we ransack our deep and false hearts, find out our secret enemies, buckle with them, expel them, arm ourselves against their re-entrance. By this, we make use of all good means, fit ourselves to all good duties; by this we descry our weakness, obtain redress, prevent temptations, cheer up our solitariness, temper our occasions of delight, get more light to our knowledge, more heat to our affections, more life to our devotion: by this we grow to be (as we are) strangers upon earth; and, out of a right estimation of all earthly things, into a sweet fruition of invisible comforts: by this, we see our Saviour with Stephen, we talk with God as Moses, and by this we are ravished with the blessed Paul into paradise and see that heaven which we are loathe to leave, which we cannot utter. This alone is the remedy of security and worldliness, the pastime of saints, the ladder of heaven and, in short, the best improvement of Christianity: learn it who can and neglect it who list; he shall never find joy, neither in God nor in himself which doth not both know and practise it. And however of old some hidden cloisterers have engrossed it to themselves, and confined it within their cells, who indeed, professing nothing but contemplation through their immunity from those cares which accompany an active life, might have the best leisure to this business; yet seeing there is no man so taken up with action as not sometimes to have a free mind; and there is no reasonable mind so simple as not to be able both to discourse somewhat and to better itself by her secret thoughts; I deem it an envious wrong to conceal that from any whose benefit may be universal. Those that have but a little stock had need to know the best rules of thrift.

Chapter. II. The description and kinds of meditation.

The rather for that whereas our divine meditation is nothing else but a bending of the mind upon some spiritual object, through diverse forms of discourse, until our thoughts come to an issue; and this must needs be either extemporal and occasioned by outward occurrences offered to the mind, or deliberate and wrought out of our own heart; which again is either in matter of knowledge for the finding out of some hidden truth and convincing of an heresy by profound traversing of reason, or in matter of affection for the enkindling of our love of God: the former of these two last we sending to the schools and masters of controversies, search after the latter; which is both of larger use, and such as no Christian can reject as either unnecessary or over difficult. For, both every Christian had need of fire put to his affections, and weaker judgments are no less capable of this divine heat, which proceeds not so much from reason as from faith.

One says (and I believe him) that God's school is more affection than understanding; both lessons very needful, very profitable; but for this our age, especially the latter. For if there be some that have much zeal, little knowledge, there are more that have much knowledge without zeal. And he that hath much skill and no affection may do good to others by information of judgment, but shall never have thank either of his own heart or of God; who useth not to cast away his love on those of whom he is but known, not loved.

Chapter. III. Concerning meditation extemporal.

Of extemporal meditation there may be much use, no rule: forasmuch as our conceits herein vary according to the infinite multitude of objects and their diverse manner of proffering themselves to the mind, as also for the suddenness of this act. Man is placed in this stage of the world to view the several natures and actions of the creatures; to view them, not idly, without his use, as they do him: God made all these for man, and man for his own sake; both these purposes were lost if man should let the creatures pass carelessly by him, only seen, not thought upon. He only can make benefit of what he sees; which if he do not, it is all one as if he were blind or brute. Whence it is that wise Solomon puts the sluggard to school unto the ant, and our Saviour sends the distrustful to the lily of the field.

In this kind was that meditation of the divine Psalmist, which, upon the view of the glorious frame of the heavens, was led to wonder at the merciful respect God hath to so poor a creature as man. Thus our Saviour took occasion of the water fetched up solemnly to the altar from the well of Shiloh, on the day of the great hosanna, to meditate and discourse of the water of life. Thus holy and sweet Augustine, from occasion of the watercourse near to his lodging, running among the pebbles, sometimes more silently, sometimes in a baser murmur, and sometimes in a shriller note, entered into the thought and discourse of that excellent order which God hath settled in all these inferior things. Thus that learned and heavenly soul of our late Estye, when we sat together and heard a sweet consort of music, seemed upon this occasion carried up for the time beforehand to the place of his rest, saying, not without some passion, What music may we think there is in heaven! Thus lastly (for who knows not that examples of this kind are infinite?) that faithful and reverend Deering, when the sun shined on his face, now lying on his deathbed, fell into a sweet meditation of the glory of God and his approaching joy. The thoughts of this nature are not only lawful, but so behoveful that we cannot omit them without neglect of God, his creatures, ourselves. The creatures are half lost if we only employ them, not learn something of them: God is wronged if his creatures be unregarded; ourselves most of all, if we read this great volume of the creatures and take no lesson for our instruction.

Chapter. IV. Cautions of extemporal meditation.

Wherein yet caution is to be had that our meditations be not either too far-fetched or savouring of superstition. Far-fetched I call those which have not a fair and easy resemblance unto the matter from whence they are raised; in which case our thoughts prove loose and heartless, making no memorable impression in the mind. Superstitious, when we make choice of those grounds of meditation which are forbidden us as teachers of vanity, or employ our own devices (though well-grounded) to a use above their reach; making them, upon our own pleasures, not only furtherances but parts of God's worship: in both which our meditations degenerate and grow rather perilous to the soul. Whereto add that the mind be not too much cloyed with too frequent iteration of the same thought, which at last breeds a weariness in ourselves and an unpleasantness of that conceit which at the first entertainment promised much delight. Our nature is too ready to abuse familiarity in any kind: and it is with meditations as with medicines, which, with over-ordinary use lose their sovereignty and fill, instead of purging. God hath not straited us for matter, having given us the scope of the whole world, so that there is no creature, event, action, speech which may not afford us new matter of meditation. And that which we are wont to say of fine wits, we may as truly affirm of the Christian heart, that it can make use of anything. Wherefore as travellers in a foreign country make every sight a lesson, so ought we in this our pilgrimage. Thou seest the heaven rolling above thine head in a constant and unmovable motion; the stars so overlooking one another that the greatest show little, the least greatest, all glorious; the air full of the bottles of rain, or fleeces of snow, or diverse forms of fiery exhalation; the sea under one uniform face full of strange and monstrous shapes beneath; the earth so adorned with variety of plants

that thou canst not but tread on many at once with every foot; besides
the store of creatures that fly above it, walk upon it, lie in it. Thou idle
truant, dost thou learn nothing of so many masters? Hast thou so long
read these capital letters of God's great book and canst thou not yet
spell one word of them? The brute creatures see the same things with
as clear, perhaps better eyes; if thine inward eyes see not their use, as
well as thy bodily eyes their shape, I know not whether is more
reasonable, or less brutish . . .

Chapter. XII. Of the matter and subject of our meditation.

Now time and order call us from these circumstances to the matter
and subject of meditation, which must be divine and spiritual, not evil,
nor worldly. O the carnal and unprofitable thoughts of men! We all
meditate: one how to do ill to others; another how to do some earthly
good to himself; another to hurt himself under the colour of good, as
how to accomplish his lewd desires, the fulfilling whereof proves the
bane of the soul, how he may sin unseen, and go to hell with least noise
of the world. Or perhaps some better minds bend their thoughts upon
the search of natural things; the motions of every heaven and of every
star; the reason and course of the ebbing and flowing of the sea; the
manifold kinds of simples that grow out of the earth and creatures that
creep upon it; with all their strange qualities and operations. Or
perhaps the several forms of government and rules of state take up
their busy heads; so that while they would be acquainted with the
whole world, they are strangers at home; and while they seek to know
all other things, they remain unknown to themselves. The God that
made them, the vileness of their nature, the danger of their sins, the
multitude of their imperfections, the Saviour that bought them, the
heaven that he brought for them, are in the meantime as unknown, as
unregarded, as if they were not.

Thus do foolish children spend their time and labour in turning over
leaves to look for painted babes, not at all respecting the solid matter
under their hands. We fools, when will we be wise, and turning our
eyes from vanity, with that sweet singer of Israel, make God's statutes
our song and meditation in the house of our pilgrimage?

Earthly things proffer themselves with importunity; heavenly things
must with importunity be sued to. Those, if they were not so little
worth, would not be so forward; and being so forward need not any
meditation to solicit them; these, by how much more hard they are to

entreat, by so much more precious they are being obtained; and therefore worthier our endeavour. As then we cannot go amiss so long as we keep ourselves in the track of divinity; while the soul is taken up with the thoughts, either of the deity in his essence and persons (sparingly yet in this point, and more in faith and admiration than inquiry), or of his attributes, his justice, power, wisdom, mercy, truth; or of his works, in the creation, preservation, government of all things, according to the Psalmist, *I will meditate of the beauty of thy glorious majesty, and thy wonderful works.* So, most directly in our way and best fitting our exercise of meditation are those matters in divinity which can most of all work compunction in the heart, and most stir us up to devotion. Of which kind are the meditations concerning Christ Jesus, our mediator, his incarnation, miracles, life, passion, burial, resurrection, ascension, intercession, the benefit of our redemption, the certainty of our election, the graces proceeding of our sanctification, our glorious estate in paradise lost in our first parents, our present vileness, our inclination to sin, our several actual offences, the temptations and sleights of evil angels, the use of the sacraments, the nature and practice of faith and repentance: the miseries of our life, with the frailty of it, the certainty and uncertainty of our death, the glory of God's saints above, the awfulness of judgment, the terrors of hell, and the rest of this quality: wherein both it is fit to have variety (for that even the strongest stomach doth not always delight in one dish) and yet so to change that our choice may be free from wildness and inconstancy.

16. From Andrew Marvell, *The Rehearsal Transpros'd: or, Animadversions Upon a Late Book, Entitled, A Preface Showing What Grounds There Are of Fears and Jealousies of Popery* (1672):

But is it not a great pity to see a man in the flower of his age, and the vigour of his studies, to fall into such a distraction, that his head runs upon nothing but Roman empire and ecclesiastical policy? This happens by his growing too early acquainted with *Don Quixote*, and reading the bible too late: so that the first impressions being most strong, and mixing with the last, as more novel, have made such a medley in his brain-pan that he is become a mad priest, which of all sorts is the most incurable. Hence it is that you shall hear him anon instructing princes, like Sancho, how to govern his island: as he is busied at present in vanquishing the Calvinists of Germany and Geneva. Had he no friends to have given him good counsel before his understanding were quite unsettled? Or if there were none near, why did not men call in the neighbours and send for the parson of the parish to persuade him in time, but let it run on thus till he is fit for nothing but Bedlam, or Hogsdon? However though it be a particular damage, it may tend to a general advantage: and young students will I hope by his example learn to beware henceforward of overweening presumption and preposterous ambition. For this gentleman, as I have heard, after he had read *Don Quixote* and the bible, besides such school books as were necessary for his age, was sent early to the university: and there studied hard, and in a short time became a competent rhetorician, and no ill disputant. He had learned how to erect a thesis, and to defend it *pro* or *con* with a serviceable distinction: while the truth (as his camarade Mr Bays hath it on another occasion)

Before a full pot of ale you can swallow,
Was here with a whoop and gone with a hollow.

And so thinking himself now ripe and qualified for the greatest undertakings, and highest fortune, he therefore exchanged the narrowness of the university for the town; but coming out of the confinement of the square cap and the quadrangle into the open air, the world began to turn round with him: which he imagined, though it were his own giddiness, to be nothing less than the quadrature of the circle. This accident concurring so happily to increase the good opinion which he naturally had of himself, he thenceforward applied to gain a like reputation with others. He followed the town life, haunted the best companies; and, to polish himself from any pedantic roughness, he read and saw the plays, with much care and more proficiency than most of the auditory. But all this while he forgot not the main chance, but hearing of a vacancy with a nobleman, he clapped in, and easily obtained to be his chaplain. From that day you may take the date of his preferments and his ruin. For having soon wrought himself dexterously into his patron's favour, by short graces and sermons, and a mimical way of drolling upon the puritans, which he knew would take both at chapel and table; he gained a great authority likewise among all the domestics. They all listened to him as an oracle: and they allowed him by common consent, to have not only all the divinity, but more wit too than all the rest of the family put together. This thing alone elevated him exceedingly in his own conceit, and raised his hypochondria into the region of the brain: that his head swelled like any bladder with wind and vapour. But after he was stretched to such an height in his own fancy, that he could not look down from top to toe but his eyes dazzled at the precipice of his stature; there fell out, or in, another natural chance which pushed him headlong. For being of an amorous complexion, and finding himself (as I told you) the cock divine and the cock wit of the family, he took the privilege to walk among the hens: and thought it was not impolitic to establish his new-acquired reputation upon the gentlewomen's side. And they that perceived he was a rising man, and of pleasant conversation, dividing his day among them into canonical hours, of reading now the *Common Prayer*, and now the romances; were very much taken with him. The sympathy of silk began to stir and attract the tippet to the petticoat and the petticoat toward the tippet. The innocent ladies found a strange unquietness in their minds, and could not distinguish whether it were love or devotion. Neither was he wanting on his part to carry on the work; but shifted himself every day with a clean surplice, and, as oft as he had occasion to bow, he directed his reverence towards the gentlewomen's pew. Till, having before had enough of the libertine, and undertaken his calling only for preferment; he was transported now with the sanctity of his office, even to ecstasy: and like the bishop over Magdalen College altar, or like Magdalen de la Croix, he was seen in his prayers to be lifted up sometimes in the air, and once particularly so high that he cracked his skull against the chapel ceiling. I do not hear for all this that he ever practised upon the honour of the ladies, but that he preserved always the civility of a platonic knight errant. For all this courtship had no other operation than to make him still more in love with himself: and if he frequented their company, it was only to speculate his own baby in their eyes. But being thus, without competitor or rival, the darling of both sexes in the family and his own minion; he grew beyond all measure elated, and that crack of his skull, as in broken looking-glasses, multiplied him in self-conceit and imagination . . .

For the English have been always very tender of their religion, their liberty, their propriety, and (I was going to say) no less of their reputation. Neither yet do I speak of these things with passion, considering at more distance how natural it is for men to desire to be in office, and no less natural to grow proud and intractable in office;

and the less a clergyman is so, the more he deserves to be commended. But these things before mentioned, grew yet higher, after that Bishop Laud was once not only exalted to the see of Canterbury, but to be chief minister. Happy had it been for the king, happy for the nation, and happy for himself, had he never climbed that pinnacle. For whether it be or no, that the clergy are not so well fitted by education, as others for political affairs, I know not; though I should rather think they have advantage above others, and even if they would but keep to their bibles, might make the best ministers of state in the world; yet it is generally observed that things miscarry under their government. If there be any counsel more precipitate, more violent, more rigorous, more extreme than other, that is theirs. Truly I think the reason that God does not bless them in affairs of state, is, because he never intended them for that employment. Or if government, and the preaching of the gospel, may well concur in the same person, God therefore frustrates him, because though knowing better, he seeks and manages his greatness by the lesser and meaner maxims. I am confident the bishop studied to do both God and his majesty good service, but alas how utterly he was mistaken. Though so learned, so pious, so wise a man, he seemed to know nothing beyond ceremonies, Arminianism, and Manwaring. With that he begun, and with that ended, and thereby deformed the whole reign of the best prince that ever wielded the English sceptre.

For his late majesty being a prince truly pious and religious, was thereby the more inclined to esteem and favour the clergy. And thence, though himself of a most exquisite understanding, yet thought he could not trust it better than in their keeping. Whereas every man is best in his own post, and so the preacher in the pulpit. But he that will do the clergy's drudgery, must look for his reward in another world. For they having gained this ascendant upon him, resolved whatever became on't to make their best of him; and having made the whole business of state their Arminian jangles, and the persecution for ceremonies, did for recompence assign him that imaginary absolute government, upon which rock we all ruined.

For now was come the last part of the Archbishop's indiscretion; who having strained those strings so high here, and all at the same time, which no wise man ever did; he moreover had a mind to try the same dangerous experiment in Scotland, and sent thither the book of the English liturgy, to be imposed upon them. What followed thereupon, is yet within the compass of most men's memories. And how the war broke out, and then to be sure hell's broke loose. Whether it were a war of religion, or of liberty, is not worth the labour to enquire. Whichsoever was at the top, the other was at the bottom; but upon considering all, I think the cause was too good to have been fought for. Men ought to have trusted God; they ought and might have trusted the king with that whole matter. The arms of the church are prayers and tears, the arms of the subjects are patience and petitions. The king himself being of so accurate and piercing a judgment, would soon have felt where it stuck. For men may spare their pains where nature is at work, and the world will not go faster for our driving. Even as his present majesty's happy restoration did itself, so all things happen in their best and proper time, without any need of our officiousness.

17. From Desiderius Erasmus, *The Praise of Folly*, translated by Sir Thomas Chaloner (1559):

But now I return to my matter. Ye have heard my name then (O my friend). What addition shall I give you? What? but my most foolish friend? For what more mannerly surname may the goddess Folly call her servant and allies? But now seeing all folk know not of what lineage I am descended so help me the muses as I intend to declare the same unto you. My father therefore was neither Chaos, nor Orcus, nor Saturnus, nor any other of that old and rusty race of gods, but Plutus the golden god of riches, and the only sire of gods and man, though Hesiodus, Homer, yea and Jupiter himself stand never so stiffly against me. At whose only beck as aforetimes, so now also both holy, and unholy things be turned topsy-turvy. At whose arbitrement, war, peace, kingdoms, counsels, judgments, assemblies, marriages, covenants, leagues, laws, sciences, games, earnest matters (my breath faileth me) to be short, all public, and private doings of men are administered. Without whose aid, the whole rout of the poetical gods, yea I will say further, those that be the chosen gods should either not be at all, or live else with a mess of slender cheer; that whomso he is aggrieved with, Pallas is not able to protect him. And whoso hath him on his side, may (if it like him) defy Jupiter, with all his thunder. And such a father (lo) do I glory in. Who neither begat me of his brain, as Jupiter did that unamiable, scowling goddess Pallas, but of Youth, a nymph above all others most fair and goodly. Neither was he (I warrant you) at the time of my begetting clogged with the heavy yoke of wedlock, wherein Vulcan that limphalt smith was born, but rather mixed in love (as my Homer saith) which I take to be a copulation not a little more pleasant than the other is. Further, to the end that ye mistake nothing, I do ye to wit that Plutus begat me not in his old days, when he was blind and scarce able to go for age and goutiness, as the poet Aristophanes describeth him; but in his prime years, when as yet he was sound and full of hot blood, but much fuller of nectar drink, which sitting at board with the other gods, he had sipped then by chance somewhat more than enough.

Now and if ye look to be instructed also of my birthplace, insomuch as nowadays men think how the country where one is born doth not a little impart towards his nobility, ye shall understand that I was brought forth neither in floating Delos, as Apollo; nor amongst the waving seas, where Venus took her beginning; nor yet in hollow rocks underground, as was the great god Jupiter, but even amids the Islands, which of their singular fertility and fruitfulness are called Fortunatae, whereas all things grow unsowed and untilled. In which isles neither labour, nor age, nor any manner sickness reigneth, nor in the fields there do either nettles, thistles, mallows, brambles, cockle, or such like baggage grow, but instead thereof gillyflowers, roses, lilies, basil, violets and such sweet-smelling herbs, as whilom grew in Adonis' gardens, do on all sides satisfy both the scent and the sight. Thus born in these delights, I began not my life with leaves, but straightways smiled sweetly on my mother, an evident argument and token of good luck as these birth-lotters say.

Further as concerning my bringing up, I am not envious that Jupiter the great god had a goat to his fortress, seeing two so pleasant nymphs, as Drunkenness daughter unto Bacchus and Rudeness the daughter of Pan were my nurses. Whom ye may see here also amongs my other women and handmaids about me. Whose names in case ye list to know, I am very well content to rehearse them unto you. For this maid truly, whom ye may behold with brows upcast, looking ever as if she wondered at something, is called Self-love. This next her that fareth as if she flixed upon you and clappeth her hands together, is Adulation. This sluggard and drowsy head is named Oblivion. This then that leaneth on her elbows, clasping her hands together, is called Litherness. This besides her with the rose garland on her head, and all to perfumed with sweet savours, is cleped Voluptuousness. This with the rolling and unsteadfast eyes, is Madness. This other with the slick skin and fair-feed body, is called Delicacy. As for these two gods which ye may see also in the fellowship of my other train, the one is named Belly-cheer, the other Soundsleep. Now if you ask me, what stead these stand me to? I answer that through the trusty aid of such a band as this is, I subdue all the world under my dominion, bearing empire over emperors themselves. Ye have heard me thus declare unto you my lineage, my education, and my family. But lest now I might causeless seem to challenge the name of a goddess, hearken ye therefore attentively, with how great commodities I endue both gods and men, and how largely my power stretcheth. For and if a certain author wrote not much amiss, *how this was properly the office of a god, to do benefit to mortal men*; further, if such have worthily been ascribed to the senate of the gods, as were first inventors of wine, of corn and such like commodities for your living: why should not I then rightfully be taken and set tofore them all, who only am the giver of all things, to all men?

For first (I ask) what may be sweeter or more dearer unto you than is your life? But the original spring and plantation of the same, whom should ye thank for but me only? In as much as neither the spear of Pallas, ne yet the shield of Jupiter, called *aegis*, is it that engendreth mankind; but the self Jupiter, father of the gods: and king of kings, who with his only beck, can shake all heaven, must lay down his three-forked thunder and also his grim countenance, wherewith when him listeth, he can make all the gods to tremble; yea, and like a player must disguise himself into another personage, in case he would do the thing that almost he always practiseth (which is) to get children. Again, amongs mortal men, the stoics count themselves to be next the gods in perfection. But bring me one, admit he be four, or five, or (if you list) six hundred times a stoic, and yet must he lay down, if not his long beard, betokening wisdom (which natheless goats have also), at least (I say) lay aside his grave and frowning look, he must calm and explain his forehead, he must cast away those his ironlike lessons and precepts of doctrine; it is I, it is I (believe me) whom that wise and sage stoic must have recourse unto in case he would be a father.

And why should I not commune more familiarly with you, according to my custom? I pray you, is it the head? the face? the breast? the hands? or the ears? which parts of the body are named honest, that engender gods and men? I trow no. Nay, it is even that silly member, so fond and foolish, as may not without laughter be spoken of, which is the only planter of mankind. That is the only fountain whence all things receive life, a great deal sooner than from Pythagoras' quaternion. As concerning the use whereof, who is he (suppose ye) would take in his mouth the snaffle of wedlock, if (according as these wisemen are wont to do) he should first cast and reckon with himself the discommodities of that trade of life? Or what woman would yield unto a man, if she either knew or thought upon the perilous throes of childbearing, or travail of their bringing up? What and if ye owe your lives to wedlock, and wedlock ye owe to my damsel Madness; now ye may soon guess, what ye owe and should refer to me. Then, who is she, that after one assay, would eftsoons venture childbearing, ne were it not through the encouragement of Oblivion. No not Venus herself (whatever Lucretius writeth) will deny, but that her might in engendure remaineth void and of small effect without th'access of mine aid. So that to conclude, I say how of this my drunken and ridiculous game are procreate (omitting vulgar folk) both grave philosophers, whom such succeed now, as ye call monks, and purpre princes, and holy priests, and these holy bishops, at once, all the whole rout of the poetical gods, so swarming, as scarce all heaven is able to contain them, be it never so large of room.

18. From Niccolò Machiavelli, *The Prince*, translated by E. D. (1640):

Chapter 25: How great power fortune hath in human affairs, and what means there is to resist it.

It is not unknown unto me how that many have held opinion, and still hold it, that the affairs of the world are so governed by fortune, and by God, that men by their wisdom cannot amend or alter them; or rather that there is no remedy for them: and hereupon they would think that it were of no avail to take much pains in anything, but leave all to be governed by chance. This opinion hath gained the more credit in our days, by reason of the great alteration of things, which we have of late seen, and do every day see, beyond all human conjecture: upon which, I sometimes thinking, am in some part inclined to their opinion: nevertheless not to extinguish quite our own free will, I think it may be true that fortune is the mistress of one half of our actions; but yet that she lets us have rule of the other half, or little less. And I liken her to a precipitous torrent, which when it rages overflows the plains, overthrows the trees and buildings, removes the earth from one side, and lays it on another, everyone flies before it, everyone yields to the fury thereof, as unable to withstand it; and yet however it be thus, when the times are calmer, men are able to make provision against these excesses, with banks and fences, so that afterwards when it swells again, it shall all pass smoothly along, within its channel, or else the violence thereof shall not prove so licentious and hurtful. In like manner befalls it us with fortune, which there shows her power where virtue is not ordained to resist her, and thither turns she all her forces, where she perceives that no provisions nor resistances are made to uphold her. And if you shall consider Italy, which is the seat of these changes, and that which hath given them their motion, you shall see it to be a plain field, without any trench or bank; which had it been fenced with convenient virtue, as was Germany, Spain, or France; this inundation would never have caused these great alterations it hath, or else would it not have reached to us: and this shall suffice to have said, touching the opposing of fortune in general.

But restraining myself more to particulars: I say, that today we see a prince prosper and flourish, and tomorrow utterly go to ruin; not seeing that he hath altered any condition or quality; which I believe arises first from the causes which we have long since run over, that is because that prince that relies wholly upon fortune, ruins as her wheel turns. I believe also, that he proves the fortunate man whose manner of proceeding meets with the quality of the times: and so likewise the unfortunate, from whose course of proceeding the times differ: for we see that men, in the things that induce them to the end (which everyone propounds to himself, as glory and riches), proceed therein diversely; some with respects, others more bold and rashly; one with violence, and th'other with cunning; the one with patience, th'other with its contrary; and everyone by several ways may attain thereto. We see also two very respective and wary men, the one come to his purpose, and th'other not; and in like manner two equally prosper taking diverse courses, th'one being wary, th'other headstrong; which proceeds from nothing else, but from the quality of the times, which agree, or not, with their proceedings. From hence arises that which I said, that two working diversely, produce the same effect; and two equally working th'one attains his end, th'other not. Hereupon also depends the alteration of the good; for if to one that behaves himself with wariness and patience, times and affairs turn so favourably that the carriage of his business prove well, he prospers; but if the times and affairs change, he is ruined; because he changes not his manner of proceeding. Nor is there any man so wise that can frame himself hereunto; as well because he cannot go out of the way from that whereunto nature inclines him; as also, for that one having always prospered, walking such a way, cannot be persuaded to leave it: and therefore the respective and wary man, when it is fit time for him to use violence and force knows not how to put it in practice, whereupon he is ruined: but if he could change his disposition with the times and the affairs, he should not change his fortune.

Pope Julius the Second proceeded in all his actions with very great violence, and found the time and things so conformable to that his manner of proceeding that in all of them he had happy success. Consider the first exploit he did at Bologna, even while John Bentivoglio lived: the Venetians were not well contented therewith; the king of Spain likewise with the French had treated of that enterprise; and notwithstanding all this, he stirred up by his own rage and fierceness, personally undertook that expedition: which action of his put in suspense and stopped Spain and the Venetians, those for fear, and th'others for desire to recover the kingdom of Naples; and on th'other part drew after him the king of France; for that king seeing him already in motion and desiring to hold him his friend, whereby to humble the Venetians, thought he could no way deny him an open injury. Julius then effected that with his violent and heady motion which no other pope with all human wisdom could ever have done; for if he had expected to part from Rome with his conclusions settled, and all his affairs ordered beforehand, as any other pope would have done, he had neither brought it to pass; for the king of France would have devised a thousand excuses, and others would have put him in as many fears. I will let pass his other actions, for all of them were alike, and all of them proved lucky to him; and the brevity of his life never suffered him to feel the contrary: for had he lit upon such times afterwards that it had been necessary for him to proceed with respects, there had been his utter ruin; for he would never have left those ways, to which he had been naturally inclined.

I conclude then, fortune varying, and men continuing still obstinate to their own ways, prove happy, while these accord together: and as they disagree, prove unhappy: and I think it true, that it is better to be heady, than wary; because fortune is a mistress and it is necessary, to keep her in obedience, to ruffle and force her: and we see, that she suffers herself rather to be mastered by those, than by others that proceed coldly. And therefore, as a mistress, she is a friend to young men because they are less respective, more rough, and command her with more boldness.

19. Gerrard Winstanley, *The True Levellers' Standard Advanced* (1649):

A declaration to the powers of England and to all the powers of the world, showing the cause why the common people of England have begun and gives consent to dig up, manure and sow corn upon George Hill in Surrey; by those that have subscribed, and thousands more that gives consent.

In the beginning of time, the great creator reason made the earth to be a common treasury, to preserve beasts, birds, fishes and man, the lord that was to govern this creation; for man had domination given to him, over the beasts, birds and fishes; but not one word was spoken in the beginning, that one branch of mankind should rule over another.

And the reason is this, every single man, male and female, is a perfect creature of himself; and the same spirit that made the globe dwells in man to govern the globe; so that the flesh of man being subject to reason, his maker, hath him to be his teacher and ruler within himself, therefore needs not run abroad after any teacher and ruler without him; for he needs not that any man should teach him, for the same anointing that ruled in the Son of Man teacheth him all things.

But since human flesh (that king of beasts) began to delight himself in the objects of the creation, more than in the spirit reason and righteousness, who manifests himself to be the indweller in the five senses of hearing, seeing, tasting, smelling, feeling; then he fell into blindness of mind and weakness of heart, and runs abroad for a teacher and ruler. And so selfish imagination, taking possession of the five senses and ruling as king in the room of reason therein, and working with covetousness, did set up one man to teach and rule over another; and thereby the spirit was killed and man was brought into bondage, and became a greater slave to such of his own kind, than the beasts of the field were to him.

And hereupon the earth (which was made to be a common treasury of relief for all, both beasts and men) was hedged into enclosures by the teachers and rulers, and the others were made servants and slaves: and that earth, that is within this creation made a common storehouse for all, is bought and sold and kept in the hands of a few, whereby the great creator is mightily dishonoured, as if he were a respecter of persons, delighting in the comfortable livelihood of some, and rejoicing in the miserable poverty and straits of others. From the beginning it was not so.

But this coming in of bondage is called Adam, because this ruling and teaching power without doth dam up the spirit of peace and liberty, first within the heart, by filling it with slavish fears of others; secondly without, by giving the bodies of one to be imprisoned, punished and oppressed by the outward power of another. And this evil was brought upon us through his own covetousness, whereby he is blinded and made weak, and sees not the law of righteousness in his heart, which is the pure light of reason, but looks abroad for it, and thereby the creation is cast under bondage and curse, and the creator is slighted; first by the teachers and rulers that sets themselves down in the spirit's room, to teach and rule, where he himself is only king. Secondly by the other, that refuses the spirit, to be taught and governed by fellow creatures; and this was called Israel's sin in casting off the Lord and choosing Saul, one like themselves, to be their king, whenas they had the same spirit of reason and government in themselves as he had, if they were but subject. And Israel's rejecting of outward teachers and rulers to embrace the Lord, and to be all taught and ruled by that righteous king that Jeremiah prophesied shall rule in the new heavens and new earth in the latter days, will be their restoration from bondage, Jeremiah 23. 5,6.

But for the present state of the old world that is running up like parchment in the fire, and wearing away, we see proud imaginary flesh, which is the wise serpent, rises up in flesh and gets dominion in some to rule over others, and so forces one part of the creation, man, to be a slave to another; and thereby the spirit is killed in both. The one looks upon himself as a teacher and ruler, and so is lifted up in pride over his fellow creature. The other looks upon himself as imperfect, and so is dejected in his spirit, and looks upon his fellow creature of his own image as a lord above him.

And thus Esau, the man of flesh which is covetousness and pride, hath killed Jacob, the spirit of meekness and righteous government in the light of reason, and rules over him: and so the earth, that was made a common treasury for all to live comfortably upon, is become through man's unrighteous actions one over another to be a place wherein one torments another.

Now the great creator, who is the spirit reason, suffered himself thus to be rejected and trodden underfoot by the covetous proud flesh for a certain time limited; therefore, saith he, *The seed out of whom the creation did proceed, which is myself, shall bruise this serpent's head and restore my creation again from this curse and bondage; and when I the king of righteousness reigns in every man, I will be the blessing of the earth, and the joy of all nations.*

And since the coming in of the stoppage, or the Adam, the earth hath been enclosed and given to the elder brother Esau, or man of flesh, and hath been bought and sold from one to another; and Jacob, or the younger brother, that is to succeed or come forth next, who is the universal spreading power of righteousness that gives liberty to the whole creation, is made a servant.

And this elder son, or man of bondage, hath held the earth in bondage to himself not by a meek law of righteousness, but by subtle selfish counsels and by open and violent force; for wherefore is it that there is such wars and rumours of wars in the nations of the earth? And wherefore are men so mad to destroy one another? but only to uphold civil property of honour, dominion and riches one over another, which is the curse the creation groans under, waiting for deliverance.

But when once the earth becomes a common treasury again, as it must, for all the prophecies of scriptures and reason are circled here in this community, and mankind must have the law of righteousness once more writ in his heart, and all must be made of one heart and one mind:

Then this enmity in all lands will cease, for none shall dare to seek a dominion over others, neither shall any dare to kill another, nor desire more of the earth than another, for he that will rule over, imprison, oppress and kill his fellow creatures, under what pretence soever, is a destroyer of the creation, and an actor of the curse, and walks contrary to the rule of righteousness: *Do as you would have others do to you; and love your enemies, not in words but in actions.*

Therefore, you powers of the earth, or Lord Esau the elder brother, because you have appeared to rule the creation, first take notice that the power that sets you to work is selfish covetousness and an aspiring pride, to live in glory and ease over Jacob, the meek spirit; that is, the seed that lies hid in and among the poor common people or younger brother, out of whom the blessing of deliverance is to rise and spring up to all nations.

And reason, the living king of righteousness, doth only look on and lets thee alone that, whereas thou counts thyself an angel of light, thou shalt appear in the light of the sun to be a devil, Adam, and the curse that the creation groans under; and the time is now come for thy downfall and Jacob must rise, who is the universal spirit of love and righteousness that fills and will fill all the earth.

Thou teaching and ruling power of flesh, thou hast had three periods of time to vaunt thyself over thy brother. The first was from the time of thy coming in, called Adam or a stoppage, till Moses came; and there thou, that wast a self-lover in Cain, killed thy brother Abel, a plain-hearted man that loved righteousness. And thou by thy wisdom and beastly government made the whole earth to stink till Noah came, which was a time of the world like the coming in of the watery seed into the womb, towards the bringing forth of the man-child.

And from Noah till Moses came thou still hast ruled in vaunting, pride and cruel oppression: Ishmael against Isaac, Esau against Jacob; for thou hast still been the man of flesh that hath ever persecuted the man of righteousness, the spirit reason.

And secondly, from Moses till the Son of Man came, which was a time of the world that the man-child could not speak like a man, but lisping, making signs to show his meaning; as we see many creatures that cannot speak do. For Moses' law was a language lapped up in types, sacrifices, forms and customs, which was a weak time. And in this time likewise, O thou teaching and ruling power, thou wast an oppressor; for look into scriptures and see if Aaron and the priests were not the first that deceived the people. And the rulers, as kings and governors, were continually the ocean-head out of whose power burdens, oppressions and poverty did flow out upon the earth: and these two powers still hath been the curse, that hath led the earth (mankind) into confusion and death by their imaginary and selfish teaching and ruling, and it could be no otherwise; for while man looks upon himself as an imperfect creation, and seeks and runs abroad for a teacher and a ruler, he is all this time a stranger to the spirit that is within himself.

But though the earth hath been generally thus in darkness since the Adam rise up, and hath owned a light and a law without them to walk by, yet some have been found as watchmen in this night-time of the world, that have been taught by the spirit within them and not by any flesh without them, as Abraham, Isaac, Jacob and the prophets: and these and such as these have still been the butt at whom the powers of the earth in all ages of the world, by their selfish laws, have shot their fury.

And then thirdly, from the time of the Son of Man, which was a time that the man-child began to speak like a child growing upward to manhood, till now that the spirit is rising up in strength, O thou teaching and ruling power of the earthy man, thou hast been an oppressor, by imprisonment, impoverishing and martyrdom; and all thy power and wit hath been to make laws and execute them against such as stand for universal liberty, which is the rising up of Jacob; as by those ancient enslaving laws not yet blotted out, but held up as weapons against the man-child.

O thou powers of England, though thou hast promised to make this people a free people, yet thou hast so handled the matter through thy self-seeking humour that thou hast wrapped us up more in bondage, and oppression lies heavier upon us; not only bringing thy fellow creatures, the commoners, to a morsel of bread, but by confounding all sorts of people by thy government of doing and undoing.

First, thou hast made the people to take a covenant and oaths to endeavour a reformation and to bring in liberty every man in his place; and yet while a man is in pursuing of that covenant, he is imprisoned and oppressed by thy officers, courts and justices, so-called.

Thou hast made ordinances to cast down oppressing, popish, episcopal, self-willed and prerogative laws; yet we see that self-will and prerogative power is the great standing law that rules all in action, and others in words.

Thou hast made many promises and protestations to make the land a free nation: and yet at this very day the same people, to whom thou hast made such protestations of liberty, are oppressed by thy courts, sizes, sessions, by thy justices and clerks of the peace (so-called), bailiffs, committees, are imprisoned and forced to spend that bread that should save their lives from famine.

And all this because they stand to maintain an universal liberty and freedom, which not only is our birthright which our maker gave us, but which thou hast promised to restore unto us, from under the former oppressing powers that are gone before, and which likewise we have bought with our money, in taxes, free quarter and blood shed; all which sums thou hast received at our hands, and yet thou hast not given us our bargain.

O thou Adam, thou Esau, thou Cain, thou hypocritical man of flesh, when wilt thou cease to kill thy younger brother? Surely thou must not do this great work of advancing the creation out of bondage; for thou art lost extremely, and drowned in the sea of covetousness, pride and hardness of heart. *The blessing shall rise out of the dust which thou treadest under foot, even the poor despised people, and they shall hold up salvation to this land and to all lands, and thou shalt be ashamed.*

Our bodies as yet are in thy hand, our spirit waits in quiet and peace upon our Father for deliverance; and if he give our blood into thy hand for thee to spill, know this, that he is our almighty captain. And if some of you will not dare to shed your blood, to maintain tyranny and oppression upon the creation, know this, that our blood and life shall not be unwilling to be delivered up in meekness to maintain universal liberty, that so the curse on our part may be taken off the creation.

And we shall not do this by force of arms, we abhor it, for that is the work of the Midianites, to kill one another; but by obeying the Lord of Hosts, who hath revealed himself in us and to us, by labouring the earth in righteousness together, to eat our bread with the sweat of our brows, neither giving hire nor taking hire but working together and eating together as one man or as one house of Israel restored from bondage. And so by the power of reason, the law of righteousness in us, we endeavour to lift up the creation from that bondage of civil propriety which it groans under.

We are made to hold forth this declaration to you that are the great council, and to you the great army of the land of England, that you may know what we would have and what you are bound to give us by your covenants and promises; and that you may join with us in this work and so find peace. Or else, if you do oppose us, we have peace in our work and in declaring this report: and you shall be left without excuse.

The work we are going about is this, to dig up George's Hill and the waste ground thereabouts and to sow corn, and to eat our bread together by the sweat of our brows.

And the first reason is this, that we may work in righteousness and lay the foundation of making the earth a common treasury for all, both rich and poor, that everyone that is born in the land may be fed by the earth his mother that brought him forth, according to the reason that rules in the creation. Not enclosing any part into any particular hand, but all as one man working together and feeding together as sons of one father, members of one family; not one lording over another, but all looking upon each other as equals in the creation; so that our maker may be glorified in the work of his own hands, and that everyone may see he is no respecter of persons but equally loves his whole creation and hates nothing but the serpent, which is covetousness, branching forth into selfish imagination, pride, envy, hypocrisy, uncleanness; all seeking the ease and honour of flesh and fighting against the spirit reason that made the creation; for that is the corruption, the curse, the devil, the father of lies, death and bondage, that serpent and dragon that the creation is to be delivered from.

And we are moved hereunto for that reason and others which hath been showed us, both by vision, voice and revelation.

For it is showed us that so long as we or any other doth own the earth to be the peculiar interest of lords and landlords, and not common to others as well as them, we own the curse, and hold the creation under bondage; and so long as we or any other doth own landlords and tenants, for one to call the land his or another to hire it of him, or for one to give hire and for another to work for hire; this is to dishonour the work of creation; as if the righteous creator should have respect to persons, and therefore made the earth for some and not for all. And so long as we or any other maintain this civil propriety, we consent still to hold the creation down under that bondage it groans under, and so we should hinder the work of restoration and sin against light that is given into us, and so through the fear of the flesh (man) lose our peace.

And that this civil propriety is the curse is manifest thus: those that buy and sell land, and are landlords, have got it either by oppression or murder or theft; and all landlords live in the breach of the seventh and eighth commandments, *Thou shalt not steal nor kill.*

First by their oppression: they have by their subtle imaginary and covetous wit got the plain-hearted poor or younger brethren to work for them for small wages, and by their work have got a great increase; for the poor by their labour lift up tyrants to rule over them; or else by their covetous wit they have outreached the plain-hearted in buying and selling, and thereby enriched themselves but impoverished others: or else by their subtle wit, having been a lifter up into places of trust, have enforced people to pay money for a public use, but have divided much of it into their private purses; and so have got it by oppression.

Then secondly for murder: they have by subtle wit and power pretended to preserve a people in safety by the power of the sword; and what by large pay, much free quarter and other booties which they call their own, they get much moneys, and with this they buy land and become landlords; and if once landlords, then they rise to be justices, rulers and state governors, as experience shows. But all this is but a bloody and subtle thievery, countenanced by a law that covetousness made; and is a breach of the seventh commandment, *Thou shalt not kill.*

And likewise thirdly a breach of the eighth commandment, *Thou shalt not steal*; but these landlords have thus stolen the earth from their fellow creatures, that have an equal share with them by the law of reason and creation, as well as they.

And such as these rise up to be rich in the objects of the earth. Then by their plausible words of flattery to the plain-hearted people whom they deceive, and that lies under confusion and blindness, they are lifted up to be teachers, rulers and lawmakers over them that lifted them up; as if the earth were made peculiarly for them, and not for others' weal. If you cast your eye a little backward, you shall see that this outward teaching and ruling power is the Babylonish yoke laid upon Israel of old under Nebuchadnezzar; and so successively from that time the conquering enemy have still laid these yokes upon Israel to keep Jacob down. And the last enslaving conquest which the enemy got over Israel was the Norman over England; and from that time kings, lords, judges, justices, bailiffs and the violent bitter people that are freeholders, are and have been successively: the Norman bastard William himself, his colonels, captains, inferior officers and common soldiers, who still are from that time to this day in pursuit of that victory, imprisoning, robbing and killing the poor enslaved English Israelites.

And this appears clear. For when any trustee or state officer is to be chosen, the freeholders or landlords must be the choosers, who are the Norman common soldiers, spread abroad in the land. And who must be chosen but some very rich man, who is the successor of the Norman colonels or high officers? And to what end have they been thus chosen but to establish that Norman power the more forcibly over the enslaved English, and to beat them down again whenas they gather heart to seek for liberty?

For what are all those binding and restraining laws that have been made from one age to another since that conquest, and are still upheld by fury over the people? I say, what are they but the cords, bands, manacles and yokes that the enslaved English, like Newgate prisoners, wears upon their hands and legs as they walk the streets? by which those Norman oppressors and these their successors from age to age have enslaved the poor people by, killed their younger brother, and would not suffer Jacob to arise.

O what mighty delusion do you, who are the powers of England, live in! That while you pretend to throw down that Norman yoke and Babylonish power, and have promised to make the groaning people of England a free people, yet you still lift up that Norman yoke and slavish tyranny, and hold the people as much in bondage as the bastard conqueror himself and his council of war.

Take notice that England is not a free people till the poor that have no land have a free allowance to dig and labour the commons, and so live as comfortably as the landlords that live in their enclosures. For the people have not laid out their moneys and shed their blood that their landlords, the Norman power, should still have its liberty and freedom to rule in tyranny in his lords, landlords, judges, justices, bailiffs and state servants; but that the oppressed might be set free, prison doors opened, and the poor people's hearts comforted by an universal consent of making the earth a common treasury, that they may live together as one house of Israel, united in brotherly love into one spirit; and having a comfortable livelihood in the community of one earth, their mother.

If you look through the earth, you shall see that the landlords, teachers and rulers are oppressors, murderers and thieves in this manner. But it was not thus from the beginning. And this is one reason of our digging and labouring the earth one with another, that we might work in righteousness and lift up the creation from bondage. For so long as we own landlords in this corrupt settlement, we cannot work in righteousness; for we should still lift up the curse and tread down the creation, dishonour the spirit of universal liberty, and hinder the work of restoration.

Secondly, in that we begin to dig upon George Hill to eat our bread together by righteous labour and sweat of our brows, it was showed us by vision in dreams and out of dreams that that should be the place we should begin upon. And though that earth in view of flesh be very barren, yet we should trust the spirit for a blessing. And that not only this common or heath should be taken in and manured by the people, but all the commons and waste ground in England and in the whole world shall be taken in by the people in righteousness, not owning any propriety; but taking the earth to be a common treasury, as it was first made for all.

Thirdly, it is showed us that all the prophecies, visions and revelations of scriptures, of prophets and apostles, concerning the calling of the Jews, the restoration of Israel and making of that people the inheritors of the whole earth, doth all seat themselves in this work of making the earth a common treasury; as you may read, Ezekiel 24.26,27,etc. Jeremiah 33.7 to 12. Isaiah 49.17,18, etc. Zechariah 8. from 4 to 12. Daniel 2.44,45. Daniel 7.27. Hosea 14.5,6,7. Joel 2.26,27. Amos 9. from 8 to the end. Obadiah 17.18,21. Micah 5. from 7 to the end. Habakkuk 2.6,7,8,13,14. Genesis 18.18. Romans 11.15. Zephaniah 3. etc. Zechariah 14.9.

And when the Son of Man was gone from the apostles, his spirit descended upon the apostles and brethren, as they were waiting at Jerusalem; and the rich men sold their possessions and gave part to the poor; and no man said that aught that he possessed was his own, for they had all things common, Acts 4.32.

Now this community was suppressed by covetous proud flesh, which was the powers that ruled the world; and the righteous Father suffered himself thus to be suppressed for a time, times and dividing of time, or for forty-two months, or for three days and half, which are all but one and the same term of time. And the world is now come to the half day; and the spirit of Christ, which is the spirit of universal community and freedom, is risen, and is rising, and will rise higher and higher, till those pure waters of Shiloh, the wellsprings of life and liberty to the whole creation, do overrun Adam and drown those banks of bondage, curse and slavery.

Fourthly, this work to make the earth a common treasury was showed us by voice in trance and out of trance, which words were these, 'Work together, eat bread together, declare this all abroad.'

Which voice was heard three times. And in obedience to the spirit we have declared this by word of mouth, as occasion was offered. Secondly, we have declared it by writing, which others may read. Thirdly, we have now begun to declare it by action, in digging up the common land and casting in seed, that we may eat our bread together in righteousness. And everyone that comes to work shall eat the fruit of their own labours, one having as much freedom in the fruit of the earth as another. Another voice that was heard was this, 'Israel shall neither take hire nor give hire.'

And if so, then certainly none shall say, 'This is my land, work for me, and I'll give you wages.' For the earth is the Lord's, that is, man's, who is lord of the creation, in every branch of mankind; for as diverse members of our human bodies make but one body perfect; so every particular man is but a member or branch of mankind; and mankind living in the light and obedience to reason, the king of righteousness, is thereby made a fit and complete lord of the creation. And the whole earth is this lord's, man, subject to the spirit: and not the inheritance of covetous proud flesh, that is selfish and enmity to the spirit.

And if the earth be not peculiar to any one branch or branches of mankind, but the inheritance of all: then it is free and common for all, to work together and eat together.

And truly, you councillors and powers of the earth, know this, that wheresoever there is a people thus united by common community of livelihood into oneness, it will become the strongest land in the world, for then they will be as one man to defend their inheritance; and salvation (which is liberty and peace) is the walls and bulwarks of that land or city.

Whereas on the other side, pleading for propriety and single interest divides the people of a land and the whole world into parties, and is the cause of all wars and bloodshed and contention everywhere.

Another voice that was heard in a trance was this, 'Whosoever labours the earth for any person or persons that are lifted up to rule over others, and doth not look upon themselves as equal to others in the creation: the hand of the Lord shall be upon that labourer: I the Lord have spoke it, and I will do it.'

This declares likewise to all labourers or such as are called poor people, that they shall not dare to work for hire for any landlord or for any that is lifted up above others; for by their labours they have lifted up tyrants and tyranny; and by denying to labour for hire they shall pull them down again. He that works for another, either for wages or to pay him rent, works unrighteously and still lifts up the curse; but they that are resolved to work and eat together, making the earth a common treasury, doth join hands with Christ to lift up the creation from bondage, and restores all things from the curse.

Fifthly, that which does encourage us to go on in this work is this: we find the streaming out of love in our hearts towards all, to enemies as well as friends; we would have none live in beggary, poverty or sorrow, but that everyone might enjoy the benefit of his creation: we have peace in our hearts and quiet rejoicing in our work, and filled with sweet content, though we have but a dish of roots and bread for our food.

And we are assured that in the strength of this spirit that hath manifested himself to us, we shall not be startled, neither at prison nor death while we are about his work; and we have been made to sit down and count what it may cost us in undertaking such a work, and we know the full sum and are resolved to give all that we have to buy this pearl which we see in the field.

For by this work we are assured, and reason makes it appear to others, that bondage shall be removed, tears wiped away, and all poor people by their righteous labours shall be relieved and freed from poverty and straits. For in this work of restoration there will be no beggar in Israel. For surely, if there was no beggar in literal Israel, there shall be no beggar in spiritual Israel the antitype, much more.

Sixthly, we have another encouragement that this work shall prosper, because we see it to be the fullness of time. For whereas the Son of Man, the Lamb, came in the fullness of time, that is, when the powers of the world made the earth stink everywhere by oppressing others under pretence of worshipping the spirit rightly, by the types and sacrifices of Moses' law; the priests were grown so abominably covetous and proud that they made the people to loathe the sacrifices and to groan under the burden of their oppressing pride.

Even so now in this age of the world that the spirit is upon his resurrection, it is likewise the fullness of time in a higher measure. For whereas the people generally in former times did rest upon the very observation of the sacrifices and types, but persecuted the very name of the spirit: even so now professors do rest upon the bare observation of forms and customs, and pretend to the spirit, and yet persecutes, grudges and hates the power of the spirit; and as it was then, so it is now: all places stink with the abomination of self-seeking teachers and rulers. For do not I see that everyone preacheth for money, counsels for money and fights for money, to maintain particular interests? And none of these three, that pretend to give liberty to the creation, do give liberty to the creation; neither can they, for they are enemies to universal liberty; so that the earth stinks with their hypocrisy, covetousness, envy, sottish ignorance and pride.

The common people are filled with good words from pulpits and council tables, but no good deeds; for they wait and wait for good and for deliverances, but none comes. While they wait for liberty, behold greater bondage comes instead of it; and burdens, oppressions, taskmasters, from sessions, lawyers, bailiffs of hundreds, committees, impropriators, clerks of peace and courts of justice (so-called) does whip the people by old popish weather-beaten laws, that were excommunicate long ago by covenants, oaths and ordinances; but as yet are not cast out, but rather taken in again, to be standing pricks in our eyes and thorns in our side; beside free quartering, plundering by some rude soldiers, and the abounding of taxes; which if they were equally divided among the soldiery, and not too much bagged up in the hands of particular officers and trustees, there would be less complaining: besides the horrible cheating that is in buying and selling, and the cruel oppression of landlords and lords of manors and quarter sessions. Many that have been good housekeepers (as we say) cannot live, but are forced to turn soldiers and so to fight to uphold the curse, or else live in great straits and beggary. O you Adams of the earth, you have rich clothing, full bellies, have your honours and ease, and you puff at this; but know, thou stout-hearted Pharaoh, that the day of judgment is begun, and it will reach to thee ere long. Jacob hath been very low, but he is rising, and will rise, do the worst thou canst; and the poor people whom thou oppresses shall be the saviours of the land. For the blessing is rising up in them, and thou shalt be ashamed.

And thus, you powers of England and of the whole world, we have declared our reasons why we have begun to dig upon George Hill in Surrey. One thing I must tell you more, in the close, which I received *in voce* likewise at another time; and when I received it, my eye was set towards you. The words were these: 'Let Israel go free.'

Surely, as Israel lay 430 years under Pharaoh's bondage, before Moses was sent to fetch them out: even so Israel (the elect spirit spread in sons and daughters) hath lain three times so long already, which is the antitype, under your bondage and cruel taskmasters. But now the time of deliverance is come, and thou proud Esau and stout-hearted covetousness, thou must come down and be lord of the creation no longer. For *now the king of righteousness is rising to rule in and over the earth.*

Therefore, if thou wilt find mercy, *Let Israel go free*; break in pieces quickly the band of particular propriety, disown this oppressing murder, oppression and thievery of buying and selling of land, owning of landlords and paying of rents, and give thy free consent to make the earth a common treasury, without grumbling: that the younger brethren may live comfortably upon earth, as well as the elder: that all may enjoy the benefit of their creation.

And hereby thou wilt *Honour thy father and thy mother*: thy father, which is the spirit of community, that made all and that dwells in all; thy mother, which is the earth, that brought us all forth: that as a true mother loves all her children. Therefore do not thou hinder the mother earth from giving all her children suck, by thy enclosing it into particular hands, and holding up that cursed bondage of enclosure by thy power.

And then thou wilt repent of thy theft, in maintaining the breach of the eighth commandment, by stealing the land as I say from thy fellow creatures, or younger brothers: which thou and all thy landlords have and do live in the breach of that commandment.

Then thou wilt *own no other God*, or ruling power, *but one*, which is the king of righteousness, ruling and dwelling in everyone and in the whole; whereas now thou hast many gods: for covetousness is thy god; pride and an envious murdering humour (to kill one by prison or gallows that crosses thee, though their cause be pure, sound and good reason) is thy god; self-love and slavish fear (lest others serve thee as thou hast served them) is thy god; hypocrisy, fleshly imagination, that keeps no promise, covenant nor protestation, is thy god; love of money, honour and ease is thy god. And all these, and the like ruling powers, makes thee blind and hardhearted, that thou does not nor cannot lay to heart the affliction of others, though they die for want of bread in that rich city, undone under your eyes.

Therefore once more, *Let Israel go free*, that the poor may labour the waste land and suck the breasts of their mother earth, that they starve not. And in so doing thou wilt keep the sabbath day, which is a day of rest, sweetly enjoying the peace of the spirit of righteousness; and find peace, by living among a people that live in peace. This will be a day of rest which thou never knew yet.

But I do not entreat thee, for thou art not to be entreated, but in the name of the Lord that hath drawn me forth to speak to thee, I, yea I say, I command thee to *let Israel go free* and quietly *to gather together into the place where I shall appoint; and hold them no longer in bondage.*

And thou Adam that holds the earth in slavery under the curse: if thou wilt not *let Israel go free* (for thou being the antitype will be more stout and lusty than the Egyptian Pharaoh of old, who was thy type), then know that whereas I brought ten plagues upon him, I will multiply my plagues upon thee, till I make thee weary and miserably ashamed. And *I will bring out my people with a strong hand and stretched-out arm.*

Thus we have discharged our souls in declaring the cause of our digging upon George Hill in Surrey, that the great council and army of the land may take notice of it, that there is no intent of tumult or fighting, but only to get bread to eat with the sweat of our brows; working together in righteousness and eating the blessings of the earth in peace.

And if any of you that are the great ones of the earth, that have been bred tenderly and cannot work, do bring in your stock into this common treasury as an offering to the work of righteousness, we will work for you, and you shall receive as we receive. But if you will not, but Pharaoh-like cry, *Who is the Lord that we should obey him?* and endeavour to oppose, then know that he that delivered Israel from Pharaoh of old is the same power still, in whom we trust and whom we serve; for this conquest over thee shall be got, *not by sword or weapon, but by my spirit, saith the Lord of Hosts.*

William Everard,	Gerrard Winstanley,
John Palmer,	Richard Goodgroome,
John South,	Thomas Starre,
John Courton,	William Hoggrill,
William Taylor,	Robert Sawyer,
Christopher Clifford,	Thomas Eder,
John Barker,	Henry Bickerstaffe,
	John Taylor, etc.

FINIS.

20. From Anna Trapnel, *The Cry of a Stone* (1654):

Upon the tenth day of the eleventh month, 1653. The relator coming into the chamber where [Anna Trapnel] lay, heard her first making melody with a spiritual song, which he could not take but in part, and that too with such imperfection, as he cannot present any account of it to the understanding of others. After her song, she without intermission uttered forth her spirit in prayer, wherein among many other, she expressed the passages following:

'What is marvellous or can be in the eyes of the Lord? The resurrection of Jesus was marvellous in our eyes; but not with the Lord, for nothing could keep down a Jesus; thy people could never have come out of their graves, had it not been for the resurrection of Jesus; as thou risedst, so should they, as thou diedst, so should they, thou wilt make all things death before them. What endeavourings were there to have kept thee in the grave? Oh, but what fastness, what locks, what bolts that could keep in a Jesus? Oh, but they thought that the Lord Jesus was but a man, they understood not that the divine nature was wrapped up in him in the human nature. When thy time came the sepulchre was open and the Lord Jesus came forth with great power and majesty. Oh blessed be the Lord that brought forth the Son, the heir, him that was victorious over his enemies, so shall there be a declaration against all things that would keep thine down: faith is that victory. How so? because faith brings into the bosom, and it draws forth the death and resurrection of Jesus upon us; thou art abringing forth a great resurrection, Jesus Christ is upon his appearing. There are some do think so, but they say it is not yet begun, God will bring it about another way, and another time; but the Lord says, he will cut short his work in righteousness; thou knowest who are the Babylonians that are now about thine; as thou didst to thy people of old, thou wilt come forth speedily.

'Thy thoughts are so exceeding high and glorious that none is able to reach them; man cannot bring forth his own thoughts, they are so tumultuous, and run unto the ends of the earth; oh then what are thy thoughts O Lord?

'Though the enemy begin to jeer them concerning those blessed songs; well says God, are my people jeered concerning their excellencies, their songs, their hallelujahs that are of my own making, that are before my throne? The Lord cannot endure that these excellencies of his saints should be trampled upon, which are so perfect, so pure; how pleasant are the songs of thine, when they are brought forth out of the churches of thine enemies.

'Tis not all the force of the world that can strike one stroke against thine, but thou sufferest them to come forth to try thine; oh that thine could believe thee for thy breakings of them, as well as for thy bindings up; all things under the sun, all things before you, in you, shall work for your good; when they come to understand more of the mystery and of the entrails of scripture, how will they praise thy highness? The enemies are strong, Satan is strong, instruments are strong, temptations they are strong, what strengths are against thy flock! They cannot be without the lion, and lion-like creatures; oh if thy servants suffer, let them not suffer passion or rash words, but as lambs. There is a zeal which is but from nature, a man's own spirit may prompt him to, but the zeal of God is accompanied with meekness, humility, grief for Christ.

'Since thy handmaid is taken up to walk with thee, thy handmaid always desired that she might be swift to hear, slow to speak; but now that thou hast taken her up into thy mount, who can keep in the rushing wind? Who can bind the influences of the heavenly Orion, who can stop thy spirit? It is good to be in the territories, in the regions, where thou walkest before thy servant; oh how glittering and glorious are they, what sparklings are there!

'Thou hast a great gust to come upon the earth, a great wind that shall shake the trees that now appear upon the earth, that are full of leaves of profession; but they have nothing but outward beauty, an outward flourish; but thy trees O Lord, they are full of sap. A great number of people said, oh let our oaks stand, let them not be cut down: oh but, says the Lord, I will make you ashamed in the oaks you have chosen; and because you will have these oaks, I will now give you other oaks, and what are they? A first, a second and a third power, and thou breakest them one after another; oh thine own have had a great hand in these things; thine have said, we will have oaks and gardens, how have they run to and fro! says the Lord now, I will give you gardens, but they shall have no springs in them, they shall be as dry, chapped ground; they shall be as the fallow ground: what loveliness is there to walk upon fallow ground? You shall have stumbling walkings upon them, you shall have no green grass in these gardens; what have all the gardens of the earth been? They have been to thine places of stumbling: oh thou wilt by these thy strange ways, draw up thine into thy upper and nether springs. Thou hast deceived thy saints once again about these gardens, let them now run after them no more, but be ashamed and abashed: we have hankered from mountain to hill, we have said salvation is in this hill and in that, but let us say so no longer; when we shall thus be drawn up to thee, then we shall prosper, and thou wilt give us vineyards, and gardens, and trees of thine own which shall abide.

'Thou calledst thy servant to come sometimes near this place to witness against some, who said that the kingdom was already given up to the Father and contemned the man Christ: but now hast thou sent thy servant again to witness for thee, for the kingdom of thy Son.'

Having uttered much more in prayer, which the relator because of the press of people in the chamber could not take, she delivered the further enlargements of her heart in a song: so much whereof as could be taken is presented to you as follows:

'When Babylon within, the great and tall,
With tumults shall come down:
Then that which is without shall fall,
And be laid flat on ground.

'O King Jesus thou art longed for,
Oh take thy power and reign,
And let thy children see thy face,
Which with them shall remain.

'Thy lovely looks will be so bright,
They will make them to sing.
They shall bring offerings unto thee,
And myrrh unto their king.

'For they know that thou dost delight
To hear their panting soul;
They do rejoice in the marrow,
And esteem it more than gold.

'Therefore thou hearing their heart's cry,
Thou sayest, oh wait a while!
And suddenly thou wilt draw near,
The world's glory to spoil.

'Oh you shall have great rolls of writ
Concerning Babylon's fall,
And the destruction of the whore,
Which now seems spiritual.

'Come write down how that Antichrist,
That is so rigid here,
Shall fall down quite, when Christ comes forth,
Who suddenly will appear.

'Come write down how those sparkling ones,
Which Antichrist are too:
Those notioners, oh do write down,
How he will make them rue.

'Come write also that great powers shall,
From off their thrones be cast:
Oh the Lord he will batter them,
Though they mount up so fast.

'Oh write that those great counsellors,
That now against Christ agree,
How Christ will never own at all
Nor give them any fee.

'Write how that protectors shall go,
And into graves there lie:
Let pens make known what is said, that,
They shall expire and die.

'Oh write also that colonels
And captains they shall down,
Be not afraid to pen also,
That Christ will them cast down.

'Because they have not honoured God,
They have not paid their vows:
But only blustering oaks have been,
Great tall branches and boughs.

'Which have no spirit or moisture, then,
How can they longer stand,
Though a while they have active been:
Yet they must out o'th'land.

'The Lord will reckon with them all,
And set their words before:
They have not brought forth righteousness,
Nor relief to the poor.

'Which they said they would chiefly eye,
But their words do not speak:
But all unto their own nets, they
Do stretch themselves and creep.

'Pen down how all their gallantry,
Shall crumble into dust:
For the Lord he hath spoken, that
To dust they vanish must.

'Come sergeants, what will then you do;
When your masters are cast,
What will become then of your pay,
Which you run for so fast?

'O sergeants, some of you I have,
Look'd on to be such which
Would not have taken such a place,
Your hands forth for to reach.

'Poor sergeants that were honest men
Oh how are you fallen,
Oh how are you now taken with
The vanity of men?

'O sergeants leave off this your work,
And get some other thing,
Your pay'll be sweet to follow him,
Who is your Lord and King.

'Oh bread and water is more sweet,
Than roastmeat of this sort,
Oh meat of herbs better for you,
And of better report.

'You come and crave pardon of them,
While you dissemble in heart,
Oh call for pardon from a Christ,
When to his bar you come.

'And leave those other ways, which will
Prove injurious to you;
The Lord doth hate such practices,
And he will out them spew.

'Oh keep thy poor saints, that they may
Not run away from their Lord,
Oh let them be contented with
Th' morsels thou dost afford.

'Oh that they may not now set hands
To engagements that come,
But rather engage for the Lord,
Who is the only Son.

'Oh mind the saints, how engagements
Have become to them a snare,
That others they may not them take,
But take up to thee repair.

'Let them know tis but a short time,
That men thus shall abide,
Tis but a while that these stormy winds,
Shall bring forth such great tide.

'Though winds and waves they boisterous are,
Yet Christ will them rebuke,
He will speak to them to abate,
And they'll go at his look.'

After she had breathed forth this song with more enlargement than could be noted by the relator, she proceeded in prayer, which for the press of people crowding and darkening the chamber could not be taken. She continued that day in prayer and singing four or five hours together, and was then silent.

Notes on contributors

William Zunder teaches English at Hull University, where he specializes in the Renaissance. His publications include *The Poetry of John Donne* (1982) and *Elizabethan Marlowe* (1994). He is currently preparing the New Casebook volume on Milton's *Paradise Lost*.

Suzanne Trill teaches English at Queen's University, Belfast. Her principal interest lies in women's use of scripture in the early modern period. She is a contributor to *Women and Literature in Britain 1500–1700* and coeditor of *Voicing Women* (both forthcoming).

Mark Thornton Burnett teaches English at Queen's University, Belfast. He is coeditor of *New Essays on 'Hamlet'* (1994) and has recently completed a study of master–servant relations in the English Renaissance. He is currently editing Marlowe's plays for Everyman's Library.

Kate Chedgzoy teaches in the Department of English and Comparative Literary Studies at Warwick University. She has just completed a book on Shakespeare and gender, and is coeditor of *Voicing Women*. She has also edited a forthcoming anthology of early modern women's writing.

Tony Davies teaches English at Birmingham University. His publications include *Rewriting English* (1985), two editions of Milton's poetry and prose, and articles on Renaissance and modern writing. He is currently working on a study of humanism.

Melanie Hansen teaches English at Durham University. She is coeditor of *Voicing Women*.

John Hoyles teaches English at Hull University. He is the author of *The Waning of the Renaissance 1640–1740* (1971) and *The Literary Underground 1900–50* (1991).

Christopher Kendrick is Associate Professor of English Literature at Loyola University of Chicago. He has published *Milton: A Study in Ideology and Form* (1986) and articles on Marvell and Thomas More.

Kathleen McLuskie is Professor of English at Southampton University. Her publications include *Renaissance Dramatists* (1989) and *Dekker and Heywood* (1994). She is currently working on the commercialization of theatre in early modern England, and is editing *Macbeth* for Arden III.

Garthine Walker is a lecturer in history in the School of History and Archaeology, University of Wales College of Cardiff. Her principal interests lie in gender, crime, and the law, and in the social consequences of the English Revolution. She is coeditor of *Women, Crime and the Courts in Early Modern England* (1994).

Helen Wilcox is Professor of English Literature at Groningen University, The Netherlands. She is coeditor of *Her Own Life* (1989) and editor of *Women and Literature in Britain 1500–1700* and *Poetry of George Herbert* (forthcoming). Currently, she is writing a book on the seventeenth-century devotional lyric and editing *All's Well That Ends Well* for Arden III.

Bruce Woodcock teaches English at Hull University. He is the author of *Male Mythologies: John Fowles and Masculinity* (1984) and coauthor of *Combative Styles: Romantic Prose and Ideology* (1995). He is currently at work on a book about Peter Carey.

Marion Wynne-Davies teaches English at Dundee University. She has edited *The Bloomsbury Guide to English Literature*, *Chaucer's Tales of the Clerk and the Wife of Bath*, *The Renaissance: From 1500–1660*, and coedited *Gloriana's Face* and *Renaissance Theatre by Women*. She has also published *Women and Arthurian Literature: Seizing the Sword*.

Select bibliography

The secondary material on the English Renaissance is extensive. What follows is a selection of books and articles likely to prove most useful to students of the period.

General

HISTORICAL

Crawford, P. *Women and Religion in England 1500–1720* (London, 1993)

Dobb, M. *Studies in the Development of Capitalism*, rev. edn (London, 1963)

Guy, J. *Tudor England* (Oxford, 1988)

Hill, C. *Reformation to Industrial Revolution 1530–1780*, rev. edn (Harmondsworth, 1969); *The Century of Revolution 1603–1714*, rev. edn (Walton-on-Thames, 1980)

Kamen, H. *The Iron Century: Social Change in Europe 1550–1660*, rev. edn (London, 1976)

Koenigsberger, H. G., Mosse, G. L. and Bowler, G. Q. *Europe in the Sixteenth Century*, 2nd edn (London, 1989)

Prior, M., ed., *Women in English Society 1500–1800* (London, 1985)

Rose, M. B., ed., *Women in the Middle Ages and the Renaissance: Literary and Historical Perspectives* (Syracuse, 1986)

Wrightson, K. *English Society 1580–1680* (London, 1982)

CRITICAL

Aers, D., Hodge, B. and Kress, G. *Literature, Language and Society in England 1580–1680* (Dublin, 1981)

Beilin, E. V. *Redeeming Eve: Women Writers of the English Renaissance* (Princeton, 1987)

Bloom, C., ed., *Jacobean Poetry and Prose: Rhetoric, Representation and the Popular Imagination* (London, 1988)

Brant, C. and Purkiss, D. *Women, Texts, Histories 1575–1760* (London, 1992)

Dollimore, J. *Radical Tragedy: Religion, Ideology and Power in the Drama of Shakespeare and his Contemporaries*, 2nd edn (Hemel Hempstead, 1989)

Ezell, M. J. *Writing Women's Literary History* (Baltimore, 1993)

Farrell, K., Hageman, E. H. and Kinney, A. F., eds, *Women in the Renaissance: Selections from 'English Literary Renaissance'* (Amherst, 1990)

Greenblatt, S. *Renaissance Self-Fashioning: From More to Shakespeare* (Chicago, 1980)

Grundy, I. and Wiseman, S. *Women, Writing, History 1640–1740* (London, 1992)

Hobby, E. *Virtue of Necessity: English Women's Writing 1646–1688* (London, 1988)

Jones, A. R. *The Currency of Eros: Women's Love Lyric in Europe* (Bloomington, 1990)

Knights, L. C. *Drama and Society in the Age of Jonson* (1937; reprinted Harmondsworth, 1962)

Krontiris, T. *Oppositional Voices: Women as Writers and Translators of Literature in the English Renaissance* (London, 1992)

Lewalski, B. K. *Writing Women in Jacobean England* (Cambridge, Massachusetts, 1993)

McLuskie, K. *Renaissance Dramatists* (Hemel Hempstead, 1989)

Parfitt, G. *English Poetry of the Seventeenth Century* (London, 1985)

Parry, G. *The Seventeenth Century: The Intellectual and Cultural Context of English Literature 1603–1700* (London, 1989)

Sinfield, A. *Literature in Protestant England 1560–1660* (Beckenham, 1983)

Waller, G. *English Poetry of the Sixteenth Century*, 2nd edn (London, 1993)

Woodbridge, L. *Women and the English Renaissance: Literature and the Nature of Womankind* (Brighton, 1984)

Edmund Spenser

Bellamy, E. J. *Translations of Power: Narcissism and the Unconscious in Epic History* (Ithaca, 1992)

Goldberg, J. *Endlesse Worke: Spenser and the Structures of Discourse* (Baltimore, 1981)

Hume, A. *Spenser: Protestant Poet* (Cambridge, 1985)

MacCaffrey, I. *Spenser's Allegory* (Princeton, 1976)

Nohrnberg, J. *The Analogy of the 'Faerie Queene'* (Princeton, 1976)

Shepherd, S. *Spenser* (Hemel Hempstead, 1989)

Christopher Marlowe

Healy, T. *Christopher Marlowe* (Plymouth, 1994)

Kuriyama, C. B. *Hammer or Anvil: Psychological Patterns in Christopher Marlowe's Plays* (New Brunswick, 1980)

Sales, R. *Christopher Marlowe* (London, 1991)

Shepherd, S. *Marlowe and the Politics of Elizabethan Theatre* (Brighton, 1986)

Steane, J. B. *Marlowe: A Critical Study* (Cambridge, 1964)

Zunder, W. *Elizabethan Marlowe: Writing and Culture in the English Renaissance* (Hull, 1994)

John Donne and the metaphysical poets

Carey, J. *John Donne: Life, Mind and Art* (London, 1981)

Docherty, T. *John Donne, Undone* (London, 1986)

Mackenzie, D. *The Metaphysical Poets* (London, 1990)

Sanders, W. *John Donne's Poetry* (Cambridge, 1971)

Winny, J. *A Preface to Donne*, rev. edn (London, 1981)

Zunder, W. *The Poetry of John Donne: Literature and Culture in the Elizabethan and Jacobean Period* (Brighton, 1982)

Renaissance tragedy

Brown, C. C., ed., *Patronage, Politics and Literary Traditions in England 1558–1658* (Detroit, 1993)

Chambers, E. K. *The Elizabethan Stage*, Vol. 4 (Oxford, 1923) ['Documents of Criticism']

Clare, J. *Art Made Tongue-Tied by Authoritie: Elizabethan and Jacobean Dramatic Censorship* (Manchester, 1990)

Dessen, A. C. *Elizabethan Stage Conventions and Modern Interpreters* (Cambridge, 1984)

Dutton, R. *Mastering the Revels: The Regulation and Censorship of English Renaissance Drama* (London, 1991)

Moretti, F. 'The great eclipse: tragic form as the deconsecration of sovereignty', in *Shakespearean Tragedy*, ed. J. Drakakis (London, 1992), pp. 45–84

Tennenhouse, L. *Power on Display: The Politics of Shakespeare's Genres* (London, 1986)

Williams, R. *Modern Tragedy* (London, 1966); *Politics and Letters* (London, 1979), pp. 211–13

Narratives of land

Barnes, T. J. and Duncan, J. S., eds, *Writing Worlds: Discourse, Text and Metaphor in the Representation of Landscape* (London, 1992)

Dubrow, H. and Strier, R., eds, *The Historical Renaissance: New Essays on Tudor and Stuart Literature and Culture* (Chicago, 1988)

Ferguson, A. *Clio Unbound: Perception of the Social and Cultural Past in Renaissance England* (Durham, North Carolina, 1979)

Greenblatt, S., ed., *Representing the English Renaissance* (Berkeley, 1988)

Pocock, D. C. D., ed., *Humanistic Geography and Literature: Essays on the Experience of Place* (Beckenham, 1981)

Samuel, R., ed., *Patriotism: The Making and Unmaking of British National Identity*, Vol. 3: *National Fictions* (London, 1989)

Popular culture

Burke, P. *Popular Culture in Early Modern Europe* (London, 1978)

Laroque, F. *Shakespeare's Festive World: Elizabethan Seasonal Entertainment and the Professional Stage*, tr. J. Lloyd (Cambridge, 1991)

Reay, B., ed., *Popular Culture in Seventeenth-Century England* (London, 1988)

Storey, J. *An Introductory Guide to Cultural Theory and Popular Culture* (Hemel Hempstead, 1993)

Watt, T. *Cheap Print and Popular Piety 1550–1640* (Cambridge, 1991)

Representations of women

Dolan, F. E. *Dangerous Familiars: Representations of Domestic Crime in England 1550–1700* (Ithaca, 1994)

Henderson, K. U. and McManus, B. F., *Half Humankind: Contexts and Texts of the Controversy about Women in England 1540–1640* (Urbana, 1985)

Kermode, J. and Walker, G., eds., *Women, Crime and the Courts in Early Modern England* (London, 1994)

Lake, P. 'Deeds against nature: cheap print, protestantism and murder in early seventeenth-century England', in *Culture and Politics in Early Stuart England*, ed. K. Sharpe and P. Lake (London, 1994), pp. 257–84

Sharpe, J. A. 'Domestic homicide in early modern England', *Historical Journal*, 24 (1981), 29–48

Wiltenburg, J. *Disorderly Women and Female Power in the Street Literature of Early Modern England and Germany* (Charlottesville, 1992)

Mary Sidney and translation

Hannay, M. P. *Philip's Phoenix: Mary Sidney, Countess of Pembroke* (Oxford, 1990); ed., *Silent but for the Word: Tudor Women as Patrons, Translators, and Writers of Religious Works* (Kent, Ohio, 1985)

Haselkorn, A. M. and Travitsky, B. S. *The Renaissance Englishwoman in Print: Counterbalancing the Canon* (Amherst, 1990)

Lamb, M. E. *Gender and Authorship in the Sidney Circle* (Madison, 1990)

Zim, R. *English Metrical Psalms: Poetry as Praise and Prayer 1535–1601* (Cambridge, 1987)

George Herbert and the devotional lyric

Corns, T. N., ed., *The Cambridge Companion to English Poetry: Donne to Marvell* (Cambridge, 1993)

Greer, G., Medoff, J., Sansone, M. and Hastings, S., eds, *Kissing the Rod: An Anthology of Seventeenth-Century Women's Verse* (London, 1988)

Roberts, J. R., ed., *New Perspectives on the Seventeenth-Century Religious Lyric* (Columbia, Missouri, 1994)

Schoenfeldt, M. *Prayer and Power: George Herbert and Renaissance Courtship* (Chicago, 1991)

Summers, J. H. *George Herbert: His Religion and Art* (1954; reissued Binghamton, 1981)

Andrew Marvell

Bradbrook, M. C. and Lloyd Thomas, M. G. *Andrew Marvell* (Cambridge, 1940)

Carey, J., ed., *Andrew Marvell: A Critical Anthology* (Harmondsworth, 1969)

Hill, C. *Puritanism and Revolution* (London, 1962)

Hunt, J. D. *Andrew Marvell: His Life and Writings* (London, 1978)

Legouis, P. *Andrew Marvell: Poet, Puritan, Patriot* (1928; tr. Oxford, 1965)

Leishman, J. B. *The Art of Marvell's Poetry* (London, 1966)

Wallace, J. M. *Destiny His Choice: The Loyalism of Andrew Marvell* (Cambridge, 1968)

Wilcher, R. Introduction and Commentary to *Andrew Marvell: Selected Poetry and Prose* (London, 1986)

John Milton

Belsey, C. *John Milton: Language, Gender, Power* (Oxford, 1988)

Empson, W. *Milton's God* (London, 1961)

Hill, C. *Milton and the English Revolution* (London, 1977)

Kendrick, C. *Milton: A Study in Ideology and Form* (London, 1986)

Le Comte, E. *Milton and Sex* (London, 1978)

Nyquist, M. 'The genesis of gendered subjectivity in the divorce tracts and in *Paradise Lost*', in *Re-Membering Milton: Essays on the Texts and Traditions*, ed. M. Nyquist and M. W. Ferguson (London, 1987), pp. 99–127

Patterson, A., ed., *John Milton* (London, 1992)

Gerrard Winstanley and the Diggers

Hill, C. 'The religion of Gerrard Winstanley', in *The Collected Essays of Christopher Hill* (Brighton, 1986), 2, pp. 185–252; *The World Turned Upside Down* (Harmondsworth, 1972)

Holstun, J. 'Rational hunger: Gerrard Winstanley's *Hortus Inconclusus*', in *Pamphlet Wars: Prose in the English Revolution*, ed. J. Holstun (London, 1992), pp. 158–204

Kenney, R. W. Introduction to Gerrard Winstanley, *The Law of Freedom in a Platform* (1940; reissued New York, 1973)

Lutaud, O. *Winstanley: Socialisme et Christianisme sous Cromwell* (Paris, 1976)

Petegorsky, D. W. *Left-Wing Democracy in the English Civil War* (London, 1940)

Sabine, G. H. Introduction to *The Works of Gerrard Winstanley* (Ithaca, 1944)

Anna Trapnel and female prophecy

Berg, C. and Berry, P. ' "Spiritual whoredom": an essay on female prophets in the seventeenth century', in *1642: Literature and Power in the Seventeenth Century*, ed. F. Barker *et al.* (Colchester, 1981)

Capp, B. *The Fifth Monarchy Men: A Study in Seventeenth-Century Millenarianism* (London, 1972); 'The Fifth Monarchists and popular millenarianism', in *Radical Religion in the English Revolution*, ed. J. F. McGregor and B. Reay (Oxford, 1984)

Graham, E., Hinds, H., Hobby, E. and Wilcox, H., eds, *Her Own Life: Autobiographical Writings by Seventeenth-Century Englishwomen* (London, 1989)

Mack, P. 'Women as prophets during the English Civil War', in *The Origins of Anglo-American Radicalism*, ed. M. C. Jacob and J. Jacob (London, 1984); *Visionary Women: Ecstatic Prophecy in Seventeenth-Century England* (Berkeley, 1992)

Thomas, K. 'Women and the Civil War sects', *Past and Present*, 13 (1955)

Index

Authors and titles listed at end of chapters and referred to only as quoted sources are not included. Titles are listed under author, as well as under title where they appear in italics in the text; they also appear in italics in the index. Titles of single poems are shown in parentheses under author only. Names of characters in plays and poems are not indexed.

Translations: under English title, with translator's name following, in brackets.

Page numbers in italics indicate printed extract.